The Inspiration of the Pentateuch

An Educational Resource For Theological Students

The Inspiration of the Pentateuch

or

The Graf–Wellhausen Fallacy

An examination of the origins of the Torah,
the inadequacies and contradictions of cynical Source Criticism,
and the merits of Faithful Source, and Form Criticism.

by

M. W. J. Phelan, B.Th., M.Th., Th.D., Ph.D.

Dedicated to the memory of my late friend
and fellow researcher, Leslie F. Green.

Twoedged Sword Publications

The word of God is sharper than any twoedged sword, piercing even to the dividing asunder of soul and spirit. (Hebrews 4:12)

First published 2005

ISBN-13   978-0-9547205-6-8

ISBN-10   0-9547205-6-3

Twoedged Sword Publications
PO Box 266, Waterlooville, PO7 5ZT
www.twoedgedswordpublications.co.uk

Acknowledgement

This book was first written as my dissertation for the degree of Doctor of Theology with The European Theological Seminary and College Of The Bible. Because of this, the copyright of the work is held by the Seminary. I would like to thank Professor Doctor Gordon S. Beck, who first suggested I should tackle the subject of Pentateuchal High Criticism, and the rest of the Academic Faculty for allowing its publication by Twoedged Sword Publications.

I would also like to acknowledge the very real service I received from others in producing this book. The Reverend Professor Doctor Robert H. Creane, Vice Chancellor of the Seminary, most kindly and patiently reviewed the text, while it was a dissertation. Professors Beck and Creane graciously awarded this work the Seminary Doctoral Prize for the Academic Year 2002–2003. That was an honour I will never forget. Mrs. Ilana Tahan, curator at the Hebrew Section of the Oriental And India Office Collection at The British Library was particularly helpful in assisting me by locating *The Samaritan Pentateuch* in their *Cotton Collection*, and in suggesting folio numbers for my use. Mr. Howard Simons of the Reproductions Department, and Ms. Christine Campbell of the Reproduction Permissions Department were also extremely helpful in supplying photographic material and permission to use it. I am also particularly grateful for the technical advice and practical work of Mr. John Collyer and Mr. Steve Sajnog of *Focus Photography*, Southwick, West Sussex in reproducing the image. I acknowledge also the helpfulness and generosity of Liz Cooper, Copyright Manager, and Mary Bergin-Cartwright, of the Permissions Department of Oxford University Press, in granting permission to use the English translation of the whole of IV Ezra 14 as found in R. H. Charles' *Apocrypha And Pseudepigrapha Of The Old Testament*. I wish also to acknowledge the willing services of the librarians of University College Chichester, as well as those of the West Sussex County Library Service, whose contributions enabled me to complete the sections dealing with the literary forms of Genesis, and the Ugaritic alphabet, and in the latter case, located the article in *The Times* on the speed of light referred to in Supplement Two.

Many Christian writers have inspired me in my researches. Perhaps the greatest help has been derived from Duane Garrett, R. K. Harrison, Isaac M. Kikawada and Arthur Quinn, Edward Robertson, P. J. Wiseman, Friedrick Weinreb, and Gordon Wenham. I am profoundly grateful to the Lord for the excellent works they have produced.

The unstinting labours of Paul Rose of Twoedged Sword Publications must also be acknowledged. Owing to the necessity of revising the work prior to publication, Paul had a very severe workload to deal with. I drew upon his reserves of patience and concentration more than I ought to have done, and I thank him for his tolerance and forbearance while under pressure. The quality of his Christian character became very evident through the imposition of this extra work. The maps to be found in Supplement One are Paul's work, and display his ability very well. Thank you Paul!

Finally, and in the place of honour, I thank my wife Joy Marion, who despite poor health, has shown a keen interest in the progress of this work, insisted I strive for the highest standard I might achieve, and has been a real source of encouragement throughout.

Opening Thoughts

"The success of the sceptical movement is not due to the strength of the attack, but to the weakness of the defence."

Sir Robert Anderson, K.C.B., LL.D.

"It was needful for me to write unto you, and exhort you that ye should earnestly contend for the faith."

The Epistle of Jude, verse 3.

"A careful study of the evidences makes intelligent believers."

Arthur T. Pierson, D.D.

Contents

Part Seven   Appendices, Glossary, And Bibliography

Illustrations

Introduction

The problem

Bible-based Christianity claims to be a revelation from God, in fact it claims to comprise the most comprehensive collection of truths concerning the nature and purposes of God, and the nature and destiny of mankind that has ever been revealed. It claims that this revelation was made to mankind by Divinely Inspired, and therefore, utterly inerrant writings that have been transmitted to us through what is popularly known as The New Testament. However, this collection of documents rests upon the previously existing collection of documents which comprise the Hebrew Canon, referred to by Christians as the Old Testament, and therefore is itself acutely vulnerable to any assault made upon the Hebrew Canon, or Old Testament.

The very foundation of the Hebrew Canon, in terms of the claimed sequence of writing, historical events narrated, and theological importance, is the Torah, or Pentateuch, or Five-Books-Of-Moses; namely, Genesis, Exodus, Leviticus, Numbers, and Deuteronomy.

It is not surprising then, that while there is continuing debate about the so-called Synoptic Problem, the authorship and placement of the Pastoral Epistles, the provenance of the Book of Daniel, the authorship of the Book of Isaiah, and many of the Psalms, it is the Pentateuch that has been the target of the most unremitting assaults of sceptics and Critics down the years, and the Book of Genesis has suffered the most brutal of these attacks. It is these assaults upon the Pentateuch that form the subject of this dissertation.

Scope

While it is true that since the rise of popular evolutionary hypotheses, and uniformitarian geology, attacks have been made upon the Scriptural accounts of the Creation, the global Flood, and the dispersal of the nations from Babel, this dissertation is concerned primarily with an older assault upon the Hebrew Canon; an assault which is traceable to the first days of Christianity, although its current form dates from the middle of the seventeenth century.

This assault has been undertaken during the last three and a half centuries through what is known as the Higher Criticism, or Source Criticism. While the Lower Criticism often referred to as Textual Criticism, deals with issues relating to the written text, and examines such matters as the canon, and variant readings in extant manuscripts, copies, ancient versions, and citations from Lectionaries and the 'Fathers' dating from antiquity, the Higher Criticism seeks to go behind the text, to examine such matters as authorship, literary sources, the date and place of writing, the purpose and manner of composition, theological tendency and historicity.[1] It must be said that both areas of enquiry are perfectly legitimate, being right and proper fields of research for genuine believers, but in the main, they have been taken over by the sceptic with an agenda that sets out to discredit the Scriptures. To this extent then it might be said that the Higher Criticism has become *tendentious*. Nevertheless, it ought to be understood that in calling the latter field of Criticism, *Higher*, no intrinsic spirit of arrogance is implied, although it may well be present in the writings of many a sceptic. Nor is the word *criticism*, necessarily and inevitably a negative term, although again there is very frequently a negative tendency to be found in the writings of sceptics.[2]

This trend is clearly visible in the course taken by Biblical scholarship in the Post-Reformation Period. Influenced by the so-called Age-Of-Enlightenment, Biblical scholarship generally, and with notable exceptions, has moved away from the confessional, towards the rationalistic, and destructively critical. As Sir Robert Anderson has pointed out, the main reason for the dominance, or near monopoly of

---

[1] See Adeney, W. F., in the article *Criticism*, in *Dictionary Of The Bible*, edited by Hastings, J., & Selbie, J., Edinburgh, T. & T. Clark, 1909.

[2] Ibid. In fact it is true to say that the term *Higher Criticism* is used less now than formerly, giving way to the alternative *Biblical Criticism*, mainly because it is thought to possess a pejorative resonance. So also the term *Lower Criticism* has given way more and more to the term *Textual Criticism*. See Soulen, R. N., and Kendall Soulen, R., *Handbook Of Biblical Criticism*, Louisville, Kentucky, U.S.A., Westminster John Knox Press, 2001, p. 108.

the sceptical variety of Higher Criticism, is not to be looked for in the strength of the sceptic's arguments, but in the weakness of the defence of the veracity of God's Word, by believers.[3] It is greatly to be regretted that believers generally shy away from the attacks made upon the Word-of-God by sceptics, intimidated by their so-called learning.

The most frequently encountered mode of the Higher Criticism that the believer is liable to encounter in connection with the Pentateuch, is that built upon what has become known as the Graf–Wellhausen Hypothesis, or the New Documentary Hypothesis. It is the credibility of this type of Literary Higher Criticism, as opposed to the Form Criticism of Dibelius, Gunkel, Mowinckel, Von Rad, Noth, Rendtorff and the Uppsala School that is examined in this brief dissertation, although what I have termed Positive Form Criticism will be dealt with in Chapters Nine and Ten.

It is not my intention for this work to be presented as an apologia for Post-Critical Interpretation, nor should it be understood as such, nonetheless there are some areas of agreement between Post-Critical Interpretation and my own stance. In common with Post-Critical Interpretation, I look to the Scriptures to interpret themselves, yet am also keen to understand the most ancient forms of exegesis, as will become apparent later. Again, as with Post-Critical Interpreters generally, I agree that just as we cannot now be the same after the discoveries at Qumran, and Nag Hammadi, so too, we cannot ignore the rise of Critical Methods, as some of the questions Critics pose are genuine, and do require investigation. I also hold in common with the views of Post-Critical Interpreters, the belief that both Higher and Lower Criticism may be used in a constructive manner, but believe that they are by themselves inadequate to the task of understanding literature that is *Divinely Inspired.* Unless we come by faith to the Ultimate Author of the Written Word, we will never be able to handle it aright. Understanding the Word of God, may only begin, after we acknowledge the supreme place of honouring faith in the Living Word.

---

[3] Anderson, Sir Robert, *The Bible And Modern Criticism,* London, Hodder & Stoughton, 1902, p. 257.

My aims

In examining the claims of source Critics I have three main aims. These are;

1. I hope to demonstrate to the reader how inconsistent the schemes of Higher Criticism are, and how thoroughly they are based upon ignorance of ancient literary practice, special pleading, and the labours of many supposed and anonymous redactors whose existence may neither be proved or disproved.

2. I hope to show that over the years many independent researchers have discovered these serious weaknesses within the hypotheses advocated by sceptical Higher Critics.

3. Finally, I hope to reveal the genuine existence of viable and attractive alternatives to the schemes advocated by sceptical Source and Form Critics, which accept the Pentateuchal text at face value. These alternatives do actually confront the real problems of the Pentateuch, but nonetheless, reveal its immense value, and display its utter trustworthiness.

The question of objectivity

This work is an unashamed apologia for accepting the books of Genesis, Exodus, Leviticus, Numbers, and Deuteronomy as the Inspired Word of God. How then may my work be objective and uncompromised? Have I not already decided upon my conclusions, and am merely embarking now on a search for evidence to bolster my own private beliefs? How do I answer such charges?

In the undertaking of such an exercise I believe three categories of evidence should be considered. Firstly, the internal evidence offered by the Pentateuch itself must be reviewed; that is, the characters and script it is written in, its literary style and forms, its vocabulary, its literary structures, its supposed difficulties, and so-called duplications, and similar matters.

Secondly the relevant external evidence must also be considered; such as, the existence and nature of the Samaritan Pentateuch, various relevant ostraca, legends of the Jews, archaeological discoveries demonstrating the great antiquity of the age of writing, and the various techniques employed in the most ancient forms of literature.

But I also believe that with the books of Scripture, there is above and beyond this, a third category of evidence; that is, the impact the Scriptures have had upon humanity, collectively, and individually. When I first began to read the Scriptures, it was in total isolation from any Jewish or Christian individual or organisation. I did not even know that the book I had purchased, entitled *Good News For Modern Man,*[4] was a New Testament. As I read its pages, I was drawn more and more deeply into the heart of its teaching until I reached a definite point where an event of recognition occurred. Without the aid of any other human, immediately and comprehensively, I was granted the realisation that what I was reading was absolutely and eternally True. The impact this recognition made upon me was life-changing, and brought a feeling of joy combined with wonder and awe. For me, there could be no going back: from that moment on, I knew I was reading words that forever were true, and must be lived by, and, if need be, died for. This most potent power of the Scriptures, of witnessing for the Truth of God, is for me a genuine property or attribute of the Scriptures, and is equally present in all Scripture, including the books under consideration in this dissertation. Thus I believe that this power itself may also be offered as evidence for consideration, and is certainly evidence that I have personally encountered, and which any with an open mind may encounter also. My conclusions have of course been made since the discovery of the Power to which I refer, and were made by the leading of this Power.

If a study of humanity were to be based solely upon the anatomy and physical attributes of human kind, to the exclusion of ordinary human life and relationships, its conclusion would be flawed by incompleteness and consequent bias. So too with Scripture; exclusive consideration of the text, and a failure to consider the Life flowing through it will produce a similarly biased conclusion. Of course, once the Life or testifying Power flowing through Scripture has been found, it is impossible for it to become 'unfound' so that the subject

---

[4] The New Testament portion of what is now known as *The Good News Bible*, London, The Bible Societies, 1976.

may be returned to a position of neutrality for the purposes of research. Inevitably my search began after I had found and been changed by this higher Life of the Scriptures, but I submit that this does not weaken my research, but rather that it enhances it, as I have considered evidence that no true sceptic has experienced, but which each and every true sceptic might experience, were his or her prior conclusions suspended, and a genuine enquiry into the existence and force of this testifying Power honestly made. Thus Critics themselves do not begin always, or even *often*, from a position of neutrality, and inevitably they are not able to consider as much evidence as am I. There will be more on this matter in Chapter Ten, but for the moment my answer is that an agnostic is unable to consider this third category of evidence, and is therefore, under-equipped, which leads inevitably, even if unconsciously and unintentionally, to bias.

Plan of the work

In Part One, comprising Chapters One and Two, I give a brief survey of the Modern Critical Movement. It was difficult to know quite where to begin this survey, but the Post-Reformation era seems to mark a definite turning point, in that the new-found faith in the Scriptures that dates from that time, and that had been so greatly assisted by the invention of printing, had begun to subside, and the dawning of the so-called Age of Enlightenment was beginning to make its mark on European intellectual life. Additionally, if P. J. Wiseman is correct, the very term Higher Criticism is traceable to this era. After a few opening comments concerning the Gnostics, I begin this survey therefore from the middle of the seventeenth century, a time, when ironically, the English Puritan Movement was at its height. I was encouraged in this respect to find that this too is the point from which Soulen, and Kendall Soulen in their *Handbook* date the rise of Modern Criticism.[5] The first part of this survey takes us down to the time of Graf. The second part covers the Period from Graf onwards.

It was equally difficult to know where to conclude the survey. Should I bring it up to the present day? stop at Graf–Wellhausen? examine the Form Criticism of Gunkel, Noth, Von Rad, and Rendtorff, and the

---

[5] Op. cit., p. 19.

mass of theories which carry the dissection of the Pentateuch to extremes, and the subsequent rise of Redaction Criticism? Should I give a summary of the attacks on Graf–Wellhausen by Cassuto, Robertson, Wiseman, Thompson, Harrison, Whybray, Wenham, and Kikawada and Quinn?

In the end, I decided on a compromise solution. I conclude with the afterglow derived from the apotheosis of Source Criticism, when Graf–Wellhausen-type hypotheses had won such acceptance by academia that it was virtually impossible for any who held to the views of plenary Inspiration to receive a position of note in any college, university or seminary in the West. I have however, included brief notices concerning the insidious attacks made by Form Criticism, which really merit a separate study; the trend of multiplying sources for the Pentateuch; and the supposed labours of the so-called Deuteronomists. I give also a very brief statement regarding the situation as it is today.

Inevitably such a survey in a dissertation as slim as this may only skim the surface, and some may feel I could, perhaps *should*, have included other individuals and schemes within its scope. I have had to exercise my own judgement as to whom and what I should include and exclude, and ask the reader's indulgence where my judgement differs from his or hers.

Within this survey I have inserted occasional numbered observations. Inevitably this survey contains many technical terms, so I have included a glossary on page 423.

In Part Two, I offer my basic objections to Graf–Wellhausen-type hypotheses. Chapter Three shows from the discoveries of Ashurbanipal's Library, Tel El Armana, Ugarit, or Ras Shamra, and Ebla, that contrary to what had been believed in the early days of the Modern Critical Movement, the dawning of the age of writing presents no obstacles at all to accepting a Mosaic provenance for the Pentateuch. Crucially this is evidence that Wellhausen could not have been ignorant of, but chose to ignore, as it militated against his views. A lesson even Martin Noth and other 'moderns' seem not to have learned. In Chapter Four, I show from evidence gleaned from the ancient characters used in the Samaritan Pentateuch, from certain errors in its text, as well as certain peculiarities in the Masoretic Text, and from evidence derived from other fields as well, that both the Samaritan and Masoretic Texts descend from a vorlage that goes back at least to the time of Hezekiah, and probably much earlier. This of course disproves the assertion made occasionally by sceptics that the Torah was lost at the Fall of Jerusalem. I also show that the Pentateuch is a literary corpus in its own right, and that the so-called Octateuch, Hexateuch, or Tetrateuch, have no objective existence.

In Chapter Five I demonstrate from the complex of highly detailed literary patterns of many different types that are to be found in the Pentateuch, that it is a work of literary unity, and that modern Source Criticism is utterly overthrown by a serious consideration of this compelling evidence. It is also shown that the unity of the Pentateuch means that all five books must be at least as old as the age of Hezekiah. This assertion by itself is sufficient to stand Higher Criticism on its head, yet the believer in Divine Inspiration requires much more, and further evidence follows.

In Part Three I discuss the origins of the Pentateuch, and begin with the book of Deuteronomy which recent discoveries have shown to be a work of literary unity, and which is likely to be so ancient, that a Mosaic provenance is far from unreasonable. This finding has important consequences for the books at the heart of the Pentateuch, Exodus, Leviticus and Numbers. I show that there are good reasons for the puzzling form these books exhibit, and that far from being a problem, their unique form, along with other factors suggest a Mosaic provenance for these works too. Finally I consider the book of Genesis, and examine in particular the occurrence, and meaning of the Hebrew word *toledoth,* which is found throughout the book, is usually translated as *generations*, and provides a most valuable but rarely used key to the book. The use of this key enables the elusive literary sources of Genesis finally to be identified and even *named*.

In Part Four, using the findings of Duane Garrett, Isaac M. Kikawada and Arthur Quinn, the literary forms of Genesis and the rest of the Pentateuch are examined. This technique proves most rewarding, and enables us to move from Higher Criticism, to the Highest Appreciation of the Pentateuch, through understanding it to comprise

Inspired Scripture, which, like all Scripture, is a profound and supreme testifier to the Lord Jesus Christ.

In Part Five, I offer five definite Propositions which together I believe account for the origins of the five books of Moses.

In Part Six I give two Supplementary Studies. The first of these examines an issue which is closely intertwined with The New Documentary Hypothesis, namely, the rôle of the Levites. A strong attraction of Wellhausen's views for many is the way he related the alleged Documentary Sources of the Pentateuch to what he saw as the evolution of Hebrew Religion. He believed that the priesthood changed radically in form from the period of the Judges, throughout the monarchical period, and during the days of Ezra, and that these changes in the priesthood, which he claims are discernible in the Hebrew Canon, and the scheme of alleged Documentary Sources, corroborate one another. In my examination I show that Wellhausen and his followers have never understood the rôle of the Levites with precision, and that when this is done, support for the New Documentary Hypothesis evaporates.

The second Supplementary Study looks at the non-literary problems involved in accepting the book of Genesis as being literally true, and gives ideas for those interested in pursuing these matters.

Finally in Part Seven, I give a series of Appendices which give background information on matters raised in the study itself, followed by the Glossary, and Bibliography.

Assumptions

The only intended assumptions made in this work are that my readers are familiar with the content of the Scriptures, understand Hebrew and Greek orthography, are willing to consider evidence honestly, and do not have closed minds. I would be pleased indeed were this work to become a springboard for further research in this field.

A note on the sub-title

The sub-title of this work, *The Graf–Wellhausen Fallacy*, was the title of the original dissertation. This title was a deliberate echo of the name given to the New Testament Source Criticism argument, attributed to Lachmann, that makes *Urmarkus* the Primary source, and Q the Secondary source of the Synoptic Gospels. It was said that Mark preserves best the order of *Urmarkus*, and that when either Matthew or Luke departed from that order, the other adhered to it. It was thought that this proved that both Matthew and Luke were dependent on Mark. This argument, because it has now been exploded, is known as *The Lachmann Fallacy*.[6] To be fair to Lachmann, it is actually a distortion of what he said, nevertheless the name continues to be used widely. I borrowed the idea behind the title, and applied it instead to Old Testament Source Criticism, implying thereby that it is now high time that the myth of Graf–Wellhausen and its legion of kindred hypotheses was exploded! Indeed, it seems as if the attacks made by Robertson, Wiseman, Cassuto, Thompson, Harrison, Whybray, Wenham, Garrett, and Kikawada and Quinn, may quite soon, actually achieve this. For Graf–Wellhausen, I believe, time has all but run out. A new title was thought to be appropriate for its publication by Twoedged Sword, nevertheless, the retention of the sub-title maintains the connection with the doctoral dissertation from which it was born.

---

[6] Soulen and Kendall Soulen, op. cit., in. loc.

Part One

The origin and nature of the Graf–Wellhausen Hypothesis

Chapter One

Pre-Grafian Higher Criticism

The Antecedents Of The Modern Critical Movement

Ever since Eve listened to, and accepted the serpent's lie concerning the veracity of God's Word,[7] it has been quite contrary to the nature of mankind to believe in it (Genesis 3:4). The Word of God is opposed to the condition of men and women in their *natural*, or, *unregenerate* state. "The natural man receiveth not the things of the Spirit of God: for they are foolishness unto him: neither can he know them, because they are spiritually discerned (I Corinthians 2:14)."

This natural predisposition of mankind not to believe in God's Word, is seen with the most dreadful clarity in some apologias for the Higher Criticism. One such example is the intelligently and subtly written book, *The Bible And Criticism*.[8] W. H. Bennett, one of the two co-authors of this book, using the most plausible and seductive language possible, presents the destructive and cynical type of Higher Criticism in the most flattering of lights, and appeals to his readers' sense of reasonableness and fair-mindedness. He begs them not to dismiss the centuries of allegedly detailed, methodical and disinterested work, undertaken by men who are presented as being not only equally reasonable and fair-minded, but above all, professional and scientific, while at the same time being *devout believers* [*sic*].

Without doubt, this writer, as well as his heroes, Robertson-Smith, Cheyne, Eichhorn, Ewald, et cetera, are ravening wolves in sheep's clothing (Matthew 7:15). It is one of the most dangerous books I have ever read, as, like the serpent in Eden appealing to Eve, it presents unbelief and the denial of God's Word, as being reasonable, sane, and the natural, or even *inevitable* response of the educated and

---

[7] Genesis 3:13, II Corinthians 11:3, & I Timothy 2:14.

[8] Bennett, W. H., and Adeney, W. F., *The Bible And Criticism*, London, T. C. and E. C. Jack, undated.

enlightened mind. Such a writer would seem to know nothing of the Spiritual insight the acceptance of God's Word brings, because, while with terrible sadness, we may have to accept that the denial of God's Word is indeed the natural response of the mind educated and enlightened only by the resources of a fallen and sin-ridden world, were these Higher Critics *truly* devout as is claimed,[9] they would have been transformed by the *renewing* of their minds (Romans 12:2); they would have known that the Word of God *quickens* those who accept and delight in it (Psalm 119:50).

The acceptance of God's Word gives an illumination and *understanding* that the natural man or woman, however highly educated, and even with the greatest of natural abilities, may know nothing of. "The entrance of Thy Words giveth light; it giveth *understanding*." (Psalms 119:130) This vital, and Divinely given *understanding*, which by the grace of God is available to all believers, is always capable of defeating the unaided, or purely *natural* intellect, because "It is written, I will destroy the wisdom of the wise, and will bring to nothing the understanding of the prudent (even that of the Higher Critics) (I Corinthians 1:19)." It would appear to be inevitable that true believers will have to contend for the faith (Jude 3), but there is no need to fear this situation, as all who place every atom of their faith solely in the revealed Word of God will triumph over the serpent's lies, pulling down the seeming strongholds of merely natural wisdom, and "every high thing, (including Higher Criticism) that exalteth itself against the knowledge of God (II Corinthians 10:5)."

Given the above, it is not surprising then that the very first attacks made upon ordinary believers for accepting the Hebrew Canon as Divinely Inspired, go back to the first days of Christianity, to the time of the Gnostics. The so-called *Clementine Homilies* record Simon Magus repudiating the Hebrew Canon in a theological debate with the Apostle Peter.[10] While the contest with Peter that this episode in the *Homilies* describes may well be merely legendary, it is certainly the

---

[9] Ibid., p. 13.

[10] *The Clementine Homilies*, translated by Roberts & Donaldson, Edinburgh, published by T. & T. Clark, as Volume XVII of the *Anti-Nicene Christian Library*, 1870, pp. 248f.

case that the Gnostics as a whole regarded the Hebrew Canon as being quite inaccurate.[11]

It was the very able and scholarly, but sadly heretical and Gnostic Marcion who might be called the first real High Critic. He, in common with Gnosticism generally, considered the Hebrew Canon revealed a god who is lower in rank than the Father Who was revealed by Christ, and rejected the Old Testament outright.[12] He analysed systematically the text of the Hebrew Canon setting it out in different columns in order to present his perverse results.[13] While it is not until many centuries later that we encounter the beginnings of the Modern Critical Movement, the Graf–Wellhausen Hypothesis, and Source Criticism, it is revealing to discover that its own origins lie in a wisdom-based, and antichristian movement, appealing to those who had received a particular type of *knowledge.*

The Beginnings Of The Modern Critical Movement

It was in the middle of the seventeenth century that the Modern Critical Movement really began, with the suggestion made by the Deistic[14] philosopher Thomas Hobbes (1588–1679), that very large portions of the Pentateuch post-date the age of Moses by a considerable margin.[15] Shortly after this, in 1670 Baruch Spinoza (1632–1677) published his *Tractatus Theologico-Politicus,* in which he rejected outright any Mosaic contribution to the Pentateuch,

---

[11] See any good work on Gnosticism, for example, Jonas, Hans, *The Gnostic Religion*, Boston, U.S.A., Beacon Press, 1958, and also any work covering early Church History, for example, *The History Of Christianity*, edited Dowley, Tim; Briggs, John; Linder, Robert; & Wright, David, Berkhamsted, Hertfordshire, Lion Publishing, 1977, p. 103.

[12] Pagels, Elaine, *The Gnostic Gospels*, Harmondsworth, Middlesex, Penguin Books, 1986, pp. 55ff.

[13] Mead, G.R.S., *Fragments Of A Faith Forgotten*, New York, University Books, 1960, pp. 241ff.

[14] Deism is a philosophical system that teaches that God is a Remote Creator, who leaves the universe to run according to the laws He built into it, and does not intervene directly, thus eliminating the miraculous. See *The Hodder Pocket Dictionary Of Theological Terms*, edited by Grenz, Guretzki, & Nordling, London, Hodder & Stoughton, 1999, in. loc.

[15] Harrison, R. K., *Introduction To The Old Testament*, London, Tyndale Press, 1970, pp. 9–10.

attributing it all to Ezra, along with Joshua, Judges, Ruth, I & II Samuel, and I & II Kings. Spinoza sought to ascertain not just the date of composition of the books he considered, but also the reasons behind their composition, and the circumstances and character of the author.[16] According to Wiseman, the name Higher Criticism, is traceable to Hobbes and Spinoza.[17]

In 1678, the Roman Catholic theologian and Professor of Philosophy, Richard Simon (1638–1712) published his *Histoire Critique Du Vieux Testament*, in which he too concluded that the Pentateuch as we know it, could not be attributed to Moses, but is to be placed much later. Simon utilised the techniques of literary criticism in his work, in which he also suggested that the historical books had been the subject of a lengthy process of compilation and redaction. The Arminian Le Clerc replied to Simon's work in 1685, in his *Sentiments De Quelques Théologiens De Hollande Sur L'Histoire Critique Du Vieux Testamen,* but Le Clerc himself ascribed to the Torah an even later date![18]

Astruc's Clue, And The Older Document Hypothesis

In 1689 in an early attempt at Source Criticism, Campegius Vitringa in his *Observationes Sacrae*, made the suggestion that Moses had available to him, records dating from the Patriarchal Period, which he had used in producing the Pentateuch.[19] As will be shown later, this is a view I hold to myself, but Vitringa's suggestions have been used to undermine the credibility of the Scriptures as we shall see.

Twenty-two years later in 1711, H. B. Witter published his *Jura Israelitarum In Palestina*, in which he argued that the different Names of God encountered in the book of Genesis; viz *Elohim,* (Hebrew אלהים), and *Jehovah* (Hebrew יהוה), could be used to identify

---

[16] Ibid, p. 10.

[17] Wiseman, P. J., *New Discoveries In Babylonia About Genesis*, London, Marshall, Morgan & Scott, the seventh edition of 1958, p. 119.

[18] Harrison, op. cit., pp. 10–11.

[19] Ibid., p. 11.

material from different sources that had been put together to form the book of Genesis, which was then presented falsely as an unity.[20]

These two suggestions were taken up by one who has since become infamous for his furthering of the sceptic's work, namely, Jean Astruc (1684–1766). In 1753 he published his impressively entitled, *Conjectures Sur Les Mémoires Originaux Dont Il Parait Que Moyse S'est Servi Pour Composer Le Livre De La Genèse. Avec Des Remarques Qui Appuient Ou Qui Éclaircissent Ces Conjectures.* Astruc argued that Moses had gathered together a large collection of oral as well as written material, and from this collection had produced the book of Genesis. Astruc cited as evidence for his views, what he termed duplications in the Creation and Flood narratives,[21] as well as the use of the different Names for God referred to by Witter. According to Astruc, whoever had compiled what we now know as Genesis had got the material into a confused state, resulting in certain episodes being presented out of their chronological sequence.

Astruc proposed that this confusion of material could be resolved by resorting to the clues given by the occurrences of the different Names for God. Ironically this practice is now often referred to as *Astruc's Clue*, when really it was Witter's![22] He identified all the passages in which *Elohim* occurred and located them in a column in his reorganised text, which he designated as column (A). By this technique he believed he had displayed the documentary source for this material, which he named *Elohist*. He then examined all the material which referred to God as *Jehovah*, and placed it in a parallel column designated (B), having in the process, he believed, identified a second documentary source which he referred to as *Jehovist*. He then added column (C) into which he placed material that he labelled as duplications, and column (D), in which he placed what he regarded as non-Israelite material. As Kaiser observes, this approach has

---

[20] Ibid., p. 12. It should be pointed out that אלהים, *Elohim,* is not a name at all, but a *title,* and that the anglicised word *Jehovah* is completely invalid as it is a hybrid of the consonants of יהוה and the vowels of אדון, the Hebrew for *Lord.*

[21] The unity of the two accounts of the Creation, and of the Flood narrative will be demonstrated later.

[22] See for example, Kaiser, Walter C. Jnr., *The Old Testament Documents*, Leicester, InterVarsity Press, 2001, p. 334.

ecome the main criterion in Source Criticism.[23] Astruc's view that the different Divine Names indicate different documentary sources is now known as the Older Document Hypothesis.[24]

Astruc initially convinced himself that he had revealed the sources Moses had used in the compilation of Genesis, but ultimately he came to realise that his proposals were inadequate for such a task. Difficulties arose because it became apparent that some verses, which it was seen had to have been written by the same person, actually contained *both* Names, and therefore could be traced to either documentary source! To overcome this difficulty, it was proposed that an editor had amalgamated texts that had originated from different sources. Another difficulty arose when it was realised that material which contained the title *Elohim*, seemed to be *Jehovist* in every other respect. It was then proposed that another editor had somehow changed the Divine names.[25] The supposed existence of this editor however undermined the entire thesis, as through his assumed activities we would never know which Divine Names the editor had changed, and which he had left alone, and therefore, sorting the text by these Divine Names would be reduced to a most laborious yet fruitless exercise![26]

Observation 1. As will become apparent, it seems to be a feature of many critical schemes, that appeals are made to the work of unnamed editors and redactors, whose existence may neither be proved or disproved. Although there are times when a researcher must hypothesise, his or her hypothesis must be minimalist and *tenable*, but the recourse that is made by many Critics to such editors and redactors whose existence may only be *presumed*, does appear to be so easy, frequent, and above all *convenient*, as to make us wonder how scientific the method employed really is! It is of course, notoriously

---

[23] Ibid.

[24] Ibid.

[25] Many interesting examples of the literary knots and muddles produced by this viewpoint are given in Hills, E. F., *The King James Version Defended! A Space Age Defence Of The Historic Christian Faith*, Des Moines, Iowa, U.S.A., third edition, 1979, p. 74.

[26] Harrison, op. cit., pp. 12–13, and Wiseman, op. cit., pp. 109–110.

difficult to prove a negative. The existence of these proposed editors and redactors then may never be *dis*proved, which means that such claims are virtually immune to any forensic tests, and enable Critics to call upon their services to paper over the cracks in their own hypotheses. The reader is urged to remember therefore, that such proposals must be regarded as general, and extremely vague *opinions* which may be offered by anyone for any purpose with almost complete impunity, rather than as specific and detailed assertions, the veracity of which may be either demonstrated or refuted.

Semler

About the middle of the eighteenth century, J. S. Semler (1725–1791), a Protestant Professor at Halle, translated into German, Simon's *Histoire Critique Du Vieux Testament*, referred to above, and utilised Simon's methods himself.[27] He is mainly remembered for having been credited, if that is an appropriate term, with destroying the concept that the Hebrew Canon is an unified corpus of authoritative teaching. This notion was, he argued, based upon misconceptions, and should be replaced by ideas based solely upon a true understanding of the historical *development* of the Scriptures.[28]

Partly as a reaction to Semler, the poet J. G. Von Herder (1744–1803), published in 1783 his *Vom Geist Der Hebräischen Poesie*. Herder was drawn to the earlier work of Spinoza, but is most noteworthy for being the first to examine the Scriptures in the context of other near eastern cultures.[29] A technique that Hermann Gunkel was to pursue years later as we shall see.

Johann Gottfried Eichhorn

J. D. Michaelis had attempted to enable the traditional ecclesiastical view of the Old Testament, to become broad enough to accept much of the work of the critical schools, but without much success, however, Eichhorn (1752–1827), the next contributor to Old

---

[27] Harrison, op. cit., p. 13.

[28] Childs, Brevard, *Introduction To The Old Testament As Scripture*, London, SCM Press, 1979, p. 35.

[29] Harrison, op. cit., p. 13.

Testament criticism we must consider is something of an enigma, inasmuch as he too attempted to win back to Christianity the educated classes, yet the tactics he adopted, contributed enormously to the invalidation of the Scriptures in the minds of many. Eichhorn, who, as we will see shortly, had been influenced greatly by many of his predecessors, attempted to broaden the appeal of the Old Testament Scriptures by seeking to remove from them, any hint of the miraculous. He did this in order to render the Scriptures more agreeable to the anti-supernaturalism of his times.[30]

He is remembered particularly for his *Einleitung In Das Alte Testament*, which appeared in the years 1780–1783, initially in three volumes, with another two added later. Although it is reported that Eichhorn was impressed greatly by the literary quality of the Hebrew Scriptures, it is clear he did not regard them as comprising the Word of God. He accepted the basis of Astruc's earlier work in Source Criticism, but enlarged it to embrace divergent literary styles, and the use of particular words and phrases, by which the supposed different sources could be identified.[31]

Childs writes of Eichhorn, "[He] combined the insights of several of his predecessors. He devoted an entire section [of his *Einleitung In Das Alte Testament*] to an exhaustive investigation of the history of the Hebrew text and versions, in which he fully supported Cappellus[32] against Buxtorf. Again, he followed Herder's lead in classifying his material according to literary genres and, abandoning the older dogmatic categories, he treated prophecy as a special disposition of the human spirit. He approached the Old Testament as an independent record of antiquity, a source from the distant past from which one could reconstruct the early stages in the education of the human race. Moreover, he pursued vigorously the direction initiated by Simon in attempting to trace the development of Israel's literature, and in setting out the source theory of the Pentateuch as it had been analysed by

---

[30] Anderson, Sir Robert, *A Doubter Doubts About Science And Religion*, London, Pickering & Inglis, third edition, undated, p. 145.

[31] Harrison, op. cit., pp. 13–14, Childs, op. cit., pp. 35–36, & Wiseman, op. cit., pp. 90–91.

[32] Held to have discredited the Masoretic Text, by showing it to contain many corruptions, see Childs, op. cit., p. 34.

Astruc and others. Finally, the important influence of Semler's study of the canon is everywhere evident. Eichhorn abandoned completely the theological concern with the canon, stating at one point: 'it would have been desirable if one had never even used the term canon.' (4th. Ed., vol. I, p. 106). He replaced the term with a purely historical definition. He was concerned only with the historical process by which the ancient literature was collected. Only occasionally does one see vestiges of the older position. His defence of the 'genuineness of the sources', by which he meant that the literature was not a forgery, was soon to be re-defined in terms of historicity and authorship [The words in square brackets are my own]."[33]

Eichhorn is frequently referred to as the 'father' of Old Testament Criticism,[34] and is said by some to be the first actually to use the term Higher Criticism.[35]

The Fragment Hypothesis

After Eichhorn, the next significant contribution came from a Scottish Roman Catholic theologian, named Alexander Geddes (1737–1802), who, in 1792, published a translation of the Pentateuch and Joshua, which was followed in 1800 by another work entitled, *Critical Remarks On The Hebrew Scriptures*. Geddes suggested that the Pentateuch dated only from the days of Solomon, and was the consequence of an editor working from a mass of fragments, some of which pre-dated Moses. While he accepted Astruc's suggestion about the Divine Names identifying different sources, or, in his case, *different series of fragments*, he rejected the view, accepted by Eichhorn, that they identified actual documents.[36] This was a reaction to the development of Higher Criticism which by then had identified so many so-called discrepancies, that, in the opinion of Geddes, the Pentateuch was clearly the product of a large amount of sources,

---

[33] Childs, op. cit., pp. 35–36.

[34] Harrison, op. cit., p. 14, attributes this saying to the British Higher Critic, T. K. Cheyne.

[35] In the preface to the second edition of his *Einleitung In Das Alte Testament* in 1787. Harrison, op. cit., p. 26.

[36] Harrison, op. cit., p. 14.

rather than a few documents.[37] He was the first to suggest that Joshua belonged with the Pentateuch to form a Hexateuch, as he held that they were worked on by the same redactor. The name Hexateuch has since become commonplace in critical circles.[38]

In 1805 Johann Severin Vater (1771–1826) developed Geddes' *Fragment Hypothesis,* suggesting in his *Commentar Über Den Pentateuch*, that there were as many as forty different fragmentary sources to be found in the Pentateuch. While Vater agreed that some of these fragments would pre-date Moses, and thought that most were cöeval with Moses, the Pentateuch in its final form he dated to the time of the Exile.

Observation 2. It should be pointed out that the so-called Hexateuch is an example of wrongly dividing The Word Of Truth (II Timothy 2:15).[39] The book of Joshua, together with Judges, (I & II) Samuel, and (I & II) Kings form the Division of the Hebrew Canon known as the *Former Prophets*, (in Hebrew, נביאים ראשונים). By consulting Zechariah 7:7, it will be seen that this Grouping is a valid Division of Scripture, inasmuch as Scripture itself utilises the term. Removing the book of Joshua from its context, and aligning it with the Torah, Pentateuch, or five books of Moses, has no Scriptural warrant at all.[40] The fact that there may nonetheless be a noticeable

---

[37] Whybray, R. N., *The Making Of The Pentateuch: A Methodological Study*, being Supplement Number 53 of *The Journal For The Study Of The Old Testament*, Sheffield, Sheffield University Press, 1987, p. 25.

[38] Harrison, op. cit., p. 14.

[39] As is, of course, the so-called Octateuch; that is the Pentateuch, plus, Joshua, Judges, and Ruth. The latter book is taken from the Kethuvim, or Writings, and not even from the Prophets. See Appendix I.

[40] In fact Joshua 24:26 seems to show that even in the days of Joshua himself, the Pentateuch was regarded as a distinct corpus. Although this same verse shows that Joshua seemingly may have contributed a small amount to the Pentateuch, such as the *Post-Mosaica*, or *A-Mosaica* of Deuteronomy 34:5–12, which gives the details of the death of Moses, and Numbers 12:3 which is a reference to the character of Moses, the main point is that the Pentateuch had received recognition as a particular body of literature, very shortly after its completion, making a proposed Hexateuch an impossibility. This concept is expressed particularly clearly in the traditional Jewish designation of the books of the Torah as חמשה חומשי תורה, *The Five Fifths Of The Law,* thereby demonstrating their belief that it is a body of literature to which no other book may be added (or taken away).

similarity of style between the writings of Moses and Joshua, is readily accounted for by the fact that they shared very many common experiences, over several decades, and that Joshua was chosen to succeed Moses. It would be strange indeed if a pupil showed no likeness to his master with whom he had spent forty years (cf. Matthew 10:25a). Thus, again, whatever similarity of style may be seen when comparing Joshua and the Pentateuch is accounted for by the Pentateuchal narrative itself, rather than by appealing to unknown, and unknowable editors or redactors; an obvious merit I believe.

De Wette's Clue

The most prominent follower of the Fragment Hypothesis was Wilhelm Martin Lebrecht De Wette (1780–1849). His *Beiträge Zur Einleitung In Das Alte Testament*, published in 1807 is his most well-known work. He proposed that the earliest portions of the Pentateuch go back only as far as David, and that the different books were the work of different redactors who utilised independent fragmentary sources. De Wette was the first to suggest that the Book of the Law found in the reign of Josiah was the legal heart of Deuteronomy, *and is to be dated to the time of Josiah*. He made this suggestion after comparing II Kings 22f. with Deuteronomy 12. This proposal, known as De Wette's Clue,[41] is now very widely accepted in critical circles. Nonetheless, De Wette felt that the Documentary Theory of Astruc and Eichhorn had some merits which the Fragment Hypothesis lacked, and as a consequence, proposed an Elohistic type of document as a source for Genesis, and the first six chapters of Exodus. Following Herder's lead, he believed that much of Genesis has the nature of epic poetry.[42]

In fact De Wette's most controversial suggestions were that the Pentateuch contained *no genuine history at all*, only epic poetry and

---

[41] Cheyne, T. K. & Wellhausen, Julius, in the article, *Hexateuch*, in *Encyclopædia Biblica*, edited by Cheyne, T. K. & Sutherland Black, J., London, A. & C. Black, 1903, and Rendle Short, A, *Modern Discovery And The Bible*, London, Inter-Varsity Fellowship, fourth edition, reprinted 1955, p. 167.

[42] Harrison, op. cit., p. 15, & Cheyne, T. K. & Wellhausen, Julius, op. cit., in. loc.

legends! The history they revealed, according to his book *Kritik Der Mosaischen Geschichte* also published in 1807, is not the history they claim to give the details of; that is, the history of the Patriarchs and Moses, but the history of the era De Wette said they were actually composed in. In the previous year, he had published *Kritischer Versuch Über Die Glaubwürdigkeit Der Bücher Der Chronik* in which he claimed that the Torah was unknown during the years covered by the books of Samuel and Kings. Chronicles, he claimed, was a re-writing of the same history, but was aimed at supporting the false claims concerning the Mosaic provenance of the Torah, by the insertion of material purporting to show the presence of the Torah, when, according to De Wette, it never existed.[43] De Wette's work constituted a pioneering contribution to what has become known as Historical Criticism. Among those influenced by De Wette was the famous German Hebraist, H. W. F. Gesenius of Halle, the author of the well-known Hebrew Grammar, and Hebrew Lexicon.[44]

Observation 3. These startling claims by De Wette, in which he alleged that Chronicles was written in an attempt to delude innocent believers, as well as his assertion that the Pentateuch itself contains no real history at all, show how false are Bennett's words in his book *The Bible And Criticism.* Bennett complains that those who oppose the Higher Criticism charge Higher Critics with implying that some books of Scripture are forgeries, written to deceive, and that this attack is not valid.[45] Well De Wette's views certainly do seem to demonstrate that such claims are extremely valid; they appear to offer a perfectly apt description of the charge De Wette brought against the Pentateuch and Chronicles at least; namely that they are fabrication. Sceptical Higher Criticism ought at least be honest about itself, what it stands for, and its motives, but it is not. Hence my earlier remarks about ravenous wolves in sheep's clothing! We may only conclude that Sceptical Higher Criticism is dishonest, disingenuous, and charges Scripture with containing forgeries.

---

[43] Cheyne, T. K. & Wellhausen, Julius, in the article, *Hexateuch*, in *Encyclopædia Biblica*, op. cit., in. loc.

[44] Ibid.

[45] Op. cit., p. 12.

The Supplement Hypothesis

The Fragment Hypothesis had a relatively short life. It was undermined by Heinrich Georg August Ewald, the pupil of Eichhorn,[46] in his *Die Komposition Der Genesis Kritisch Untersucht* published in 1823. He showed how the book of Genesis has an unity about it which eliminated the concept of it being the consequence of a collection of fragments. Ewald also pushed the date of the composition of Genesis further back in time than his predecessors had done, but stopped short of placing it in the days of Moses. He maintained that the Elohistic Source was the foundation of the Hexateuch, but that it had been supplemented by older material, such as the Decalogue. Subsequently, according to Ewald's scheme, an editor used the Elohistic Document as a basic framework, but occasionally inserted material from a Jehovist Source into this foundational Elohistic document thus *supplementing* it. This Foundation Document became known as the Grundschrift,[47] and the new theory was known as the Supplement Hypothesis.

Ewald's early dating of the Grundschrift was contested by Wilhelm Vatke in his *Die Biblische Theologie Wissenschaftlich Dargestellt* of 1835, who placed it during the Exile. Ewald's principle of the Supplement Hypothesis did however, win backing from De Wette, who from 1840 onwards adhered to the view that the Elohistic Grundschrift had been supplemented by both Jehovistic material, and material from the Deuteronomist. J. J. Stähelin in 1843, in his *Kritische Untersuchungen Über Den Pentateuch*, added that there had been a redaction of the Hexateuch during the monarchy, possibly undertaken by Samuel.[48] Finally, J. C. F. Tuch in 1838, in his *Kommentar Über Die Genesis,* saw two documentary sources in the Pentateuch, the Elohistic Grundschrift, to which had been added material from the Jehovist Ergänzer, or Supplementer, in the Solomonic age.[49]

---

[46] Anderson, Sir Robert, *The Bible And Modern Criticism*, op. cit., p. 40.

[47] Not to be confused with Martin Noth's *Grundlage*, a word coined by him in 1948, to designated the common basis of J & E. Soulen & Kendall Soulen, op. cit., in. loc.

[48] Harrison, op. cit., pp. 15–16, & Wiseman, op. cit., p. 92.

[49] Harrison, op. cit., pp. 16–17.

Observation 4. I think believers have nothing to fear from a proposed recension of the Torah, and Joshua and Judges by Samuel. To my mind this hypothesis is both minimalist and tenable, as the very strong Scriptural association of Samuel with reform (I Samuel 4–7), makes it extremely likely that he would have had a very keen interest in bringing a real knowledge of the Scriptures to as many of the people of Israel as possible.

It is seen from Church history, that a desire to circulate the Scriptures, and bring a real knowledge of them to the common people, is usually the forerunner of a revision of the translation of the Scriptures, so as to bring them up-to-date by the introduction of current day place names, the elimination of little known words and phrases and so on. Thus, this proposed recension, by a *named* individual constitutes a tenable hypothesis I submit.

The Crystallisation Hypothesis

The Supplement Hypothesis too was superseded. It was demonstrated by J. H. Kurtz in 1846 in his *Die Einheit Der Genesis*, that much of the Elohistic Grundschrift, presupposed material that was held to have originated from the Solomonic Ergänzer! However, the most telling blow to the Supplement Hypothesis, surprisingly came from Ewald himself, who, in a considerable realignment of his views, proposed in 1843, in *Geschichte Des Volkes Israel*, that certain passages of the Pentateuch originated from a source that was distinct from the Elohistic, Jehovistic and Deuteronomist documents. These passages included *The Book Of Covenants,*[50] which he said dated from the Period of the Judges, a *Book of Origins,*[51] dating from the Solomonic Age, and the work of three separate narrators, dating from circa 500 B.C.E. This view became known as the Crystallisation Hypothesis.

Hupfeld And The New Documentary Hypothesis

In 1853, Hermann Hupfeld published his *Die Quellen Der Genesis Und Die Art Ihrer Zusammensetzung Von Neuen Untersucht.* Hupfeld

---

[50] Exodus 20:22–23:19, see Bennett, W. H., & Adeney, W. F., op. cit., p. 22.

[51] Genesis 1:1–2:4a, ibid., p. 24, and Driver, S. R., *The Book Of Genesis*, London, Methuen & Co., fourth edition, 1905, p. iv.

argued that the Grundschrift was not an unity after all, as suggested by Ewald, but was an amalgam of two separate sources. Both of these were Elohistic inasmuch as they both used Elohim instead of Jehovah. The first of these contributors to the Grundschrift, called Die Urschrift, clearly showed Priestly tendencies, and therefore was designated P,[52] and relates to the first nineteen chapters of Genesis. The second and therefore younger Elohist's work commenced at Genesis 20, and was far closer than the first to the Jehovistic Source. This second Elohist was named E. Added to this was J, the Jehovistic source, and D, the Deuteronomist. E, through what seems to be a partial return to the Fragment Hypothesis, was now considered to be a compilation. Hupfeld then proposed that a redactor or many redactors produced the Hexateuch as we now know it from these four distinct sources.[53]

Another milestone was reached when Eduard Riehm in 1854 applied Hupfeld's theory to the entire Pentateuch, and thereby created what became known as the Four-Source Document Theory, of P, E, J, and D, which, in a modified form, was later embraced by Abraham Kuenen, and Karl Heinrich Graf, to whom we shall turn very shortly.[54]

Hupfeld's position was challenged by Nöldeke, who in 1869 published his *Untersuchungen Zur Kritik Des Alte Testament.* Nöldeke argued that there were after all only two main sources of the Pentateuch, apart from Deuteronomy, as according to his views, the Second Elohist and the Jehovist are to be counted as one Source, (JE), and the Grundschrift (P), another. He also showed to his satisfaction, how the Grundschrift permeates the Hexateuch.

Conclusion To Chapter One

The Modern Critical Movement's spiritual roots are similar to the roots of Gnosticism, not because the Higher Critics have recourse to intuitive thought as opposed to analytical thought, but inasmuch as they lay claim to a special method of interpreting the Scriptures that is a

---

[52] Harrison, op. cit., pp. 17–18, Hills, op. cit., p. 74 & Kaiser, op. cit., p. 135. P was at first it was named Q, see Whybray, op. cit., p. 25.

[53] Harrison, op. cit., pp. 17–18, Hills, op. cit., p. 74 & Kaiser, op. cit., p. 135.

[54] Kaiser, op. cit., p. 135.

consequence of their having received a special form of knowledge. Upon examination, however, it becomes clear that this special method of interpreting the Scriptures, is but a special method of doubting the Scriptures, or in De Wette's case, repudiating the Scriptures. This wisdom-based interpretation, like Gnosticism of old, is elitist, as it elevates those who understand Critical Method, from ordinary believers who are uninitiated, and, again like Gnosticism, it leads so reasonably and easily, to a denial of the very basic tenets of Christianity.

At this stage in our investigation it has also become apparent that Sceptical Higher Criticism is dependent upon the supposed labours of a whole host of unnamed editors and redactors, who were so inefficient and careless as to confuse hopelessly the texts they had received from many different sources. Higher Criticism, suggests among others, the existence of R^{JE}, the redactor who amalgamated, J & E; R^{D}, who merged JE & D; and R^{P}, who brought together JED & P.[55]

The muddle these unknown editors produced was so thorough it is alleged, that it was not until the Age of Enlightenment, that specially trained minds were able to begin the task of untangling the mess. Earlier generations, which inevitably included the Apostles and Christ HimSelf, were either ignorant of the reality of the situation, or accommodated their statements concerning the Pentateuch, to the unlearned masses around them. Thus, the Sceptical Higher Criticism forces believers to choose between Apostles and a Son of God who were profoundly ignorant of the origins of the Scriptures, or Apostles and a Son of God who were not ignorant at all, but chose to mislead the masses, just as De Wette's chronicler did! That this is the true position is evidenced by the fact that this concept has been given a particular name; it is referred to as the Accommodation Theory, a name coined by Semler.[56] This consequence of Sceptical Higher Criticism should reveal much to ordinary believers about the sinister character of the movement.

---

[55] Garrett, Duane, *Rethinking Genesis*, Fearn, Ross-shire, Scotland, Christian Focus Publications, 2000, pp. 12–13.

[56] Wiseman, op. cit., p. 120.

Chapter Two

Post-Grafian Higher Criticism

Part A:
The Development Of
The New Documentary Hypothesis

Reuss, Graf, Colenso, And Kuenen

Karl Heinrich Graf is remembered for his very late dating of the Grundschrift, but it appears to have been an idea he borrowed from his teacher Eduard Reuss, who in the university of Strasbourg, in the summer of 1834, had suggested to his students that the Elohistic source was not an early source at all, but was the *latest* source that underpinned the Pentateuch. Graf was attracted by this suggestion, and in 1865, in his *Die Geschichtlichen Bücher Des Alt Testament: Zwei Historisch-Kritische Untersuchungen* stated that the Priestly interests evident in the Elohistic Document meant it must be dated to the time of Ezra, and his promulgation of the Law. The so-called Holiness Code, that is Leviticus 17–26, and referred to as H, he placed in the time of Ezekiel. Graf still adhered to the Supplement Hypothesis, and believed that the Jehovist additions to the Grundschrift underwent redaction by the Deuteronomist.

Rendle Short gives a very good synopsis of Graf's scheme, which is also known as Graf's Clue. He writes, "(According to Graf's Clue) there are three stages in the development of Israelitish religion. JE corresponds to a stage, running up to the time of Josiah, when God might be worshipped anywhere at any shrine; any layman could offer his sacrifice, and images of Jehovah were tolerated. D corresponds to a stage when worship was centralised at Jerusalem, and priests and

Levites only might minister at the altar. After the Exile, a full and complicated ritual was laid down by P, and only priests could minister."[57]

At about the same time, the Anglican Bishop of Natal, John William Colenso entered the field. Between 1862 and 1879 he published seven treatises entitled *The Pentateuch And The Book Of Joshua Critically Examined*. He believed that the highly detailed priestly organisation found in Leviticus and Numbers was evidence of its very late date. He also suggested that the book found by Hilkiah in the temple was Deuteronomy, and that Chronicles was written as propaganda to exalt the status of the priesthood.

Colenso was severely disciplined for his writings, but, nonetheless, they were not without their admirers. The Dutch scholar, Abraham Kuenen was in broad agreement with Colenso's views, and suggested that the prophetic passages of Genesis, Exodus and Numbers were far older than the Grundschrift. In 1870 Kuenen published *De Godsdienst Van Israel*. He argued that the Jehovistic material was the basis of the Pentateuch, and that it had been supplemented by additional material from an Elohistic source, Deuteronomy, which he dated to the time of Josiah, the Holiness Code and similar material, dating from the exile, as well as material from the Priestly source.

This gave great support to the views of Graf. A real revolution had occurred. Before, Reuss, and Graf, the supposed order of sources had been P, E, J, D, after their contributions, it was held to be J, E, D, P.[58] The Supplement Theory was still considered to be viable, but in a revised form of course, owing to the rearranged sequence of the Sources as outlined above.

Wellhausen

Just as Ewald was Eichhorn's most well known student, so Julius Wellhausen (1844–1918), was Ewald's most renowned pupil. Wellhausen studied under Ewald at Göttingen. There is no doubt at all

---

[57] Rendle Short, op. cit., p. 168. For a discussion on the rôle of the priests and Levites see Supplement One.

[58] Harrison, op. cit, pp. 19–20.

that Wellhausen possessed a first class mind, winning wide acclaim for his study on the books of Samuel.[59] He has been compared with Charles Darwin, as in keeping with the spirit of the age that saw Darwin introduce the concept of evolution by means of natural selection into the field of biology, following the philosophy of G. W. F. Hegel (1770–1831),[60] as well as Herder, and the ideas of Wilhelm Vatke, another follower of Hegel, Wellhausen brought the concept of evolution to the study of the Scriptures.

In combining the developmental views of the Hegelian Vatke, which he applied to the Israelite priesthood, with the alleged evolution of Israelite ritual laws proposed by Graf, Wellhausen believed he had shown the necessity of a late placement of the Priestly Source. According to Harrison, Wellhausen did not undertake a critical enquiry into Graf's views, but took them to what he thought was their logical conclusion. This resulted in him viewing the Pentateuch as being built up from J, the Jehovist Source (ninth century B.C.E.); a distinct Elohist Source, E, (a century later); D, the book of Deuteronomy, more or less as we know it today (datable to the time of Josiah, 640–609 B.C.E.); and P, the Priestly Source, which he placed in the fifth century B.C.E. In his *Die Komposition Des Hexateuchs*, which was published in 1877, he maintained that the Jehovist writer complied a narrative by combining J and E, which in the days of Josiah was supplemented by the addition of D. In the time of Ezekiel, the Holiness Code, known as H, and comprising Leviticus 17–26 was added to the Priestly Source, the rest of which was contributed by Ezra. At about 200 B.C.E., the entire collection was revised resulting in the Pentateuch as we have it today.[61]

---

[59] Der Text Der Bücher Samuelis Untersucht, published in 1871.

[60] A brief description of Hegel's views, and reactions to Kant are given in Hills, op. cit., pp. 48–49., See also *Historical Selections In The Philosophy Of Religion*, edited Smart, N, London, SCM Press, 1962, pp. 290–305.

[61] Harrison, op. cit., pp. 21–22. It is interesting to note how widely the Hegelian concept underpinning the Graf–Wellhausen Hypothesis spread. It affected the study of ancient literature generally, including the works of Homer, which according to Wilamowitz was a "wretched patchwork." More recently however the Documentary approach to Homer has been overturned by Schadewaldt, who is said to have brought a century and a half of German scholarship crashing to the ground by his researches showing the literary unity of the Iliad! See Kikawada, Isaac, M., & Quinn, Arthur, *Before Abraham Was: A*

Wellhausen's Presentation Of The History Of Israel

For Wellhausen the Scriptural narratives concerning Patriarchal religious practices were simply untrue. Following the evolutionary theories of Hegel, he proposed that the earliest period of Israelite history was marked by religious impulses that were primitive and animistic. He further proposed that after the conquest, the adaptation of the Israelites to the religion life of Canaan, marked a step forward on their way towards monotheism, which was brought about by the activity of the prophets. He believed that the work of the prophets also brought about the creation of a central shrine in Jerusalem, which occurred only during the days of Josiah. After the exile and return, the Priestly codes were drawn up.[62]

Hills gives a very good synopsis of the effect of Wellhausen's views on the understanding of the Scriptural narrative. He writes, "In 1878 Julius Wellhausen published his famous *Prolegomena to the History of Ancient Israel*.[63] This was a complete reconstruction of Old Testament history in agreement with Graf's hypothesis, which accordingly was renamed the Graf–Wellhausen hypothesis. The history of Israel, Wellhausen maintained, began at Mt. Sinai, where Moses persuaded the Israelites to adopt Yahweh (Jehovah) as their tribal god. Ever afterwards they felt themselves to be Yahweh's people, and this feeling gave them a sense of national unity. But Moses gave them no laws. These were developed later after they had settled in the land of Canaan. This primitive legal code was transmitted orally until about 850 B.C. Then it was written down and incorporated in the J narrative and is now found in Exodus 20–23.

Around 750 B.C., according to Wellhausen, a tremendous transformation of the religious thinking of ancient Israel began to take place. Mighty, prophetic reformers arose, such as Amos, Hosea, and the first Isaiah, who publicly proclaimed that Yahweh was not a tribal deity but a righteous God who ruled all nations and would punish

---

Provocative Challenge To The Documentary Hypothesis, Nashville, U.S.A., Abingdon Press, 1985, pp. 11–12.

[62] Harrison, op. cit., pp. 21–22.

[63] Hills here gives the title of the American translation of the sixth German edition. In German it was *Prolegomena Zur Geschichte Israels*, see Kaiser, op. cit., p. 84, note 1.

them for their sins, who would chastise even Israel. This reform movement finally culminated in an exciting event which occurred around 621 B.C. Hilkiah the high priest found in the Temple the book of the law, which had been lost. This book was brought to King Josiah, who accepted it as genuine and called an assembly of the people in which he and the whole nation made a solemn covenant before Yahweh to keep all the commandments written in this book. This action, Wellhausen asserted, marked the entrance of the covenant-concept into Jewish thought. The covenant which Josiah made with Yahweh came to be regarded as typical. Ever after the Jews though of themselves as Yahweh's covenant people. According to Wellhausen, however, the book that produced this profound effect was not an ancient book, as Josiah was led to believe, but the book of Deuteronomy, which had been written only a short time before by the leaders of the reform movement and placed in the Temple for the express purpose of being 'discovered.'"[64]

Observation 5. It is astounding to think that Wellhausen really thought that he was in a better position than Josiah, to judge the provenance of the book Hilkiah brought to him! It follows that we are also obliged to think Josiah enormously naïve, compared with the shrewd Wellhausen. This one episode shows the breathtaking arrogance of Wellhausen and those of his ilk.

Wellhausen did not add much to Graf's views, but enlarged their application, and then presented them in such a way that their appeal to the intelligentsia of the day, immersed as they were in the evolutionary theories of Hegel, and Darwin, and bolstered by the promotion of uniformitarian geology by Charles Lyell, and the political and economic theories of Marx, which like Hegelianism were based on dialectic, made them irresistible.[65] Wellhausen was in step with the views of his time.

---

[64] Hills, op. cit., pp. 75–76.

[65] This dependence upon dialectic paradigms is observable in New Testament criticism of the same period as well. F. C. Bauer, Professor of Church History and dogmatics at Tübingen from 1826 to 1860, in 1850 proposed that the thesis of the Jewish Gospel of Matthew, was opposed by the antithesis of the Gentile Gospel of Luke; the two views being reconciled by the synthesis of Mark. What is important about this is not so much the interpretation of each Gospel, so much as the Dialectic framework, which was very

From then on the Graf–Wellhausen Hypothesis became the dominant literary critical theory of Old Testament origins. It very much suited the spirit of its age that embraced the ideas of slow development from primitive beginnings as being characteristic of every area of life. Together with Darwinism, Marxism, and in later years, cosmic evolutionary theories, it contributed towards a multifaceted attack on the veracity of the Scriptures that has continued into the current Post-Modernist Liberal Age.

Wellhausen eventually turned his attentions to the Gospels, but was succeeded amongst others, by Smend, Stade, Budde, Cornill, and Kautzsch, the famous editor of Gesenius' *Hebrew Grammar*.[66] The Graf–Wellhausen Hypothesis gained a stranglehold on academia, as senior posts in seminaries and universities in Europe, and ultimately in America too, were reserved only for those progressive theologians who embraced the latest literary-critical methods.[67]

Wellhausen's Disciples

In Britain, the most noteworthy followers of Graf and Wellhausen were A. B. Davidson, the famous Hebraist, T. K. Cheyne, one of the editors of *Encyclopædia Biblica*, S. R. Driver, author of *An Introduction To The Literature Of The Old Testament*, and a very famous commentary on Genesis, and W. Robertson-Smith, to whom the *Encyclopædia Biblica* is dedicated. Robertson-Smith became one of the so-called martyrs of the Higher Criticism, as after an article he had written which supported the Graf–Wellhausen Hypothesis was accepted by the *Encyclopædia Britannica*, he was tried for heresy, and was expelled from The Free Church College of Aberdeen, in 1881. In the same year he published a series of lectures on *The Old Testament In The Jewish Church*. This was followed in 1882 by *The Prophets Of Israel*, in 1885 by *Kinship And Marriage In Early Arabia*, and in 1889 by *The Religion Of The Semites*. However, while there is no doubt about Robertson-

---

much in vogue at the time, and constitutes what Robinson rightly calls in the case of the synoptics, an *imposition*. See Robinson, J. A. T., *Redating The New Testament*, London, SCM Press, 1976, pp. 3–4.

[66] Harrison, op. cit., p. 24.

[67] Ibid., p. 28.

Smith's literary ability, it was S. R. Driver who really advanced the cause of Graf–Wellhausen in Britain.[68]

---

[68] Ibid., pp. 27–28.

Part Two:
Reactions To
The New Documentary Hypothesis

It is fair to say that since the appearance of the Graf–Wellhausen Hypothesis, most scholars and researchers have tended to accept its major principles. Amongst the ranks of its supporters over the last fifty years would be found De Vaux in 1953, John Marks in 1961, Speiser in 1964, Otto Eissfeldt in 1965, Georg Fohrer also in 1965, David Green in 1968, Cazelles in 1973, Soggin in 1976 Smend (the younger) in 1978, Schmidt in 1979, George Coats in 1984, and Westermann again in 1984[69] There have been those however, who have sought to modify the theory in one way or another, while others have challenged its fundamental concepts.

The Revival Of The Fragment Hypothesis And The Rise Of Redaction Criticism

One serious attempt at modifying the Graf–Wellhausen Hypothesis is to be found in the attempts to fragment the various source documents. The division of the J source is typical of a whole class of competing systems which have become more and more absorbed with dissecting the alleged different sources of the Pentateuch. Rudolph Smend in 1912 published his *Die Erzälung Des Hexateuchs Auf Ihre Quellen Untersucht* in which he developed the views of a Charles Bruston. Smend proposed two J sources; J^1 & J^2. These two sources permeated the Hexateuch according to Smend. Eichrodt took up this suggestion in 1918 in his *Der Quellen Der Genesis*, and analysed the Patriarchal narratives in order to validate the theory. The theory was developed yet again by Otto Eissfeldt in 1922 in his *Hexateuch-Synopse*.

---

[69] Whybray, op. cit., pp. 31–34, and Garrett, op. cit., p. 262, n. 1.

Eissfeldt maintained that J^1 was older than J^2 and constituted what he called a Laienquelle, or Laity-source, which was the absolute opposite of the Priestly source, or P.[70] This Laity-source is sometimes referred to as L. In addition to this Pfeiffer refers to a Southern Source he calls S, while Morgenstern and Fohrer suggested their own additional sources known as K and N respectively![71]

The supposed E and P documents have also been viewed as but amalgamations of different sources in what amounts to a small revival of the Fragment Hypothesis, although recently there has been serious debate as to whether P is really a redaction rather than a source![72] A reaction induced by the dissecting of the sources J, E, and P into ever smaller and smaller fragments is the rise of what is called Redaction Criticism, a term that was only coined as late as 1954.[73] This discipline claims to examine the proposed series of redactions the literary sources or oral traditions were subjected to.[74]

Alternative Systems

The rise of Form Criticism was caused by the recognised inadequacies of the Graf–Wellhausen Hypothesis,[75] but it was more than a mere criticism of the system, but was a serious attempt at producing an *alternative* system. Hermann Gunkel (1862–1932) and his followers attempted to trace the origins of the stories in the Scriptural narrative back to presumed oral traditions, such as are encountered in folktales, and actually employed the same methods

---

[70] Harrison, op. cit., pp. 38–39.

[71] Kidner, D. *Genesis: An Introduction And Commentary*, London, The Tyndale Press, 1973, p. 18. Kidner also points out that in addition to L, J, E, D, H, & P, R. H. Pfeiffer has added S, & O, designated Edomite sources! (p. 18). See also Whybray, op. cit., p. 31.

[72] Alexander, T. Desmond, *Abraham In The Negev: A Source-Critical Investigation Of Genesis 20:1–22:19*, Carlisle, Paternoster Press, 1997, p. 11ff.

[73] See Soulen, & Kendall Soulen, op. cit., in. loc.

[74] Ibid.

[75] See Wright, G. Ernest, *The Old Testament Against Its Environment*, being Number 1, in the original series of *Studies In Biblical Theology*, London, SCM Press, 1962 impression pp. 60ff.

that are used in the analysing of folklore,[76] including what have become known as Olrik's Laws, named after Axel Olrik who was a Danish Folklorist who devised a series of 'Laws' to which Oral Narrative is said to conform.[77]

Gunkel analysed the Hittite, Egyptian, and Mesopotamian mythologies in order to see to what extent they had influenced what he regarded as Hebrew myths which underlay the stories in the Scriptures. Gunkel taught that the accounts of the Patriarchs were originally sagas told around camp fires, and tended to centre around the activities of particular individuals. Some considerable time later they were committed to writing to form the basis of the Elohist and Jehovist documents.

Surprisingly, Gunkel wished to rediscover the religious significance of the Hebrew Scriptures, which the clinically analytical approach of Graf and Wellhausen had smothered. Ironically, Gunkel also claimed actually to support Graf–Wellhausen, yet it is very clear that his approach had a lot in common with the earlier Fragment Hypothesis of Geddes and Vater, and that his early dating of the roots of the narrative through tracing it to an alleged oral tradition undermined totally the very late dating Graf and Wellhausen had given P![78]

Martin Noth And The Deuteronomists

The most well known Form Critic of modern times, is Martin Noth (pronounced *Note*) who, like Gunkel, viewed himself as a firm supporter of Graf–Wellhausen.[79] Noth, (1902–1968), was a prodigious writer, who became Professor of Old Testament Studies in

---

[76] An excellent survey of the history (and follies) of sceptical Form Criticism is to be found in Whybray, op. cit., Part II, i.e., pp. 133–219.

[77] For a list of these so-called Laws, see Whybray, op. cit., pp. 146–147.

[78] Kaiser gives an excellent introduction, and scholarly challenge to Gunkel's Form Criticism in *The Old Testament Documents,* op. cit., cap. 4. For an excellent rebuttal of Gunkel's views on Genesis 1, see Young, E. J., *Studies In Genesis One*, Philadelphia, U.S.A., Presbyterian And Reformed, 1964. See also Garrett, op. cit., pp. 32–45, & Harrison, op. cit., pp. 35ff.

[79] See Whybray, op. cit., p. 32, & Noth, Martin, *A History Of Pentateuchal Traditions*, translated Anderson, Englewood Cliffs, New Jersey, U.S.A., Prentice–Hall, 1972, pp. 228ff.

Königsberg in 1930, and afterwards in Bonn in 1945, and from 1965 till 1968 was Director of the Institute For The Study Of The Holy Land in Jerusalem. He held that Israel only came into being as the consequence of a tribal amphictyony, after the tribe of Joseph had invaded Canaan, and that the pre-history of Israel cannot be known with any certainty, owing to the complete lack of reliable information.

In spite of his professed allegiance to Graf–Wellhausen, Noth detached the book of Deuteronomy from the Pentateuch, to leave a Tetrateuch, and attached it as a Preamble to Joshua, Judges, I & II Samuel, and I & II Kings, thus forming a group of books which he termed the Deuteronomist History. The terms Deuteronomists, and Deuteronomist History are now common in Biblical studies. He is also remembered for his proposal of a common basis, or Grundlage for the supposed J and E sources. The Grundlage is referred to by the siglum G.[80] Recently however, there appears to have been a decline in the popularity of Noth's views.[81]

Later developments of Form Criticism have become even more obscure with John Van Seters using the practices and methods of Yugoslavian bards as detailed in Albert. B. Lord's *The Singer Of Tales*, to explain the making of the Pentateuch, for which he received the criticism of the later writer, Patricia Kirkpatrick.[82]

Winnett, Wagner, And Redford

Van Seters was a pupil of F. V. Winnett, who has also proposed an alternative to Graf–Wellhausen, an alternative that was later taken up and modified by two more of his pupils, Wagner, and Redford. Winnett held that Exodus and Numbers were based on 'a continuous Mosaic tradition', to use Harrison's phrase, which originated in the Northern Kingdom of Israel. With the fall of the Northern Kingdom, this tradition was transferred to the Southern Kingdom, where it was revised in accordance with the views that prevailed in Judah. In the

---

[80] Soulen & Kendall Soulen, op. cit., pp. 46–47, 70, & 123.

[81] See Garrett, op. cit., pp. 39–41.

[82] Garrett, op. cit., pp. 38ff. For more information on Van Seters, see Alexander, op. cit., pp. 20ff., Garrett, op. cit., Cap. 2, and Whybray, op. cit., Part II.

seventh century B.C.E., the Mosaic tradition was recast in the form of Deuteronomy, which after the Return from the Babylonian Exile, the Priesthood attempted to harmonise with the earlier Mosaic tradition. A key factor for Winnett, was the presence of a theme to be found within the Pentateuch, of the exaltation of the Jerusalem priesthood over that of the Samaritans.[83]

Rendtorff And Blum

In 1969 the Form Critic Rolf Rendtorff began his assault upon the New Documentary Hypothesis which exposed some very serious inherent weaknesses. It is my opinion that this assault, and that of Whybray, to which we shall turn shortly, have together undermined the credibility of the theory to such an extent, that it may truly be said, that the Graf–Wellhausen Hypothesis is now seen to be a failure, and that we may be said to be entering a Post-Documentary Hypothesis Era. Indeed Alexander even talks of "the present demise of the Documentary Hypothesis,"[84] while Garrett states that it has already been "demolished," and refers to its incompatibility with the findings of Form Critics and archaeological data.[85]

Rendtorff identified specific problems for the New Documentary Hypothesis which Alexander gives as follows;

1. There is nothing remotely like a scholarly consensus on the exact formulation of The New Documentary Hypothesis. This poses a severe challenge to its validity. It cannot win universal acceptance even from those who ought to be its natural supporters.

2. Tradition-historical research has indicated that the Pentateuch has been built up from independent units rather than the supposed parallel documents of Graf–Wellhausen. This is absolutely true I believe, as I will show later in this study.

---

[83] Harrison, op. cit., pp. 70–71, and Alexander, op. cit., pp. 22–22.

[84] Alexander, op. cit., p. 131.

[85] Garrett, op. cit. p. 11.

3. It is an impossibility to build up coherent documentary sources from the material assigned to J and P.

4. Gross inconsistency is found in the selection criteria used to attribute particular portions of text to the alleged sources J, E, & P. Words and phrases said to be indicative of one source, are found in material awarded to other sources.

5. Material that is as fundamentally different in nature as Genesis 12:10–20 (the first instance of the *wife-as-sister-deception*), 24:1–67 (the acquisition of a wife for Isaac), & 37:2–50:26 (the Joseph narrative), cannot be attributed to the same J source as is the case with Graf–Wellhausen. Again, I applaud Rendtorff for his perspicacity here, and later on will make definite proposals which resolve this situation.

From all of these shortcoming, Rendtorff, and his pupil, Blum, concluded that the New Documentary Hypothesis was completely unworkable.[86] His own theories, reviewed helpfully by Garrett[87] and Alexander[88] are not irresistibly attractive however.

He regards Genesis 12–50 as comprising separate units of narrative that are linked together by three different types of Divine Promises; Promises of *offspring*, *land*, and *guidance*. Given his most valid criticism of the New Documentary Hypothesis, in a way which to the uncharitably minded might seem rather hypocritical, these Promises are categorised by certain key words. The Promises of offspring are categorised by whether they refer to *seed*, or contain references to being *fruitful*, or *increasing*. Similarly, Promises of land are categorised by occurrences of the phrases *to you*, or *to you and your seed*, or by the occurrence of *to your seed*, but with the absence of *to you*. Rendtorff builds up the Pentateuch on the basis that the smallest literary units must be the oldest, but this strange assumption is completely unscientific.[89]

---

[86] Alexander, op. cit., pp. 22–25.

[87] Garrett, op. cit., pp. 241–244.

[88] Alexander, op. cit., pp. 22–25.

[89] Garrett, op. cit., pp. 241–244.

R Norman Whybray

In 1987 Whybray published his ground-breaking *The Making Of The Pentateuch: A Methodological Study*. Whybray conducted a very thorough investigation of the New Documentary Hypothesis and the Form Criticism of Gunkel, Noth, Rendtorff and Blum, and like Rendtorff, found major problems with current-day Source Criticism.

I list below some of the weaknesses he found with the New Documentary Hypothesis. Direct quotations from Whybray are in double quotations marks. The words in square brackets are my own. The emphases are his throughout.[90]

1. Although adherents of the New Documentary Hypothesis believe it accounts satisfactorily for the entire Pentateuch, the Law Codes are not dealt with adequately, as even Wellhausen acknowledged.

2. "The hypothesis was unduly dependent on a particular view of the history of the religion of Israel."

3. "The authors of the documents [J, E, P, & D.] are credited with a consistency in the avoidance of repetitions and contradictions which is unparalleled in ancient literature (and even in modern fiction), and which ignores the possibility of the deliberate use of such features for aesthetic and literary purposes. At the same time, the documentary Critics were themselves frequently inconsistent in that they ignored such features *within* the documents which they had reconstructed."

4. "The breaking up of narratives into separate documents by a 'scissors and paste' method not only lacks true analogies in the ancient literary world, but also often destroys the literary and aesthetic qualities of these narratives, which are themselves important data which ought not to be ignored."

5. "Too much reliance was placed, in view of our relative ignorance of the history of the Hebrew language, on differences of language and style. Other explanations of

---

[90] Whybray, op. cit., pp. 129–131.

variations of language and style are available, e.g. differences of subject-matter requiring special or distinctive vocabulary, alternations of vocabulary introduced for literary reasons, and unconscious variation of vocabulary."

6. "The hypothesis depends on the occurrence of 'constants', i.e. the presence *throughout* each of the documents of a single style, purpose and point of view or theology, and of an unbroken narrative thread. These constants are not to be found. The use of the analogical argument to claim otherwise 'neutral' passages for one or other of the documents, and the making of assumptions about 'missing' parts of a document are dubious procedures."

This is such a broadside attack upon the basics of Graf–Wellhausen, that, coming as it does on top of Rendtorff's criticism, I believe the theory is now seen to be full of holes, and must in the end sink without any rescue in prospect. Whybray, who is most certainly not a conservative, goes on to argue for a single authorship of the Pentateuch, although he makes this single author very late indeed, placing him in the sixth century B.C.E.

Alexander makes some most relevant remarks about Whybray. He writes, "While many of the shortcomings of the Documentary Hypothesis highlighted by Whybray have already been noted by others, his work is noteworthy for two reasons. First, his rejection of the Documentary Hypothesis is not motivated by an underlying theological conservatism. Indeed, he concludes that the narrative sections of the Pentateuch were probably composed in the sixth-century by a single author who, while drawing upon some recent traditions, relied mainly upon his own imagination. Second, Whybray offers a generally comprehensive assessment of the Documentary Hypothesis. While some issues are dealt with briefly, he demonstrates that the Documentary Hypothesis rests on unacceptable presuppositions, inadequate criteria for distinguishing the different sources, and a method of literary composition for which there is no analogy elsewhere. Rejecting the Documentary Hypothesis he favours the idea that the Pentateuch was composed by a single individual. Significantly, however, although Whybray's criticism is compelling, he nowhere attempts to demonstrate the literary unity of the

Pentateuch by a detailed exposition of the entire text, or even a part of it. Thus, while he may have gone some way to demolishing the idea that the Pentateuch was composed of continuous parallel documents, his study does not exclude the possibility of either a fragmentary or supplementary explanation for the composition of the Pentateuch."[91]

Clearly Alexander is aware of the potency of the assault by Whybray, but it is interesting to note his last point, namely, that Whybray allows for the single author to have used multiple sources. This is indeed the case I believe, as later chapters will reveal.

Other Assaults On Graf–Wellhausen

Ever since the New Documentary Hypothesis first appeared there have been a minority of commentators who have opposed it. Prominent among the early challengers to Graf–Wellhausen was the erudite and very kindly-mannered William Henry Green of Princeton, a most competent Hebrew scholar who in 1863 published his *The Pentateuch Vindicated From The Aspersions Of Bishop Colenso*, and in 1883 his, *Moses And The Prophets*, in which he opposed Kuenen's treatment of the so-called Hexateuch. Three years later this was followed by an assault upon Wellhausen's presentation of the Israelite festivals in his *The Hebrew Feasts*, and in 1895 he published two challenging works, *The Unity Of The Book Of Genesis*, and *The Higher Criticism Of The Pentateuch,* in which he undermined the entire methodology of Graf–Wellhausen.[92]

P. J. Wiseman made a novel assault on the New Documentary Hypothesis by means of credible literary arguments, with his *New Discoveries In Babylonia About Genesis,* already referred to, which was published in 1936.[93] Wiseman, as we shall see later, showed how many of the so-called duplications and repetitions identified by the Critics, were essential features found in ancient texts that were used to link together different clay tablets. The excellent Hebraist, Umberto Cassuto, also joined the fray basing his attack on credible

---

[91] Alexander, op. cit., pp. 26–27.

[92] Harrison, op. cit., p. 32, & Alexander, op. cit., pp. 17f.

[93] Garrett, op. cit.

literary grounds with his *The Documentary Hypothesis And The Composition Of The Pentateuch*, published in Hebrew in 1941, and translated into English in 1961.[94] His work is now a recognized source for later writers.

In 1943, Oswald T. Allis published *The Five Books Of Moses,* in which he argued cogently for accepting the Mosaic authorship of the Pentateuch,[95] while in 1949, the much respected E. J. Young published his *An Introduction To The Old Testament*, in which the prevailing critical theories were subjected to a genuinely scholarly and searching scrutiny.[96]

The year 1950 saw the publication of Edward Robertson's fascinating *The Old Testament Problem,*[97] which also displayed many of the shortcomings of The New Documentary Hypothesis, and in 1979, Brevard S. Childs indicated even more of these in his scholarly *Introduction To The Old Testament As Scripture*. Britain's most famous Egyptologist, Kenneth Kitchen published his *Ancient Orient And Old Testament,* in 1966, in which he showed that the techniques used by the supporters of Graf–Wellhausen are to his mind totally unworkable, and are certainly alien to how ancient historians work.

More recently, in 1985, Gordon Wenham published his *Genesis 1–15,*[98] in which he too shows the unity of the first part of Genesis, providing viable answers to the challenges of sceptical Higher Criticism. In the same year, Isaac Kikawada and Arthur Quinn had produced jointly a work whose findings I shall use in Chapter Eight, entitled, *Before Abraham Was: A Provocative Challenge To The Documentary Hypothesis,*[99] in which they show through some very clear evidence, that the first eleven chapters of the book of Genesis are a collection of

---

[94] Cassuto, Umberto, *The Documentary Hypothesis And The Composition Of The Pentateuch*, Jerusalem, Magnes, 1961.

[95] Harrison, op. cit., p. 70.

[96] Ibid.

[97] Robertson, Edward, *The Old Testament Problem*, Manchester, Manchester University Press, 1950.

[98] Wenham, Gordon, *Genesis 1–15*, being Volume I of the *Word Biblical Commentary* series, Waco, Texas, Word Books, 1987.

[99] Op. cit.

recognized ancient literary forms, which span the supposed Documentary Sources. The strength of their argument lies in the fact that these literary forms are genres recognized and used by researchers of other types of ancient literature. Theories such as the Documentary Hypothesis which cut right across these recognized literary forms are thereby utterly discredited as they fly-in-the-face of the canons of established literary criticism. to the immense discomfiture of sceptical Source Critics. Interestingly, the same year saw the release of a computer-based analysis by Yehuda T. Radday and Shore Haim entitled, *Genesis: An Authorship Study,* which analysed linguistic variations. These results were then compared with the proposals of the New Documentary Hypothesis. The authors conclude, "With all due respect to the illustrious Documentarians past and present, there is massive evidence that the pre-Biblical triplicity [i.e. the alleged documentary sources, J, E, & P.] of Genesis, which their line of thought postulates to have been worked over by a late and gifted editor into a trinity, is actually a unity."[100]

Professor Duane Garrett, in 1991 published his now famous work *Rethinking Genesis,*[101] a key source book for this work, in which, building on Whybray, Wenham and Kikawada and Quinn to a certain extent, he demonstrates in an extremely comprehensive manner the literary unity of Genesis specifically, and the Pentateuch generally. One of Garrett's key contributions is to show the intrinsic tensions and contradictions to be found within sceptical Source Criticism. Of course, there will be much more on this matter later.

Even more recently, Doctor T. Desmond Alexander published in 1997 his *Abraham In The Negev: A Source-Critical Investigation Of Genesis 20:1–22:19,*[102] in which, through an analysis of the passage named in the title, he shows very persuasively that the theories of the New Documentary Hypothesis are unsustainable.

---

[100] Cited from Garrett, op. cit., p. 28.

[101] Op. cit.

[102] Op. cit.

Conclusion To Chapter Two

Zophar, in the book of Job asks the rhetorical question, "Canst thou by searching find out God?" (Job 11:7) I suggest that we might modify this to read, "Canst thou by *researching alone* find out God?" The writer to the Hebrews says, "He that cometh to God must believe that He is, and that He is a rewarder of them that diligently seek Him." (Hebrews 11:6) Here we see two qualities are required: 1) *Belief*, and 2) *Diligent seeking*, or, to use Zophar's word, *searching*. We might put this another way, and say that *both our hearts and our minds* must be employed in fathoming the things of God. Christ said to the lawyer, "Thou shalt love the Lord thy God with all thy heart, and with all thy soul, and with all thy mind." (Matthew 22:37). Both heart and mind must be used *together* in dealing with the things of God, so that belief, that is, that which pertains to the heart, is not *mindless*, and our thought, that is, that which pertains to the mind, is not *heartless*.

With the Higher Criticism now almost entirely destructive, we see *heartless thinking*, opposed to and by, what so often, is *mindless belief*. We are not being true to the Scriptures, if we rely solely upon our hearts, or solely upon our minds. The destructive Higher Criticism referred to above, is the fruit of the heartless mind of unregenerate mankind. It is hopelessly inconstant, with one theory being attacked by, and giving way to another, because of its own inadequacies, and has continually to resort to the services of many unknown but presumed editors and redactors who are called upon at will to answer each and every difficulty. Their employment is merely a technique of evasion, used to escape the consequences of the manifold shortcomings of these cherished theories.

Moreover, as we will see later, the Modern Critical Method, was, despite its boasting, born in an age of profound ignorance, when it was genuinely believed by most educated people, that the art of writing was unknown in the days of Moses. We now know that this is so utterly erroneous, that modern-day Critics are often embarrassed by this gaping void in the knowledge of their predecessors. It was this common though profoundly mistaken view, which made them believe that it was a real *impossibility* for any writing to be placed as early as Moses. With the enormous archaeological discoveries of the last two centuries, we now know it is extremely credible. Above all, however, destructive Higher Criticism is an attempt to deny the power of the Scriptures by accommodating them to the taste of unregenerate mankind. Eichhorn tried to do this in his attempt at eliminating the miraculous from the Scriptures, that we saw earlier. The Historical Criticism of De Wette is also an attempt to do just that, as it seeks to present the Scriptures as an invention of interested parties, who produced them as a tool to advance their own causes. As such they are reduced to the level of propaganda, and therefore at best present a distortion of the truth; at worst, lies. Finally, with Gunkel and Van Seters, we see the Scriptures reduced merely to the lowly status of anthologies of myths, legends, and folklore. Where do we go from here?

Part Two

Basic Objections To The Graf–Wellhausen Hypothesis

Chapter Three

The Antiquity Of The Age Of Writing

Ashurbanipal's Library

As was noted above, although the Modern Critical Movement began in what is often called the Age of Enlightenment, compared with our knowledge of today, it was an Age of Ignorant Speculation. It was seriously questioned whether the art of writing, one of the hallmarks of civilisation, even existed in the days of Moses. This real uncertainty about the dawning of the age of literature led many to conclude that the Critics must be correct when they asserted so forcibly and with such seeming authority, that Moses could never have written the Pentateuch, and that it must have been based upon a purely oral tradition.[103]

Surprisingly, it was not until the middle of the nineteenth century, that the magnitude of this error began to be exposed, by the discovery of many tens of thousands of clay tablets from the library of the ancient Assyrian king, Ashurbanipal, and from many other hoards. Although the library of Ashurbanipal, who may be the king of Assyria mentioned in II Chronicles 33:11, who took Manasseh captive,[104] dates only from the seventh century B.C.E.,[105] the startling fact that quickly became apparent is that very many of these tablets were of *great antiquity even in Ashurbanipal's time!* He had amassed a library

---

[103] It must be admitted that Ewald was reasonable enough to agree that Moses may have been aquatinted with writing, but ruled this out for the Patriarchs. The Patriarchs' ignorance of writing was being urged even as late as 1893 by Higher Critics. See Wiseman, op. cit., pp. 10–11, & 35ff., Anderson, *A Doubter Doubts About Science And Religion,* op. cit., p. 148, and Kenyon, F. G., *Our Bible And The Ancient Manuscripts Being A History Of The Text And Its Translations,* London, Eyre & Spottiswoode, 1895, pp. 17ff.

[104] See the article, *Ashurbanipal,* by Clay, A. T., in *The International Standard Bible Encyclopædia,* edited by Orr, Nuelson, Mullins, Evans & Kyle, Grand Rapids, Michigan, U.S.A., Eerdmans, revised edition, 1946.

[105] See Rohl, David, *Legend: The Genesis Of Civilisation,* London, Arrow Books, 1998, p. 39.

of the most ancient texts he could trace, including the now famous tablets of the Creation,[106] and the *Epic Of Gilgamesh,* an ancient account of the Flood.[107]

David Rohl in his book *Legend: The Genesis Of Civilisation* refers to tablets K-3050 and K2964 held in the British Museum which contain the following, "I [Ashurbanipal] have read the artistic script of Sumer and the dark obscure Akkadian, which is hard to master (and I now) take pleasure in the reading of the stone inscriptions from before the flood."[108]

This exciting discovery described so vividly by Wiseman in his *New Discoveries In Babylonia About Genesis,*[109] and by N. K. Sanders in the Penguin edition of *The Epic Of Gilgamesh,*[110] pushed the age of writing back so far into the past, centuries before Moses in fact, that the Modern Critical Method's original basis was demolished overnight. Not only that, but even the Form Criticism of Gunkel and the Uppsala School was under threat, as no longer was there any need to propose an ancient oral tradition of folktales prior to the current literary form of the Hebrew Canon. Writing went back to before the time of the Patriarchs themselves, and in the very homeland of Terah, Lot, and Abraham![111]

More and more tablets were discovered over the years, with enormous crate loads being sent back to the leading museums of the West.[112] The tablets were made of an exceptionally fine clay, into which

---

[106] A photograph and translation of the first of these tablets is given in *Aids To The Student Of The Holy Bible*, edited Ball, C. J., London, Eyre And Spottiswoode, 1897, plate 25.

[107] Wiseman, op. cit., p. 20, & Rohl, op. cit., p. 16.

[108] Ibid., p. 16. The words in round brackets are found in Rohl's work. I have added the name Ashurbanipal in square brackets.

[109] Op. cit., pp. 14–45.

[110] *The Epic Of Gilgamesh*, translated and introduced by Sanders, N. K., Harmondsworth, Penguin Books, revised edition, printed 1971, pp. 9–13.

[111] See Wiseman, op. cit., pp. 22ff. The earliest tablets, including *The Epic Of Gilgamesh*, the ancient Mesopotamian account of the Flood, date back to the time Biblical Chronology would place the Flood itself, and so are centuries before the time of Moses. See Rohl, op. cit., p. 39, cf. p. 151.

[112] Wiseman, op. cit., pp. 17ff.

impressions from wedge shaped styli had been pressed after the clay had been moistened. This wedge shaped writing was known as cuneiform. When the text was complete, the tablets had then either been sun or kiln baked, sometimes with chalk added to give extra durability, The result was the most robust form of written records ever discovered. Concrete-hard documents that could and did survive for millennia, where vellum, or papyrus would either become covered in mould, eaten by insects, or burned by fire.[113]

The discovery ultimately changed our view of ancient history. It became apparent that life in the remotest antiquity was complex, not simple; that the written record was an essential part of business, governmental, and even private life; and that in the time of Abraham and before, there was no dependence on mere oral tradition.

Although the evidence for the great antiquity of writing was not available to the early Higher Critics, crucially it was available to Wellhausen. The problem for Wellhausen and his followers was that it militated against their Hegelian evolutionary views, which demanded only a gradual development from savagery to a point where civilisation was sufficiently far advanced for writing to develop. The knowledge that writing was centuries older than Moses invalidated his views totally.

Wellhausen's reaction to the evidence is most revealing. In spite of the overwhelming evidence that opposed his views, Wellhausen persisted in maintaining that the art of writing was not to be found within Israel until the monarchical period. We now know, and, crucially, it was known in Wellhausen's day, that this view is utterly false. The Hebrews had the ability to produce written records from before the time of Abraham. Harrison shows clearly how a sophisticated system of writing, including logograms, syllabic signs, and determinatives spread from the Sumerians, to cover the whole of the Middle-East, assisting greatly the processes of government, and economic development amongst the peoples of antiquity.[114]

---

[113] Ibid., pp. 36–37.

[114] Harrison, op. cit., pp. 201–202. See also, Wiseman D. J., *Illustrations From Bible Archaeology,* London, The Tyndale Press, 1958, the essay by Walker, C. B. F., entitled

Thus, at a stroke, the references that speak of the writings of Moses, who we remember, "was learned in all the wisdom of the Egyptians" (Acts 7:22) that occur so frequently in the Hebrew Canon, and even in the Gospel of John (1:45 & 5:46–47) are seen to be completely credible. It is remarkable that current-day Higher-Criticism still speaks of the pre-literary period when discussing the so-called Pentateuchal Sources, showing that even today, the genuine antiquity of the age of writing is not acknowledged by sceptics.[115]

Conclusion 1. This discovery in the mid-nineteenth century of thousands upon thousands of cuneiform clay tablets, showing that writing goes back to the time even *before* Abraham, removes a key foundation-stone upon which the Modern Critical Movement's argument of a non-Mosaic Pentateuch is based. This situation of course, applies also to Form Criticism.

Conclusion 2. The fact that Wellhausen ignored real evidence that witnessed against his views, means that his approach ought not be dignified by the adjective 'scientific'. It is anything but scientific to ignore inconvenient but highly relevant evidence, and is suggestive of an attachment to his hypothesis that is based more upon subjectivity, emotion, and special pleading, than objectivity and rationality; the qualities Higher Criticism claims as its own. Thus the Graf–Wellhausen Hypothesis fails when judged by its own criteria.

The El Armana Tablets

In 1887, a peasant woman purely by chance came upon a hoard of cuneiform tablets at Tell el Amarna in Egypt.[116] The Amarna archive she had discovered included tablets that were letters written from leaders of foreign nations to the XVIIIth Dynasty Pharaoh, Akhenaten, the first of the Amarna Kings of Egypt. There were also

---

Cuneiform in *Reading The Past: Ancient Writing From Cuneiform To The Alphabet*, London, British Museum Publications, 1990, and Naveh, Joseph, *Origins Of The Alphabet*, London, Cassell & Co., 1975.

[115] See Anderson's *Introduction* to Noth, Martin, *A History Of Pentateuchal Traditions*, translated Anderson, Englewood Cliffs, New Jersey, U.S.A., published by Prentice–Hall Inc., 1972, pp. xv–xvi.

[116] See Harrison, op. cit., p. 318, & Rohl, David, *A Test Of Time: Volume One, The Bible-From Myth To History*, London, Century, 1995, p. 195.

many copies of his replies. The New Kingdom Pharaoh Akhenaten is usually dated to the 14th Century, B.C.E.[117] Recently this dating has been credibly challenged by the independent researcher David Rohl in his book and Channel 4 television series, *Pharaohs And Kings: A Test Of Time*. Rohl argues persuasively, that the Amarna letters are to be placed at a later date, at around 1000 B.C.E.,[118] a date my own findings relating to the dating of the Exodus corroborated,[119] and which the recent dating of the Ugarit solar eclipse also validates.[120] This would mean that some of the tablets contained in the archive may well be letters from Saul, the first king of Israel.[121]

Ras Shamra

Eleven years after the death of Wellhausen, in May of 1929, the French excavators, MM Schaeffer, and Chenet began work at Ras Shamra, the ancient Phœnician city of Ugarit, on the coast opposite Cyprus. What they were to find dealt another devastating blow to the Graf–Wellhausen Hypothesis. They unearthed a temple library dated at circa 1400 B.C.E, although accepting David Rohl's dating, I would put this a few centuries later, in the Solomonic age.[122] Sir Charles Marston writes, "There were tablets at Ras Shamra that had been used for dictionaries or works of reference; there was a register of ships that used the seaport; and there were quantities of other tablets in eight languages and scripts. The most important for our present purpose, were a series of tablets in cuneiform which

---

[117] Rohl, op. cit., p. 20.

[118] Ibid., p. 330.

[119] Phelan, M. W. J. *The Dating Of The Exodus*, Birmingham, The European Theological Seminary, 2001.

[120] Rohl, op. cit., pp. 237ff.

[121] Ibid., pp. 195–202.

[122] Ibid., pp. 173, cf. 330. Coincidentally, this dating, which makes Ras Shamra cöeval with Solomon, means that there is no longer a problem with a version of Psalm 29, attributed by its title to David, that was found in the texts, praising Baal, instead of YHWH. It could easily have been, borrowed from Israel, and used at Ugarit. The same dating also solves a similar problem with Psalm 104, said to be an Israelitish adaptation of the Egyptian *Hymn To The Sun*, dating from the time of Akhenaton. That too would, by Rohl's dating, be placed a generation after David, and, therefore, could have been used by the Egyptians. For Psalm 29, see Soulen & Kendall–Soulen, op. cit., p. 156, for Psalm 104, see Kaiser, op. cit., p. 149.

employed only twenty-eight different characters, instead of the far larger number used in ordinary cuneiform writing."[123] Rendle-Short remarks, "In 1949 M. Claude Schaeffer discovered a tablet containing the oldest known alphabet, from the fourteenth century B.C., with thirty characters, including the twenty-two letters of the Hebrew alphabet, in the same order."[124]

Harrison points out that the languages of the texts discovered at Ras Shamra included a Hurrian dialect, and a Semitic tongue, never previously encountered that was strikingly similar to pre-Mosaic Hebrew! The significance for furthering our knowledge of the Hebrew Scriptures was evident right from the start. It soon became abundantly clear that the Masoretic Text had preserved idiosyncrasies of Canaanite speech-forms and grammatical structures which generally had been lost following the close of the Armana Age. Nineteenth century Critics had tended to regard these faithful preservation in the Masoretic Text of the ancient forms as textual _corruptions_. The very opposite is the case, as now it is realized, showing again the ignorance of the Critics who dismissed the Hebrew Text as being impure. The discoveries at Ras Shamra have also assisted greatly in our understanding of the Psalms, and the usage of Hebrew verbs.[125]

The tablets make reference to a milk-charm ritual of boiling a kid in its mother's milk, a practice which Exodus 23:19, and Deuteronomy 14:21 both outlaw, showing that the Israelites were being warned not to emulate the ways of the ancient Canaanites.[126] Clearly this meant that the alleged late Documents underpinning the Pentateuch were particularly relevant to times far earlier, and were actually _connected_ to those earlier times linguistically and thematically.

The cumulative effect of all that was unearthed at Tell el Amarna and Ras Shamra had a profound effect on the Graf–Wellhausen

---

[123] Marston, Sir Charles, *The Bible Comes Alive*, London, Eyre & Spottiswoode, 1937, p. 73.

[124] Rendle–Short, op. cit., p. 151. I illustrate this alphabet in Appendix II.

[125] Harrison, op. cit., p. 246.

[126] Marston, op. cit., p. 74.

Hypothesis. Harrison reports that René Dussand, the conservator of the Louvre in Paris, and a true scholar, pointed out that the discoveries at Ras Shamra had far-reaching implications for the Graf–Wellhausen hypothesis. Referring to the significance of the Ugaritic finds for advancing our understanding of Phoenician–Canaanite culture, he made the point that the Ras Shamra texts had demonstrated that followers of Graf–Wellhausen had placed their supposed sources later than the evidence suggests, and that they had underestimated by a considerable amount, the merit of Israelite tradition. He went on to say that the exciting finds at Ras Shamra had revealed the need for a fundamental revision of the Graf–Wellhausen hypothesis. Small wonder, therefore, that J. Coppens could declare that, "even for the faithful, *the magnificent critical edifice was palpably rocking on its foundations.*"[127]

A similarly scathing conclusion was reached by Soulen and Kendall–Soulen concerning the finds at Ras Shamra. They comment bluntly, "the texts *disproved* Wellhausen's evolutionary theory of cultic development, which gave a post-exilic date to the P: Priestly Code." (Emphasis mine)[128]

Ebla

More recently, an exciting find at the site of ancient Ebla, modern-day Tell Mardikh in Northern Syria, made in the 1970s has contributed further to our knowledge of ancient writing. Italian archaeologists have discovered many thousands of cuneiform texts written in Sumerian, and what has become known as 'Eblaite', which appears to be very similar to ancient Hebrew. These tablets date from the third millennium B.C.E., the time of the Patriarchs themselves, and show again, if more evidence were necessary, that the Patriarchs lived in the middle of a highly literate society. Soulen and Kendall–Soulen report the texts include economic–administrative texts, lexical texts, historical and juridical texts, literary and religious texts, and

---

[127] Harrison, op. cit., p. 65.
[128] Op. cit., p. 156.

syllabaries.[129] It seems they even refer to Eber, from whom the Hebrews take their name, the great grandson of Shem, great great grandson of Noah, and ancestor of Abraham (Genesis 11:10–27).[130]

A. H. Sayce

The career of Professor A. H. Sayce is very relevant to all of this. Initially he was so enthusiastic about the German Higher Criticism, that Gladstone prevented him succeeding E. B. Pusey who had died in 1882, to the Regius Professorship in Hebrew at Oxford. Instead, the position went to S. R. Driver, who, ironically, championed cynical Higher Criticism as we saw above. Sayce, however took up archæology, and what he discovered there turned him against the German Higher Criticism totally! Sayce used the results of the science of archæology to examine certain key Old Testament problems, a course of action which resulted in him abandoning his support of Higher Criticism, and adopting instead, views which were much more conservative. This illustrates well just how unscientific Higher Criticism is. He is particularly remembered for his books *The "Higher Criticism" and the Verdict of the Monuments* (1894), *Early Israel and the Surrounding Nations* (1899), and *Monument Facts and Higher Critical Fancies* (1904).[131]

Conclusion 3. The finds at Tell el Amarna, Ras Shamra, and Ebla provide evidence, that not only was the art of writing widespread during the time of Abraham and Moses, but that its practice was preserved amongst the Hebrews, right the way through the period of the Judges, and down to the time of the monarchy. This is what we would expect from the Scriptural narrative itself, that refers to the art of writing during the time of Joshua (8:9, & 24:26), and during the rule of the Judges. "Out of Zebulun (came) they that handle the pen (or stylus) of the writer." (Judges 5:14, cf. 8:14).

---

[129] Op. cit., in. loc. See also, *The Applied Bible Dictionary*, edited Richards, Eastbourne, Kingsway Publications, 1990, in. loc.

[130] Magnusson, M., *BC: The Archaeology Of The Bible Lands*, London, BCA, 1977, pp. 25–26.

[131] Harrison, op. cit., pp. 29–30.

Conclusion 4. It is now widely accepted that the dating of the alleged sources of the Pentateuch by Wellhausen, is hopelessly late. This means also that the Hegelian evolutionary concept enshrined in the Graf–Wellhausen hypothesis has also been discredited.

Conclusion 5. The references to the early Canaanite milk-charm ritual of boiling a kid in its mother's milk, in the Ras Shamra texts, and Deuteronomy 14:21, draws Deuteronomy away from a Josianic setting, and implies it is much earlier, thereby invalidating the Graf–Wellhausen dating of D.

Conclusion To Chapter Three

Whybray points out[132] how common it was for the early Critics to assume that the Israelites could not have made written records, and that their assumed continuous nomadic existence was one reason for this. He makes the point that the antiquity of the age of writing shows that this was a truly enormous misconception, and that the insistence on a nomadic existence of the early Israelites, and the supposed consequent separation of them from centres of culture where writing was practiced was a gross distortion of reality. Thus, the very basis of Higher Criticism was completely unsound. The supposed literary sources for the Pentateuch must be late it was thought, simply because they could not have been early! There was no factual basis to this, and we now know better, but the views based on these misconceptions persist in spite of their foundation being removed by archaeology. While it is true that the early leaders of the Modern Critical Movement may not be blamed for what they did not know, the later leaders are responsible for not checking the direction of the movement once the antiquity and widespread use of the art of writing had became known. It is almost as if the two centuries of development of Higher Criticism had propagated a momentum which the discovery of inconvenient archæological facts could not stop. Perhaps pride, and the human trait of not wishing to be corrected had a part to play as well.

---

[132] Op. cit., pp. 139–142.

However, it would seem that the temperament of Wellhausen was a factor here as well. He is described by Whybray in his *The Making Of The Pentateuch* as being of an "isolationist temperament" which manifested itself "in his persistence in ignoring scholarly work in other related fields."[133] On the following page Whybray notes, "At the time when Wellhausen wrote his works on the Pentateuch very much less was known about the cultures, civilisations and thought-processes of the peoples of the ancient Near East than is now known. But what knowledge did exist on these subjects was mainly ignored by him and his immediate successors."[134] In contrast with the antiquity of writing, the next fact we will examine is something even the pioneers of the Modern Critical Movement ought to have considered thoroughly, but, apparently, it was simply dismissed.

---

[133] Ibid., p. 45.
[134] Ibid., p. 46.

Chapter Four

The Antiquity Of The Pentateuch

Part A

The Samaritan Pentateuch

In 1616, Pietro della Valle, acting for a M. de Saucy, who was then the French Ambassador to Constantinople, and afterwards, Archbishop of St. Maloes, obtained a copy of an ancient text from a community of Samaritans then living in Damascus.[135] It was a find that was to transform textual criticism. The text was a copy of a work known to Origen, Eusebius of Cæsarea, Cyril of Jerusalem, Jerome, the Greek church Fathers, and the Talmudists, but which had then disappeared for a thousand years. It was the Samaritan Pentateuch, now known by the siglum SP.[136] Della Valle presented it to the Paris Oratory in 1623,[137] and in 1631–1633 it was printed for the first time in the *Paris Polyglot Bible* under the editorship of Jean Morin of the Oratory.[138] Since 1616, several other copies have been unearthed, both scrolls and codices, including six copies obtained by the famous Archbishop Ussher, one of

---

[135] Hartwell Horne, Thomas, *An Introduction To The Critical Study And Knowledge Of The Holy Scriptures*, Volume II Part I, London, Cadell, in five volumes, 1839, p. 43.

[136] See the article, *Pentateuch, The Samaritan*, by Thomson, J. E. H., in *The International Standard Bible Encyclopædia*, op. cit., in. loc.

[137] Ibid.

[138] Kenyon, op. cit., p. 45, and Hartwell Horne, op. cit., Volume II, Part I, p. 90. This MS was designated Codex 363.

which, *Cotton Claudius B VIII*, is kept in the British Library. The illustration in Figure 1 is taken from this manuscript. These copies are now located in the world's leading museums. It would appear that they all derive from what is known as the Nablus Roll or Scroll. This is a large, handsomely decorated scroll of very great age that is closely guarded by the small and dwindling community of Samaritans living in Nablus, the site of ancient Shechem.[139] This community seems to have lived there since the days of the Babylonian Captivity. As Lofthouse notes, "They form, as has often been observed, the oldest religious community in the world."[140]

The Nablus Roll, and very many other scrolls and codices have a most startling claim embedded in the text, by a literary device called a tarikh. A tarikh is a message formed by the occasional insertion of letters into an otherwise blank central column on the pages of a manuscript. When read downwards, these letters form words and sentences. The tarikh in the Nablus roll referred to above occupies three columns in the book of Deuteronomy and reads, "I Abishua, son of Phinhas [Phinehas] son of Eleazar, son of Aharun [Aaron] the priest, have written this holy book in the door of the tabernacle of the congregation in Mt. Gerizim, in the 13th year of the rule of the children of Israel in the land of Canaan." [141] It is thought to be highly unlikely that this claim has any substance.

The Nablus Roll itself may perhaps be as old as the tenth century C.E.,[142] but the text it represents, while unlikely to date back to the thirteenth year of the occupation of Canaan, is nevertheless of great antiquity as we shall see.

---

[139] Thomson, op. cit. in *The International Standard Bible Encyclopædia*, op. cit., in. loc.

[140] Lofthouse, W. F., *Israel After The Exile*, Oxford, Oxford University Press, 1928, p. 232.

[141] Thomson, op. cit., I have given in full those words which are abbreviated in the article, to make for easier reading. Patterson Smyth renders it slightly differently, offering instead, "I Abishua, son of Phinehas, son of Eleazar son of Aaron the priest–upon them be the grace of Jehovah! To his honour have I written this holy Law at the entrance of the Tabernacle of Testimony on Mount Gerizim, Beth El, in the thirteenth year of the taking possession of the land of Canaan. Praise Jehovah!" He then states that these lines have *not* been found in the Nablus Roll. Patterson Smyth, J., *The Old Documents And The New Bible*, London, Samuel Bagster, 1890, p. 120.

[142] Ibid.

Figure 1 Folio 217v, of Cotton Claudius B VIII, The Samaritan Pentateuch. By permission of the British Library.

The Script

The most interesting and important feature of the Samaritan Pentateuch, is the script, or style of Hebrew characters employed by the scribes who produced and copied it (see Figure 1). J. E. H. Thomson, a recognized authority on the Samaritans writes, "The reader on opening one of the codices of the Samaritan Pentateuch recognizes at once the difference of the writing from the character in an ordinary Hebrew Bible. The Jews admit that the character in which the Samaritan Pentateuch is written is older than their square character. It is said in the Talmud (*Sanhedrin 21b*) "The law at first was given to Israel in *'ibri* letters and in the holy tongue and again by Ezra in the square [*'ashurith*] character and the Aramaic tongue. Israel chose for themselves the *'ashurith* character and the holy tongue: they left to the hedhyototh ["uncultured"] the *'ibri* character and the Aramaic tongue—'the Cuthians are the hedhyototh,' said Rabbi Hasda.'" The Cuthians is the name by which the Jews normally refer to the Samaritans. Thomson then refers to the bitter hatred that blighted relations between the Jews and the Samaritans, and the utter disdain shown to the latter by the Pharisees, and concludes that for the Jews to make such an acknowledgement, it actually serves as "a demonstration."[143] Quite so, and it has very important consequences for our investigation as we shall see.

Harrison also makes some extremely important observations. He states, "The antiquity of the archetype [of the Samaritan Pentateuch] appears evident from the confusion found in the oldest extant manuscript between the consonants ד and ר, and also between the letters ם and ב, a situation that would normally not have arisen in a post-exilic archaizing type of script. Confusion of this sort is much more likely to have occurred in the very early angular Sidonian characters, in the letter-forms of the Moabite Stone,[144] or in the Siloam

---

[143] Thomson, op. cit. in *The International Standard Bible Encyclopædia*, op. cit., in. loc. I have given in full those words which are abbreviated in the article, to make for easier reading.

[144] The ninth century B.C.E. Moabite Stone or Mesha Stela was erected by Mesha king of Moab to celebrate his rebellion against Ahab (II Kings 3:4–7). See Wilson, I., *The Bible Is History*, London, Weidenfeld & Nicolson, 1999, p. 143.

inscription from the time of Hezekiah.[145] Word dividers in the Samaritan Pentateuch were of a kind commonly employed in early Aramaic, Moabite, and Hebrew inscriptions, which points to an early date for the prototypal manuscript. The Samaritans evidently did not enunciate their gutturals. This may constitute a dialectical peculiarity indicating that their pronunciation dated from the time of Ahab and his successors in Israel, when the non-guttural Phoenician was popular in the northern kingdom as opposed to the Judaean dialect preserved in the Masoretic text."[146]

The great British authority on the Samaritans, Edward Robertson says of the script in the Samaritan Pentateuch, that it is "written in the ancient Hebrew script—almost identical with that found recently on the Lachish potsherds, dating from the time of Jeremiah."[147]

F. F. Bruce agrees, saying, "The palaeo-Hebrew is of the same general style as the script found on the Moabite Stone, the Siloam Inscription, and the Lachish Letters."[148]

The View Of The Critics

There appears to be no doubt at all that the Samaritan Pentateuch is a witness of an extremely ancient text, a text that pre-dates Ezra, and the

---

[145] This is the oldest known inscription that is written in Hebrew and that is of significant length. Fortunately its very nature makes it datable (eighth century B.C.E.), as it is taken by common consent to record the work described in II Kings 20:20. See, Masterman, in the article *Siloam*, in Volume IV of *The International Standard Bible Encyclopædia,* op. cit., in. loc.

[146] Op. cit., pp. 223–224. Thomson makes the same point about the gutturals, op. cit., in. loc.

[147] See the essay, *Law And Religion Amongst The Samaritans*, by Robertson, Edward, in *Judaism And Christianity,* Volume III, *Law And Religion*, edited by Rosenthal, Erwin I. J., London, The Sheldon Press, 1938, p. 74.

[148] Bruce, F. F., *The Books And The Parchments,* London, Marshall Pickering, Revised Edition, 1991, p. 120. The Lachish Letters are the potsherds referred to by Robertson, as they are written on *ostraca*, or broken pots. There is a photograph and very clear reproduction of the text of the Siloam Inscription by Euting in Gesenius, *Hebrew Grammar*, edited Kautzsch, translated Cowley, Oxford, Oxford University Press, from the corrected sheets of the second edition, 1966, pp. xviii–xix. The content of the Inscription is given also in the square Aramaic characters for comparison. The result is extremely striking. The enormous difference between the two scripts is seen with the utmost clarity. One would hardly believe them to be different expressions of the same language.

supposed P source by a considerable margin, and even D as well. Unlike the archæological evidence for the antiquity of the art of writing, the discovery of the Samaritan Pentateuch predated the *beginnings* of the Modern Critical Movement, meaning that even the earliest of the Modern Critics could not ignore its existence, however unhelpful it might prove to their hypotheses. H. B. Swete, who compares the text of the Septuagint with that of the Samaritan Pentateuch, records the fact that Simon, Eichhorn, and Gesenius, the acolyte of De Wette, all wrote on the subject.[149] Gesenius, in fact, carried out a very comprehensive and now famous analysis of the Samaritan Pentateuch.[150] The standard view amongst Higher Critics however, is that the Samaritan Pentateuch dates only from the time of Ezra, and is dependent on the text in use amongst the Jews at that time.

Kenyon gives this standard view of the Critics in the following words, "The most probable account [of the origin of the Samaritan Pentateuch] is that it takes its rise in the events described in Neh. 13. 23–30, namely, the expulsion by Nehemiah of those Jews who had contracted marriages with the heathen. Among those expelled was a grandson of the high-priest Eliashib, whose name, as we learn from Josephus, was Manasseh. This Manasseh, in indignation at his expulsion, took refuge amongst the Samaritans, and set up among them a rival worship to that at Jerusalem. The Samaritans, whom we know from 2 Kings 17. 24–41 to have been foreigners imported into the country of the Ten Tribes by the king of Assyria, and there, presumably, to have mingled with the scanty remnant of Israelites, had at first incorporated the worship of Jehovah, as the God of the land, into the worship of their own gods; and later, on the return of the Jews from captivity, had been willing to join in the rebuilding of the Temple at Jerusalem, but had been refused permission. Since this repulse they had been bitterly hostile to the Jews, and the schism of Manasseh gave them a head and a rival

---

[149] Swete, H. B., *An Introduction To The Old Testament In Greek*, Peabody, Massachusetts, U.S.A., 1989, p. 438. The works Swete refers to are, Simon, R., *Histoire Critique Du Vieux Testament;* Eichhorn; *Einleitung In Das Alte Testament;* and Gesenius, H. W. F., *De Pentateuchi Samaritani Origine Indole Et Auctoritate Comm.*

[150] See Kenyon, op. cit., p. 46, and Thomson, op. cit. in *The International Standard Bible Encyclopædia,* op. cit., in. loc.

worship, which embittered and perpetuated the quarrel. Manasseh obtained leave from Darius Nothus, king of Persia, to set up a temple on Mount Gerizim, which became the centre of the new religion and the rival of Jerusalem. He had brought with him, it is believed, the Hebrew Pentateuch, and this, with certain alterations (notably the substitution of Gerizim for Ebal in Deut. 27. 4 as the hill on which the memorial altar should be placed), became the sacred book of the Samaritans [The words in square brackets are my own]."[151]

This story suits the Higher Critics very well indeed, as it removes the problems which otherwise are insurmountable. Providing it may be believed that the Samaritan Pentateuch originated in the days of Ezra and Nehemiah, and is nothing more than a *copy* of the Hebrew text as it *then* existed, with a few alterations made in order to promote the status of Mount Gerizim, the existence of the Samaritan Pentateuch does not threaten any part of Higher Criticism from Astruc's Clue, to Graf–Wellhausen; but, is the story credible? I think not.

The View Of The Critics Is Contrary To The Evidence

Modernists tend to view the Samaritans as a quasi-Jewish sect, which dates only from the Return under Ezra, when the Samaritans' request to help in the rebuilding of the Temple was refused. Professor of Semitic Languages and Literatures, Edward Robertson contested this view vehemently, and reported that Doctor Gastor, a Jew, who therefore might be thought not likely to give support to the Samaritan cause unless it was absolutely valid, repeatedly denounced this view. Gastor, according to Robertson, showed irrefutably that the Samaritans must have existed long before the Return under Ezra, and must also have been in possession of the Torah for very many years prior to his day. He challenged the Modernist view by asking how the Samaritans could have had any grounds at all for approaching the Jews of the Return and offering their assistance, if they had not shared a common heritage in religious belief and practice. Gastor believed that the Samaritans, (who regard themselves as descendents of the Northern Kingdom of Israel) invited the Jews to worship at their own Temple in Mount Gerizim, and to accept it as the true Temple, but

---

[151] Kenyon, op. cit., pp. 44–45.

they met with an unequivocal refusal of the Jews. To propose then as Modernists do, that the Samaritans, generally despised by the Jews, would have received their Holy Scriptures and religious practices from the Jews, and at the very moment of their humiliating rejection by the Jews, is simply fantastic, and quite beyond belief. This idea is made even more incredible by a consideration of the well-known fact that the Samaritans referred to Ezra, as the 'cursed Ezra'! Their existence as a religious community cannot be related to the return under Ezra, it must antedate that event by a considerable margin as both Gastor and Robertson maintain. Professor Robertson remarked, "*That they* [the Samaritans] *could ever have taken over a copy of the teaching prepared by one whom they called the 'cursed Ezra,' surpasses belief.* The very fact that they possess the Torah written in the ancient Hebrew script—almost identical with that found recently on the Lachish potsherds, dating from the time of Jeremiah—is a strong argument on the Samaritan side (emphases mine)."[152] It is noteworthy that elsewhere Robertson points out that the Samaritans "prided themselves on their name, which they aver has no connexion with Samaria. They are *Shomerim*—that is, 'keepers' of the Law of God."[153] This last fact is confirmed by A. E. Cowley, the translator of Gesenius, in the *Encyclopædia Biblica*. Cowley writes, "The Samaritans are called once in the OT (2 K. 17 29) Someronim (שמרנים), a name which becomes common later. It is a gentilic form from שמר. In Rabbinical literature they are called kuthim (כותים), a term intended to be contemptuous, referring to the colonists from Cuthah. The Greek Σαμαρειται properly means inhabitants of the district of Σαμαρεια. They call themselves בני ישראל, or specifically שמרים from שמר, properly *keepers*, sc. of the Law."[154] This, again, implies that they regarded the Jews as the heretics, and assumes a practice in conformity with what we now call the Samaritan Pentateuch, for a long period of time before Ezra.

---

[152] Robertson, op. cit., pp. 72–74.

[153] Ibid., p. 76. Anderson makes a very similar point. See Anderson, *A Doubter Doubts About Science And Religion*, op. cit., pp. 151–154.

[154] See Cowley, A. E., in the article *Samaritans*, in *Encyclopædia Biblica* op. cit., columns 4256–4257.

Purely on the grounds of genuine Historical Criticism then, it seems quite incredible to propose that the Samaritan Pentateuch goes back only to the time of Ezra and Nehemiah, and it appears to be equally fantastic to make it dependent on the Hebrew text of that time. There is evidence available from another field however, which seems almost to prove the very great antiquity of the Samaritan Pentateuch, driving it back in time at least to the days of Hezekiah, and maybe earlier still.

Textual Evidence

Thomson in the article previously cited, examines the differences between the Samaritan and the Masoretic Texts, and criticises Gesenius for the methodology he used in his study which assumed the Samaritan to be the later text. This assumption of Gesenius is most helpful to Higher Critics of course, as it leaves undisturbed the supposed source sequence of J, E, D, & P. A Samaritan Pentateuch that predated the Return under Ezra by very many years would do serious damage to the hypothesis, as the P source, and possibly the D source as well, would then become *later* than the completed Pentateuch!

While I agree with Gesenius that the Samaritan text is generally speaking, and with notable exceptions, less accurate that the Masoretic, that does not mean it must be later, Thomson, in his analysis, divides the variations between the texts into two general classes, namely, *accidental* and *intentional*. In the latter would be those divergences in the Samaritan Pentateuch that promote the interests and status of Mount Gerizim. The former class however, provides a real clue as to the great antiquity of the Samaritan Pentateuch, and shows it to be far older than Higher Criticism's current theories may allow. Owing to constraints on space, I may only give a few examples.

Errors In The Samaritan Text

Thomson points out that in Genesis 19:32, the Samaritan text reads *tabhinu* which is utterly meaningless, instead of *'abhinu* which means 'our father'. It is very difficult to conceive of a situation where such an error could be made were the text to have been copied from one made after the Return when Ezra had caused the Torah to be re-written in the Square or Aramaic script that we see in Hebrew Bibles today. In these Square Characters the two letters concerned are completely different; ח, and א, but in the so-called Angular Script of the Siloam Inscription the letters are very similar indeed, as Appendix III shows. Again in Genesis 25:29 the Samaritan text reads *çazdh* instead of *yazdh* meaning to 'seethe'. As with the previous example, such a mistake could hardly occur in a text originally composed of Square Characters as the letters concerned are so different; י, and צ; but in the Samaritan, and the older Angular script, they are very alike (see Appendix III).

Errors In The Masoretic Text

Now it could be argued that the Samaritan text was copied from a post-exilic square charactered text, but written in the Samaritan script, and that after a few generations, owing to poor scribal standards, one Samaritan character was mistaken for another, thus accounting for the errors mentioned above, while still allowing a late date for the Samaritan Pentateuch. Our next piece of evidence however, shows this to be unlikely.

In Genesis 27:40 there seems to a mistake in the Masoretic Text. Thomson writes, "The RV rendering is 'When thou shalt break loose, thou shalt shake his yoke from off thy neck.' This rendering does violence to the sense of both verbs and results in a tautology. In the Hiphil the first verb *rudh* ought to mean 'to cause to wander,' not 'to break loose,' and the second verb *parak* means 'to break,' not 'to shake off.' The Samaritan has 'When thou shalt be mighty, thou shalt break his yoke from off thy neck.' The Masoretic Text mistake may be due to the confounding of $\wedge$, *a*, with $\wedge$, *t*, [see Appendix III] and the transposition of ⌐, *d*, and ⌐, *b* [see Appendix III]. The verb *'adhar*, 'to be strong,' is rare and poetic, and so unlikely to suggest itself to reader or scribe."[155] This type of error implies that the Square Charactered text was made from a text written in Angular Script, or at least, the same style in which the Samaritan text has been preserved, and thus suggests a pre-exilic provenance. Thus *both* Samaritan and

---

[155] Thomson, op. cit., in *The International Standard Bible Encyclopædia*, op. cit., p. 2315. I have given in full those words which are abbreviated in the article, to make for easier reading.

Square Charactered texts seem to emanate from an Angular script, pointing to a pre-exilic provenance.

Errors In The 'Angular' Text

Thomson has shown that there exist some confusions which relate to characters which are similar in form only when written in the Angular Script. He gives as examples the writing of pithon instead of pithom in Exodus 1:11, and לשכן, *l'shakken* in Deuteronomy 12:21, instead of לשום, *lasum*. By referring to the table of alphabets in Appendix III it will be seen that *m* and *n* might only be confused in the Siloam Script, and that *waw* and *kaph* could also easily be confused in this script. This indicates that the vorlage underpinning the Masoretic and Samaritan Texts, dates back to an Angular type of script, from at least the time of Hezekiah.[156] It is very interesting and relevant that the error in Deuteronomy, is in what Higher Critics regard as one of the latest sources, D, which is now seem to be just as early as the supposed J, & E.

We have already seen that the discoveries at Ras Shamra have shown that the Masoretic text has preserved peculiarities of Canaanite grammar, which had died out by the time of the Armana Period, and which had been thought of as textual corruptions by nineteenth century Critics. Thus we see mounting evidence for an extremely early vorlage, perhaps as early as the age of Solomon, for both the Samaritan and Square Charactered text.

An Alternative View

Given that so many indicators suggest that the Samaritan Pentateuch originated from a text written in Angular Script dating from the time of Hezekiah or earlier, it is at least conceivable that it dates from the incident recorded in II Kings 17:24ff. Here we find that after the carrying away of the Northern rebel tribes by Assyria, the land was troubled by lions, which the Assyrian King ascribed to a lack of knowledge of the God of the land. Accordingly, in verse 27 we read, "The King of Assyria commanded, saying, 'Carry thither one of the

---

[156] Ibid.

priests whom ye brought from thence; and let them go and dwell there, and let him teach them the manner of the God of the land.' Then one of the priests whom they had carried away from Samaria came and dwelt in Bethel, and taught them how they should fear the Lord." Who is to say that this priest did not use a copy of the Torah to teach from, when it seems that the Samaritan Pentateuch goes back at least to this age?

That this is a credible theory is seen from the following evidence which shows that the Torah was recognised and referred to as a distinct body of teaching at that time. The Septuagint, a Greek copy of the Hebrew Scriptures made by *Jews*, has the following reading at Amos 4:5, "And they read the Torah (Greek νομο) without, and called for public professions." Here we have a claim of the Torah being read throughout the Northern Kingdom of Israel in the days of Amos! Nor is this an isolated instance. In Hosea 4:6 we find the following words addressed to the Northern tribes, "My People are destroyed for lack of knowledge: because thou hast rejected knowledge, I also will reject thee, that thou shalt be no priest to me: seeing thou hast forgotten the Torah of thy God, I will also forget thy children." In Amos 2:4, Amos says of Judah, "they have despised the Torah of the Lord."

These are among the clearest references in the prophets to the Torah, which, according to Graf–Wellhausen, came *after* the prophets! But there are many other references, particularly in Isaiah and Jeremiah.[157] Edward Robertson, at one time Professor of Semitic Languages and Literatures at Manchester University, writing in his *The Old Testament Problem*, says this of the references to the Torah in Amos and Hosea, "The advocates of the Graf–Wellhausen theory are driven in its support to place the eighth-century prophets prior in time to the Torah in its present form. In consequence it is very awkward for them that the name Torah is found in the prophetic writings of that period. The Critics take refuge in the argument that the word here is not Torah with a capital T, but the common noun meaning 'teaching', and the word is used in a general sense. But the evidence cannot so easily be

---

[157] See for example, Isaiah 1:10, 2:3, 5:24, 8:16, 8:20, 24:5, 30:9, 42:4, 42:21, 42:24, 51:4, 51:7; Jeremiah 2:8, 6:19, 8:8, 9:13, 16:11, 18:18, 26:4, 31:33, 32:23, 44:10, 44:23; Ezekiel 7:26, 22:26; Hosea 4:6, 8:1, 8:12; Amos 2:4.

brushed aside. When Hosea complains that the children of Israel (meaning by that the Northern Kingdom) have forgotten the 'Torah of Yahweh' (4⁶), it is reluctantly conceded that he must be speaking of some system of legislation, and when, as the mouthpiece of Yahweh, he says, 'Even if I should write a myriad (copies) of my Law', or it may be translated 'my Law in 10,000 precepts' [Hosea 8:12] (the text is uncertain at this point), it has to be admitted that he can only mean a written body of law. When Amos chides Judah for rejecting 'the Torah of Yahweh, not keeping his statutes' (2⁴) he has clearly a well-known body of law in mind [the words in square brackets are my own]."[158]

To this could be added the fact that in Hosea 12:2–5, and 12:12 there are definite references to the personal history of Jacob recorded in Genesis, that 11:1, and 12:13 relate clearly to the Exodus, while 4:2 and 13:4 are distinct references to the Decalogue. In addition to this, the following table lists clear parallels between certain verses in Hosea, and Deuteronomy 32.

Hosea	Deuteronomy 32
1:9	21
5:14	39
8:14	15, 18, & 22
9:10	10
13:5–8	10, 15 & 24

It has been pointed out that these parallels are significant, as all the Deuteronomic references emanated from the same chapter, but those from Hosea are distributed throughout his book. Umberto Cassuto correctly points out how much more likely it is that Hosea made regular use of the poem of Deuteronomy 32, a self-contained literary whole, than to propose that the writer of Deuteronomy "cherry-picked" isolated verses from across the whole of Hosea's book, without displaying the core message of Hosea, namely the thought that God's love for Israel is as that of a groom for his bride. Cassuto concludes from his whole study that "There is nothing in the entire Book of Hosea to compel us to suppose that the Pentateuchal

---

[158] Robertson, op. cit., p. 51.

material existed in his day in a form different from that before us today." He goes on to claim that much of the Pentateuch "already existed in its present form in Hosea's time and was known to broad circles of people."[159]

What do the supporters of Graf–Wellhausen have to say to the clear message of the prophets, that the forsaking of the Torah is what led to the demise of both Israel and Judah? It formed after all, an essential element of what is known as the *Prophetic Protest*. They have to agree that if they are right, Israel and Judah were disobedient to that which had not been revealed to them, and that God is therefore unjust! It is simply not tenable to suggest that the Prophets pre-date the Torah!

Conclusion 6. There is evidence for the antiquity of the Samaritan Pentateuch from;

1. the infamous animosity between the Jews and the Samaritans suggesting its independence from the Square Charactered text;

2. the character and origin of the script of the Samaritan Pentateuch;

3. the errors within the Samaritan and Masoretic Texts which presuppose an Angular vorlage, and;

4. the references to the Torah in the prophets.

Taken together, these separate lines of evidence show that the Pentateuch predates the exile by very many years, and is traceable at least to the eighth century B.C.E., thus invalidating firstly the order, and secondly the dating of sources J, E, D, and P of the Graf–Wellhausen Hypothesis. The finds from Ras Shamra show also that the Masoretic Text has preserved literary archaisms that predate the Armana Period, and pertain therefore at least to the age of Solomon, and probably earlier still.

---

[159] Garrett, op. cit., p. 51. Garrett quotes from Cassuto, Umberto, *The Prophet Hosea And The Books Of The Pentateuch,* found in *Biblical And Oriental Studies*, translated Abrahams, Volume I, Jerusalem, published in two volumes by Magnes, 1973, p. 100.

Part B

The Allegation That The Torah Was Lost At The Fall Of Jerusalem

The findings associated with the previous Objection, lead us naturally into the next topic. Occasionally, a Higher Critic will make the claim that the Pentateuch, and the rest of the Hebrew Canon, must originate from the time of Ezra, as the Hebrew Sacred books were all destroyed at the fall of Jerusalem. What we possess now, it is claimed, is the work of Ezra. Evidence for this is said to be found in the apocryphal book of IV Ezra.

W. H. Bennett, became so desperate to support the Graf–Wellhausen hypothesis, that in the book he co-authored with Adeney, he peddled this old story. The late apocryphal text asserts that five associates of Ezra sat down and wrote the Pentateuch, and the other canonical books that orthodoxy claims predate Ezra, completely from scratch, and under dictation from Ezra, after he had drunk what amounts to a magic potion. It is very much less common now for Critics to use this ancient tale, so it is possible the reader is unacquainted with the story. For this reason I will allow Bennett to tell it in his own words.

Bennett writes, "The Fourth Book of Ezra, an apocalyptic work of the first century A.D., told how the law had been burnt and Ezra was inspired to dictate to five companions the contents of the twenty-four books (presumably of the Old Testament) and seventy others. The story represents an opinion that the Old Testament as we have it rests on the authority of Ezra, as editor and publisher, so to speak, rather than of the original writers. Other traces are found of this idea."[160]

---

[160] Bennett & Adeney, op. cit., p. 16.

Bennett has watered-down this story enormously. In the book of IV Ezra itself, the account has an air of the fabulous about it. I give the full text in Appendix IV. Those who are unfamiliar with the story are urged to read it in full so as to understand the fairy-story nature of the account Bennett rests so much weight upon.

I was surprised to find that even Dodd gives some support to this story, albeit highly qualified,[161] but what does it really tell us? Does it really prove that the Hebrew Canon is a concoction of Ezra's, and that we would be fools to believe it?

Ezra, And The Change Of Script

I believe that there are grains of truth in the legend, but that it has been manipulated for partisan purposes as I will explain later. It was certainly around the time of the Return under Ezra and Nehemiah, that the Scriptures were written for the first time in the Square Characters we find in printed Hebrew Bibles today. This occurred at that time, because, during the Babylonian Captivity, the Jews had had to use these characters instead of the type found in the Samaritan Pentateuch, and, consequently, for the generation that returned from Exile to the Land of Promise, the Square Characters were the letters they were familiar with.

Edersheim writes, "Altered circumstances had brought many changes to the new Jewish State. Even the language spoken and written, was other than formerly. Instead of the characters anciently employed, the exiles brought with them, on their return, those now common, the so-called square Hebrew letters, which gradually came into general use."[162]

Necessity then forced the change in script, and caused the change to occur when it did. It is also from this time, and for this reason, that the practice of producing paraphrases, or Targums, dates.[163]

---

[161] Dodd, C. H., *The Authority Of The Bible*, London, Nisbet & Co., 1928, pp. 154–155.

[162] Edersheim, Alfred, *The Life And Times Of Jesus The Messiah,* Volume I, London, published in two volumes by Longmans, Green, & Co., 1899, p. 10. See also, Rotherham, J. B., *Our Sacred Books Being Plain Chapters On The Inspiration, Transmission And Translation Of The Bible*, London, H. E. Allenson, 1903, pp. 28ff.

[163] See, Kenyon, op. cit., pp. 29ff.

Ezra, is renowned for being "a ready scribe in the Law of Moses." (Ezra 7:6, cf. vv 10–12.) His ambition, given in Ezra 7:10, was "to seek the Law of the Lord, and to do it, and to teach in Israel statutes and judgements." Given then Ezra's desire to teach the people the statutes and judgements of the Law of the Lord, his ability as a "ready scribe", and the fact that the Scriptures were written in a script which most people then could not understand, it would be very surprising indeed, if Ezra himself was not employed in transcribing the Scriptures from the old style of script, into the style the people understood, namely, the Square Characters. This is precisely what Hebrew tradition says in fact.

In Volume IV of Ginzberg's *Legends Of The Jews* we read, "In the realisation of his second hope, the spread of the Torah, Ezra was so zealous and efficient that it was justly said of him: 'If Moses had not anticipated him, Ezra would have received the Torah.' In a sense he was indeed a second Moses. The Torah had fallen into neglect and oblivion in his day, and he restored and re-established it in the minds of his people. It is due to him chiefly that it was divided into portions, to be read annually, Sabbath after Sabbath, in the synagogues, and it was he likewise, who originated the idea of re-writing the Pentateuch in 'Assyrian characters.'"[164]

Here we notice two elements that appear in the apocryphal story; firstly the comparison with Moses; secondly the introduction of the Assyrian, or Square Characters. Ginzberg, who himself gives his own account of the story told in IV Ezra, including the more fanciful portions omitted from II Esdras,[165] equates these Square Characters to the "characters which they knew not," referred to in IV Ezra 14:42 (see Appendix IV).

Thus, not only is it highly probable that Ezra would have copied out the Torah, and the rest of the Scriptures into the new Square Charactered script from the old; but there is a strong tradition that he did just that. We find also, that there are traditional accounts that many books were indeed lost at the fall of Jerusalem. Milman, in his

---

[164] *The Legends Of The Jews*, compiled by Ginzberg, Louis, Volume IV, Baltimore, U.S.A., published in seven volumes by Johns Hopkins University Press, pp. 355–356.

[165] Ibid., pp. 356–358.

History Of The Jews writes, "Ezra, who had been superseded in the civil administration by Nehemiah, had applied himself to his more momentous task—the compilation of the Sacred Books of the Jews. Much of the Hebrew literature was lost at the time of the Captivity; the ancient Book of Jasher, that of the Wars of the Lord, the writings of Gad, and Iddo the Prophet, and those of Solomon on Natural History. The rest, particularly the Law, of which, after the discovery of the original by Hilkiah, many copies were taken; the historical books, the poetry, including all the prophetic writings, except those of Malachi, were collected, revised, and either at that time, or subsequently, arranged in three great divisions: the Law, comprising the five Books of Moses; the Prophets, the historical and prophetic books; the Hagiographa, called also the Psalms, containing Psalms, Proverbs, Ecclesiastes, and the Song of Solomon. Job, Daniel too, are now found among these Ketubim. At a later period, probably in the time of Simon the Just, the books of Malachi, Ezra, Nehemiah, and Esther were added, and what is called, the Canon of Jewish Scripture finally closed."[166]

The above quote is most interesting as it draws our attention to the certain destruction of many books that were treasured by the Jews. Were Ezra to have re-written under Divine Inspiration, all the books of the Hebrew Canon, as is alleged in IV Ezra, we need to know why the writings of Gad, Iddo, Nathan and many others, were not re-written as well. Even if it is asserted that Ezra simply concocted the books we now regard as Canonical, this question still has to be answered. Surely a forger who was prepared to produce so many fakes, would continue his work, and include pseudepigrapha in the names of these prophets as well. As it stands, some books were really lost to us it seems, but many were saved, and ultimately re-written in the new Square Characters, including those books we now regard as canonical.

The Preservation Of The Torah

The Hebrew tradition is quite emphatic about this. Ginzberg records the tradition that Ezra brought back with him, from exile in Babylon,

---

[166] Milman, H. H., *The History Of The Jews*, Volume I, London, published in two volumes by J. M. Dent & Sons, 1943, pp. 345–346.

a copy of the Law, which would have been written in the Angular style of script of course, similar to the script used in the Samaritan Pentateuch. It is said that Ezekiel had located this copy in the Temple, in the time of Jehoiakim before the burning of Jerusalem, and had then taken it to Babylon, where it was acquired by Ezra. Before Ezekiel found it, this copy of the Law is reputed to have been in the hands of the prophets for some time.[167] This would be anathema to the Higher Critics, of course, who maintain, contrary to all Scriptural logic, that the prophets preceded the Torah, but it would explain the references in the prophets to the Torah dealt with above. It also means that the suggestion of James Angus, that the Samaritan Pentateuch originated from a copy of the Torah dating back to the days of Rehoboam, may be possible, especially as the finds from Ras Shamra show the very great antiquity of at least parts of the Hebrew text we have inherited.[168]

We have no way now of authenticating this tradition, but at least it accords with the textual facts established above, which show that the Square-Charactered text we have inherited, was copied from an earlier text written in an Angular Style of script, and that this Angular text would have predated Ezra, in whose time, the Square Characters were first introduced.

The Acceptance Of The Torah As Scripture

Thus we have on the one hand, the Higher Critics, and a garbled apocryphal story from the Second Century C.E., which say that the Law dates only from the time of Ezra; on the other hand we have the firm textual evidence of the copying of the Canon into Square Characters in the time of Ezra from a pre-existing Angular Script manuscript, that is supported by tradition, that would account for the notices in the prophets to the Torah, and could also account for the apocryphal story found in IV Ezra, which might be a highly embroidered version of real events. We must choose between these two scenarios.

---

[167] Ginzberg, op. cit., Volume VI, p. 220.

[168] Angus, James, *The Bible Handbook: An Introduction To The Study Of Sacred Scripture,* London, The Religious Tract Society, undated, p. 35.

The deciding factor for me, is the need to account for the fact that the books we are discussing comprise the absolute foundation of Judaism. As they are today in orthodox circles, they were anciently held in such high esteem, that during the Maccabæan Period, thousands were prepared to suffer outrageously, and give their very lives for their preservation. To think that mere forgeries could so easily be foisted upon an entire nation, and engender such an air of reverence; is to presume a triumph of propagandists that was so emphatic and unchallenged, so decisive and above all *sudden*, that even the regimes of the Third Reich, and Communist Russia or China, would not be capable of emulating it. By comparison with Ezra the supposed Master Forger of documents, their sinister manipulations and distortions would have to be regarded as little more than the efforts of bumbling amateurs. Is such a scenario credible?

I will let Professor Robertson answer for me. He wrote the following words of the Documentary Hypothesis, that proposes, as we saw above, the cutting-and-pasting together of disparate works to form the Torah in the days of Ezra. This foundation of the Documentary Hypothesis is according to Robertson its greatest weakness. Robertson wrote that according to the followers of the New Documentary Hypothesis, "behind the composition of the Pentateuch there has been an extended and intricate process of literary drafting and editorship. In our search for the documents we are introduced under its guidance to a literary world in which we meet with a variety of authors and compilers. Copyists in their weak moments make errors in the text. Redactors rectify and manipulate. Glossators annotate in the margin, and we have all the paraphernalia of literary record and dissemination in the manuscript age. But [most of this] is a reflex of the age of the printing press, of independent authors, of editors, of editions of books and of their publication and acceptance by a reading public. But is it conceivable that a religious community even in the present day could adopt as their sacred Scriptures documents which they are left to select in the haphazard way implied by the Critics? Scholars, who speak easily of documents and fragments of documents being fused, incorporated, interpolated, interwoven and the whole edited and accepted as Holy Writ as if such were a commonplace operation, seem to forget that in the Pentateuch we are dealing with the very core of Hebrew religious life. It is so easy to fall into the error of imagining that the circulation of such a document even if limited to priestly circles, would promote appreciation of its spiritual value and its consequent acceptance as Scripture. But religious communities and sects do not act in this way. Scriptures, creeds and confessions of faith do not drift into acceptance through literary merit alone. Yet no Old Testament critic seems to have offered to explain how the diverse documents of the Pentateuch which they discover or create, acquired their sanctity and authority. But surely this is of the very essence of the whole matter [The words in square brackets are my own.]"[169]

The Purpose Of IV Ezra 14

I believe the whole intention behind the writing of IV Ezra 14, is to present Ezra as a Second Moses. Even a superficial reading of the passage will reveal many intended parallels between real events in Moses' life, and what is predicated of Ezra. I give some of these below;

Real Event In Moses' Life		Parallel Event In Ezra's Life According To IV Ezra 14	
A	The Divine Utterance from a bush. (Exodus 3:3–4)	a	The Divine Utterance from a bush. (vv. 2–4)
B	The period of forty days with the Lord. (Exodus 24:18)	b	The period of forty days required for writing the Law. (vv. 36 & 44)
C	The mystery surrounding the burial of the body of Moses by the Lord. (Deuteronomy 34:5–6)	c	The assumption into heaven of Ezra. (vv 9 & 49)
Events Said In IV Ezra 14 To Have Occurred In The Time Of Moses		Parallel Events In Ezra's Life According To IV Ezra 14	
D	The revealing of hidden knowledge to Moses that was not to be published. (vv 5–7)	d	The revealing of hidden knowledge to Ezra that was not to be published. (vv 26 & 44–46)
E	The failure of ancient Israel to keep the Law. (vv. 29–30)	e	The failure of Israel in Ezra's day to keep the Law. (v. 30)

---

[169] Robertson, *The Old Testament Problem*, op. cit., pp. 35–36. These words of Robertson were published in 1950. For years his seemed to be a lone voice until in 1987 Whybray made a very similar point, concerning the anachronisms and cultural assumptions of Source Criticism (op. cit., pp. 46f.).

The comparison of Ezra with Moses begins right at the beginning of IV Ezra 14, when it is alleged, the Lord called out from a bush, "Ezra, Ezra!" (verse 1). Ezra responds in verse 2, "Here am I Lord," thus the calling of Moses, and Moses' answer recorded in Exodus 3:4 are paralleled unmistakably. The Lord continues, "I did manifestly reveal myself in the bush, and talked with Moses when my people were in bondage in Egypt: and I sent him, and led my people out of Egypt, and brought them to Mount Sinai; and I held him by me for many days (verses 3–4)." Clearly the Mosaic parallels are much in evidence here. IV Ezra 14 continues, "I told him [Moses] many wondrous things... The signs that I have shewed thee, the dreams which thou hast seen, and the interpretations which thou hast heard—lay them up in thine heart! For thou shalt be taken up from among men (verse 5–9)." There is probably yet another connection with Moses here, for in spite of the account of the death of Moses in Deuteronomy 34:5–6, Jewish legend speaks of him ascending into heaven.[170] Thus, the same is predicated here of Ezra. The "wondrous things" told to Moses is an allusion, of the very widespread belief amongst Jews, and also amongst Theosophists and Kabbalists that Moses received an Oral Torah as well as a Written Torah at Mount Sinai.[171] This Oral Torah contained doctrine that was kept secret from the ordinary people. Similarly Ezra is granted "signs" and "dreams".

More Mosaic parallels follow as Ezra is told to secure writing tablets and five capable scribes, as over a forty day period, he will be given a special revelation. This is facilitated by Ezra drinking a magic potion, after which he dictates for forty days to the five scribes. The casting of Ezra in the rôle of a Second Moses is conspicuously obvious through these parallels, but the most significant parallels relate to a corpus of secret doctrine. After the forty days were over, Ezra and his scribes had produced two groups of books; the first comprising twenty-four, the second, seventy. Ezra was told to take the twenty-four, the number of books of the Hebrew Canon, and to give them to both the "worthy" and the "unworthy" (verse 46). Thus the Scriptures

---

[170] See Abbot, *A Critical And Exegetical Commentary On The Epistle To The Ephesians*, Edinburgh, T. & T. Clark, 1897, pp. 112f.

[171] Scholem, Gershom, *On The Kabbalah And Its Symbolism*, translated Manheim, New York, Schocken, 1996, cap. II, *The Meaning Of The Torah In Jewish Mysticism*.

of the Hebrew Canon or Old Testament were for general distribution. When it came to the seventy however, Ezra was told to deliver them only to the "wise" (verse 46), because they contained, "the spring of understanding, the fountain of wisdom, and the stream of knowledge" (verse 47).

Dale Allison investigated these parallels between Moses and Ezra found in IV Ezra 14 and concluded that they served as a means of legitimising certain esoteric literary works. Just as Moses was the means of bringing revelation to Israel, so too was Ezra, and the story told about him validated the esoteric literature, including IV Ezra, and the secret doctrines this literature contained.[172]

I agree wholeheartedly with Allison here. Having been attracted by the occult in my pre-Christian days, I am keenly aware of how much importance is placed by Hermetists Theosophists and Cabbalists on the alleged existence of a *Secret Doctrine*, originally an *unwritten* or *Oral Torah*[173] said to have been given to Moses on the Mount.[174] It must be remembered that the date normally given to IV Ezra, coincides with the reappearance of Gnosticism, this time as a Christian heresy, and Gnosticism has many parallels with Hermetism, Theosophy and Cabbalism. As Allison says, it is the purpose of IV Ezra to give authority to certain esoteric works, said to embody this hidden knowledge or Secret Doctrine. A provenance was being created for spurious occult and apocalyptic writings. In order to do this, Ezra had to resemble Moses as closely as possible, and the giving of the Law to Israel was merely a necessary adjunct to this. To accept IV Ezra as a genuine presentation of textual history, is seriously to misunderstand it. The evidence that we have seen of copying from an Angular Script vorlage that is evident in the Square Charactered text we now use, shows how completely synthetic is the history presented by IV Ezra.

---

[172] Allison, Dale C., *The New Moses: A Matthean Typology*, Edinburgh, T. & T. Clark, 1993, pp. 62–64.

[173] Referred to as the *Torah-Shebe'al-Peh*, whereas the Written Torah is known as the *Torah-Shebiktav*, see *Textual Sources For The Study Of Judaism*, translated Alexander, Philip S., Manchester, Manchester University Press, 1984, p. 2.

[174] See, Scholem, op. cit., cap. II, and Edersheim, op. cit., p. 99.

Conclusion 7. There is no evidence to support the story that every copy of the Torah perished at the fall of Jerusalem. Our previous findings, summarised in Conclusion 6 above, show how credible is the Hebrew Tradition that many copies were made of the Torah before Jerusalem fell, and that at least one of these was taken into Babylon, and returned to Jerusalem with Ezra.

Part C

Does The Hexateuch Really Exist?

An outstanding characteristic of the Samaritans is that they accepted as canonical, only the Five Books Of Moses. It is true that they have a Chronicle as well,[175] but their Bible is restricted to what we know as Genesis, Exodus, Leviticus, Numbers, and Deuteronomy. This one fact alone argues strongly against the existence of a Hexateuch, as Higher Critics who claim a post-exilic origin of the Samaritan Pentateuch, inevitably either have to believe that at that very late date, the book of Joshua was not attached in any way to the Pentateuch, or that the Samaritans deliberately detached it. Given that the book in question exalts the status of their Ephraimite hero Joshua, this is most unlikely. There are other considerations however, that give further evidence that the Pentateuch is a distinct literary corpus, and that the existence of the Hexateuch, Octateuch or even Tetrateuch, is a myth created by Higher Critics.

The Book Of Psalms

That the Torah comprised a recognised corpus, was the belief not just of the Samaritans but of the Jews as well, is evident from the long recognised fivefold division of the book of Psalms, corresponding to *The Five Fifths Of The Law*. Although a detailed analysis of the structure of the book of Psalms is beyond the scope of this work,[176] I refer to it now simply to demonstrate that the Jews from antiquity have regarded the Torah as comprising five books, and have associated no other book with it at all.

---

[175] Thomson, op. cit., in *The International Standard Bible Encyclopædia* op. cit., p. 2317.

[176] Those interested should consult Boys, Thomas, *A Key To The Psalms*, edited Bullinger, E. W., London, Eyre & Spottiswoode, 1890.

The division of the Psalms is as follows: Psalms 1–41, relating to Genesis; Psalms 42–72, relating to Exodus; Psalms 73–89, relating to Leviticus; Psalms 90–106, relating to Numbers; and Psalms 107–150, relating to Deuteronomy. This fivefold structure is referred to in every work I have consulted on the Psalms,[177] and always with the same divisions, which are marked by the doxologies of Psalms 41, 72, 89, and 106, the first three also ending, uniquely, with a *double 'amen'*, the last, again uniquely, with, *Amen-Hallelujah.*

McCullough makes the point that these divisions antedate the Septuagint,[178] into which they were carried over.[179] The notes in *The Companion Bible* include the following, "Manuscript and Masoretic authorities, the Talmud (*Kiddushin* 33a) as well as the ancient versions, divide the Psalms into five books. The *Midrash* on Ps. 1. 1 says, 'Moses gave to the Israelites the five books of the Law; and corresponding with these David gave them the five books of the Psalms.'"[180]

The Fivefold book of Psalms is not the only canonical work that reflects The Five Fifths Of The Law. In Appendix I of his fascinating book *The New Moses: A Matthean Typology*, Dale C. Allison discusses the view that the Gospel of Matthew has a fivefold structure reflecting that of the Torah.[181] From this we see that for centuries the Jews and the Samaritans regarded the Pentateuch as a distinct corpus, and, apparently have never regarded any other books so highly. It may be also that the Megilloth, or Five Scrolls of The Song Of Songs, Ruth, Lamentations, Ecclesiastes, and Esther, relate to the Five books of Moses. Certainly Ben Sira regarded them as distinct from the other

---

[177] For example. Maclaren, *The Psalms*, forming a part of *The Expositors Bible*, edited Robertson Nicoll, W., London, Hodder & Stoughton, 1845; Delitzsch, F., *Psalms*, translated Martin, J., being Volume V, of Keil & Delitzsch' *Commentary On The Old Testament*, Grand Rapids, Michigan, U.S.A., 1976, Bullinger, E. W., *The Names And Order Of The Books Of The Old Testament*, Shetland, The Open Bible Trust, 1996, & Rotherham, J. B., *Studies In The Psalms*, London, Allenson, 1911.

[178] McCullough, W. Stewart, in the *Introduction* to the Psalms in *The Interpreter's Bible*, edited by Buttrick, G. A., Bowie, W. R., Schere, P., Knox, J., Terrien, S., & Harmon, N. B., Volume IV, Nashville, published in Twelve Volumes by The Abingdon Press, 1955, p. 5.

[179] Swete, H. B., op. cit., p. 254.

[180] *The Companion Bible*, London, The Lamp Press, undated, in. loc.

[181] Allison, Dale C., op. cit., pp. 293–298.

writings.[182] Edersheim even states that, compared with the Pentateuch, "all else—even the teaching of the Prophets and of the Hagiographa, as well as the oral tradition—bore the general name of *Qabbalah*"![183]

It is for this reason that the Jews frequently refer to the Torah as *The Five Fifths Of The Law*, indicating its completeness, and the impossibility of adding to it. We see that this belief goes back to the days of the Samaritan Pentateuch, which is dependent on an Angular-Script vorlage which seems to date at least from the days of Hezekiah, and possibly even earlier.

Similarities And Differences

The similarities in style that are noticeable between the Pentateuch and the book of Joshua then, are, as was suggested earlier, merely because Joshua was for forty years, a key, and very senior assistant to Moses. How would it be possible to spend so long a time in the company of one who had received the highest human education that the world then could offer (Acts 7:22), and who had encountered the Living Lord HimSelf on more than one occasion, and for such far-reaching purposes as the execution of the Exodus from Egypt, the crossing of the Sea-of-Passage, the establishment of the Chosen Nation, and the Giving-of-the-Law, and remain uninfluenced by him? It is small wonder that there are similarities, but what Higher Criticism seldom admits, is that there are differences too, notably the literary archaisms that are found in the Pentateuch, but not in the book of Joshua,[184] yet, if the same Documentary Sources which allegedly underlie the Pentateuch, underlie Joshua also, this is not what would be expected. This is not the only literary feature that is found in the Pentateuch, but not in Joshua, as we will see later.

Martin Noth

It is true that Martin Noth's contributions to Source Criticism in which he attached Deuteronomy to the books from Judges to Kings to

---

[182] See *The Prologue Of The Wisdom Of Jesus The Son Of Sirach*, being the second prologue to Ecclesiasticus.

[183] Edersheim, op. cit., Volume I, p. 102.

[184] Thomson, op. cit., in *The International Standard Bible Encyclopædia* op. cit., p. 2317.

form the so-called *Deuteronomist History*, leaving only a *Tetrateuch* have tended to suppress the usage of the term Hexateuch in recent years, but the arguments detailed above militate just as robustly against this so-called Tetrateuch, as against the Hexateuch, and just as clearly for a Pentateuch.[185]

An Inconsistent Approach

Before we sum up our findings concerning the antiquity of the Pentateuch, I would like to point out how enormously inconsistent Higher Criticism is. We have just seen how easy it is to see that the dating of the supposed D and P is hopelessly inaccurate, but the principle on which they rest is to my mind most unsound. The basic assumption is that the alleged other sources of the Pentateuch, J, and E, are discernible through Astruc's Clue, namely, their use of different Divine Names. J would consistently use Jehovah, while E would just as consistently use Elohim. In fact, this belief is perhaps the greatest assumption made by Higher Critics as we saw in Part One.

The redactors however, must be made by these same Higher Critics, to do *precisely and systematically the exact opposite!* They must be believed to be so careless and lacking in understanding, that they thoroughly confuse the material the different Divine Names supposedly identify, so that the Critics inherit an interwoven mess which it is their task to untangle. But as a consequence, Higher Criticism depends upon one group, the redactors, doing precisely what it is assumed as an article of faith the sources could and would never do, and that they did it repeatedly, and even habitually!

Far from being sympathetic to the material they edit, the redactors must be believed to be hopelessly naïve, and woefully ignorant of what the learned Higher Critics are astute enough to detect. Of course had the redactors been wise enough to understand the glaring inconsistencies their work produced, and as a consequence, eliminated the evidence of their cutting-and-pasting, Higher Criticism would not have been possible! It seems therefore, that Higher

---

[185] See Soulen and Kendall Soulen, op. cit., p. 123.

Criticism's viability *depends* on the repeated inefficient workings of a group of people whose existence may not be demonstrated.

But there is even more. Where supposed narrative duplications occur, it is said that a redactor has set out in parallel different accounts of the same story. Yet at other times redactors are said to fuse together into one account, material that originally was found in different documents. Thus the redactors that are so indispensable to the existence of Higher Criticism must be capable of undertaking any and every task Higher Critics require in order to maintain the credibility of their theories. It is well worth quoting Professor of Hebrew and Old Testament Studies, Norman Whybray at this point. Accepting Higher Criticism's views on documentary sources for the sake of his argument, He writes, "With regard to the *motives* of the redactors, some of the sharpest criticism of the hypothesis came from Sandmel, who, writing about R^{JE} [the supposed redactor who combined J and E], asked what reason there can have been for dovetailing two works covering the same ground to form a single work if nothing essentially new was created as a result. He rejected the frequently used analogy of Tatian's harmonising of the four Gospels in his *Diatessaron* on the grounds that the Gospels had already been canonized: to unite their conflicting accounts [*sic*] into a single harmonious one while losing nothing essential from any of the original books may have been seen as an apologetical necessity. But there was no such necessity in the case of J and E, and Sandmel could find no satisfactory motive for the work of R^{JE}. It is true that it has been frequently suggested that the motive was the combination of the traditions of Judah (J) with those of northern Israel (E). However, apart from the fact that doubt has recently been expressed about the correctness of the attribution of these two documents to south and north respectively, it is not at all clear that either party would have accepted a new version of Israel's origins which both omitted parts of its own traditions and also introduced new material unknown to it, especially since the documentary Critics themselves maintained that each version had its own bias which was in some respects unfavourable to the other group. In fact *the historical circumstances which could have inspired* *the work of R^{JE} are extremely difficult to discover* [emphasis mine, the words in square brackets are my own]."[186]

Conclusion To Chapter Four

Chapter Three showed that the evidence for the antiquity of the art of writing does not make it either necessary or inevitable that the Torah must be placed centuries after Moses. There is nothing inherently improbable in believing that Moses, "learned in all the wisdom of the Egyptians (Acts 7:22)" could easily have been in a position to write a set of documents as long as the Pentateuch. The preservation of the knowledge of writing during the period of the Judges also removes any such obstacle concerning the books of Joshua, Judges, Samuel, and Ruth.

Now, in Chapter Four, we have seen that the Prophets referred to the Torah as a distinct body of teaching, and, claim that it was read to the people of Israel, and that Israel and Judah were both scolded for their failure to adhere to the Torah. We have seen that the Samaritan Pentateuch derives from a source that is independent from, and earlier than, the Square Charactered text of Ezra; and that both texts descend from an Angular Scripted pre-exilic vorlage. The literary evidence we have examined shows definite indications, albeit occasional, although they are also quite distinct and consistent, that this vorlage is likely to be of very great antiquity. It would seem to be at least as early as Hezekiah; and may even be as old as the Judges. By themselves, these indicators do not demonstrate a Mosaic authorship of the entire Pentateuch, of course, but they certainly do undermine the credibility of the claims made by the more extreme Higher Critics. This applies especially to the references in the prophets to the Torah. They also show that accepting the Mosaic authorship of the Pentateuch is not as naïve as often it is thought to be.

It is true that the critic may well retort that certain fragments of the Pentateuch may indeed be of very great age, but that this does not disprove Graf–Wellhausen at all, as such genuinely early fragments could easily have been worked into a much later literary production

---

[186] Whybray, op. cit., p. 121.

102

via the labours of the very convenient redactors Higher Critics love to appeal to. Here again, however, the prophets' reference to the Torah does not help their case, nonetheless, it seems clear that the next subject we tackle ought to be the *unity* of the Pentateuch, for if it could be shown that there is evidence for the literary unity of the Five Fifths Of The Law, the evidence for great antiquity that we have recently seen, would make *the entire corpus* early, not merely certain alleged fragments, and would also have profound effects on the dating, and even the existence of the supposed literary sources J, E, D, and P.

Chapter Five

The Unity Of The Pentateuch Seen From Its Literary Construction

Part A

There are many remarkable phenomena attending the literary construction of the Pentateuch which witness for its unity. The first that we will examine is the existence of literary *Correspondences*, or *Structures*, as they are now more commonly referred to.

What Is A Structure?

A Structure is a portion of Scripture, which may be as small as a single verse, or as large as a complete book, series of books, or, even the entire compass of Scripture, in which correspondences between the different elements of which that portion is comprised are exhibited. It is presented to the reader so as to give emphasis to these correspondences, enabling more meaningful exegesis. I give below a basic Structure of Philippians 2:9–11,[187] in which it is very easy to see the form of Structure often called an *Introversion*, or a *Chiasmus*.[188]

---

[187] Taken from Welch, C. H. *The Prize Of The High Calling,* London, The Berean Publishing Trust, undated, p. 83.

[188] See Watson, Wilfred G.E., *A Review Of Kugel's 'The Idea Of Biblical Poetry,'* in *Journal For The Study Of The Old Testament*, Issue 28, Sheffield, The University Of Sheffield, 1984, p. 89–98.

Philippians 2:9–11

A) Verse 9; The Name above every name,

    B) Verse 10a; Every knee shall bow,

        C) Verse 10b; Things in heaven,

            D) Verse 10c; Things in earth,

        c) Verse 10d; Things under the earth,

    b) Verse 11a; Every tongue confess,

a) Verse 11b; Jesus Christ is Lord.

Here,

> **A** corresponds with **a**, the Name of the Lord Jesus Christ is the Name above every Name;
>
> **B** corresponds with **b**, both statements concern the submission of all to the Lordship of Christ;
>
> **C** corresponds with **c**, the submission of all to Christ will include those in heaven and those under the earth;
>
> finally those on earth form the centre of the Structure, **D**.

Far more highly detailed Structures may be produced for this passage, but this will serve as an illustration of the principle. The relevance for our investigation is that a Structure is evidence of a literary plan, and therefore highly suggestive of commonality of authorship throughout the passage concerned. Now some structures are immensely long, and fantastically detailed, giving evidence thereby of commonality of authorship over a great extent of Scripture. Were such Structures to be found that span passages alleged to derive from *different* literary sources, the obviously common literary plan would militate firmly against the existence of such separate sources, in a way which it would be extremely difficult to gainsay. This, I believe is the reason that Structures receive so little notice. They provide important and measurable literary evidence against Graf–Wellhausen in an emphatic manner. Like so many other Scriptural phenomena, the existence of literary Structures in the Pentateuch was known of for centuries by learned Jews before it became known by Gentile students of the Word.

The Discovery Of Literary Structures

Andrew Morton in his booklet, *The Principle Of Structure In Scripture,* traces the knowledge of Structures back to the Jewish community of Spain, and in particular to Isaac Ben Jehudah Abarbanel, born in Lisbon in 1437, and the famous Azariah de Rossi of Ferrara, born in 1513.

It was the Bishop of London, and one-time Professor of Poetry at Oxford, Robert Lowth (1710–1787) who took the first major steps in bringing this knowledge to ordinary Gentile believers. Using the work of de Rossi, in 1753 he published his *Sacra Poesi Hebraeorum Praelectiones Academicae,* which illustrated the existence of Structures, and won acclaim across Europe. In a later work, he published a translation of chapter 60 of de Rossi's *Meor Enayim,* or *Light Of The Eyes.* Lowth was succeeded by Bishop John Jebb, who in 1820 published his *Sacred Literature,* which promoted the views of Lowth. Four years later, Thomas Boys (1792–1880) published a landmark work entitled *Tactica Sacra* in which he gave many impressive examples of literary Structure to be found in the Scriptures. Boys went on to publish another such work entitled *Key To The Book Of Psalms,* and after his death, Doctor Ethelbert W. Bullinger, using pencilled notes in Boys' Hebrew Bible, published *A Key To The Psalms,* which very clearly shows the Structure of each individual Psalm.[189]

Bullinger then expanded on this, to show not merely that Structures exist in every Psalm, and many other places in the Word of God, but that the entire body of Scripture is Structured. It proves to be what we would now term a *fractal* type of phenomenon, whereby the same pattern-types are in evidence at every level of scale. Individual verses are structured, as are, whole passages, books, collections of books, and the entire corpus of Scripture![190]

---

[189] Morton, Andrew, *The Principle Of Structure In Scripture,* Worthing, Sussex, published privately by the author, 1950. See also Bullinger, E. W., *How To Enjoy The Bible,* London, Eyre & Spottiswoode, 1928, pp. 199–226.

[190] The results of his findings are to be seen in the *Companion Bible,* in which every verse is located in its Structural position in a manner which is particularly impressive. London, The Lamp Press, undated.

The Dispensationalists, Welch, and Knoch, have perhaps undertaken the greatest amount of research into Structures, but by no means is the work confined to Dispensationalists, although it is one of the greatest contributions made to Scriptural study by Dispensationalism. Duane Garrett in his extremely useful book, *Rethinking Genesis,*[191] refers to many very scholarly researchers who employ Structures in their work, often to the great discomfort of Higher Critics. The academics Kikawada and Quinn also undermine many arguments of Higher Critics through the employment of structures.[192] Their genuine existence is even acknowledged by Soulen and Kendall Soulen in their *Handbook Of Biblical Criticism.*[193]

Evidence Ignored

As with the evidence for the antiquity of the art of writing, the evidence provided by the phenomenon of literary Structures was not available to the first Higher Critics, but was certainly available by the time of Wellhausen, but was again ignored. Had this evidence not been locked up in the Hebrew tongue, and confined to learned Jewish circles, it would have revealed the Old Documentary Hypothesis to be completely untenable I believe, as I will now show. In the following pages I give the Structure for each book of the Pentateuch, followed by that for the Pentateuch itself, based on those given in *The Companion Bible.*

---

[191] Op. cit.

[192] Op. cit.

[193] See under *Chiasmus*, op. cit., in. loc.

Genesis

The structure of the book as a whole

A¹ 1:1–2:3   The Introduction.
A² 2:4–50:26 The eleven toledoths (*books of generations*).

Genesis 1:1–2:3 (A¹ above)
The Introduction

A¹   A) 1:1–2 The earth, without form, and empty or void.

          B) 1:2 The Spirit of God upon the face of the waters.

    A) 1:2–25 In the six days, the earth is given form, and given fulness, so that is it no longer void.

          B) 1:26–2:3 The Image of God upon the face of the earth.

Genesis 2:4–50:26 (A² above)
The eleven toledoths (*books of generations*)

Concerning all people:

A²   C   E) The heavens and the earth 2:4–4:26

          F) Adam 5:1–6:8

            G) Noah 6:9–9:29

              H) The sons of Noah 10:1–11:9

                I) Shem 11;10–11:26

                  D) Terah 11:27–25:11

Concerning the Chosen People:

    C   *E*) Ishmael 25:12–18

          F) Isaac 25:19–35:29

            G) Esau 36:1–8

              H) The sons of Esau 36:9–43

                I) Jacob 37:1–50:26

Exodus

A) 1:1–2:10 The bondage of Israel begun.

B) 2:11–14:31 Freedom given.

A) 15:1–21 The bondage of Israel ended.

B) 15:22–40:38 Freedom used.

Leviticus

A^1) 1:1–7:38 The offerings and their laws.

B^1) D) 8:1–10:20 Priesthood.

E) 11:1–15:33 Ceremonial laws (Promulgation).

C) 16;1–34 Israel's Fast: The Day Of Atonement.

A^2) 17:1–16 The offerings and their requirements.

B^2) *E)* 18:1–20:17 Ceremonial laws (Penalties).

D) 21:1–22:33 Priesthood.

C) 23:1–25:55 Jehovah's Feasts.

A^3) 26:1–27:34 The offerings and their charges.

Numbers

A^1) 1:1–4:49 Numeration and orders. Encampment and service.

B^1) 5:1–9:23 Laws and events.

A^2) 10:1–36 Journeyings and order. March.

B^2) 11:1–25:18 Events and laws.

A^3) 26:1–27 Numeration and orders. Inheritance.

B^3) 27:1–31:54 Events and Laws.

A^4) 32:1–36:12 Journeyings and order. Division of Land.

Epilogue 36:13

Deuteronomy

A   1:1–5 Introduction.

     B   C 1:6–32:47 The Tribes: their administration.

            D 32:48–52 Moses: his death announced.

     B   *C* 33:1–29 The Tribes: their blessing.

            D 34:1–7 Moses: his death accomplished.

A   34:8–12 Conclusion.

The Pentateuch as a whole

A   GENESIS: The beginning. All produced by The Word Of God. Israel as a Family.

     B   EXODUS: History. The journey from Egypt to Sinai. Israel emerging from families and tribes, to a nation. Called 'Hebrews' according to their 'tongue.'

         C   LEVITICUS: Worship. Mount Sinai. Jehovah in the midst. He is Israel's God; they are His People.

     B   NUMBERS: History. The journey from Sinai to Canaan. Israel now a nation; numbered and blessed as such.

A   DEUTERONOMY: The end. All depending on The Word Of Jehovah. Israel regarded as in the Land.

The Flood Narrative

Although these structures which relate to the separate books of the Pentateuch show evidence of a common literary plan for each book, and the collection as a whole, it is often the Structures found in smaller portions of Scripture that prove most interesting, and frequently for High Criticism, the most challenging. A fine example of this is to be found in the Flood narrative of Genesis 6:1–9:19. Isaac Kikawada and Arthur Quinn give the classical Documentary analysis of the Flood narrative in their book, *Before Abraham Was* as given in the table below.[194] The narrative is divided into no less than *twenty-three* different fragments from which it is said, the so-called

---

[194] Op. cit., pp. 22–29.

J and P narratives may be rebuilt. Critics believe that the narrative found in the book of Genesis has been 'cobbled together' artificially, in order to produce the account we know so well.

The Flood Narrative According To Graf–Wellhausen

P	J
	6:5–8
6:9–22	
	7:1–5
7:6	
	7:7–8
7:9	
	7:10
7:11	
	7:12
7:13–16a	
	7:16b–17
7:18–21	
	7:22–23
7:24–8:2a	
	8:2b–3a
8:3b–5	
	8:6–12
8:13a	
	8:13b
8:14–19	
	8:20–22
9:1–17	
	9:18–19

The Findings Of Gordon Wenham

Higher Criticism divides this seemingly straightforward narrative up into the twenty-three different portions above. However, the commentator Gordon Wenham, has detected a fascinating and highly detailed Structure which encompasses the *whole* of the Flood narrative in a way which reveals the utter unity of the passage. It accomplishes this, beautifully, majestically, and emphatically. Wenham's work has been confirmed by Bernard Anderson,[195] Duane Garrett,[196] and Kikawada and Quinn,[197] and is given below.

The symmetry of this complex Structure shows how absurd it is to claim that the narrative that reveals it is a patchwork of fragments obtained from different sources, that was then crudely stitched together. Plainly there is literary continuity, a plan and a purpose revealed here, and neither the Old or New Documentary Theories of J and P are adequate to the task of explaining its origin. The evidence of the planning of the Structure is seen as Wenham has pointed out, in the way the seven day period of waiting for the Flood is *twice* referred to (H & I), in order to balance the later period of fourteen days (I' & H'). Further, Kikawada and Quinn have shown that the Hebrew text reveals a large number of deliberate word-plays that span the alleged seams between the supposed sources, which offers even more evidence for the unity of the narrative.[198]

---

[195] Cited in Garrett, op. cit., p. 24.

[196] Ibid.

[197] Op. cit., pp. 97–104.

[198] Ibid., pp. 97f.

The Structure Of The Flood Story (6:1–9:19)

A   Noah (6:10a)

 B   Shem, Ham, and Japheth (10b)

  C   Ark to be built (14–16)

   D   Flood announced (17)

    E   Covenant with Noah (18–20)

     F   Food in the ark (21)

      G   Command to enter the ark (7:1–3)

       H   7 days waiting for flood (4–5)

        I   7 days waiting for flood (7–10)

         J   Entry to ark (11–15)

          K   Yahweh shuts Noah in (16)

           L   40 days flood (17a)

            M   Waters increase (17b–18)

             N   Mountains covered (19–20)

              O   150 days water prevail ([21]–24)

               P   GOD REMEMBERS NOAH (8:1)

              O'   150 days waters abate (3)

             N'   Mountain tops visible (4–5)

            M'   Waters abate (5)

           L'   40 days (end of) (6a)

          K'   Noah opens window of ark (6b)

         J'   Raven and dove leave ark (7–9)

        I'   7 days waiting for waters to subside (10–11)

       H'   7 days waiting for waters to subside (12–13)

      G'   Command to leave ark (15–17[22])

     F'   Food outside the ark (9:1–4)

    E'   Covenant with all flesh (8–10)

   D'   No flood in the future (11–17)

  C'   Ark (18a)

 B'   Shem Ham and Japheth (18b)

A'   Noah (19)

The Life Of Jacob

Garrett refers to another Structure, covering the life of Jacob, running from Genesis 25:19 to 35:22, found originally by Michael Fishbane, with further details located by Gary Rendsburg. This shows how the details of the life of Jacob conform also to a Chiasmus.[199] Although it does not contain as many elements as the one given above relating to the Flood, its consequences are significantly more far-reaching as it covers a much greater span of the Scriptures, and encompasses material supposed to derive from E, as well as J, and P. Higher Criticism divides this section of Scripture into a staggering 136 different fragments! The truth is, as the Structure will show, that there is again, clear literary continuity, arguing strongly for common authorship of the entire passage. Higher Criticism's 136 fragments are detailed in the table below, which is based on S. H. Hooke's commentary on Genesis.[200]

Fragment no.	J	E	P
1			25:19–20
2	25:21–25a		
3		25:25b	
4	25:26a		
5			25:26b
6		25:27	
7	25:28		
8		25:29–34	
9	26:1–3a		
10		26:3b–5	
11	26:6–14		
12		26:15	
13	26:16–17		
14		26:18	

---

[199] Op. cit., p. 110.

[200] Op. cit., p. 176.

Fragment no.	J	E	P
15	26:19–33		
16			26:34–35
17	27:1a		
18		27:1b	
19	27:2–3		
20		27:4a	
21	27:4b		
22		27:5a	
23	27:5b–7a		
24		27:7b–14	
25	27:15		
26		27:16–18a	
27	27:18b–20		
28		27:21–23	
29	27:24–7		
30		27:28	
31	27:29a		
32		27:29b	
33	27:29c–30a		
34		27:30b–31a	
35	27:31b–34		
36		37:35–41a	
37	27:41b–42		
38		27:43a	
39	27:43b		
40		27:44	
41	27:45a		
42		27:45b	
43			27:46–28:9
44	28:10		

Fragment no.	J	E	P
45		28:11–12	
46	28:13–16		
47		28:17–18	
48	28:19		
49		28:20–21a	
50	28:21b		
51		28:22–29:1	
52	29:2–14		
53		29:15–23	
54			29:24
55		29:25	
56	29:26		
57		29:27–28a	
58			29:28b–29
59		29:30	
60	29:31–35		
61		30:1–3a	
62	30:3b–16		
63		30:17–20	
64			30:21–22a
65		30:22b	
66	30:22c–23a		
67		30:23b	
68	30:24–25		
69		30:26	
70	30:27		
71		30:28	
72	30:29–31a		
73		30:31b–33	
74	30:34–38a		

Fragment no.	J	E	P
75		30:38b	
76	30:39–40a		
77		30:40b	
78	30:40c–31:1		
79		31:2	
80	31:3		
81		31:4–9	
82	31:10		
83		31:11;12a	
84	31:12b		
85		31:13–16	
86	31:17–18a		
87			31:18b
88		31:19–24	
89	31:25		
90		31:26	
91	31:27		
92		31:28–30	
93	31:31		
94		31:32–42	
95	31:43–44		
96		31:45	
97	31:46		
98		31:47	
99	31:48		
100		31:49	
101	31:50		
102		31:51–32:2	
103	32:3–7a		
104		32:7b–13a	

Fragment no.	J	E	P
105	32:13b–22a		
106		32:22b–23a	
107	32:23b–29		
108		32:30	
109	32:31–33:17		
110		33:18a	
111			33:18b
112		33:18c–20	
113			34:1–2a
114	34:2b–3a		
115			34:3b
116	34:3c		
117			34:4
118	34;5		
119			34:6
120	34:7		
121			34:8–10
122	34:11		
123			34:12–18
124	34:19		
125			34:20–25
126	34;26		
127			34:27–29a
128	34:29b–31		
129		35:1–4	
130			35:5–6a
131		35:6b–9a	
132			35:9b–13
133	35:14		
134			35:15

Fragment no.	J	E	P
135	35:16–22a		
136			35:22b

We see in the above breakdown of Higher Criticism's analysis of this section of Genesis, that on four different occasions, individual verses are broken into no less than three separate fragments! One of these, 30:22, is not only broken up into three, but then has each of its three alleged portions awarded to different sources. 30:22a is attributed to P; 30:22b to E; and 30:22c to J! According to this view the following phrase, "And God (Elohim) remembered Rachel (Genesis 30:22a)," is derived from P, the next phrase, "and God (Elohim) hearkened to her (30:22b)" from E, and the concluding words, "and opened her womb (3:22c)" from J. Anyone familiar with Hebrew literary style however, will recognise here a very good example of Hebrew Parallelism, whereby an idea is gradually built up by separate, complimentary statements.[201] Bullinger gives numerous examples in his *Figures Of Speech Used In The Bible*.[202] This too is a literary style found very frequently throughout the Canon of Scripture, and which de Rossi wrote about in his *Light Of The Eyes*, and has been recognized by students of Hebrew prose and poetry for very many years. A reading of the Hebrew text will also reveal that all three parts of the verse are united by two occurrences of waw-copulative,[203] showing the verse's unity. The unsympathetic manhandling of Hebrew style, by cynical gentiles, utterly ignorant of Hebrew literature and Jewish Tradition is what has led to the absurd results given above. I now give the Structure of Jacob's life below, but unlike Garrett's presentation of it, I have indented it in order to emphasise the chiastic form.

---

[201] Soulen & Kendall–Soulen, op. cit., in. loc.

[202] Bullinger, E. W., *Figures Of Speech Used In The Bible*, Grand Rapids, Michigan, U.S.A., 1968, pp. 349ff. This work, which draws on de Rossi and other Jewish exegetes, is one of the very best introductions to the Hebrew literary forms found in the Scriptures.

[203] Waw-copulative is the equivalent of the English conjunction, *and*, and is the letter ו prefixed to a word, normally with the Sh'va underneath it (like our colon, :), as in our case. See *The Hebrew Student's Manual,* London, Samuel Bagster, undated, p. 92.

The Life Of Jacob

A Word of the Lord sought, the struggle at birth, birth of Jacob. (25:19–34)

 B Parenthesis: Rebekah in foreign palace, settlement with foreigners (26:1–34)

  C Jacob's fear of Esau: Jacob's escape. (27:1–28:9)

   D The Angels (28:10–22)

    E Jacob settles in Haran (29:1–30)

     F The fecundity of Jacob's wives. (29:31–30:24)

     F' The fecundity of Jacob's flocks. (30:25–43)

    E' Jacob escapes from Haran (31:1–54)

   D' The Angel (32:1–32)

  C' Jacob's fear of Esau: Jacob's return. (33:1–20)

 B' Parenthesis: Dinah in foreign palace, settlement with foreigners (34:1–31)

A' Word of the Lord fulfilled, the struggle at birth, Jacob becomes Israel (35:1–22)

Here again we find that one literary Structure spans the many alleged fragments numbering more than 130 (!)[204] of Higher Criticism, showing how lacking in credibility the Documentary Hypothesis is. It could only develop and thrive in an environment of ignorance of Hebrew method. Unlike the allegations of Source Criticism, these Structures have *real* existence, an existence that may be *demonstrated*, and which any reader of the Scriptures who is acquainted with its fundamentals, may prove for himself or herself. These Structures show the foolishness of Higher Criticism's bold assertions as well as the truth of Christ's remark, "The Scripture cannot be broken." (John 10:35) I give below as examples, two more of the Structures which Duane Garrett refers to in his excellent book, *Rethinking Genesis*.[205] As with the previous occasions, Higher Criticism alleges these texts have been built up from many different fragments; thirty-nine and one-hundred-and-six fragments respectively.[206]

---

[204] See Hooke, S. H., in the article, *Genesis*, in *Peake's Commentary On The Bible*, edited, by Black, Matthew, & Rowley, H. H., London, Thomas Nelson, 1977, p. 176.

[205] With minor changes to give greater emphasis to the chiastic structure. Garrett, op. cit., pp. 114–115.

[206] Hooke, S. H., op. cit, in *Peake's Commentary On The Bible*, op. cit., p. 176.

The Story Of Abraham

A   Terah's Genealogy. (11:27–32)

  B   Abram's Spiritual Journey begins. (12:1–9)

    C   Sarai as Abram's sister, peaceful conclusion, departure of Lot. (12:10–13:18)

      D   Abram intervenes for Sodom and Lot. (14:3–24)

        E   Abram and the Covenant of the pieces, birth of Ishmael. (15:1–16:16)

        E'   Abraham and the Covenant of circumcision, birth of Isaac foretold. (17:1–18:15)

      D'   Abraham intervenes for Sodom and Lot. (18:16–19:13)

    C'   Sarah as Abraham's sister, peaceful conclusion, departure of Ishmael. (20:1–21:34)

  B'   Abraham's Spiritual Journey reaches its fulfilment. (22:1–19)l

A'   Nahor's Genealogy. (22:20–24)

I give below a table showing the thirty-nine fragments Higher Critics say that the material used in the structure shown above is built up from.[207]

Fragment No.	J	E	P
1			11:27.
2	11:28–30.		
3			11:31–32.
4	12:1–4a.		
5			12:4b–5.
6	12:6–13:5.		
7			13:6a.
8	13:6b–11a.		
9			13:11b–12a.
10	13:12b–18		
11	chapter 14 = source unknown.		
12		15:1–2.	
13	15:3–4.		

---

[207] Based on Hooke, op. cit., in *Peake's Commentary*, op. cit., p. 176. No source is attributed by Hooke to 21:3–5.

Fragment No.	J	E	P
14		15:5.	
15	15:6–15.		
16		15:16.	
17	15:17–19.		
18			15:19–16:1a.
19	16:1b–2.		
20			16:3.
21	16:4–8.		
22		16:9–10.	
23	16:11–14.		
24			16:15–17:27.
25	18:1–19:28.		
26			19:29.
27	19:30–38.		
28		20:1–17.	
29	20:18–21:2.		
30		21:6.	
31	21:7.		
32		21:8–27.	
33	21:28–30.		
34		21:31–32.	
35	21:33.		
36		21:34–22:14.	
37	22:15–18.		
38		22:19.	
39	22:20–24.		

The Story Of Joseph

A   Joseph and his brothers, Jacob and Joseph part. (37:1–36)

  B   Parenthesis: Joseph not present. (38:1–30)

    C   Reversal: Joseph found guilty, Potiphar's wife found innocent. (39:1–23)

      D   Joseph hero of Egypt. (40:1–41:57)

        E   Two trips to Egypt. (42:1–43:34)

          F   Concluding test. (44:1–34)

            F'   Conclusion of test. (45:1–28)

          E'   Two accounts of migration to Egypt. (46:1–47:12)

        D'   Joseph hero of Egypt. (47:13–27)

      C'   Reversal: Ephraim firstborn, Manasseh secondborn. (47:28–48:22)

    B'   Parenthesis: Joseph nominally present. (49:1–28)

  A'   Joseph and his brothers, Jacob and Joseph part. (49:29–50:26)

I give below a table showing the one-hundred-and-six fragments Higher Critics say that the material used in the structure shown above is built up from.[208]

Fragment no.	J	E	P
1			37:1–2a.
2	37:2b.		
3			37:2c.
4	37:2d–4.		
5		37:5–11.	
6	37:12–13a.		
7		37:13b–14a.	
8	37:14b.		
9		37:15–18a.	
10	37:18b.		
11		37:19–20.	

---

[208] Based on Hooke, op. cit., in *Peake's Commentary*, op. cit., p. 176.

Fragment no.	J	E	P
12	37:21.		
13		37:22–25a.	
14	37:25b–27.		
15		37:28a.	
16	37:28b.		
17		37:28c–31.	
18	37:32a.		
19		37:32b–33a.	
20	37:33b.		
21		37:34.	
22	37:35.		
23		37:36.	
24	38:1–39:4a.		
25		39:4b.	
26	39:4c–5.		
27		39:6a.	
28	39:6b.		
29		39:6c–7a.	
30	39:7b–23.		
31		40:1–41:30.	
32	41:31.		
33		41:32–33.	
34	41:34.		
35		41:35a.	
36	41:35b.		
37		41:36a.	
38	41:36b.		
39		41:37–40.	
40	41:41–45a.		
41			41:45b–46a.

Fragment no.	J	E	P
42	41:46b–49.		
43		41:50–55.	
44	41:56a.		
45		41:56b.	
46	41:57.		
47		42:1.	
48	42:2.		
49		42:3.	
50	42:4–5.		
51		42:6.	
52	42:7a.		
53		42:7b–26.	
54	42:27–28a.		
55		42:28b–37.	
56	42:38–41:13.		
57		43:14.	
58	43:15–45:1a.		
59		45:1b–2a.	
60	45:2b.		
61		45:3.	
62	45:4–5a.		
63		45:5b.	
64	45:5c.		
65		45:5d–8.	
66	45:9–11.		
67		45:12.	
68	45:13–14		
69		45:15–18.	
70	45:21a.		
71		45:21b–27.	

Fragment no.	J	E	P
72	45:28–46:1a.		
73		46:1b–5.	
74			46:6–27.
75	46:28–47:4.		
76			47:5–6a.
77	47:6b.		
78			47:7–11.
79	47:12–27a.		
80			47:27b–28.
81	47:29–31.		
82		48:1–2a.	
83	48:2b.		
84			48:3–7.
85		48:8–9a.	
86	48:9b–10a.		
87		48:10b–12.	
88	48:13–19.		
89		48:20–22.	
90			49:1a.
91	49:1b–24a.		
92		49:24b–26.	
93	49:27.		
94			49:28–33a.
95	49:33b.		
96			49:33c
97	50:1–11.		
98			50:12–13.
99	50:14.		
100		50:15–17.	
101	50:18.		

Fragment no.	J	E	P
102		50:19–20.	
103	50:21.		
104		50:22–3.	
105	50:24.		
106		50:25–26.	

Those interested in pursuing the study of Structures will find *The Companion Bible*, and the works of Bullinger and Welch of invaluable help.

Conclusion 8. The four Structures we have examined very briefly cover the vast majority of the book of Genesis. Between them they cover chapters 6:1–9:19, 11:27–22:24, 25:19–35:22, & 37:1–50:26, or 80% of Genesis. The evidence from *The Companion Bible* and the writings of Bullinger and Welch will show however, that *all* of Genesis, and all of Scripture in fact, is interwoven with many Structures, some of which overlap in complex ways! Such a matrix or tapestry of Structures argues strongly for the intrinsic unity of Genesis, and the Pentateuch as a whole. To suggest that such coherent and detailed design could emerge from a patchwork of fragments pasted together is absurd, and only serves to show the intellectual poverty of Graf–Wellhausen!

Part B

If the Structures shown above illustrate the unity of the book of Genesis that Higher Criticism would break up into dozens upon dozens of fragments, the next piece of evidence derived from the literary construction of the Pentateuch calls into question the very existence of the alleged sources J, E, and P.

The Twenty-Six Generations

Just as the antiquity of the art of writing and the existence of Structures was unknown to the earliest Higher Critics, so our next consideration is almost completely unknown today, outside of Jewish exegetical groups. As with the above mentioned factors, this too militates against Higher Criticism, and at a foundational level. We saw earlier that Astruc's Clue is perhaps the most basic assumption of Higher Criticism. So then, if this were found to be untenable, the whole superstructure would collapse. That, I believe, is the spectacle that awaits us.

The Hebrew Tradition shows how the Sacred Name, revealed in the Tetragrammaton יהוה, Yahweh, usually rendered Jehovah is revealed in the number of generations from the Creation until the time of Moses. As with ancient Greek, every letter of the Hebrew alphabet has a numeric, as well as a linguistic value.[209] The numeric values of the letters of the Tetragrammaton total 26, as ה, of which there are two in the Name, = 5; ו, = 6; and י, = 10. As Hebrew is read from right to left, were the Name to be read as numerals instead of letters, it would read, 10, 5, 6, 5. Now let us see how many generations Scripture reveals between the Creation and Moses. In Genesis 5:3–29

---

[209] Ifrah, Georges, *The Universal History Of Numbers*, translated Bellos, Harding, Wood, & Monk, London, Harvill Press, 1998, pp. 212–263.

we find there are ten generations from the Creation to the Flood; Adam, Seth, Enos, Cainan, Mahalaleel, Jared, Enoch, Methuselah, Lamech, and Noah. According to Higher Criticism, verses 3–28 pertain to P, but verse 29 pertains to J.[210] From the Flood until the Division of Tongues, in the days of Peleg, there are five generations, as we see from Genesis 5:32; 10:22, and 10:24–25. These are Shem, Arphaxad, Salah, Eber, and Peleg. Higher Criticism attributes these verses to P, P, & J respectively.[211] From the Division of Tongues, until the birth of Isaac, the Child of Promise, there are six generations, as shown by Genesis 11:18–26 and 21:1–8. These are Reu, Serug, Nahor, Terah, Abram, and Isaac. The sources proposed for these passages are P, for the first, and a combination of J and E for the second.[212] Finally, from Isaac to Moses there are again five generations. We find these in Genesis 25:20–26, 29:21–34, and Exodus 6:16–20. They are Jacob, Levi, Kohath, Amram, and Moses. The alleged sources for these verses are for the first passage, a combination of P and J; for the second, an amalgam of, E, P, E, J, E, P, E, and J; and for the last passage, P.[213] Thus Higher Criticism proposes nineteen different fragments for the passages which cover the lists of the generations from the Creation to Moses; 6 from J; 6 from E; and 7 from P. But now let us look more closely at these generations, and what they reveal. There are, we saw, a total of twenty-six generations from the Creation until Moses. Thus, Moses was in the twenty-sixth generation from the Creation, the generation that equalled the gematria value of the Sacred Name, the full significance of which had not been revealed to the previous twenty-five generations! With the fulfilment of the number of generations which equated to the gematria value of the Sacred Name, the meaning of the Sacred Name itself was revealed! To my mind these parallel facts cannot be coincidental.[214]

---

[210] Hooke, op. cit., in Peake's Commentary op. cit., p. 176.

[211] Ibid.

[212] Ibid.

[213] Ibid, and Stalker, in the article, *Exodus*, in *Peake's Commentary On The Bible*, edited, by Black, Matthew, & Rowley, H. H., London, Thomas Nelson, 1977, p. 215.

[214] As will have been noticed, I understand Exodus 6:2–3 to relate to the *meaning* of the Sacred Name, rather than to the existence of the Name. There will be more on this later.

But we saw also that the pivotal events of the Flood, the Division of Tongues, and the birth of Isaac, the Child of Promise, divided these twenty-six generations into four groups, just as there are four letters in the Sacred Name. Further, *the four groups of generations contain respectively, 10, 5, 6, and 5 generations. These four groups of generations correspond to the gematria value of each of the individual letters of the Sacred Name, and even appear in the same order, spelling out the Sacred Name!*

Conclusion To Part B

The significance of this is immense. For E, the Elohist, and P the Priestly Source, and another Elohist, are now seen to be at least as Jehovist, if not more so, as J himself! Did all three sources conspire together to weave the Divine Name, alleged to be avoided by E and P altogether, into the very fabric of the narrative! This finding removes utterly the basis of Astruc's Clue, as the P narrative, and especially the E narrative, were distinguished from the J material by the avoidance of the Name Jehovah. But now we see the most majestic, subtle and creative use of that Divine Name woven together from all three of the alleged sources, destroying the foundation of both the Old and New Documentary Hypotheses. The impact of this design on Graf–Wellhausen, whereby the Sacred Name is woven into the fabric of human history in the pattern of the generations, should not be underestimated, as it shows that Astruc's Clue is meaningless. All three alleged sources, J, E, and P are Jehovist and each and every attempt to divide the Hebrew Canon into documentary sources based upon the use or avoidance of the Name Jehovah, is now seen to be based upon complete ignorance of the sublime occurrence of that Name in passages attributed to both E and P. This most remarkable occurrence of the Sacred Name was undetected by the Higher Critics, who it seems were unsympathetic to, and uninterested in, Hebrew method. Even if it is asserted that a clever redactor or redactors had been responsible for this phenomenon, where is the evidence? and, were redactors to be this clever, where would be the need for the original sources? The redactors would do all the work themselves! This astounding find of the Sacred Name written into the generations from Adam to Moses is nowhere within Scripture given any emphasis at all, and is hardly known of even today outside of certain Jewish circles. Were it to be the work of a redactor, we must ask why he would go to so much trouble, and then *hide* his literary creation so well that few today are aware of it. As it is, it stands as a stubborn fact, that once seen, is very obvious indeed, and that disproves Graf–Wellhausen utterly. The *theological* import of this phenomenon, understandable only since the Incarnation of the Word of God in human flesh, also speaks against it being a human contrivance. For here we catch an unmistakable glimpse of the manifestation within time and history, within the generations of humanity, of Israel's God. Would any pre-Christian redactor produce such a result? We see from this that Higher Critics like the Sadducees "do err, not knowing the Scriptures, nor the power of God!" (Matthew 22:29) I give an illustration of the twenty-six generations below.[215]

---

[215] The Masoretes point out also the Tetragrammaton is concealed in very remarkable ways in the book of Esther. An extremely clear presentation of this is given in Appendix 60 of the *Companion Bible,* op. cit.

The Twenty-Six Generations				
First Period Of Ten Generations				
׳	10	Adam Seth Enos Cainan Mahalaleel	Jared Enoch Methuselah Lamech Noah	The creation to The flood
Second Period Of Five Generations				
ה	5	Shem Arphaxad Salah Eber Peleg	The flood to Babel	
Third Period Of Six Generations				
ו	6	Reu Serug Nahor Terah Abraham Isaac	Babel to Jacob/Israel	
Fourth Period Of Five Generations				
ה	5	Jacob Levi Kohath Amram Moses	Jacob/Israel to Moses	
Total =	26	Generations	Adam to Moses	

Conclusion 9. The pattern of the twenty-six generations of human history from the Creation until the revelation of the Nature of the Sacred Name, and which, letter by letter, spell out that very Name, undermines the entire basis of Astruc's Clue, the very foundation of Higher Criticism, making invalid the so-called Documentary Hypothesis.

Part C

The Two Accounts Of The Creation

The next piece of evidence for the unity of the Pentateuch based on its literary construction, actually shows the unity of the whole compass of Scripture, and like the evidence of the twenty-six generations is based upon the little-known methods of Hebrew Traditional exegesis.

Ironically, this is most clearly seen in the first two chapters of Genesis which contain separate accounts of the Creation, which according to Higher Criticism, are completely contradictory, and are often paraded as Higher Criticism's greatest evidence.[216] The first is alleged to derive from P, the second from J.[217] However, it is never explained by Higher Critics, why, if these separate accounts are as contradictory as they maintain, that the redactors they also insist must have existed, left such blatant contradictions in the text without spiriting them away through the means of yet another supposed redaction!

It is a pity that believers so rarely tackle Higher Critics on this particular issue, as unfortunately the impression is sometimes created that believers have no answer to give, and that the field of conflict must be abandoned to the cynic and the critic, but this is not the case at all.

Hebrew Traditional Exegesis

In order to provide what I believe is the best answer to the critic, I must now digress into the realms of Hebrew Traditional thought before returning to our primary task, and ask for the reader's patience

---

[216] See for example, Knapp, Charles, *The Old Testament: Studies In Teaching And Syllabus*, Volume I, London, Thomas Murby, 1926, pp. 83ff.

[217] See Hooke, S. H., in the article, Genesis, in *Peake's Commentary On The Bible*, op. cit., p. 176.

in this. The result, I believe, will be well worth while. It is likely that the reader will be unfamiliar with the methods of Traditional Hebrew exegesis that I will resort to in the following pages, and, if that is so, I ask him or her, to read this section through at least twice.

I would now also ask the reader kindly to interrupt the reading of this dissertation, and to open his or her Bible and read the account of the creation in Genesis chapter 1 carefully, and as if for the first time, and to be on the alert whilst reading, for any patterns that might suggest themselves. Please do not study the table on the next page until this has been done, so that you are familiar with the entire chapter, before you read the diagram overleaf.

The Scheme Of Genesis 1: First Phase

Verses	Primary Duality	Day	Secondary Duality
1–2	Heaven Earth		
3–5	Light Darkness	1	
6–8	Waters above the firmament Waters below the firmament	2	
9–10	Sea Land	3	
11–13	Seed yielding plants Fruit yielding plants	3	Male and female implied
14–19	Sun Moon and stars	4	
20–23	Life in waters beneath Life up to waters above	5	Male and female implied: "be fruitful and multiply"
24–25	Domestic animals (cattle) Wild animals	6	Male and female Male and female
36–31	Man Woman	6	Male and female Stated explicitly

So often we do not see the wood for the trees. In the table above we see that Genesis 1 contains a series of *dualities*; light and darkness, waters above and waters below, sea and land, seed yielding plants and fruit yielding plants, the light to rule the day, and the lights to rule the night, marine and winged life, domestic and wild animals, and finally, man and woman. We see *contrast* here; pairs of opposites; thus creation introduces polarity, a feature we encounter continually in physics, chemistry and mathematics. This is the primary duality present from the very beginning, but a secondary duality of gender manifests itself in time, beginning on the third day, with the creation of seed and fruit yielding plants which implies masculinity and femininity, and moving on to the marine and winged life, commanded to be fruitful and multiply, and finally it is stated explicitly with the creation of man and woman. This is a feature we encounter continually in botany and biology.

The duality of Genesis 1 runs deeper than this however. Turn back to the previous page, and look again. What do you see? Day 1 relates to light and darkness, as does day 4, where the sun is to rule the day, and the moon is to rule the night when the stars also may be seen. The second day is associated with the waters above and beneath the firmament; a feature not heard of again until we reach day 5. The third day relates for the first time to two creative acts; firstly, the emergence of the dry land from the sea, completing the conditions required for the subject of the second creative act of that day, the creation of plant life. It is not until we reach day 6 that we find again two distinct creative acts on the same day. Firstly, the creation of animal life, completing the conditions required for the next creative act on the same day, the creation of humanity.

So then we see a correspondence between two sets of three day periods. The first, second and third days seem to relate to the fourth, fifth and sixth days respectively. But the second triad of days seems to be an advance on the first triad of days. They give fulness to the forms created in the first triad of days. In each triad of days, the first two days contain only one act of creation, while in the last day, two acts of creation occur.[218] Thus we see another Structure appear, which ordinarily might be set out as indicated below;

The Six Days Of Genesis 1 Set Out As A Normal Structure

A) Light and darkness.

    B) Waters above and waters beneath the firmament.

        C. I) Sea and land.

        C. II) Seed yielding plants and fruit yielding plants.

a) Sun, and the moon and stars.

    b) Life in the waters beneath, and up to the waters above the firmament.

        c. i) Domestic and wild animals.

        c ii) Man and woman.

---

[218] The fundamentals of this scheme are set out in Sarna, Nahum M., *The JPS Commentary: Genesis,* Philadelphia, The Jewish Publication Society, 1989, p. 4., and Kikawada & Quinn, op. cit., pp. 74–80.

The Hebrew Traditional Scheme

The Hebrew Tradition has its own way of setting out this structure which gives emphasis to those days on which the greatest emphasis was given to the Creator, because they relate to two creative acts each, rather than one. This traditional scheme, places the last element of each triad of days in the centre of the scheme. Because Hebrew is read from right to left, the scheme must be read from the right hand side; the reader then crosses to the left hand side, and then descends to the centre of the scheme, the place of emphasis. Thus the order is, the right hand side, the left hand side, and finally the centre. After this, the cycle begins again.

I have set out the same Structure given above in accordance with the Hebrew Traditional method below.

The Scheme Of Genesis 1: Second Phase[219]

Day 2   Day 1

<u>Waters above</u>   <u>Light</u>
Waters beneath   Darkness

Day 3

<u>Sea</u> Conditions for
Land plant life

<u>Seed yielding plants</u> Plant life
Fruit yielding plants

Day 5   Day 4

<u>Life up to waters above</u>   <u>Sun</u>
Life in waters beneath   Moon & stars

Day 6

<u>Domestic Animals</u> Conditions for
Wild Animals human life

<u>Man</u> Human life
Woman

Straightaway we see three parts to the scheme, the right hand side, the left hand side and the centre. At the centre, in the place of emphasis, are the man and the woman. The central truth of Genesis 1 then, is the Creation of the Image and Likeness of God and its placement within the earth. Thus, the centre of the scheme is where *we* belong, where we find *ourselves*, or, where we *ought* to find ourselves.

According to the Tradition, this scheme is fundamental, and recurs throughout the Scriptures and nature. Some even claim that it is discernible in the Periodic Table of elements, a claim which I think is

---

[219] This chart is based on a similar chart found in Weinreb, F., *Roots Of The Bible*, Braunton, Devon, Merlin Books, 1986, p. 21.

not unreasonable.[220] We notice that the right hand side is concerned with light, and the two lights. This is said always to be the characteristic of the right hand side; *light, fire, heat, burning.* The left hand side however is related to *water*, while the centre is concerned with life on earth, *plant, animal and human life.* The right hand side is also said to be the side of the male and is associated with the sun and daylight. The left hand side is associated with the female, and the moon and darkness, while the centre is the place of the child, and sometimes displays the characteristics, as do most children, of both the male and female that produced it. Thus we see that Genesis 1 is not merely a list of events, but the presentation of a system or scheme. I have shown elsewhere that this system permeates the Scriptures, and is found even in the Christian Canon,[221] but there is no time here to go into the subject in as much depth as it deserves. In the Scheme of the six days, every act of creation is preceded by the formula, "and God said," but there are two more occasions in Genesis 1 where this formula occurs, making ten "commandments" altogether. These occur at verses 28 and 29. The first is the command to be fruitful and multiply, and to replenish the earth and subdue it. The second concerns the granting of the herbs and fruit to the man and woman for food. Thus the complete Scheme for the six days of Genesis 1 will be as set out below.

---

[220] Weinreb, F., op. cit., pp. 108–109.

[221] In a series of taped messages available from the author.

The Scheme Of Genesis 1: Final Phase

Day 2   Day 1

<u>Waters above</u>   <u>Light</u>
Waters beneath   Darkness

Day 3

<u>Sea</u>   Conditions for
Land   plant life

<u>Seed yielding plants</u>   Plant life
Fruit yielding plants

Day 5   Day 4

<u>Life up to waters above</u>   <u>Sun</u>
Life in waters beneath   Moon & stars

Day 6

<u>Domestic Animals</u>   Conditions for
Wild Animals   human life

<u>Man</u>   Human life
Woman

Be fruitful & multiply
Replenish the earth and subdue it

Herbs for food
Fruit for food

Genesis 2

We must now turn to the account of the creation in Genesis 2, and see if there is after all any consistency between it, and Genesis 1, in spite of what the Critics say. Ten times in Genesis 1 we read the formula, "and God said," thus the tenth occasion completes the account. Here in Genesis 2, perhaps to the surprise of some, we again find ten specific actions of God, these are;

1. The mist rising from the earth to water it (verse 6).

2. The forming of man (verse 7).

3. The planting in Eden of a Garden in which the man is placed (verse 8).

4. The appearance of trees, including the tree-of-life and the tree-of-the-knowledge-of-good-and-evil (verse 9).

5. The river parted into four (verses 10–14).

6. The command to the man to dress the Garden and keep it (verse 15).

7. The freedom granted to man to eat from every tree in the Garden, except the tree-of-the-knowledge-of-good-and-evil (verses 16–17).

8. The declaration that the man is alone, and that this is not good (verse 18–20).

9. The Deep Sleep which falls upon Adam (verse 21), leading up to,

10. The making of Woman (verse 22).

We must now see if these ten features fit the same Scheme as Genesis 1, or not. To the dismay of the critic they do, and have been set out in the diagram below.

The Scheme Of Genesis 2

2	1
Man.	Mist.

3

The Garden in Eden.

4

The trees
Especially the Two Trees.

6	5
Man in the Garden to dress and keep it.	The 1 river dividing into 4 streams.

7

What to eat and
What not to eat.

8

The man alone
The animals brought to him.

9

The Deep Sleep.

10

The Woman.

Here we see again that the first set of features; A) water in the form of mist, B) the man, C) the Garden and the trees, correspond with, and are complemented by the next set; a) water in the form of the one river and four streams, b) man in the Garden to dress and keep it, and c) the proper attitude to the trees. Thus this basic double triadic pattern exists in both Genesis 1 and 2.

Looking now at the right hand side, we see that it is the side of water, firstly as mist, secondly as the one river and four streams. The left hand side twice features man, firstly he himself is *formed*, and then he is placed in Eden, to give *form* to the Garden. The centre of the Scheme, as with Genesis 1, is concerned with plant, animal and human life. In the centre man is divided into male and female so that human history may begin. In the left hand column, he is still an unity, the potential woman still a part of him. Thus we see that the Scheme does appear to be working out in Genesis 2 as well, but we notice also some differences.

We see there is nothing in this Scheme which speaks of light, fire, heat, or burning. Quite the contrary in fact, for the mist and the man at the top of the right and left hand sides respectively, seem to be related by what is said in verses 5 and 6. There we are told that the _mist_ arose because no rain had fallen, and there was no _man_ to till the ground. Thus, man and mist seem related. We are told twice that God put man in the Garden (verses 8 & 15) and in between these two references is the account of the watering of the Garden by the river. Thus, man and water, firstly as mist, secondly as a river, alternate here in the sequence; (1) man, mist, man; (2) man, river, man.

The Hebrew for the word _mist_, is _ed_, אד, or aleph-daleth. These are the first and fourth letters of the Hebrew alphabet and, consequently represent the numbers 1 and 4. We noticed above a link between the mist watering the earth, and the 1 river parting into 4 that watered the Garden. Now we see that the link is more than just water. The principle of 1:4, which is veiled within the Hebrew word for _mist_, is brought out in a more concrete way in the 1 river, which parts into 4 streams. Up to this point, it has probably not seemed to be very important or relevant that the river divided into 4 streams. For all we knew, it would have made no difference had it divided into 3 or 5, or none at all. It was merely an accident of geography caused by the shape and contours of the land. But now we see that in order to make the link, and to be a concretisation of the mist, it has to part into 4 streams; neither more, or less.

I go much further into this matter elsewhere, but for now, I will only say that man, at the head of the left hand column, is in Hebrew, _Adam_, אדם. This is 1, 4, 40, a development of 1:4. Furthermore the two trees also conform to this pattern, as I show below.

The Hebrew for *tree-of-life*, is

ע צ ה ח י י ם   The gematria total of this is

40 10 10 8 5 90 70   233

The Hebrew for tree-of-the-knowledge-of-good-and-evil is;

ע צ ה ד ת ע ט ו ב ו ר ק   The gematria total of this is

70 200 6 2 6 9 400 70 4 5 90 70   932

The ratio of these totals is 1:4, as 932 ÷ 233 = exactly 4![222]

These facts show that the construction of the Scheme in Genesis 2 is legitimate, and, therefore, show also that Genesis chapters 1 and 2 conform to the same pattern, and therefore suggest commonality of authorship. As this is the Second appearance of the Scheme it has the character of the second place of the first appearance of the Scheme, namely *water*. The *whole Scheme* is characterised in this way, further, it is most definitely the side of the female, for this is *The Story Of Woman*. Chapter 2 leads up to the creation of woman, and the next chapter, chapter 3 is again the story of woman. Woman has the initiative. She converses with the serpent, is the first to take the forbidden fruit, which Adam eats at *her* bidding. The remedy for this situation is again related to the woman, as One is promised who is described as The-Seed-of-the-woman (3:15). We saw also that the second place of the first Scheme was the place of darkness, so too this is the side of sin, of the Fall of man, of the serpent, and of death too. The next chapters, 4 and 5 as would be expected, occupy the place-of-the-child, and here we find the accounts of the *children* of Adam and Eve. The killing of Abel by Cain, and the two distinct lines of Seth and Cain, showing duality. Here too, the cycle is concluded in ten creative acts, as there are ten generations which conclude this opening section of human history with the onset of the Flood, and the coming of the Second Federal Head of Mankind, Noah.

---

[222] These and other features are explained in Weinreb, op. cit.

The first Federal Head of mankind, Adam, comes to us from the side of *Light*, as he was made directly by the 'hand' of God, had life breathed into him directly by God, and existed at first in an unfallen condition. The Second Federal Head of mankind, Noah, unquestionably comes to us from the side of *Water*. Finally, the third Federal Head of mankind will be in the centre of the Scheme, the place of the child, the place where we must be ourselves, and the place of duality. Whereas Adam was created as a mature man, and Noah became the Second Federal Head of humanity as a mature man, Christ, the Third and Last Federal Head of mankind entered this world as a Child. The duality of this position is seen in the two advents of Christ, a situation that did not pertain either to Adam or Noah. Furthermore, it is absolutely imperative for our salvation that we ourselves are found in the centre of the Scheme, not within Adam (or Noah) but *within Christ*. If we are not, we will perish (I Corinthians 15:22).

There is much more that may be said about the Traditional Hebrew exegesis which is found in the Christian Canon also, but here we see that there is an amazing consistency within the first two chapters of Genesis, and that instead of contradicting one another, they compliment each other, the rest of the Pentateuch, and whole Canon of Scripture as well. I have set out the Scheme as it reveals and categorises the Three Federal Heads of mankind below.

2   1

NOAH,   ADAM,

comes to us in the place   comes to us in the place
of Water   of Light

3

CHRIST,

comes to us in the place
of the Child.

DUALITY.

Christ has two advents.

The Centre of the
Scheme;

this is where we must be
positioned (within Christ)

A Secondary Connection Between Genesis 1 And 2

It is unusual to encounter any who are aware of the Hebrew Traditional Scheme which connects the first two chapters of the Scriptures, yet the next commentator I will refer to, Jacques Doukhan, is such a person. Interestingly, while Doukhan acknowledges the double-triadic structure of Genesis I referred to above, he has also found another set of links between the two accounts of the creation. Doukhan's basic link is heptadic. While the heptadic form is unavoidably conspicuous in Genesis 1, being revealed by the six days of Creation, followed by the Sabbath, it is far more subtle in Genesis 2. Doukhan maintains that the second heptad is revealed by the use of what is known as the waw-copulative,[223] where אלהים יהוה, YHWH-Elohim, translated in the English Authorized Version as *Lord God*, is the subject. I give Doukhan's Scheme below.

Genesis 1	Genesis 2
Introduction. 1:1–2.	Introduction. 2:4b–6.
1. Light/Darkness. 1:3–5.	1. Man/Dust. 2:7.
2. Firmament in heaven. 1:6–8.	2. Garden on earth. 2:8.
3. Water and Land; Plants. 1:9–13.	3. Plants; Water and Land. 2:9–15.
4. Luminaries separate days and seasons. 1:14–19.	4. Tree of the-knowledge-of-good-and-evil separated from other trees. 2:16–17.
5. First creation of animal life. 1:20–23.	5. First concern for a companion for man. 2:18.
6. Creation of animals continued, and the creation of man. 1:24–31.	6. Concern for a companion for man continued. 2:19–22.
7. Pattern. 2:1–3: a. End of process. b. Divine involvement. c. Separation of Sabbath. d. Blessing of Sabbath.	7. Pattern: 2:23–24. a. End of process. b. Divine involvement. c. Separation of couple from parents. d. Unity of couple.

---

[223] Put simply, this is the use of the Hebrew letter waw, ו, as a conjunction, whereby it is attached to the word conjoined as a prefix. See any good Hebrew Grammar, e.g., *The Hebrew Student's Manual*, op. cit., pp. 92 & 113.

The Process Of Separation

It should also be noted that Genesis 2 sees several separations, or parturitions that are of basic importance. Firstly, the four streams part from the one river. Secondly, the woman, related by the tradition to the number 4, is parted from the man. The two trees are separated, so that man who has tasted of the tree-of-the-knowledge-of-good-and-evil may not taste of the tree-of-life, its way being guarded by the kerubim (3:24). So too, the Tradition teaches, the Figure of Yahweh, emerges from the Godhead of Elohim to deal directly with the man and woman. This pattern of parturition shows then that the emergence of the Sacred Name, the tetragrammaton, the Name of the 4 letters, occurs not because the J narrative has begun, and the P narrative has ended, but because the entire context and 'plot' requires it, thus there exists an unity about the entire pericope of Genesis 1–2, which again, undermines Astruc's Clue, and with it the Documentary Hypothesis which is the *sine-qua-non* of Graf–Wellhausen![224]

Conclusion 10. There is a basic unity to be found linking, and permeating Genesis chapters 1 & 2, which renders invalid what is often thought to be the best evidence for the Old and New Documentary Hypotheses.

---

[224] For validation of what I have said concerning the Hebrew Traditional Exegesis, which is surprisingly 'Christian' in outlook, see Weinreb, op. cit., cap. 1–15. The details of Doukhan's Scheme are taken from Garrett, op. cit., pp. 193–197.

Part D

Equi-Distant Letter Sequences

The next category of evidence relating to the literary construction of the Pentateuch only began to enter the public domain in the 1980s, and only became widely known in the 1990s. It is unreasonable therefore, to censure Higher Critics for not taking it into account when producing their theories, but now that the evidence *is* available, it ought to induce a major re-assessment of Modernist views. We must observe the activities of the various critical schools to see if any such re-assessment takes place or not. The evidence I refer to concerns what is now popularly known as *The Bible Code*, or, more correctly, Equi-Distant Letter Sequences. This is a method of discovering words or even messages embedded in the Inspired text, by recognising only certain characters of that text. Each character that is recognised is separated from the next such character by a regular interval, measured by the number of intermediate characters that are skipped over to reach the next in the series. As is usual with the literary phenomena of the Scriptures, it has been up till very recently the exclusive province of Jewish exegetes who have guarded this treasure very closely indeed.

It seems that something of this phenomenon was known by one of the most famous Rabbis who has ever lived, Moses Ben Nachman, or Nachmanides, or The Ramban.[225] When it is realised that Nachmanides lived in the *twelfth* century,[226] we begin to understand how many Scriptural secrets the Jews have kept hidden from gentile eyes over the centuries, and how detrimental to Christian exegesis, anti-Semitism is!

---

[225] See Satinover, Dr. Jeffrey, *The Truth Behind The Bible Code*, London, Sidgwick & Jackson, 1997, pp. 2ff.

[226] Ibid.

Who knows what other information has yet to be released by them? Unlike the revealing of other literary devices, however, the timing of this particular revelation does have its benefits, coinciding as it does, with the widespread availability of affordable high-powered computers, and software applications which may be used to reveal the messages embedded in the text.

The News Breaks

The earliest reference I have to the Code is a newspaper article by Jonathan Margolis, entitled, *In The Beginning Was The Word (and it was in code)*, which appeared in *The Mail On Sunday* of August 4th 1985, in the *Analysis* feature.[227] Margolis explained how Rabbi David Ordman from Israel and some colleagues had discovered a series of codes hidden in the text of the Torah, the complexity of which indicated at least to him, that they could not be of human contrivance. Margolis then considered the implications of Ordman's discoveries for the standard view of scholars we have previously examined, and concluded that the codes presented them with a most severe challenge. Margolis wrote that the discovery "raises the possibility, frankly an awesome one even for religious people who 'believe', *that it is really all true: that the Torah is the work of Someone or Something Out There*." [Emphasis his.]

Twelve years later, Michael Drosnin published his first sensationalist book on the subject, entitled *The Bible Code*,[228] which was reviewed widely on television programmes and in the press, raising the profile of the subject in an unprecedented, albeit controversial manner. One good point about Drosnin's first book, is that in an appendix, he includes the full text of a paper by the Jewish researchers, Doron Witztum, Eliyahu Rips, and Yoav Rosenberg that was published in the American Journal, *Statistical Science*, Volume 9, Number 3 in August 1994, and which, when Drosnin wrote, had not been rebutted.[229] The paper claims

---

[227] Available from the Dispensationalist researcher, Mr. Geoff Wright at Bible Numerics U.K., 16, Bedford Road, Letchworth, Hertfordshire, SG6 4DJ

[228] Drosnin, Michael, *The Bible Code* London, Weidenfeld & Nicolson, 1997.

[229] There have been attempts at rebuttal since, but while I believe that some of Drosnin's claims have been shown to be questionable, I do not think that those of Rips have yet faced serious challenge.

to offer *mathematical proof* for the existence of Equi-Distant Letter Sequences in the Torah, and has been accepted as a challenge by the fraternity of the world's top mathematicians who usually are of a cynical disposition, and who are engaged on a mission to destroy the evidence submitted by the paper through finding an error in the maths, so far without success. I would like to make it clear however that I dissociate myself entirely from Drosnin's dramatic claims, especially those made in his second book.[230] I concern myself here exclusively with the sober work of Jewish and Christian exegetes.

In the same year that Drosnin published *The Bible Code*, Dr Jeffrey Satinover published his much more scholarly and detailed work, *The Truth Behind The Bible Code*,[231] the following year Grant Jeffrey's *The Signature Of God,* became available in the U.K.,[232] so that now knowledge of the existence of the so-called Bible Code is very common indeed, even if the facts of the statistical evidence are not.[233]

What Do The Equi-Distant Letter Sequences Reveal?

For Christian believers, perhaps the most significant Equi-Distant Letter Sequences are those that Grant Jeffrey refers to in *The Signature Of God*. The first of his examples is found in Psalm 22. This, of course, is a Psalm that is full of references to the crucifixion of Christ. Verse 17 is referred to in Matthew 27:35, "They parted My garments among them, and upon My vesture did they cast lots," but it is also alluded to in Matthew 27:39 (verse 7), 27:42 (verse 6), 27:43 (verse 8), and in Matthew 27:46, while at the height of His agony, Christ recited the words of the first verse of Psalm 22, "My God, My God, why hast Thou forsaken Me?"

---

[230] Drosnin, Michael, *Bible Code 2*, London, Weidenfeld & Nicolson, 2002.

[231] Satinover, Dr. Jeffrey, *The Truth Behind The Bible Code*, London, Sidgwick & Jackson, 1997.

[232] Jeffrey, Grant, *The Signature Of God: Astonishing Biblical Discoveries*, London, Marshall Pickering, 1998.

[233] Surprisingly, there has been an attempt by a believer to cast doubt upon the existence of Equi-Distant Letter Sequences, but I have to say I believe it to be very poorly researched, and am not surprised that it now seems never to be mentioned. See Stanton, Phil, *The Bible Code: Fact Or Fake*, Eastbourne, Kingsway Publications, 1997.

Here, in this Psalm, at 22:15–17, the Name ישוע, *Jesus* has been found embedded in the text. Furthermore, the code is found by beginning at the י of היה, and then counting every 26th letter. 26 is the gematria value of יהוה, Yahweh, which I have shown elsewhere relates to the Greek word Κυριος, *Lord*, the title used of Christ in the New Testament.[234] The Name ישוע [Jesus] has also been found in Psalm 41:8–9, Zechariah 9:9, Isaiah 53:10, and Daniel 9:25–26. The passage in Psalm 41 relates to the betrayal of Christ, and is referred to in John 13:18. Zechariah 9:9 refers to the Triumphal entry of Christ, and is cited in Matthew 21:4–5, Isaiah 53 is very well known as offering the most complete depiction in the prophets of the Passion of Christ, being referred to in Matthew 27:31 (verse 7), 27:38 (verse 9), and 27:60 (verse 9 again), while Daniel 9:25–26, concerns the crucifixion of Christ, and is one of the few Old Testament verses which uses the word Messiah! Thus even the cipher texts relate directly to Christ.[235]

Equi-Distant Letter Sequences And The Pentateuch

The significance in Equi-Distant Letter Sequences for us however, lies in a most remarkable pattern that has been detected in the Pentateuch, and which confirms its unity. The Hebrew word *Torah*, is embedded in the opening verses of Genesis, Exodus, Numbers and Deuteronomy.

The first letter of the Hebrew word Torah is ת. Beginning at the first occurrence in the book of Genesis of this letter, which is found in the last letter of the first word, and then counting forward fifty letters, we find the second letter of Torah, which is ו. Moving forward another fifty letters we find the third letter ר, while after another fifty letters the last letter ה, is located. Thus the complete word תורה, Torah is spelt out.

The same feature is found in the book of Exodus, in exactly the same manner. Beginning with the first occurrence of the letter ת, which this

---

[234] See Phelan, M. W. J. *The One True God And Pluralism Of Language*, Brighton, Paradosis, 1996.

[235] Contrary to what is usually thought, the word *cipher text*, refers to a text which *contains* an encrypted word or message. This coded word or message itself is referred to as the *plaintext*. See Satinover, op. cit., pp. 143ff.

time occurs at the end of the second word of the book, and then moving forward from that, using every fiftieth letter, as with Genesis.

With the books of Numbers and Deuteronomy however, comes a change. The word תורה appears again, but this time it is spelt *backwards* as הרות. With the book of Numbers, the count begins with the third occurrence of ה, and is again based on an Equi-Distant Letter Sequence of fifty. With the book of Deuteronomy, the count is based on a sequence of forty-nine instead of fifty, and begins with the fourth ה in verse 5. (That is, at the end of the Preamble, as will become clear in chapter 6).

This leaves the central book of Leviticus sandwiched between Genesis and Exodus, both of which spell out the word *Torah* in the normal manner in their respective opening verses, and Numbers and Deuteronomy, both of which spell out the same word in their respective opening verses, but backwards. Thus the first two books taken as a pair, and the last two books, taken as another pair, direct the reader towards the central book of Leviticus, in a way which emulates that of the Structure for the Pentateuch given above. When we come to this central book of the Torah, Leviticus, to which the other four books direct the reader, we find that the Sacred Name itself, YHWH, is spelt out based on a letter skip of eight, and commencing at the first י of the book. Thus at the heart of the Pentateuch is the Name of the Lord!

The Implications

This is a most remarkable pattern indeed, and has important implications. The relevant verses of Genesis, Leviticus and Numbers are attributed to P, those of Exodus to P & J, while those of Deuteronomy are awarded to D.[236]

This means;

1. The unity of the narratives attributed by the Documentary Hypothesis to all four supposed literary sources is very

---

[236] See *Peake's Commentary On The Bible*, op. cit., in. loc.

clearly demonstrated by this pattern, providing yet another challenge to the viability of Graf–Wellhausen.

2. The Divine Name alleged to be the Hallmark of J, is spelt out by an Equi-Distant Letter Sequence in Leviticus in material attributed to the Elohist source P, thus invalidating Astruc's Clue yet again, as P is supposed to avoid the Sacred Name!

3. The existence of the Torah-Code confirms the Structure of the Pentateuch found in *The Companion Bible*, and which is given above.

4. The presence of the Torah-Code in every book of the Pentateuch, and its absence from Joshua, is another indicator that the Hexateuch and Octateuch of Higher Criticism have no objective reality. Similarly its presence in Deuteronomy shows that Noth's Tetrateuch is also invalid.

If it be suggested that the Torah-Code is the work of a late redactor, then as with the twenty-six generations, we would expect the attention of the reader to be drawn to it in some way or another, even if it was only through the means of the *literæ majusculæ, minusculæ, suspensæ* or similar techniques,[237] but this is not the case. Besides this, the codes are so numerous, that they occur *throughout* the Scriptures, but particularly in the Pentateuch.

Further, to conceive of a redactor whose ability would facilitate the introduction of all the complex, and often overlapping literary Structures of the Pentateuch, while at the same time preserving the array of the twenty-six generations, and simultaneously creating these amazing codes, without disturbing the sense of the narrative, is to suggest the existence of a literary genius of towering, and unparalleled prowess, who somehow has managed to preserve his anonymity. Indeed, such would be the abilities of this redactor if all

---

[237] These are letters that in the Masoretic Text are respectively oversize, undersize, or suspended above the level of adjacent letters. Some other letters are ornamented by crowns, others mutilated, medials are used instead of finals, and vice versa, and some are even inverted! See Gesenius' *Hebrew Grammar* for details. Op. cit., p. 31, & Kelley, Mynatt & Crawford, *The Masorah Of Biblia Hebraica Stuttgatensia*, Grand Rapids, Michigan, U.S.A., 1998, pp. 31ff.

that we have examined in this chapter were to be attributable to him, that the authors of the supposed original sources would scarcely be needed at all. Not only this, but the redactor or redactors must on the one hand be foolish enough to jumble their original material in a thoroughly amateurish manner, and yet on the other hand, clever enough to incorporate all the features this chapter has revealed. Such a suggestion is neither reasonable or credible, especially since it is only with the coming of computer technology that the more complex codes have been discovered, some of which seem to be truly prophetic.

Conclusion 11. The presence of the word *Torah* encoded within the Pentateuch provides another demonstration of the unity of the Pentateuch, and shows that the Hexateuch, Octateuch, and Tetrateuch have no existence outside the imagination of Higher Critics.

Conclusion To Chapter Five

In this chapter we have seen a four-fold assault upon the Documentary Hypothesis, and a severe undermining of Astruc's Clue. The literary Structures we have examined strike at the basis of these concepts in their very heartland, the book of Genesis. Some of these Structures span well over a hundred supposed fragments thought to derive from the alleged sources, J, E, and P, and show the absolute unity of the book of Genesis in a most impressive manner. We saw too that each book of the Torah is Structured, and that when considered together, the Pentateuch forms yet another chiastic Structure, displaying the unity of the Torah as a whole, as they witness unequivocally to a common literary plan, and therefore, a common authorship; not a fragmentary one.

The array of the twenty-six generations, spelling out letter by letter the Sacred Name, which runs from Genesis 5 to Exodus 6, thereby linking the first two books of Moses into another common literary plan, shows that the alleged Elohist narrative is as Jehovist as the supposed J narrative! The alleged contradiction between Genesis 1 and 2, supposedly providing irrefutable evidence of Astruc's Clue has also been shown to be non-existent, as both chapters conform to the same overall literary plan. Finally, the Torah-Code, shows again that the supposedly different narratives of J, E, P, and D, when examined properly appear to be uniform and complimentary, rather than diverse and contradictory. They also harmonise with the literary Structure of the Pentateuch as a whole.

But above all, it must be remembered that the literary Structures, the array of the twenty-six generations, the Scheme of Genesis 1 & 2, and the Torah-Codes, are *real textual features*, which may be examined and validated by any who will take a small amount of time and trouble. Unlike the proposals of Higher Criticism, they are not hypothetical, but have genuine existence. They may be measured and demonstrated, and therefore constitute *forensic* evidence of a single literary plan, and thereby common authorship.

It is clear that this evidence is genuine and has real credibility as a now famous study on Pentateuchal Origins, namely R. N. Whybray's *The Making Of The Pentateuch*, also concludes that current-day Source Criticism is extremely unsatisfactory. Whybray himself argues convincingly for unity of authorship of the entire Pentateuch based on literary evidence.[238] The fact that Whybray could not in any sense be called a Fundamentalist makes his testimony all the more remarkable, it is perhaps an indicator that the tide might now be turning.

When we consider the literary unity that has been clearly demonstrated, together with the evidence for the immense age of certain parts of the Torah that we noticed in the previous chapter, we are led inevitably to the conclusion that the entire Pentateuch must be of the highest antiquity, despite what Graf–Wellhausen says.

This conclusion is based purely on logic. We have seen that only the existence of an angular vorlage dating from the time of Hezekiah or even earlier will account for certain textual characteristics observable in the Samaritan and Square-Charactered text. We have seen too that it is far more probable that the Pentateuch is a literary unity, rather than an amalgam of disparate texts. Therefore if parts of this literary unity are seen to be datable to the time of Hezekiah or earlier, it follows necessarily and inevitably that *the Pentateuch as a whole* must date back to the time of Hezekiah or earlier. Thus, the prophets

---

[238] Whybray, R. N., op. cit., pp. 241–242.

may easily have referred to the teachings of the Torah, precisely as they claim in their writings to have done.

It could be argued of course that the unquestionable unity we have seen to exist in the Pentateuch is owing to major editorial work, but this makes the editors of more significance than the original sources, and there remains the interesting and highly relevant fact that the Pentateuch is written not in the Late Hebrew style of Ezra and Nehemiah, but in the earlier Standard Hebrew literary style, pointing to it being of far earlier provenance.[239] Thus it is quite reasonable to date the Pentateuch, broadly as we know it today to the time of Hezekiah.

Thus we find ourselves in a position radically different from that of the first Higher Critics. We now know that the dawning of the age of literature is of such high antiquity, that it is incapable of being a challenge to the proposal of a Mosaic provenance for the Pentateuch. We know also that the peculiarities of the Samaritan and Square-Charactered text, are explainable only by an angular vorlage, written in the script known to have existed in the days of Hezekiah, but that the finds of Ras Shamra show that what Higher Critics of the nineteenth century thought were corruptions in the text, turn out to be literary archaisms that date back to the time of Solomon! We know also that there is overwhelming evidence from the Structures, the array of the twenty-six generations, the Scheme of Genesis 1 and 2, and now Equi-Distant Letter Sequences that the Pentateuch is a single literary corpus. Thus, we are unable to accept the conclusions of the first Higher Critics who did not have the benefits of this evidence at their disposal, nor are we able to agree with the similar conclusions of the later Higher Critics who simply ignored this telling evidence. I believe it is fair to say, that had this evidence been available in the middle of the seventeenth century, Higher Criticism would never have got off the ground; ignorance alone allowed that to happen.

It is only when we have seen the evidence for the unity of the Pentateuch, that we realise the extent of the folly of Source Criticism's arguments. Source Criticism's most fundamental axiom, expressed in Astruc's Clue, is that J used YHWH exclusively, while

---

[239] Whybray, op. cit., p. 44.

E and P used Elohim exclusively. We have just seen how erroneous this belief is, but it must also be pointed out that Higher Critics are themselves conspicuously inconsistent in their methods. Supporters of The New Documentary Hypothesis must agree that the very first so-called J passage, found in the second account of the Creation beginning at Genesis 2:4b, contains very many references to YHWH–*Elohim*, showing, by their own admission that J actually used Elohim frequently! Furthermore, it is also conceded that E and P in the books of Exodus to Numbers used YHWH extremely frequently! Elohim occurs far less often in these books than it does in Genesis, YHWH being used almost universally. Thus sceptical Source Critics, routinely contradict their owns canons!

Source Critics of course are very fond of comparing the Scriptures with pagan myths, but if they were to look at the discoveries made at Ras Shamra, mentioned above, they would find that in those texts Baal is sometimes referred to as Baal, but sometimes as Hadad! Line 4, vii, 36 reads, "The foes of Baal clung to forests, the enemies of Hadad to the hollows of the rock."[240] This parallelism is a feature of ancient literature ands speaks of its unity, rather than its fragmentary nature.

Similarly, a major element of the Source Critic's argument is that the alleged different sources, J, E, and P are revealed in the so-called repetitions, and duplicate narratives found in the Pentateuch. The Flood narrative is often paraded as the critic's best example, but we have just seen from Gordon Wenham's excellent work, rightly applauded by Kikawada and Quinn,[241] as well as by Whybray[242] and Duane Garrett,[243] that the repetitions have a distinct function in the building of structures. They are not at all needless phrases that are rendered redundant through tautology, but actually facilitate the correspondences at the heart of literary structures, which reveal the key theological aspects of the narrative. Researchers have also shown how they serve to heighten the tension of the narrative, and generally

---

[240] Quoted from Whybray, op. cit., p. 68.

[241] Op. cit., pp. 103–104.

[242] Op. cit., p. 83.

[243] Op. cit., pp. 23–27.

enhance its dramatic impact, as well as assisting retention of the story in the human memory.[244] Far from being evidence of multiple sources, and bungling redactors, they seem to constitute evidence of a literary plan. One example may easily be given. In Genesis 41:1–8 there is a most well known repetition. Pharaoh has two separate dreams, each telling in different ways, the same story. Yet Joseph, when he is made aware of the two dreams refuses to see them as a duality, but says in verse 25 "the dream (singular[245]) is one." As far as Joseph was concerned the repetition did not imply a contradiction but an *enhancement*; this is the way all such repetitions should be viewed, in accordance with ancient, (and quite often modern), practice.

We are now ready to examine the individual books of the Pentateuch.

---

[244] Whybray, op. cit., p. 74–84.

[245] Davidson, op. cit., p. 259.

Part Three

The Literary Sources Of The Pentateuch

Chapter Six

The Book Of Deuteronomy

So far then, we have seen that the existence of the Pentateuch during the age of Hezekiah is not merely not unreasonable, but may even be said to be likely. Added to this is the fact that if the intimations concerning the archaisms found in the Pentateuch and the similar archaisms found at Ras Shamra have any substance, then the Pentateuch may perhaps and very tentatively be regarded as being datable to the days of the united Monarchy. Yet, the Pentateuch itself claims to be even older, to be *Mosaic* in fact. Is it possible to find a real connection with Moses? a connecting link that places the Pentateuch in his days in a credible manner? That is the challenge set in this section, and we begin with the one book of the Pentateuch which has had a particular year set for its publication by some Critics; the book of Deuteronomy.

De Wette's Clue

In Chapter One it was noticed that De Wette suggested that the Book of the Law found by Hilkiah during the days of Josiah (II Kings 22), was the book of Deuteronomy, and that it had been written very shortly before its intended, and engineered 'discovery'. This proposition is known as De Wette's Clue. There have been occasional suggestions from fundamentalists that it might have been the entire Pentateuch that was found. However, much as I sympathise with the fundamentalist view-point, and even entertained this view myself once, I have to agree with the majority opinion here, that as it seems that the book was read through twice, and maybe even three times within the day of its discovery, once perhaps by Shaphan after Hilkiah had found it (II Kings 22:8), again by Shaphan to Josiah, almost certainly in its entirety (II Kings 22:10), and, it seems a third time, perhaps in the same day at a public meeting (II Kings 23:2), this cannot be the case. It is difficult to imagine that the entire Pentateuch could have been read once in a day, let alone more than once. It must have been a smaller document that was discovered therefore, one that could be referred to as *The Book Of The Covenant* (II Kings 23:2), and *The Book Of The Law* (II Kings 22:9), and that could be read through in a day at least once, perhaps twice, or even three times. From II Kings 22:11, 13, cf. 16–20, it is obvious that Josiah was extremely upset when he discovered the content of the book, and this does indeed seem to indicate that Deuteronomy is a likely candidate.

The Identity Of 'Hilkiah's Book'

For reasons which will become clear later, Deuteronomy could certainly be described as being *The Book Of The Covenant*, but additionally Deuteronomy contains many references to the Covenant made with the Lord; for example, 4:13, 4:23, 5:2–3, 17:2, 29:1, 29:9, 29:12, 29:14, 29:21, & 29:25.[246] It could also quite legitimately be referred to as *The Book Of The Law*, given the repetition of the Ten Commandments in Deuteronomy 5, as well as other pieces of legislation.[247] Furthermore, the expression *Book Of The Law*, is _exclusive_ to Deuteronomy, being found in 28:61, 31:24, and especially 30:10 & 31:26, where Deuteronomy is actually referred to as _The Book Of The Law_. Finally, the curses of Deuteronomy 28:15–68 would make any righteous king of a backslidden Judah, who was hearing them for the first time, shudder in unmitigated terror at the thought of the evil that was being stored up for the nation. All in all, it does seem most likely that Deuteronomy was the book found by Hilkiah, and for reasons that will be given later, I believe it was the book in its *entirety*, substantially as we know it today. The suggestion that it was Deuteronomy that Hilkiah discovered does not date only from the time of De Wette of course, as Athanasius, Chysostom and Jerome all drew

---

[246] It should be pointed out that the term *Book Of The Covenant* or some such, as used by Higher Critics, is a reference to Exodus 21–23. For a comparison of the pericope with Deuteronomy, see Appendix V.

[247] It should be noted that our modern title, *Deuteronomy*, is based on a misunderstanding. In 17:18, the ruler of the nation is commanded to make a copy of the Law. The Septuagint renders this as δευτερονομιον τουτο, which means *this _second_ law*. In the Vulgate this became *deuteronomion,* whence Deuteronomy. See Thompson, J. A., *Deuteronomy: An Introduction And Commentary*, London, InterVarsity Press, 1974, p. 12.

the same conclusion.[248] The only contribution made by De Wette, if it may be called that, is that the *book itself* is to be dated only from that time, owing to it being a 'pious forgery'.

The So-Called 'Deuteronomists'

De Wette pinned the production of Deuteronomy down to the year 621 B.C.E., that being the commonly accepted date of Josiah's reforms, and the book being supposed to have been written only shortly before.[249] This very precise dating led to the creation of two distinct areas of investigation amongst Critics;

1. What portion of Deuteronomy was found in the Temple by Hilkiah? and,

2. How do the other supposed sources, J, E, and P relate chronologically to D?

This tendency is well illustrated in an article in *Peake's Commentary* by G. Henton-Davies, which also illustrates a phenomenon I mention at the close of Chapter Two, namely, that there has been an observable tendency to dissect the four classic sources, J, E, P, and D into an ever increasing number of separate sources. Although I disagree profoundly with Henton-Davies, I have found his article extremely useful, as it sums up very well the recent position on Deuteronomy, and shows how substantially the situation has changed since De Wette.

For Henton-Davies, following majority opinion, Deuteronomy is a book that has had more than one revision. He suggests that what he calls "the D of the reform" carried out by Josiah as a consequence of Hilkiah's discovery might have been limited to chapters 12 to 26 together with chapter 28; or, more likely, chapter 4 verse 44 to chapter 30 verse 20. He also makes the point that "the linguistic and conceptual similarities with the 8th-cent. Prophets, and especially with Jeremiah" indicate that it was written shortly after the days of

---

[248] See the article by Moore, G. F., entitled *Deuteronomy*, in *Encyclopædia Biblica*, op. cit., column 1079.

[249] See the article by Henton–Davies, G., *Deuteronomy* in Peake's Commentary, op. cit., p. 269.

Hezekiah. He further suggests however that there is "a long history of transmission and interpretation of really ancient material in the book."

Observation 6. We have already seen that the Pentateuch may be dated credibly to the time of the prophets, and that they claim to have read the Torah to the people, and claim constantly to have drawn attention to the fact that it was being disobeyed. It is hardly surprising therefore that there are noticeable similarities between the prophets and the Pentateuch. Further, as I will show shortly, there is a very good reason for Deuteronomy in particular to be the book that the prophets would refer to most often, so that they would echo its words and phrases. The evidence of undoubted similarity between the prophets and Deuteronomy is therefore perfectly neutral, as it may be understood both ways; either to support the traditional, or fundamentalist viewpoint, or that of cynical Higher Criticism.

Henton-Davies refers approvingly to Adam Welch who traced D material to a time before the United Monarchy. According to Henton-Davies, this has led some to suppose D to have been the foundation document of the First Temple erected by Solomon and that it might also have been the book referred to in I Samuel 10:25. He then says, "It is thus probable that the real future of the study of D lies along these lines. First, there is the long history of priestly transmission by which early material, with no doubt Mosaic utterance as the original oral nucleus, supplemented by tradition and usages from Shechem, were handed on and expanded in northern circles. D material may thus be dated from the days of Moses to those of Manasseh. Secondly, a date of composition or editing possibly in prophetic circles such as Isaiah's disciples, but more probably priestly circles, as Dt. 31:9 suggests. Von Rad has shown that such priestly circles would not be those of Jerusalem but were from the north. D may well be the work of a single Levitical preacher who was either the founder of the well-known style or its outstanding exponent. Thirdly there is the publication or appearance date of 621 in Jerusalem, with the adding of further material such as the Appendices soon after. D may no longer be conceived as a point on a date line, but as a stream of material, whose source is Moses, whose course was through some sanctuary like Shechem, and whose outlet, after diversion from the north, was the Temple at Jerusalem. This conception of D as a stream rather than a gusher involves the modification of the so-called comparative dating of D as after J and E and as before P. Rather is D the tradition of an independent use and theology existing in a northern sanctuary. The differences between D and other law codes are thus not those of chronological development but of geographical apartness, illustrating what happened at different sanctuaries, and are not to be judged in the light of some conception of unilinear development."[250]

Martin Noth

This was the state-of-play in the middle of the twentieth century, but now, fifty years later, an alternative view has appeared through the writings of the critic Martin Noth, (Noth is pronounced *Note*; 1902–1968). Noth's writings have made a considerable impact, although their influence may now be on the wane.[251] Noth claimed that Deuteronomy–II Kings (minus Ruth) was a single work by a single author, written during the exile, but based on earlier documentary and oral traditional material, and that it underwent several redactions by those of the Deuteronomist School.[252] Noth therefore maintained the tendency seen in the quote from Henton-Davies, of viewing Deuteronomy as a work detached from the rest of the Pentateuch, rather than as one of its key sources and redactors, and went even further, through attaching it to the books of Joshua–II Kings![253]

It has since been proposed that the allegedly distinct work Deuteronomy–II Kings was subject to several redactions by the Deuteronomist Historian(s) referred to as Dtr. A later redactor, who wished to connect this Deuteronomist history with the work of the prophets (DtrP) then 'processed' the material, before yet another

---

[250] Ibid., pp. 269–270.

[251] See Garrett, op. cit., pp. 39–41.

[252] See Noth, Martin, *The Deuteronomist History,* Sheffield, *Journal For The Study Of The Old Testament*, The University Of Sheffield, 1980.

[253] Noth saw Genesis–Numbers as the first great division of the Hebrew historical material, Deuteronomy–II Kings, the Deuteronomist History as the second, and I & II Chronicles, with Ezra and Nehemiah forming the third, which was a Judean History.

redactor (DtrN) who wished to present Israel's history in terms of its relationship with the Law re-worked it again.[254]

In spite of this highly complex and convoluted picture, which I have perhaps over-simplified, there are some very interesting thoughts to be detected here. These are;

1. The realisation that De Wette's Clue requires a major rethink,

2. The realisation that Deuteronomy is *The Book Of The Law*, or *The Book Of The Covenant*,

3. The realisation that there is a close connection between the prophets, the author of II Kings, and the book of Deuteronomy,

4. The realisation that somehow Deuteronomy is different from the rest of the Pentateuch, and,

5. The realisation that Deuteronomy must be made to reach back into remote antiquity, perhaps even to the days of Moses. The two means for accomplishing this that we have seen, namely, either by presenting Deuteronomy under the form of Henton-Davies' "stream" "from Moses to Manasseh", or by suggesting that it was produced from ancient oral and documentary material, perhaps going back to the time of Moses, are both erroneous, but are attempts nonetheless to satisfy what is seen to be a real need. This is an amazing admission by Critics.

It is now time to suggest an alternative to the confusion of the Higher Critics, which will take seriously the five points mentioned above, but will also show that the book of Deuteronomy is a single work, not an amalgam, or the product of a literary "stream", and that it is indeed, of very great antiquity.

The Treaty Of The Great King

It is well-known that the book of Deuteronomy has a threefold structure, as it comprises three addresses given by Moses; 1:1–4:43, 4:44–28:68, and 29:1–30:20, but there is another structure to be noted

---

[254] See Soulen & Kendall–Soulen, op. cit., pp. 46–47.

it seems. In 1955 a landmark book by George. E. Mendenhall, entitled, *Law And Covenant In Israel And The Ancient Near East* was published.[255] Mendenhall pointed out that there were very many interesting parallels between the book of Deuteronomy and Hittite treaties of the second millennium B.C.E. Basing his work on discoveries made known over twenty years earlier by V. Korosec,[256] Mendenhall proposed that Deuteronomy was a treaty between Yahweh and Israel, made along the lines of the ancient Hittite treaties. The ancient Near-Eastern treaty was structured in the following manner;

1. *The Preamble*, in which the King is introduced.

2. *The Historical Prologue*, in which the past relations between the contracting parties are reviewed.

3. *The Treaty Stipulations*;

    a. *General Principles*.

    b. *Specific Stipulations*.

4. *The Treaty Sanctions*, which detail *blessings* and *curses*.

5. *The Witnesses*, the list of gods who it was thought, would guarantee the treaty.

Mendenhall added a sixth element to this structure, which related to the provision for the deposit in the Temple of the treaty document, and the arrangements for its regular reading.[257]

The work of Mendenhall inspired many others to look at the parallels between the book of Deuteronomy and the form of ancient Middle-Eastern treaties. The most well-known work that resulted from this being Meredith Kline's *The Treaty Of The Great King*.[258] Reviewing Kline's work, Kaiser points out that these treaties were political

---

[255] It was actually a reprint of two articles published the previous year in the *Biblical Archaeologist*, (XVII, Number 2, May 1954, pp. 24–46, & XVII, Number 3, September 1954, pp. 49–76, see Thompson, J. A., op. cit., p. 17.

[256] Korosec, V., *Hethitische Staatsvertraege*, 1931, cited in Thompson, J.A., op. cit, p. 17.

[257] This treaty structure is based on that given in Thompson, J. A., op. cit., p. 17.

[258] Kline, M. E., *The Treaty Of The Great King*, Grand Rapids, Michigan, U.S.A., Eerdmans, 1963.

agreements known as suzerainty treaties, in which a subordinate or vassal state declared its allegiance to a more powerful neighbouring king who claimed lordship over the state. These treaties are found in their classic form in the Hittite Empire, although modified forms, lacking some of the classic elements have been found relating to the Assyrians of the first millennium B.C.E. The typical opening words of the treaty are *These are the words of x* (the Great King). It is particularly interesting therefore that the book of Deuteronomy opens with the phrase, אלה הדברים, *These are the words!*[259] It is true that they are the words of Moses, yet nonetheless, the context makes abundantly clear the fact that Moses is speaking for Yahweh, The Great King.[260]

Walter C. Kaiser Jr has shown that elements of this Treaty Form are discernable in the Ten Commandments. He points out that *The Preamble* may be equated to the opening words of the First Commandment, "I am the Lord thy God," found in Deuteronomy 5:6a. The following words, "Which brought thee out of the land of Egypt, from the house of bondage," Kaiser compares with an abbreviated form of *The Historical Prologue*. After these words come the Ten Commandments themselves, in Deuteronomy 5:7–21, which would relate to *The Treaty Stipulations*. Kaiser then has to go outside the Commandments themselves however, to find the remaining elements of the Treaty Form. In Deuteronomy 31:9–13 he locates the arrangements for *The Safe-Keeping and Public Reading of the Treaty. The Witnesses to the Treaty* are referred to in Deuteronomy 30:19–20, while *The Blessings and Curses* are given in Deuteronomy chapters 27–28.[261]

This in itself is most interesting, but with the Ten Commandments the Treaty Form is not immediately apparent to the reader because it is broken up into fragments. Kaiser though goes on to emphasise that *the entire book of Deuteronomy, as we know it today,* is presented to us in the Ancient Treaty Form. Were Deuteronomy to be merely an

---

[259] See Green, Jay. P. Sr., editor, *The Interlinear Bible: Hebrew-Greek-English*, Peabody, Massachusetts, U.S.A., Hendrickson, second edition, 1986, in. loc.

[260] Kaiser, op. cit., pp. 143ff.

[261] Ibid., pp. 143f.

accumulation, or an ever-widening stream of teaching built up over centuries, or an expansion of a pious forgery dating only from the days of Josiah, then the unmistakable unity of the book of Deuteronomy which the presence of the Treaty Form displays so convincingly, would be either confined to a small section of the book, or, more likely, completely undetectable. As things stand however, once the reader is shown where to look, the Treaty Form is not merely obvious, it is *unavoidable*. Kaiser presents the Treaty Form in the book of Deuteronomy as follows.

1. *Preamble* (Deuteronomy 1:1–5)

2. *Historical Prologue* (Deuteronomy 1:6–4:43)

3. *Stipulations of the Covenant* (Deuteronomy 4:44–26:19)

4. *Deposit and Public Reading* (Deuteronomy 27:1–8; 31:1–13)

5. *Curses and Blessings* (Deuteronomy 27:9–28:68)

6. *Witnesses and provision for Renewal and Succession* (Deuteronomy 29–34)[262]

He then goes on to make an interesting point. He emphasises that the Treaty Form outlined above is only to be found in Second Millennium B.C.E. treaties which follow the Hittite pattern. The later treaties of the First Millennium B.C.E. lack the Historical Prologue, thus the Critics have been proved wrong, in asserting that D belongs to the days of Josiah. Clearly, and *irrefutably*, it belongs to the Second Millennium B.C.E., which is highly suggestive of a Mosaic provenance. Of course, the concept of an oral tradition underpinning Deuteronomy is completely shattered, as treaties such as we find in Deuteronomy, were given in a written form. Kaiser cites Meredith Kline thus,

> "Now that the form critical data compel the recognition of the antiquity not merely of this or that element within Deuteronomy but of the Deuteronomy treaty in its integrity… any persistent insistence on a final edition of the book around the seventh century B.C. can be nothing

---

[262] Ibid., p. 144.

more than a vestigial hypothesis no longer performing a significant function in Old Testament criticism."[263]

There is no doubt about the tremendous impact made by this discovery upon the New Documentary Hypothesis. It blows to pieces any theory of Deuteronomy being the consequence of a "stream" of material "from Moses to Manasseh," or of it being a patchwork of material. The two prologues (1:1–4 & 1:5–4:49), for example, which had been taken as evidence of the work of two different editors, are now seen to be an essential part of the treaty format! Thus Deuteronomy is seen to be a work of absolute unity, a single literary work comprising a written agreement between Yahweh and Israel, and not for the first time, we see that the theories of Higher Criticism, are founded upon ignorance; this time ignorance of ancient Middle-Eastern treaties.

Harrison writes of the impact of this discovery, and the work of Kline, "It [Deuteronomy] can no longer be considered the product of a series of redactions of the document that produced the Josianic reformation. The so-called 'two introduction' to the book (Deut. 1–5 and 5–11) need not be regarded now as the product of two editorial hands, since in the suzerainty treaties of the ancient Near East an historical prologue regularly follows the preamble and precedes the stipulations of the agreement. In the light of this situation Deuteronomy 1:5–4:49 qualifies admirably as just such an historical prologue. Deuteronomy 5–11 must now be recognized as expounding the Covenant way of life in precisely the same manner as chapters 12 to 26, which together declare the demands of the suzerain. The differences between Deuteronomy 5 to 11 and 12 to 26 only represent for Kline variant treatments of this one theme, namely the stipulations of the suzerain in relation to his subjects. In the same manner it is possible to relate the appendix material (Deut. 31–34) to the treaty pattern discerned in earlier sections of the book, and to see in it a concern for succession rights which, according to Near Eastern parallels, were an important part of the legal deposition to which allegiance was required."[264]

---

[263] Kaiser, op. cit., pp. 144–145. The quote Kaiser makes from Kline is from p. 44 of the work mentioned above.

[264] Harrison, op. cit., p. 649.

How Should Deuteronomy, As A Treaty-Document, Be Dated?

Harrison, like Kaiser, takes up Kline's distinction between the early and later types of the treaty form, and also agrees that the absence of the historical prologue from the later treaty forms, and its unmistakable presence in Deuteronomy means that Deuteronomy must be classed as typical of an early form, and therefore seems in its entirety to date from the Mosaic age, but others are not so sure, as further evidence has now come to light. For Harrison, writing in 1969, there is good reason for him to take the line that he did, as the news of these further discoveries was then only just beginning to break, but for Kaiser, writing in 2001, it would seem that he simply did not wish to recognise the latest discoveries.

J. A. Thompson, who has himself published work on these treaty forms,[265] does however, consider this later evidence in his commentary on Deuteronomy, and makes some interesting points. In a work published in 1974, over a quarter of a century before Kaiser he noted, "When Kline wrote, the evidence seemed to point to the fact that the first-millennium treaties lacked the historical prologue. Now Deuteronomy has a historical prologue in 1:5–4:49 and thus qualifies for inclusion among the classic second-millennium treaties." He then goes on, "But the final word has not been said. The possibility must be allowed that Deuteronomy was cast in the shape of an ancient treaty by someone who wrote long after Moses' day. Alternately, Kline's proposal that only in the second-millennium treaties does one find a historical prologue has been challenged more recently. The absence of a historical prologue on the Assyrian and Aramaic treaties does not prove that the historical prologue was lacking. It may have been stated orally or have been assumed. It may even have been present on the Sefiré Aramaic documents which are broken at the top. But in fact there is a seventh-century B.C. treaty where the historical prologue occurs. Hence the fact that Deuteronomy has a historical

---

[265] Thompson, J. A., *The Ancient Near Eastern Treaties And The Old Testament*, 1964, cited in Harrison, op. cit.

introduction is not necessarily an argument for a date in the second-millennium, although it may be."[266]

Thompson is to be commended here for resisting the temptation of going beyond the evidence. We have seen remarkable evidence for the _integrity_ of Deuteronomy, and it may also indicate a Mosaic provenance, but this aspect of the evidence is at present inconclusive, although there will be further evidence of a Mosaic provenance submitted shortly. This evidence will, I believe, disprove the theory advanced by Moshe Weinfeld that Deuteronomy is an eighth or seventh century attempt to imitate the more ancient treaty form.[267]

In his assessment of the viability of the view that Deuteronomy is a treaty-document, Thompson gives Kline's presentation of the Deuteronomic treaty form as given below.

1. Preamble: The covenant mediator 1:1–5.

2. The historical prologue; covenant history, 1:6–4:49.

3. The covenant stipulations: covenant life.

    a. The great commandment, 5:1–11:32.

    b. Ancillary commandments, 12:1–26:19.

4. The covenant sanctions: covenant ratification, blessings and curses, covenant oath, 27:1–30:20.

5. Dynastic disposition: covenant continuity, 31:1–34:12.[268]

He then goes on to mention an unpublished work by Gordon Wenham entitled, _The Structure And Date Of Deuteronomy_, in which is found a slightly different view. Wenham maintains that while the Old Testament Covenant Form is strikingly similar to that of the Middle-Eastern Treaty Form, and also may be compared very favourably with a similar literary form known as the Law-Code Form, it is nonetheless

---

[266] Thompson, J. A., op. cit., pp. 51–52. The seventh century B.C.E. treaty Thompson refers to which does have the historical prologue, is cited by him from Campbell, A. F., _An Historical Prologue In A Seventh Century Treaty_, 1969.

[267] Weinfeld, M., _Deuteronomy And The Deuteronomic School_, 1972, cited in Childs, op. cit., p. 208, and Thompson, J. A., op. cit., p. 20.

[268] Thompson, op. cit., pp. 17–18.

distinct from both. Wenham argues that the Old Testament Covenant Form comprises 1) an Historical Prologue, 2) a section of Laws, and 3) an Epilogue, which contains an Historical Survey, detailing some of the achievements of the king with whom the Treaty is made, and who dictates the Laws. The Epilogue contains also the directions for the production and erection of a stele, and gives the blessings and curses for those who obey, and disobey the Treaty. Thompson presents Wenham's scheme as follows.

Law Code	O.T. Covenant	N.E. Treaty
		1. Preamble
1. Prologue	1. Historical prologue	2. Historical prologue
2. Laws	2. Stipulations (a) basic (b) detailed	3. Stipulations (a) basic (b) detailed
3. Summary/Document clause	3. Document clause	4. Document clause
4. Blessing	4. Blessing	5. God list
5. Curse	5. Curse	6. Curses and blessings
	6. Recapitulation	

He adds that the item defined as 'recapitulation' is unique to the Old Testament covenant.[269]

After presenting Wenham's views, Thompson then uses them as a basis for his own analysis of Deuteronomy. He concludes that all of Deuteronomy 1–30 has been cast in what Wenham called The Old Testament Covenant Form. He explains that this is achieved by omitting what he refers to as "editorial headings". Thompson sets out his analysis of Deuteronomy in conformity with The Old Testament Covenant Form of Gordon Wenham as follows.

---

[269] Thompson, J. A., op. cit., pp. 18–19.

1:6–3:29	Historical prologue
4:1–40; 5:1–11:32	Basic stipulations
12:1–26:19	Detailed stipulations
27:1–26	Document clause
28:1–14	Blessings
28:15–68	Curses
29:1–30:20	Recapitulation

He suggests it is now no longer necessary to propose that Deuteronomy 1–3 is a later addition by a so-called Deuteronomist. By setting to one side 4:41–49 which he designates as one of a series of headings found throughout Deuteronomy, we find that 4:1–40 is associated intimately with chapters 5–11. Further, 5:1–6 has the same features as 4:34–40, although they are reversed, indicating a very close association between Chapters 4 and 5. Thompson proposes that 4:34–40 and 5:1–6 were linked in the original of Deuteronomy, and that together they comprised an element of the basic covenant principles. 4:41–49 which he refers to as a 'heading' is, he suggests, an interpolation. This results in the following attractive sub-structure:

1.   Deuteronomy 4:1–40 parenesis,[270]

2.   Deuteronomy 5:1–6:3 narrative,

3.   Deuteronomy 6:4–8:20 parenesis,

4.   Deuteronomy 9:1–10:11 narrative,

5.   Deuteronomy 10:12–11:32 parenesis.

Thompson then moves on to Chapters 12:1–26:19 showing that they cover the Covenant Stipulations in detail, and then reveals that Chapter 27 relates to the fourth section in Korosec's scheme, namely

---

[270] An exhortation.

the controls for the safe-keeping of the Covenant and its regular public reading. This section would also correspond to the Document Clause of the Law Code literary form. Thompson adds that it is not unknown for some to remove chapter 27 from its current location, but this is absolutely unnecessary, as the Old Testament Covenant Literary Form requires its presence precisely where it is! Furthermore, while some commentators have suggested that Chapters 29–30 are merely an editorial addition, these too are now seen to be an essential element of The Old Testament Covenant Form, forming the recapitulation of the covenant, ending in Chapter 31:2–6 with a call for Israel to be faithful in war.

Thompson shows that Chapters 31–34 are distinct from the Covenant itself, but are related to it nonetheless inasmuch as they concern the renewal of the Covenant. Moses' successor, Joshua, is appointed as military leader, and is given the responsibility of dividing the Land of Promise into various tribal allotments (31:6–8). Finally Thompson deals with *The Song of Moses* (32:1–43), which is intimately associated with the Covenant. In Thompson's own words, "The introduction to the song (31:24–29) takes up themes within the song and the whole idea of appointing Joshua links back to 1:37ff.; 3:21–28, providing editorial links between the earlier and later chapters in the whole book. Similarly chapter 33 is introduced by 32:48–52 which links back to 3:27f. where Moses is commanded to ascend Pisgah (cf. 34:1ff.). The land which Moses viewed is the theme of the blessings of 33:6–28."[271]

This, to my mind, is the best presentation of the structure of the Treaty Form in the book of Deuteronomy. Interestingly, and significantly, the fact that Deuteronomy does indeed record such a Treaty between Yahweh and Israel, seems now to be beyond serious challenge. This is a most crucial and meaningful development, as the argument about the integrity of Deuteronomy now cannot seriously by countered, although the defeat of Higher Criticism on this point is not dwelt upon by cynics, who debate instead the date of the composition of Deuteronomy, a subject to which we now turn.

---

[271] Thompson, op. cit., pp. 19–20.

Conclusion 12. The overwhelming evidence that Deuteronomy is a treaty document, paralleling in its structure, the forms of other recognised legal documents, shows with the greatest degree of clarity imaginable, that the book, as we know it today, and as it was when originally written, _is a single work_, whose integrity is intact, and which details the covenant relationship between Israel and Yahweh.

We have seen that Meredith Kline's view that the presence of the Historical Prologue in the book of Deuteronomy, while it is _suggestive_ of a date cöeval with Moses, does not make such a date absolutely certain. There is other evidence however, that will be presented later, which does seem to make certain this early dating. But before we turn to this other evidence, we need to examine the reasons for the Higher Critics' late dating of Deuteronomy. Why is this late dating so important to thêm?

Wellhausen, And The Centralisation Of Worship

Central to the scheme of Wellhausen, and Higher Critics generally is the assertion that Deuteronomy insists upon the establishment of only one place of worship within Israel, and that this single location was to be at Jerusalem, which excludes a date earlier than Josiah, as prior to his day, Yahweh had been worshipped at many different locations throughout Israel. Thus this assertion also implies that Deuteronomy _contradicts_ other Scriptures which report true worship in locations other than Jerusalem.[272]

Because of this, while the _unity_ of Deuteronomy might now be conceded by the more enlightened modernists, they still will not accept a Mosaic provenance. We now need to ask whether their insistence of a Josianic date is reasonable or not.

The Practice Of Worship Presented In Deuteronomy

The plain fact of the matter is that, as many commentators have pointed out, there is nothing at all in the book of Deuteronomy that states that Jerusalem was the only site at which Yahweh might be

---

[272] For example, Joshua 4:19, 5:9, 7:6, 8:33, 18:1, 24:1; Judges 18:31, 20:18, 20:26–28, 21:2, 21:19; I Samuel 1:7, 1:24, 3:3, 3:15; & II Samuel 20:8.

worshipped. In fact, Jerusalem itself is never even referred to, nor is a Temple. If an honest search of the book is made, no such centralization of worship policy will be found; only a policy to eradicate *false* worship, including the destruction of the sites associated with false worship, and a requirement to worship Yahweh as directed. This is clearly the policy as given in 12:1–5, which is often cited as the best example of the alleged centralization policy.

Harrison writes, quite correctly, "One of the important points at issue in the discussion of the provenance and date of Deuteronomy has been the question of the centralization of worship, which for many has been held to be the principle theme of the composition. Deuteronomy 12 prescribed that all sacrifices and offerings would be brought in the Promised Land '…unto the place which the Lord your God will choose' (Deut. 12:5, 11, 14, 18, 21, 26). This matter was interpreted along Hegelian lines by Wellhausen and his followers to the point where it was assumed, quite without proof, that Jerusalem was the place where the cult was intended to be centralized. The real force of the contrast in Deuteronomy 12 is not between many altars of God and one, but between those of the Canaanites dedicated to alien deities and the place where the name of God is to be revered. As Manley has put it, the thing which is in question is not their number but their character."[273]

The Impossibility Of A Josianic Provenance For Deuteronomy

This is the key. The background to Deuteronomy is not the centralization of worship at Jerusalem attempted by Hezekiah, and accomplished by Josiah, but the elimination of the pagan cults of the Canaanites. Thus the *Sitz im Leben* of Deuteronomy cannot be the late Monarchical Period at all. If it were, surely Jerusalem would have at least one mention, but what is utterly fatal to a late Monarchical date is the command in 27:1–8 to built an altar on Mount Ebal, in territory that in Josiah's time was associated with the apostates of *the Northern breakaway tribes of Israel*! For Wellhausen to insist that the polemic behind Deuteronomy is the exaltation of Jerusalem, which is

---

[273] Op. cit., pp. 642–643.

unmentioned while there is a definite command to construct an altar in the heartland of rebel-Israel, defies all logic!

The fact is that Deuteronomy does not contradict other portions of the Pentateuch, or of Joshua, Judges and Samuel that permit worship at sites other than Jerusalem, because Deuteronomy 12:10–11 makes it abundantly plain that there should be a settled location for a sanctuary in Israel *only when the Israelites had finally overcome the Canaanites*. This text reads, "When ye go over Jordan, and dwell in the land which the Lord your God giveth you to inherit, *and when He giveth you rest from all your enemies round about,* so that you dwell in safety; then there shall be a place which the Lord your God shall choose to cause His Name to dwell there."

These circumstances were not met until David took the Jebusite stronghold of Jerusalem (II Samuel 5). It was shortly after this that David first proposed that a Temple should be built there, after he had caused the ark to be taken there from Gibeah (II Samuel 6). II Samuel 7:1–2 reads, "And it came to pass when the king (David) sat in his house, *and the Lord had given him rest round about from all his enemies:* that the king said unto Nathan the prophet, 'See now, I dwell in an house of cedar, but the ark of God dwelleth within curtains.'" There then follows David's proposal to build a Temple that was actually undertaken by his son Solomon, but notice that it was only then that the conditions stated in Deuteronomy 12:10–11 had been met. Now it could hardly be said that Josiah dwelt in safety, or had rest from his enemies as he died in battle! (II Kings 23:29–30)

Harrison writes in a very scathing manner of Wellhausen's views in connection with this. He states, "The assumption that Jerusalem was the place intended by Deuteronomy where the cultus was to be centralized is entirely subjective in nature, and has no textual warrant for it whatever. This theory has been criticized by von Rad as in fact resting upon a very slender basis. In the German original of his *Studies in Deuteronomy* he maintained that the command in Deuteronomy 27:1–8 to build an altar upon Mount Ebal and to inscribe the Law upon stones raised a 'barricade' against the centralization theory. His observation is mild to say the least, in point of fact the command relating to Mount Ebal is absolutely fatal to the position of Wellhausen and his followers. It specifically prescribes that which the Law is supposed to prohibit, and even utilizes the words of Exodus 20:24, which according to the critical viewpoint, the Deuteronomic law was intended to revoke." Harrison concludes, "Thus the centralization theory of Wellhausen—described frequently as the key-stone in his system of chronology—is evidently far from being firmly fixed. *As with so many other postulates of classical liberalism, it can only be supported by a misreading of the history, and by contrived and artificial interpretations of the Hebrew text.* [Emphasis mine]"[274]

Conclusion 13. The view of Wellhausen, that the book of Deuteronomy is to be attributed a Josianic provenance because of its alleged centralization of worship policy is unfounded. There is no policy stated in Deuteronomy proscribing worship at any particular location, nor is Jerusalem, or a Temple ever mentioned. The reference to the erection of an altar on Mount Ebal strikes a dramatic and fatal blow to his proposition, as does the constant Deuteronomic theme of the elimination of Canaanite religious practices and shrines, speaking as it does of a pre-Conquest provenance for the book.

A Pre-Conquest Provenance

This pre-Conquest provenance is very clearly indicated throughout the book as J. A. Thompson notices. He writes, "The laws of Deuteronomy refer to a simpler state of society than that which existed in the later centuries and... the Deuteronomic law fits better into the background of history and cultic practice at the close of the Mosaic age. In those days the Canaanites occupied the promised land. Their shrines were to be destroyed so as to remove temptation from Israel. The gifts and sacrifices of God's people were to be brought only to an authorized altar accompanied by proper rituals. The altar of God was not to be defiled by pagan fertility symbols (16:21f.) nor were Canaanite religious practices to be followed (12:29ff.). There was to be a central sanctuary at Shechem once Israel entered the land (27:1ff.), an idea that was meaningful in Moses' day and in the early years of the settlement. [But not in Josiah's day when the Northern Kingdom had fallen.] There is no reference whatever to Jerusalem as

---

[274] Ibid, pp. 643–644.

the central sanctuary. There is no king in Israel (17:14–17), although the nature of kingship was well understood from patterns of kingship known among the Canaanites. Many of the laws would have had meaning in the Mosaic period and shortly afterwards but would have been strange anachronisms in a later age [The words in square brackets are my own].”[275]

George Robinson in an article in *The International Standard Bible Encyclopædia* raises some particularly interesting and valid points. He asks why, if Deuteronomy is to be placed in the days of Josiah, it should contain so many laws that by his time would have been quite anachronistic, and which clearly relate to the time immediately before the Conquest of the Land of Promise? Examples include the command to eliminate the Canaanites (7:18–22), and Amalek (25:17–19), the last of whom had been destroyed in the days of Hezekiah (1 Chronicles 4:41–43). Why, he asks, is there not a single trace of any post-Mosaic literary anachronisms betraying clearly a post Mosaic, in fact, a post United Monarchy *Sitz im Leben*? Why no reference to the Disruption after the death of Solomon, and why, instead of the dangers posed by Assyria or Babylon, Israel is threatened with a return to Egypt (28:68). Why is Jerusalem never mentioned? He then goes on to emphasise how profoundly difficult it is for any writer, no matter how gifted, to eliminate utterly every last trace of the days in which he or she is writing, and to retroject himself or herself so thoroughly into a former age, that no tell-tale evidence is left behind. Yet this is what the Critics ask us to believe is what has happened. We may be sure, that were such forensic evidence available, these same Critics would be the very first to trumpet it from the rooftops. Their complete silence on this matter may be taken as the surest proof that none exists. But given the near impossibility of such a feat, over even a small tract of literature, let alone a work as long as Deuteronomy, this counts as evidence of the most compelling nature for the genuine Mosaic authorship of the book.[276]

---

[275] Op. cit., p. 50.

[276] Robinson, George L., in the article *Deuteronomy*, in *The International Standard Bible Encyclopædia,* op. cit., Volume II, p. 839.

I would also like to point out that one of the circumstances attending the discovery of Deuteronomy by Hilkiah seems to me to be a very clear indicator of the great age of the particular copy that was unearthed. It would seem from II Kings 22:8 and from the parallel account in II Chronicles 34:14–18 that Hilkiah was unable to read the book he had found, at least, he probably was unable to read much of it. He did realise it was the *Book Of The Law,* so it might be that he could discern certain key words, but could not read it fluently. This, I propose is why he gave the book to Shaphan, a trained scribe, otherwise, presumably, he would have gone straight to Josiah with his find. Thus it would appear that only a trained scribe could read the book, and I believe that this is owing to the antiquity of the script used. We must remember that this was the age of the Angular Script, that was a predecessor of the Square-Charactered Script used by Ezra. Therefore it is likely that the copy of Deuteronomy found by Hilkiah was in an even earlier type of character, which the findings from Ras Shamra or Ugarit would indicate to be cuneiform! Of the authorities I have consulted, only Robinson notices this apparent difficulty in reading the book, and its implications, although he does refer to an Egyptologist by the name of Professor Edward Naville who also is of this view.[277]

Conclusion 14. Contrary to the views of Higher Criticism, the internal evidence of the book of Deuteronomy witnesses clearly to a Mosaic provenance.

The Foundation-Treaty Of Israel

If the book of Deuteronomy exhibits a Mosaic provenance, and is a single work, in a recognised Middle-Eastern Treaty format, then surely it might be what could be termed *The Foundation Treaty of Israel as a nation.* This would be why it was this particular work that was read to Israel of course. It also explains the division of the work into three speeches. The divisions at 4:43 and 29:1 separate the Prologue and the Recapitulation from the Central Section, following the Treaty Form.

---

[277] Ibid., p. 839.

There is available some intriguing evidence that this is so from the acute observations made by Robinson, which indicate that the content of Deuteronomy was read to Israel by Moses, not once, but *twice*. These two occasions were separated by a period of thirty-eight years. The second and well-known occasion, was when Israel was encamped on the plains of Moab, and was about to enter the Promised Land, but previously, Deuteronomy it appears, had been read by Moses to the former generation that had escaped from Egypt, when they should have entered Canaan thirty-eight years earlier, but were prevented by their lack of faith. Robinson became convinced of this after studying certain key features of the text.[278]

The first of Robinson's telling points relates to the distance between the localities named in the title of Deuteronomy. The book opens thus; "These be the words which Moses spake unto All Israel on this side Jordan in the Wilderness, in the plain over against the Red Sea, between Paran, and Tophel, and Laban, and Hazeroth, and Dizahab. (There are eleven days' journey from Horeb by the way of Mount Seir unto Kadesh-Barnea.)" Robinson observes that if these words which *introduce* the book of Deuteronomy have any meaning for the book as a whole, then they indicate that the *Sitz im Leben* of the book is the *entirety* of the Wilderness wanderings, from Horeb, to the plains of Moab. What could be more natural, asked Robinson, for Moses, still expecting to enter the Land of Promise from the South, in the days when the spies were sent out, to speak to the nation as recorded in Chapters 5–26 (the Stipulations of the Covenant)? Being frustrated through the peoples' unbelief, what would be more natural, he asks again, than for Moses to reiterate this message, 38 years later, to the succeeding generation, with chapters 1–4 added as an Introduction?[279]

---

[278] Ibid.

[279] Ibid., p 837. This means that the presence of the Historical Prologue might owe more to the failure of Israel to enter immediately into Canaan, than to the rigid adherence of the early Near-Eastern treaty form as Kline suggested, meaning that Thompson is right to suggest that the treaty form found in Deuteronomy does not necessarily imply an early date through its *form*, although it is early as we have seen. It seems also to add credence to Wenham's suggestion that the Covenant treaties of the Hebrew Canon are distinct from any other known form, while being noticeably similar to them in many ways.

Robinson also refers to the provision for the cities of refuge referred to in 19:1–13. There is no reference here to the cities of refuge east of the Jordan, as when this section was read to Israel originally, Sihon and Og had not been defeated, but in 4:41–43, they are referred to, as this portion of Deuteronomy was added according to Robinson's view, specifically to meet the needs of the *later* generation.

If Robinson's intriguing suggestion is correct, and I believe it is likely to be so, then the book of Deuteronomy as it stands now is what might be called the *third edition*. The *first edition*, read at Sinai, would not have included the reference to the cities of refuge east of the Jordan. After the book had been revised preparatory to its being read to the tribes while in the plains of Moab to include the reference to these cities, the book would have been in what we might term its *second edition*. It is also almost certain of course that the minute amount of amosaica was added later by Joshua (see Joshua 24:26), and perhaps the 'headings' referred to by Thompson, meaning that the book as we now have it is the *third edition*. Thus, I agree that Deuteronomy may have undergone recension, but the editors may actually be named as firstly, Moses, the author, and secondly, Joshua (see Joshua 24:26), the appointed successor to Moses.

The importance of Robinson's suggestion is that the book of Deuteronomy may now be viewed as the foundation to the existence of Israel as a nation. In fact it is very possibly what Samuel wrote (a copy of) and laid up before the Lord after telling all the people "the manner of the Kingdom" (I Samuel 10:25) after they had demanded the establishment of a monarchy. The passage in I Samuel certainly does sound like the reading of a constitutional document, and Deuteronomy certainly did anticipate the clamour for a monarchy (17:14–20). Is it any wonder then that we find such similarity of style between Deuteronomy and the prophets as the Critics emphasise? This similarity however, is because the prophets, overwhelmingly concerned with the drift away from the Lord, would continually urge Israel and Judah to return to the Covenant-relationship with the Lord, established by the Foundation-Treaty of Deuteronomy, and so would frequently exhort the people in Deuteronomic terms, and using Deuteronomic phraseology, and imagery; not because Deuteronomy dated from the age of the Prophetic Protest, but because Deuteronomy as the Foundation-Treaty of the nation, was ancient Israel's equivalent of a modern-day Constitution, to which appeal would naturally and increasingly frequently be made, as the crisis deepened.

This constant referring to Deuteronomy extended even to the Apostle Paul. C. Marvin Pate, in his enthralling *Communities Of The Last Days*,[280] has shown how constantly, when Paul in the epistle to the Romans refers to the Law, he does so in *Deuteronomist* terms. I have shown in a recent study[281] how thoroughly Deuteronomic, the book of Romans is, and that it has a clear Israelite *Sitz im Leben*. Of course, had the Torah really been lost at the Fall of Jerusalem, with a copy only being discovered after Paul wrote the epistle to the Romans, no doubt through the Pauline references, Deuteronomy would be dated by Critics to the First Century C.E! The very plain and extremely frequent Pauline references to Deuteronomy make it abundantly clear, that systematic citation of one work in another, certainly does not demand that the two works must be contemporary.

The Cause Of The Loss Of Deuteronomy

Viewing Deuteronomy in this way makes it far more easy to understand why this Foundation-Document was eliminated in the dark days of Judah's most evil, and longest reigning king, Manasseh, or his son, and Josiah's immediate predecessor, Amon (II Kings 21). We now see that this book in particular would be the target of any who wished to suppress the worship of Yahweh in Judah as did king Manasseh. This book above all others, by its being the Foundation-Treaty of Israel would be the one that would be the most hated and the most feared, and if this book above all others could be disposed of, the nation would no longer have its foundation in Yahweh. Thus the finding of Deuteronomy in the days of king Josiah is made all the more credible by understanding that its key rôle in the establishment of Israel as the People of Yahweh, would have caused it to be the prime target of the state-police of any anti-Yahweh regime, such as existed under Manasseh and Amon.

---

[280] Pate, C. Marvin, *Communities Of The Last Days*, Leicester, Apollos, 2000, pp. 164ff.

[281] Phelan, M. W. J., *The 'Greeks' Of The New Testament*, Birmingham, The European Theological Seminary, 2001, pp. 240–269.

The Reason For The Different Style Of Deuteronomy

We see too a reason for the clear linguistic differences between Deuteronomy and the other books of the Pentateuch. Deuteronomy is not merely historical narrative, but is a Constitutional Treaty, and inevitably its different, in fact, *unique* rôle is reflected in the difference in language observable when comparing it with the other books of Moses. It has also been noted that the language of Deuteronomy resembles that of Ezra, but now we see that at the Return under Ezra, Deuteronomy would be the book most likely to be revised by being cast in what was then current-day language, so as to render it the more intelligible to the returnees. It is also equally likely that Ezra himself would have adopted what might be termed Deuteronomic language out of a determination to show fidelity to the Covenant. This could even have been subconscious of course.

Conclusion 15. By being the Foundation Treaty of Israel-as-a-nation, the book of Deuteronomy is most likely not merely to have a Mosaic provenance, but a *Sinaitic* Provenance as well!

Conclusion To Chapter Six

In this chapter we have seen that the book of Deuteronomy is a single work, whose integrity is intact, but we have also seen that it is far easier to accept it has a Mosaic, and even a Sinaitic provenance, than a Josianic provenance. Its very nature as the Foundation-Treaty of the nation also shows why its elimination would have been sought by the authorities reporting either to Manasseh or Amon.

The five points mentioned above on page 168 have also now been addressed, as is indicated below.

1. De Wette's Clue has indeed had a major rethink, to such an extent in fact, that it is now seen to be untenable.

2. Deuteronomy is not merely *The Book Of The Law*, or *The Book Of The Covenant*, but is *The Foundation-Treaty document of Israel as a nation*.

3. There is indeed a connection between the prophets, the author of II Kings, and the book of Deuteronomy, as the prophets, and the author of II Kings would have been aware of the

significance of Deuteronomy, and would have alluded to it purposely, and would have often used Deuteronomic terms and phrases. We now know that even the Apostle Paul wrote in Deuteronomic terms.

4. Deuteronomy is indeed different from the rest of the Pentateuch, by virtue of it being the *Foundation-Treaty document*.

5. The first edition of Deuteronomy not only goes back to Moses, as does the second edition, but actually goes back to Sinai in all probability.

The Use Of Form Criticism

In this chapter we have seen that it is possible to use Form Criticism in a *positive* way. The identification of the book of Deuteronomy as a Treaty Document, is an exercise in Form Criticism, as it identifies the work as corresponding to an identifiable literary genre. This shows that literary criticism is able to make valuable contributions to the study of the Scriptures, but must be undertaken in an unbiased manner, rather than to bolster a preconceived cynical position.

When we consider the unity of the Pentateuch that our previous findings have established, we see that if Deuteronomy must be given a Mosaic provenance, so must the other books of the Pentateuch. It is to these other books then that we now turn, to see whether or not they are compatible with the views I have advocated. The book of Genesis will be considered in two later chapters, so for now we turn to Exodus, Leviticus and Numbers, the books at the heart of the Torah.

Chapter Seven

The Heart Of The Torah

So far we have seen that Deuteronomy is a book of an unique character. To this extent then, Higher Critics have been correct in viewing it as being distinguishable from the rest of the Pentateuch, albeit they have not understood the real reason for its distinction. This means that using the term D purely as a literary designation, *without accepting its alleged characteristic as a Pentateuchal source*, it may be agreed that D is clearly distinguishable from the other works attributed to Moses.

But now we come to consider, Exodus, Leviticus and Numbers, we encounter material that Higher Criticism nowadays tends to attribute to two sources; the combination of J and E known either as JE, or following Martin Noth's lead, G, or the *Grundlage*, and P, sometimes viewed as an amalgam of P and a later editor P_2.[282]

Before we begin to examine the three middle books of the Torah then, it may be as well to test the foundation of the concept of the alleged different literary sources to be found in Exodus, Leviticus, and Numbers, namely Astruc's Clue. This has already been severely challenged by our previous findings, but now I hope to show that there is an utter misunderstanding by Critics of the text Astruc's Clue is supposed to be based on.

The Basis Of 'Astruc's Clue'

It is taken as axiomatic by Higher Critics that Exodus 6:3 means that the Sacred Name revealed in the tetragrammaton YHWH was unknown before the time of Moses. It is assumed to be an unchallengeable assertion, and the viability of Astruc's Clue depends on understanding the text in this way, thus, Higher Critics will seldom

---

[282] See Wenham, Gordon J., *Numbers: An Introduction And Commentary*, Leicester, InterVarsity Press, 1981, p. 19.

discuss the matter. It must be said that in most English versions the text does seem to support the Critics' position. The Authorized Version reads,

> "I appeared unto Abraham, unto Isaac, and unto Jacob,
> by the Name of God Almighty, but by My Name
> Jehovah (YHWH) was I not known to them."

This seems straightforward enough, but how then are we to understand earlier passages that use the Sacred Name? Perhaps the most famous passage of this class is Genesis 15:1–8, the introduction to the Covenant-of-the-pieces. The passage begins with the words, "After these things The Word of YHWH came unto Abram in a vision (verse 1)." In verse 2 Abram addresses the Being referred to as The Word of YHWH, as "Lord YHWH"! Later, in verses 4–5, The Word of YHWH leads Abram aside and bids him to look at the stars of Heaven, and in verse 6 it is said that Abram "believed in YHWH". In the next verse, The Word of YHWH declares to Abram, "I am YHWH", leading Abram in verse 8 to refer to Him as his "Lord YHWH".

Here we find in the clearest manner imaginable, the Sacred Name, not just in the Scriptural narrative, but on Abram's very lips! Therefore it is clear that the Scriptures depict Abram himself using the Name revealed in the Tetragrammaton, showing that we need to look again at Exodus 6:3. Nor is this an isolated incident. In Genesis 18:1 we read that YHWH appeared to Abraham, as by then he was named. But even if we go right back to the time of Seth, in Genesis 4:26, we read, "then began men to call upon the Name of YHWH". Therefore the Sacred Name was known, even when Adam was alive![283] At the other extreme, we find that the name of Moses' mother, Jochebed, is based on the Name YHWH.[284] Do these other Scriptures *contradict* Exodus 6:3, as adherents of the New Documentary Hypothesis maintain, or, instead, is there a problem with the English translation of Exodus 6:3?

---

[283] Ginzberg reports in his *Legends*, that Adam knew and used the Tetragrammaton. Ginzberg, Louis, *The Legends Of The Jews*, op. cit., Volume V, p. 83.

[284] Cole, R. Alan, *Exodus: An Introduction And Commentary*, London, InterVarsity Press, 1973, p. 84, & *The International Standard Bible Encyclopædia*, op. cit., in. loc.

The Meaning Of Exodus 6:3

Robert Young in his *Concise Critical Comments On The Holy Bible*, considers the word translated *known* in this verse, and makes some interesting remarks. He writes, "The word 'known' is in the Scriptures often used in the sense of 'appreciating, caring for, approving, experiencing,' as in Is. 53. 3, 'acquainted with sickness;' Ps. 1. 6, 'Jehovah knoweth (i.e. approveth) the way of the righteous;' Ps. 9. 11, 'those who know (i.e. appreciate) Thy name;' Ge. 39. 6, 'he hath not known (cared for) anything.' Amos 3. 2, 'you only have I known (cared for) of all the nations of the earth.'"[285]

Writing in 1685, twenty-six years before Witter in 1711 published his *Jura Israelitarum In Palestina*, and 68 years before Jean Astruc published his, *Conjectures Sur Les Mémoires Originaux Dont Il Parait Que Moyse S'est Servi Pour Composer Le Livre De La Genèse. Avec Des Remarques Qui Appuient Ou Qui Éclaircissent Ces Conjectures* in 1753, Matthew Poole made a suggestion which is not incompatible with Young's comments, and which Witter and Astruc would have done well to have paid heed to. He wrote of the statement in Exodus 6:3 as it appears in the Authorized Version, "How is this true, when God was known to them (Abraham, Isaac and Jacob), and called by the name *Jehovah?* Gen. xv. 7; xxvi. 24, &c... He speaks not of the letters or syllables, but of the thing signified by that name. For that denotes all his perfections, and amongst others, the eternity, constancy, and immutability of his nature and will, and the infallible certainty of his word and promises. And this, saith he, though it was believed by Abraham, Isaac, and Jacob, yet it was not experimentally known by them; for they only saw the promises afar off, Heb. xi. 13."[286]

Walter C. Kaiser Jr. reviewed the traditional interpretation of this verse, and came up with similar thoughts. He noted that in the Targum of Pseudo-Jonathan, it is suggested that the Patriarchs, Abraham, Isaac, and Jacob all knew the Lord as Yahweh as well as El Shaddai,

---

[285] Young, Robert, *Concise Critical Comments On The Holy Bible*, London, Pickering & Inglis, undated, pp. 47–48.

[286] Poole, Matthew, *A Commentary On The Holy Bible*, Volume I, Edinburgh, three volumes, The Banner Of Truth Trust, 1962, in. loc. A similar remark is to be found in Keil & Delitzsch, op. cit., Volume I, in. loc.

although they were unacquainted with the Shekinah Glory, that later, Israelites normally connected with the Name Yahweh. Kaiser also found that the medieval Jewish commentators understood Exodus 6:3 as indicating that the *character* of Yahweh, rather than the Name itself is what was revealed to Moses. For evidence, they looked to the Hebrew preposition, *beth*, which they took to be what grammarians refer to as *beth essentiae*. The famous Hebrew grammarian, Gesenius, who agrees the Hebrew ב is to be understood in this text as *beth essentiae,* defines the meaning of *beth essentiae* as it would be understood in this context, as signifying, *"appearing, manifesting oneself, representing, being,* in the sense of *as, in the capacity of."*[287] Based on this suggestion, Kaiser proposes that Exodus 6:3, is to be rendered as, "I appeared to Abraham, to Isaac and to Jacob *in the character of El Shaddai,* but *in the character of Yahweh* I did not make MySelf known to them."[288]

Bagster's *Comprehensive Bible* makes another interesting point. It reads, "If Abraham, Isaac, and Jacob did not know the name JEHOVAH, then Moses must have used it in Genesis by prolepsis or anticipation. But probably we should, with Mr. Locke and others, read it interrogatively, for the negative particle לֹא, lo, *not*, has frequently this power in Hebrew: 'I appeared unto Abraham, Isaac, and Jacob by the name of God Almighty, and by my name JEHOVAH was I not also made known unto them?'"[289]

A More Comprehensive Solution

This is all very well and good, and does make sound sense, yet it is also seemingly beyond question that there was something genuinely <u>new</u> being declared to Moses and the children of Israel at the revelation of God at the burning bush. To my mind this is inescapable yet none of the explanations given above seem to give an emphasis to this sense of newness here that is in any way adequate. Better by far, I believe, is the explanation offered by Duane Garrett in his *Rethinking Genesis*. The merit of this explanation which takes the

---

[287] Gesenius, *Hebrew Grammar*, op. cit., § 119, i.

[288] Op. cit., p. 139.

[289] *The Comprehensive Bible*, London, Samuel Bagster and Sons, undated, in. loc.

answers given above one crucial step further, is that while utilising the points of grammar referred to above, and thereby showing that the Patriarchs certainly did know the Name Yahweh, Garrett also provides a sufficiently meaningful answer to the need to find some genuinely new revelation associated with this verse. He provides this in a manner which satisfies this need *adequately* and *logically*, and also shows by the use of a literary structure, the sense of the verse.

Duane Garrett agrees that, superficially, the text in English translation might seem to indicate that the Patriarchs, Abraham, Isaac, and Jacob did not know the Name of Yahweh. Garrett however, appeals to the findings of Francis I. Anderson, who has pointed out the presence of what he referred to as a *non-contiguous parallelism*, which seems to have eluded at least the majority of translators. This non-contiguous parallelism is found in the phrases, "I am Yahweh... and My Name is Yahweh", in Hebrew this reads, ושמי יהוה... אני יהוה. This means that לא ('not') is to be understood as linked with that which precedes it, and as an assertion within a rhetorical question, and not as a simple negative, as Bagster's *Comprehensive Bible* suggested. (Garrett cites the following work to support this statement, Francis I. Anderson, *The Sentence In Biblical Hebrew* (The Hague: Mouton, 1974), p. 102.) Garrett found upon investigation that the entire text is built in the form of typical Hebrew poetic parallelism, above and beyond what Anderson himself suspected. The parallelism, based on Garrett's presentation, is illustrated below.

Exodus 6:2c–3

A   I am Yahweh.

B   And I made myself known to Abraham, to Isaac, and to Jacob as El Shaddai.

A   And my name is Yahweh;

B   Did I not make myself known to them?

A   אני יהוה

B   וארא אל-אברהם אל-יצחק ואל-יעקב באל שדי

A   ושמי יהוה

B   לא נודעתי להם

Garrett maintains that the text should not be understood as signifying that the Name of Yahweh was unknown to the Patriarchs, Abraham,

Isaac, and Jacob. He also shows that the presence of בּ *essentiae* implies that God had invested the Name of El Shaddai with particular significance for the Patriarchs, and that this was seen when the Abrahamic Covenant was made, and when the Land of Promise was vouchsafed to them. Now, Garrett proposes, Moses is told that the Lord will invest the Name of Yahweh with significance that actually surpasses what had happened in the time of the Patriarchs, by achieving the Israelites' deliverance from the House of Bondage. Crucially however, the text actually emphasises the <u>continuity</u> between the revelation given to the Patriarchs, and that given to Moses, and certainly does not at all imply any sense of <u>dis</u>continuity. Garrett draws attention to the final clause, "did I not make MySelf known to them [the Patriarchs]?"

Garrett again draws upon Anderson for support, emphasising how Anderson had revealed how essential it was to the successful outcome of the work of Moses, for this vital connection with the Patriarchs to be understood with clarity by the ordinary Israelite people. Thus there could be no thought here of a radical break from the past by the 'springing' upon the Israelites of a new Divine Name. The familiarity of the Name of Yahweh was vital to the success of Moses' mission.

Garrett then gives four grammatical points which favour his views.

1. The traditional rendering is invalid as it depends upon the בּ in בְּאֵל שַׁדָּי performing two distinct rôles simultaneously. It must relate not only to בְּאֵל שַׁדָּי, but also to וּשְׁמִי יהוה, a grammatical impossibility, as the different phrases are located in different clauses.

2. The niphal of יָדַע being reflective, prevents it accepting a direct object (וּשְׁמִי יהוה). (I have confirmed that נוֹדַעְתִּי is indeed the Niphal of יָדַע, which certainly does make it reflective.[290])

---

[290] Wigram, George V., *The Englishman's Hebrew And Chaldee Concordance Of The Old Testament,* Grand Rapids, Michigan, Zondervan, fifth edition, 1970, based on the 1843 and 1860 editions by Bagster, p. 505, & Kelley, Page H., *Biblical Hebrew: An Introductory Grammar*, Grand Rapids, Michigan, Eerdmans, 1992, p. 108.

3. Because it is usual for לֹא to begin a sentence in which it is found, it is highly improbable that a subordinate phrase would be found in front of it.

4. The presence of the structure illustrated above makes the possibility of a disrupted word sequence extremely unlikely, indicating again that the traditional rendition is incorrect.[291]

To my mind Garrett's proposals constitute by far and away the best solution to the question. By using only the construction of the text, Garrett citing Anderson shows that the patriarchs did know the Name of Yahweh, which, it is plain, other Scriptures demonstrate very clearly. Secondly he shows that nonetheless there is something of the greatest significance in the statement, that provides something genuinely new, that is, the *investing* of the Name with an abundance of Covenantal meaning, which prior to that point had never occurred. It is this that was new, not the Name itself. As an example, we might take the Name Emmanuel, *God-With-Us*. This Name we know for certain was known and used in ancient Judah (Isaiah 7:14). Nonetheless, who could deny, that the events of Matthew 1:23 invested that well-known Name with a significance and wealth of meaning, undreamt of before the Incarnation of Christ? So here with the redemption from the house-of-the-bondage, and the deliverance from Egypt; the crossing of the Sea-of-passage, and the giving-of-the-law; the granting of the manna, the entry into the Promised Land, and above all the Covenant made between Israel and Yahweh that we have just examined in Deuteronomy, the previously well-known Name of Yahweh, became overwhelmingly laden, or charged with majesty, glory and honour.[292]

It follows from this clearer understanding of Exodus 6:3 that is utterly consistent with Scripture as a whole, and also with the facts of Hebrew Grammar, that the Name Yahweh has been known, and used by man, since the very beginnings of human history. If proper names based upon the Tetragrammaton became more prevalent after the

---

[291] Op. cit., pp. 18–19, & 263–264. It is very plain that Gesenius supports what is said above concurning בּ essentiae. See Gesenius, H. W. F., *Hebrew Grammar*, op. cit., p. 379.

[292] Derek Kidner makes a similar remark in *Genesis: An Introduction And Commentary*, op. cit., p. 20.

Exodus, it is hardly surprising given the opulence of meaning the old Name was from that point on, seen to contain. It is not an argument for the sudden appearance of a previously unknown Divine Name, which probably would have been completely rejected by believing Israelites. As Garrett rightly says, it was the very *continuity* with the past, particularly Abraham, Isaac and Jacob that enabled Moses to be accepted. He stood as a part of a respected *tradition*, offering fulfilment of ancient promises, rather than mere novelty.

From this we see that to base any arguments of literary priority on the use or avoidance of the Name Yahweh is mere 'rainbow-chasing'. I would also point out that the Critics also fail to give any reason at all for the J Source avoiding the use of Elohim. I conclude then that they have been deluded by a mirage in the lifeless and trackless desert of cynicism that their own scepticism and unbelief has created!

Conclusion 16. Astruc's Clue, the very foundation-stone of the Graf–Wellhausen Hypothesis, and Higher, or Source Criticism generally, is founded on a misunderstanding so fundamental, that it is now seen to be utterly meaningless. This one fact consigns the New Documentary Hypothesis, and virtually every other current-day variety of Source Criticism to history's graveyard!

The Nature Of Exodus, Leviticus, And Numbers

So then, if we cannot turn to the accepted methods of Source Criticism to answer the problems of Exodus, Leviticus, and Numbers, what do we turn to? For, we must not fool *ourselves* now, as the Critics are right in one thing, namely there are real problems concerning these books that need to be answered.

The problems concern the seemingly haphazard construction of the books. If Deuteronomy has a clearly constructed literary form, then the opposite seems to apply to the works now under consideration. We see in the books before us a tapestry, the Critics would say, *confusion*, of Moses' biography, historical narrative relating the birth of Israel as a nation, all mixed in with civil, moral and ceremonial legislation. It is this commingling of history, both personal and national, with legal matters that is so peculiar about this literature, and to be fair to the Critics, they were, and are still, making a genuine attempt to solve this literary puzzle, albeit with completely inappropriate methods.

Even if we concentrate purely on the legislation found in these books, matters are far from straightforward. We find examples of decrees concerning the punishment of certain criminal activity, seemingly inserted at random into passages which otherwise concern matters of ceremony or worship.[293] Some sections which concern only one type of legislation are of considerable length,[294] others are extremely brief.[295] Some laws are repeated in more or less the same words,[296] but some in different words.[297] Some types of legislation are given in a most succinct, even 'bullet-point' manner, as for example the Ten Commandments;[298] others are given in a minutely detailed, and thoroughly comprehensive manner, as, for example the details concerning the construction of the Tabernacle, its furniture and ancillary equipment,[299] or the section concerning leprosy.[300]

The critic wants to know how this peculiar arrangement came to be? and it is fair to say this is a valid question. What then is the answer?

Different Types Of Legislation

We will tackle the subject of legislation first. The Reverend Professor Melvin Grove Kyle, a Biblical Theologian and archaeologist of great ability and standing undertook a major study of these matters and made some remarkable discoveries which, I believe, provide a logical and credible explanation for the facts referred to above. Professor

---

[293] For example Leviticus 18–20 concerns sexual crimes, and idolatry seem incongruously inserted in 16–22 which otherwise relates to the priesthood.

[294] For example, Leviticus 1–9 which concerns offerings.

[295] For example, the laws concerning childbirth, Leviticus 12:1–8.

[296] Cf. Leviticus 11:40 with 17:15.

[297] Cf. Exodus 29:36–37 with Leviticus 16:18–19.

[298] Exodus 20:1–17.

[299] Exodus 25–28.

[300] Leviticus 13–14.

Kyle's findings may be found in his article in *The International Standard Bible Encyclopædia.*[301]

In his examination of the problem, Kyle found that certain words are used of legislation in particular ways. The word תורה, *Torah,* for example, is used on thirty-two occasions in Exodus, Leviticus, and Numbers,[302] and is used of a specific type of legislation (Exodus 12:49), of ceremonial statutes (Leviticus 6:9), and, as is well known, of the *entire corpus* of legislation, and of the entire Pentateuch.

In very sharp contrast with this word of very general usage, are three words of another type which have very specific applications. The first of these is חק or חקה which is used on sixty-eight occasions in Exodus, Leviticus and Numbers,[303] and is often translated by the Authorized Version as *Statutes.* I give a list and analysis of these sixty-eight occurrences in Part A of Appendix VI, from which it is seen that whenever these words are used in connection with the Covenant made at Mount Sinai, they refer to laws concerning the worship, or the spiritual 'walk' of Israel, and were administered by the *Priests*.

The next word is משפט, שפטים, or שפט and is found on fifty-seven occasions in Exodus, Leviticus and Numbers,[304] and is frequently translated by the Authorized Version as *Judgments.* All of these instances are listed and analysed in Part A of Appendix VII. This analysis shows that when used in connection with the Covenant made at Sinai, משפט, שפטים, and שפט, refer to the Civil Law, as opposed to directions for the Worship of Israel, and that frequently they were based on *precedent*, and that they were generally administered not by the Priests, but by *Magistrates*.[305]

---

[301] In the article by Kyle, M. G., *Pentateuch, Problem of*, in *The International Standard Bible Encyclopædia*, op. cit., Volume IV, pp. 2312A–2312D.

[302] Wigram, George, *The Englishman's Hebrew And Chaldee Concordance Of The Old Testament,* Grand Rapids, Michigan, U.S.A., Zondervan, undated in. loc.

[303] Wigram, op. cit., in. loc.

[304] Ibid., in. loc.

[305] See also Margolis, Max L., & Marx, Alexander, *A History Of The Jewish People*, Philadelphia, The Jewish Publication Society Of America, 5707 (1947), p. 17f.

Finally, the word מצות occurs nineteen times in Exodus, Leviticus and Numbers,[306] and is usually translated as *Commandments* in the Authorized Version. These nineteen occurrences are listed and analysed in Part A of Appendix VIII. From this analysis it is very clear that the word had a general application, whereby it could be used of any type of commandment, and a specific application, which restricted its application to the Decalogue, or the Ten Commandments.

Kyle points out that the rare exceptions to this serve only to validate his views. Occasionally the phrase *Statute-Of-Judgment* is encountered, which I have indicated in the Appendices referred to above. A Statute is a specific direction, or instruction, while a Judgment is usually related to a precedent. Where the phrase Statute-Of-Judgment occurs it refers to a new piece of legislation, that was intended to be used as a precedent for resolving similar situations in future. Nowadays we would refer to such as a Test-Case.

Kyle argues that this technical usage of these three words is traceable through the book of Judges until the time of the United Monarchy, fell into disuse after the Disruption, and was revived again with the return under Ezra.[307] Part B of the three Appendices referred to above shows that the usage in Deuteronomy of these words is consistent with that of Exodus, Leviticus, and Numbers. (Given Kyle's findings that during the time between the Disruption and the Return the technical use of these terms was not maintained we see here further evidence that Deuteronomy is inconsistent with a Josianic provenance.)

The Uses Of These Different Types Of Legislation

Kyle points out the need for the Ten Commandments to be stated in a manner easy to remember. He noticed of these and other Commandments that they are expressed in the Hebrew text most succinctly, even *tersely*, and are stated using only nouns and verbs, with adjectives and adverbs hardly ever appearing.[308] I would add that another reason for this 'bullet-point' style is that Commandments, and

---

[306] Wigram, op. cit., in. loc.

[307] Kyle, op. cit.

[308] Ibid.

the Ten Commandments especially, would have to be known and understood by the greatest possible number of Israelites, regardless of age or ability. Thus, they would be given in a most simple and unadorned manner to facilitate ease of understanding throughout the population. Today's political and advertising slogans, designed for mass appeal, are just as elementary in construction of course.

By great contrast the details concerning the manufacture of the Tabernacle, its furniture and fittings, constitute nothing less than a full technical specification, and would need to be immensely detailed, but were to be used only by a skilled master craftsman, trained in such matters, and especially enabled by the Spirit of God (Exodus 31:1-5), and who was assisted by other recognized craftsmen (Exodus 31:6). Similarly, the Statutes concerning the Worship of Israel would inevitably be much more detailed than the Commandments, in order to ensure that the various sacrifices and offerings were carried out correctly. But these tasks were to be executed by a professional body of Priests. These Priests would make it their business to be thoroughly versed in all the minutest details of their responsibilities, and would train their successors until they too were proficient. It was unnecessary for the whole population to recall instantly and in full detail, all that pertained to each form of sacrifice, as the lay people who brought their offerings would be guided by the Priests whose frequent and continual service would ensure total familiarity with the details of every form of offering.

Somewhere in between these extremes, would be the Judgments, that were administered by another trained group, namely, the Magistrates. However, there would be a need for the population as a whole to understand the *principles* which underlay the Judgments, but the trained Magistrates could be relied upon to elucidate the finer details of the Civil Law, as and when required.

Thus we see that there were different types of legislation in the Torah, given for different purposes, and that these different purposes resulted in their being stated in different forms.

Conclusion 17. The reason for the differences of form in which different types of Torah legislation is given, is related directly to the different purposes the different types of legislation fulfilled.

The Origin Of Exodus, Leviticus, And Numbers

We have seen from our earlier findings that the books of the Pentateuch stand together. We saw that the many different types of literary construction to be found in the Pentateuch bind them together into one literary corpus. We have seen also that the book of Deuteronomy is the Foundation Treaty Document of Israel as a nation, and that it must be attributed not only a Mosaic Provenance, but even a Sinaitic Provenance as well. The ways in which the separate books of the Pentateuch are bound together, inevitably leads to the recognition that the books of Exodus, Leviticus and Numbers must also have a Mosaic Provenance, and there is real evidence that this is so. Gordon Wenham, has shown that there is real literary dependence on the book of Numbers by what I have named the *second edition* of the book of Deuteronomy, that is, the version read by Moses to the people while they were encamped on the plains of Moab. Inevitably, this literary dependence shows that Numbers itself must indeed be regarded as being Mosaic. Wenham shows this literary dependence by a comparison of the following passages.[309]

Source in Numbers	Alleged Source	Used in Deuteronomy	Content
12.	J.[310]	24:9.	Miriam's leprosy.
13:17–33.	P,J,P,J,P.	1:19–46.	The spying of the Land.
18.	P.	18:22.	Priestly duties.
20:12.	E.	32:51–52.	Moses & Aaron excluded.
20:14–21:20.	E,J,E,J,P,J,O.[311]	2:1–25.	The journeying.
21:21–35.	E.	2:26–3:10.	Conquests East of Jordan.

---

[309] Wenham, Gordon J., op. cit., p. 23.

[310] The designation of Higher Criticism's alleged literary sources is taken from Noth, Martin, *A History Of Pentateuchal Traditions*, op. cit., *Translator's Supplement*, pp. 272–275.

[311] 'O' is my own designation for *other* alleged sources.

Source in Numbers	Alleged Source	Used in Deuteronomy	Content
22–24.	P,E,J,E,J,E,J,E, J,E,J,E,J.	23:4–5.	Balaam.
30.	O.	23:21–23.	Vows.
35:9–34.	O.	19:1–13.	Cities-of-Refuge.

Now what is true of Numbers, is also true of Exodus and Leviticus, for the entire concept embodied by the book of Deuteronomy, that is, the imminent conquest of the Land of Promise by the Covenanted People of God, redeemed from the House of Bondage as detailed in Exodus, and called to serve Him, as outlined in Leviticus, shows a *conceptual* dependence on Exodus and Leviticus of the book of Deuteronomy, if not a literary dependence. Thus not only Numbers, but Exodus and Leviticus must predate the second edition of Deuteronomy, which itself predates the Conquest. This means that there is no room for the New Documentary Hypothesis in the last four books of the Pentateuch. In fact, we see from the table above that Deuteronomy assumes the intrinsic unity of passages which according to Martin Noth are an amalgam of fragments from all the alleged sources, namely J, E, and P. There is in fact no real evidence for the existence of different literary sources in the books Exodus to Numbers, and it seems as if the concept of different documentary sources thought to be identifiable in Genesis, was simply extended all the way to Deuteronomy without any real evidence, and based only on the commingling of different subject matter referred to above.

This mixture of subject matter however, is insufficient as a foundation for Source Criticism. In his commentary on Numbers, Professor Gordon Wenham refers to the inadequacy of this argument, pointing out how futile it is to suggest that a variety of subjects in the same document necessarily and inevitably proves a variety of *sources*. He goes on to argue that once the literary plan of the book of Numbers (which will be revealed shortly) is understood, the combination of historical narrative and legal material cannot be thought to imply multiple sources at all, nor does the variety of literary styles. He observes that were he to draft a law, he should use an entirely different style and vocabulary from that employed in the writing of commentaries. Poets, he adds, may also write prose, but their syntax, vocabulary and style would change to suit the type of writing produced. It is inevitable he concludes, that both the literary style and vocabulary of Numbers [and Exodus and Leviticus] will vary in accordance with the demands of the different types of subject matter encountered. Wenham emphasises how vital it is, when assessing the evidence for multiple sources, to compare like with like. Legal material must be compared with other legal material; and narrative must be compared with other narrative. When this is done, then subtle differences in style, syntax, and vocabulary may legitimately be used to assess the presence of a single source, or multiple sources. The very basic techniques used by most source-Critics however, prove nothing about different sources he argues, they reveal only the presence of different types of subject matter. Until things change he states, it is still perhaps acceptable to speak of Priestly Material (P), and Epic Material (JE), providing it is understood that this does not in any way indicate different literary sources.[312]

I conclude therefore that the provenance for the books of Exodus, Leviticus and Numbers, is indeed Mosaic, and that they were compiled in the desert, during the forty years Wandering of the children of Israel in the wilderness. This thought leads the way to the eventual solution of the problems of these books.

The Travel Journal Of Moses

Gordon Wenham points out a fact that surprisingly appears to have gone unnoticed for a long time, even though once stated, it seems to be very obvious. He notes that the material we are considering "is cast in large cycles in which three important eras of revelation, at Sinai, at Kadesh, and in the plains of Moab, are separated by two bridge passages describing the journeys from Sinai to Kadesh, and from Kadesh to the plains of Moab."[313]

It is from Kadesh Barnea that the tribes sent out the spies, and from where they should have entered the Land (Numbers 13:17–33), but, owing to their unbelief, they were doomed to trudge through the

---

[312] Wenham, op. cit., pp. 19–20.

[313] Wenham, op. cit., p. 5.

wilderness for another thirty eight years before entering Canaan from the plains of Jordan. Just as Deuteronomy was read once to the people at Kadesh Barnea, and again on the plains of Moab, so too, many statements made at Kadesh Barnea, had to be restated to the new generation on the plains of Moab. These events were I propose, recorded by Moses in some sort of travel-journal, which became what we now know as the books of Exodus to Numbers, thus accounting for some of the duplications we see in these books.

Gordon Wenham believes that the three books at the heart of the Pentateuch, Exodus, Leviticus and Numbers, are very closely related. He adds that Genesis forms the Prologue of the Pentateuch, while Deuteronomy is its epilogue. As will be seen later, this statement of Gordon Wenham describes with absolute precision the interrelationship of these books, but for the moment we must remain with the three central books of the Pentateuch. Wenham depicts the material found in Exodus, Leviticus, and Numbers as given below:

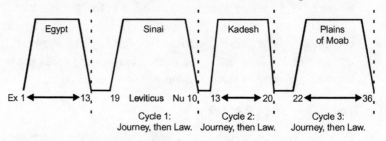

Figure 2 The Interrelationship of Exodus, Leviticus and Numbers

What Wenham has revealed here is how clearly the books of Exodus, Leviticus and Numbers are set in three great cycles, the latter two occur completely in the book of Numbers. Wenham shows that there is no mere "mechanical" repetition of the various elements that form the three cycles, and deliberately draws attention to the different natures of the material found in the first thirteen chapters of Exodus, when compared with the material which relates to Sinai, the events of Kadesh Barnea, and the time spent on the plains of Moab. Nevertheless, in spite of these real differences, the repetition of similar events and topics, in the same parts of the three cycles seems indicative of design rather than coincidence. This is further reinforced by clear references to the earlier occasions in the narrative itself (see for example, Numbers 28:6; 32:8ff.). Wenham illustrates the parallels between the three great cycles, and the three periods of law-giving (Sinai, Kadesh Barnea, The Plains of Moab) in a set of synopses as set out below.

JOURNEYS			
Topic	Red Sea to Sinai	Sinai to Kadesh	Kadesh to Moab
Led by cloud	Ex. 13:12	= Nu. 10:11ff.	
Victory over Egypt	14		cf. 21:21–35
Victory song	15:1–18	cf. 10:35f.	21:14–15
Miriam	15:20–21	= 12	= 20:1
People complain	15:23–24	= 11:1	= 21:5
Moses' intercession	15:25	= 11:2	= 21:7
Well	15:27		= 21:16
Manna and quails	16	= 11:4–35	
Water from rock	17:1–7		= 20:2–13
Victory over Amalek	17:8–16		cf. 21:1–3
Jethro	18:1–12	cf. 10:29–32	

STOPS			
Topic	Sinai	Kadesh	Moab
Divine promises	Ex. 19:3–6; 23:23ff.	Nu. 13:2	22–24
40 days	24:18	13:25	–
Rebellion	32:1–8	14:1ff.	25:1–3
Moses' intercession	32:11–13	14:13–19	–
Judgment	32:34	14:20–35	25:4
Plague	32:35	14:37	25:8–9
Laws of sacrifice	34:18ff.; Lv. 1–7. etc.	15:1–31	28–29
Trial	Lv. 24:10–23	15:32–36	27:1–11
Rebellion against priests	Lv. 10:1–3	16:1–35	–
Atonement through priests or Levites	Ex. 32:26–29	16:36–50	25:7–13
Priestly prerogatives	Lv. 6–7; 22	17–18	31:28–30; 35:1–8
Impurity rules	Lv. 11–16; Nu. 9:6–14	19	31; 35:9ff.
Census	Nu. 1–4	–	26

While some of the parallels listed above have been observed by other commentators, Wenham's particular contribution of revealing the presence in the three books at the heart of the Pentateuch of the three narrative cycles is especially significant. He shows however, that this type of structure is not confined to the books of Exodus to Numbers. Wenham writes, "Deuteronomy is based on three long speeches by Moses (1–4, 5–28, 29–30). An even closer parallel is provided by the book of Genesis. The three major cycles about the patriarchs Abraham, Jacob and Joseph, are introduced by the formula 'These are the generations of Terah, (Isaac, Jacob)' (Gn. 11:27, 25:19, 37:2), and interrupted by shorter blocks of material introduced by the same formula (25:12; 36:1). The primeval history (Gn. 2–11) follows a similar pattern: narrative (2:4–4:26), genealogy (5:1–6:8), narrative (6:9–9:28), genealogy (10:1–32), narrative (11:1–9), genealogy (11:10–26). Except in 11:1, each section begins with the formula

'These are the generations of.'"[314] These remarks are especially important for us, particularly those concerning the book of Genesis as we shall see later.

The cyclic nature of the material to be found in Exodus to Numbers would inevitably lead to some duplications, but Kyle has another suggestion to which we will now turn, which would not only account for duplications, but also for the seemingly random distribution of the various types of legislation encountered in these books.

Moses' Responsiveness To The Israelites' Needs

I have shown elsewhere that the number of Israelites that escaped from Egypt under Moses is likely to have been in the order of 2,000,000.[315] The challenges involved in teaching such a colossal number of people camping in the wilderness would have been extremely severe, and often the same material would have had to have been presented several times as different people gathered to be taught.

Kyle points out that a truly enormous amount of land would have been required by the flocks that accompanied the Israelites, and that most of the time, large numbers of people would be engaged in shepherding the flocks, away from the central camping area, which itself must have been the size of a small city. The groups that met to hear the words of Moses would presumably be organised on some sort of rota, and could well have been quite diverse in character, meaning that on some occasions the same teaching might have to be given in different wording. It is usual of course for leaders to group people according to age and ability.

Also, it would be extremely likely that the incidents arising from disputes between individuals that wilderness conditions would render almost inevitable, might cause Moses to interrupt a particular theme of teaching, in order to clarify the laws concerning particular matters of immediate concern. This would therefore account for the seemingly random distribution of some legislation. It would be a direct consequence of particular situations that developed

---

[314] Ibid., pp. 16–17.

[315] Phelan, M. W. J., *The Dating Of The Exodus*, op. cit., pp. 24–27.

spontaneously, and unpredictably, and which called for immediate clarification of the issues concerned, even at the cost of disrupting a particular course of teaching.[316]

Wenham also shows how many of the laws actually carry implicit *promises,* which low morale caused through failure of some kind, might require to be emphasised. He cites as an example Numbers 15 which explains that grain, oil, and wine must be offered with certain sacrifices.[317] This legislation of course *guarantees* that in spite of the failure recorded in the two previous chapters concerning the mission of the spies, the Israelites would certainly enter the Land that produces the plants that would enable those offerings to be made. Such encouragement would surely have been needed sorely after the refusal to enter the Land, and the consequent sentence of many years of wanderings in the wilderness. It is not unreasonable to suppose therefore that the timing of the giving of this teaching was controlled by the events of Numbers 13–14.

Exodus To Numbers As Migration Epic Literature

If Exodus to Numbers truly is based upon a journal of Moses, then what we encounter in these books approximates to the sequence in which Moses delivered to the Israelites the teaching he was entrusted with, and the reasons given above easily account for the repetitions in similar and dissimilar wording, as well as the sometimes haphazard order of teaching. In fact these characteristics may now be seen to be no less than *a badge of authenticity*, reflecting the ways our lives actually are lived out, with unpredictable events thrusting themselves into our lives, provoking interruptions and unplanned activity in our daily routines and planned schedules. We are forced to pursue the things of God amidst the hurly-burly of our mundane existence. The seeming randomness of Exodus to Numbers reflect life as it was, because in all probability they are based upon some sort of travel journal, the literary layout of which was dictated by real events, although probably Moses would have selected from his journal to give the most compact and coherent account possible. Nonetheless,

---

[316] Kyle, op. cit.

[317] Wenham, op. cit., p. 15.

these books reflect the disorder and spontaneity of ordinary human life, rather than the calm and orderliness of *imaginary* events, or the scholarly world of academia.

These answers are only available to us however, because we have already concluded from our previous findings, that the provenance of these books must indeed be Mosaic. Thus, without this foundational belief in a Mosaic provenance, there is indeed no satisfactory explanation available either for the duplications, or randomness of content, hence Higher Critics end up in the situation described earlier.

It should also be noted that the travel-journal basis I have proposed for the books of Exodus to Numbers means that these books would comply with a recognized literary form. Just as Deuteronomy conforms to the recognized literary form of a Treaty-Document, so the books Exodus to Numbers conform to what is known as a Migration Epic.[318] In Migration Epic literature, a special type of Travel Narrative, which includes also the types known as Voyage-And-Return, The Quest, and The Journey Home, we find an account of how the descendants of a Patriarch came to be in the land they occupy. The most well-known example from ancient literature of The Journey Home type of Travel Narrative, is Homer's *Odyssey*; the most well-known type of Migration Epic literature from antiquity, as Garrett says, is Virgil's *Aeneid*, in which the central character, Aeneas, escapes the wrack and ruin of Troy to found the nation of Rome. In Exodus to Numbers we find the account of the central character, Moses, escaping the collapse of Middle Kingdom Egypt, to found the nation of Israel. What the literary critic George Steiner says of *The Aeneid*, may also be said of Exodus to Numbers; "[It] is the epic of the refugee."[319] I am not trying to compare Exodus, Leviticus and Numbers with Virgil, nonetheless, the fact that these three books conform to an established literary genre, that is known to have existed in antiquity, is a highly relevant fact that Source Critics ought to take seriously, as it militates strongly against the notion that they are the consequence of the cutting and pasting together of numerous

---

[318] See Garrett, op. cit., pp. 176ff.

[319] Taken from the reviews on the rear cover of Virgil, *The Aeneid*, translated Fitzgerald, London, Penguin Books, 1990.

fragments. It speaks unambiguously of literary method, and literary unity, and, therefore, gives yet more credibility to the proposal of a Mosaic provenance for these books.[320]

Conclusion 18. The literary dependence of Deuteronomy on the book of Numbers, and its conceptual dependence on the books of Exodus and Leviticus, mean that the last three named must pre-date Deuteronomy, to which we have already attributed a Mosaic provenance. It follows, therefore, that Exodus, Leviticus and Numbers must also be awarded a Mosaic provenance.

Conclusion 19. The cyclic nature of the material found in Exodus, Leviticus and Numbers, at least partly attributable to the thirty eight years of the Wanderings, together with the need to repeat the same lessons until all the Israelites had absorbed Moses' teaching, and the need to interrupt the ordinary course of teaching to meet immediate needs induced by conflicts and other situations that arose from time to time, account fully for the way in which we encounter the mixture of different types of legislation, 'cheek-by-jowl' with personal and national history, as well as the repetitions met with in these books.

Conclusion 20. The answer given above is only available once it is realised that Exodus, Leviticus and Numbers are probably based upon some sort of travel journal of Moses, and that they reflect therefore, the conditions and events as they were encountered in the wilderness. As such they conform to the known literary classification of Migration Epic. To propose, as do Higher Critics, that they are pseudepigrapha, written centuries after the times that they purport to emanate from, means that there is no satisfactory answer available for the seeming random nature of the contents of the books, which now, ironically, appears as a badge of their authenticity.

---

[320] Garrett, op. cit., pp. 176ff.

Chapter Eight

The Book Of Genesis

Part A
Introduction

Having ascertained that the books of Exodus, Leviticus, Numbers and Deuteronomy must be attributed a Mosaic provenance, and that Graf's Clue, De Wette's Clue, and Astruc's Clue, are all meaningless, we must now confront what seems the most difficult task of all; Genesis. If Deuteronomy is the Foundation Treaty of Israel-as-a-nation, and the books of Exodus to Numbers are Migration Epic literature based upon Moses' travel journal, what do we say of Genesis, which purports to go back to "The Beginning," when "God created the heavens and the earth"?

The Non-Literary Problems Of Genesis

While the purpose of this dissertation is to examine Source Criticism, it is my belief that a key reason for the widespread acceptance of the tenets of Source Criticism by intelligent and informed seekers after truth, is that the non-literary problems of Genesis, entailed in the acceptance of it being a part of The Word Of God, that is, belief in Special Creation, the Fall of Man, the Universal Flood, the longevity of the antediluvians, and the Dispersal of the nations from Babel, seems to such people, no less than *incredible.*

The difficulties associated with current-day views of the age and size of the universe based upon such forensic evidence as Red-Shift calculations; Carbon 14 dating that seems to prove man's history to be far older than the Scriptures indicate; the Scriptures seeming to speak in terms of a flat-earth; the fossil-record that apparently proves evolution to be true; the story of every type of animal being crammed into a small boat in a flood that covered the entire world to a depth greater than the height of mount Everest; all these problems are very real. I know them to be so, as I speak from personal experience, having gone through the normal education system which implants in the developing mind, an entire and dogmatic philosophy that excludes all other world-views, which are labelled prejudicially as unscientific, superstitious, ignorance-based, primitive, and dangerous.

Because these are genuine questions, in spite of the fact that they fall outside the scope of this dissertation, I give some very brief remarks, (but nonetheless, helpful, I trust), on these matters in the second Supplement to this dissertation. The content of the Supplement will, I hope, show that genuine alternatives to the mass-programming of children and young adults by our education system in cosmic and biological evolutionary mythology, do exist, and have real scientific credibility. It should also be pointed out that advocates of these alternatives are frequently so successful in presenting their case, that orthodox evolutionists now habitually shy away from public debate with them!

In the meantime, we must commence our examination of the book of Genesis purely as a literary work. It is fair to say that in what follows I have employed speculation to a degree, but I believe it to be most reasonable speculation, based upon the known and documented literary practices of antiquity. This would place it in the sharpest contrast with much of the speculation of Higher Critics, who are unable to point to any such known practices for much of what they suggest.

Could Moses Have Gathered Information On The Matters Dealt With In Genesis?

The book of Genesis covers a huge span of human history, more than any other book in the Canon. Using the Scriptural narrative, the period covered is slightly less than 2,500 years in duration.[321] Therefore the

---

[321] Phelan, M. W. J., *The Dating Of The Exodus*, op. cit., pp. 90–95. See also any good Bible Chronology, for example; Panin, *Bible Chronology*, Vancouver, The Covenant People, undated, Evans, *Bible Chronology*, Bournemouth, published privately, undated,

first question to be asked is, Could the information that Moses might have gathered from such remote ages have any credibility?

Now this is where we have to take Genesis *on its own terms*. While this is so of all Scripture, it is particularly so with Genesis. What I mean by this, is that the problems may only be solved when we accept <u>all</u> of Genesis. Accepting only parts of Genesis, only increases the problems to such an extent, as to render them absolutely insoluble. Taking into account all we find in the book, *including the ages of the antediluvians*, opens the way to resolving the issues. I will explain.

The colossal life-spans of the antediluvians, and even of those who lived in the years immediately following the Deluge, eliminates a substantial part of the problem. From the chart found in Appendix IX, it will be seen that Shem, the son of Noah, was a contemporary of all of his descendants down to Jacob, the father of Joseph, the Vizier of Egypt, second only to Pharaoh in the days of the Middle-Kingdom.[322]

Joseph was the highest placed official in the land of Egypt, only in the throne was Pharaoh greater than Joseph (Genesis 41:40). This meant that whatever records Joseph had been able to acquire from his family, he would have been in a position to preserve safely so that, years later, when Moses was brought up in the Egyptian court, he too would have had access to them. This means that Moses could easily have acquired, the Israelites' histories going back to Abraham, in whose time we have already seen, the art of writing was very well established.

Now it is at this point that the longevity of the antediluvians comes in. As we have just noted, Shem was a *contemporary* of Terah, Abraham, Isaac, and Jacob, and of course had first-hand knowledge of the Flood, and also of the Division of Tongues at Babel, which means it is quite possible that Jacob, the father of Joseph, (who would have had very ready access to scribes and writing materials), could have received *eye witness accounts* of both the Flood and the destruction of Babel, which Moses would later have located in the Egyptian archives. But, as I show in the chart found in Appendix IX, Shem,

---

Gayer, *Old Testament Chronology*, London, Covenant Publishing Co., or Van Lennep, *The Measured Times Of The Bible*, London, Heath Cranton, 1928.

[322] For details, see my *The Dating Of The Exodus*, op. cit., and Appendix XI.

was also a contemporary of Methuselah, whose father, Enoch had been taken into the Lord's Presence without tasting death, and Methuselah was himself a contemporary, not just of Noah and Shem, but of all his ancestors back to and including _Adam_, and would have been able to pass on to Shem, the contemporary of Jacob, details of the making of Eve, the Fall of Man, the expulsion from the Garden of Eden, the murder of Abel by Cain, the development of agriculture, metal-working, the arts and sciences, and all of man's history from the birth of Cain to the taking of Enoch.

The knowledge of these events could easily have been transmitted from Methuselah to Shem, and from Shem to Abraham, in whose time they could have been committed to writing, but, I will present evidence shortly that indicates that these accounts were based on written records from the very start. It will be remembered that Ashurbanipal said he was able to read records that dated from _before_ the Flood, and these could easily have been either the same that Abraham may have been able to acquire from Shem, directly or indirectly, or copies that ultimately were dependant on the same records, although they may have become distorted during their descent. Thus from Adam to the records in Egypt available to Moses, very few links indeed are required; they need only be;

Adam to Methuselah,

Methuselah to Shem,

Shem to Jacob,

Jacob to Joseph.

Even if it is proposed that the line of descent would be;

Adam to Methuselah,

Methuselah to Shem,

Shem to Terah,

Terah to the Patriarchs and Joseph,

it remains a line of decent with remarkably few links, for we have evidence of writing dating back to the end of the life of Shem the contemporary of Methuselah, and the probability is that writing is older still. Thus, the Egyptian court, at the time of Moses could very easily have contained the material from which the book of Genesis was compiled. But is all this baseless speculation on my part, or is there real evidence to support this view?

The Structure Of Genesis

It is noticeable that the character of the text changes through the course of Genesis. In later parts of the book, Egyptian words occur commonly; but are absent in the early chapters which contain many Babylonian words, which, correspondingly, are absent later in the book. Thus the milieu seems to change from Babel to Egypt via an intermediate phase, which is absolutely consistent with the history unfolded in the narrative.[323] It is also noteworthy that the morphology of many of the words used in the text, display immense antiquity.[324]

The most significant and noticeable aspects of the structure of Genesis however, are the change in the narrative at 37:2, where the story of Joseph begins, and the occurrences of the phrase, "These are the generations of x." These phrases are usually referred to as *toledoths*, which is the transliteration into English of תולדות, the Hebrew word translated *generations*. It is not strictly accurate to speak in this way as תולדות is itself a plural word,[325] nonetheless, it is the normal practice, and the singular form is unused.[326]

We will deal with the Joseph narrative in the next chapter. We begin therefore, with an examination of the toledoths.

---

[323] See Wilson, R. D., *Is The Higher Criticism Scholarly?* London, Marshall Brothers, 1922, pp. 22ff., Rendle-Short, op. cit., pp. 161ff., and Wiseman, P. J., op. cit., pp. 58ff.

[324] Keil & Delitzsch, op. cit., Volume I, p. 23.

[325] See Davidson, Benjamin, *The Analytical Hebrew And Chaldee Lexicon*, Grand Rapids, Michigan, U.S.A., undated, in. loc.

[326] *The Hebrew Student's Manual*, op. cit., p. 23 of the section, *Genesis I–IV*.

Part B:
The Histories Found
In The Book Of Genesis

The Toledoths

The view of the Critics is that a toledoth *introduces* narrative that runs to the next toledoth. The Critic, S. R. Driver writes "The narrative of Genesis is cast into a framework, or scheme, marked by the recurring formula, *These are the generations* (lit. *Begettings*) *of...* This phrase is one which belongs properly to a genealogical system: it implies that the person to whose name it is prefixed is of sufficient importance to mark a break in the genealogical series, and that he and his descendants will form the subject of the section which follows, until another name is reached prominent enough to form the commencement of a new section." He adds that toledoths introduce genealogies.[327] His four main points are then;

1. The toledoths provide a framework for Genesis,

2. The word toledoth "belongs properly to a genealogical system",

3. Toledoths form the introductions to the different sections of the text, and,

4. The subject of a toledoth, and his descendants are the subject of what follows.

This view is tested in the chart on the following pages, which lists every genealogy and toledoth in the book of Genesis. The genealogies, which occur at 4:1–2, 4:16–22, 5:3–32, 10:2–32, 11:10b–26, 11:27b–29, 25:1–4, 25:13–18, 35:22–29, 36:2–8,

---

[327] Op. cit., p. ii, cf. Childs, op. cit., pp. 145–146.

36:10–43, & 46:8–27 are given in bold and are shaded; the toledoths which occur at 2:4–5, 5:1–2, 6:9, 10:1, 11:10a, 11:27b, 25:12, 25:19, 36:1, 36:9, & 37:2, are given in bold, and are also underlined.

Chart Representing The Text Of Genesis

1:1	6	17	3	7	21	11	18
2	7	18	4	8	22	12	19
3	8	19	5	9	23	13	20
4	9	20	6	10	24	14	21
5	10	21	7	11	8:1	15	22
6	11	22	8	12	2	16	23
7	12	23	9	13	3	17	24
8	13	24	10	14	4	18	25
9	14	4:1	11	15	5	19	26
10	15	2	12	16	6	20	27
11	16	3	13	17	7	21	28
12	17	4	14	18	8	22	29
13	18	5	15	19	9	23	30
14	19	6	16	20	10	24	31
15	20	7	17	21	11	25	32
16	21	8	18	22	12	26	11:1
17	22	9	19	7:1	13	27	2
18	23	10	20	2	14	28	3
19	24	11	21	3	15	29	4
20	25	12	22	4	16	10:1	5
21	3:1	13	23	5	17	2	6
22	2	14	24	6	18	3	7
23	3	15	25	7	19	4	8
24	4	16	26	8	20	5	9
25	5	17	27	9	21	6	10
26	6	18	28	10	22	7	11
27	7	19	29	11	9:1	8	12
28	8	20	30	12	2	9	13
29	9	21	31	13	3	10	14
30	10	22	32	14	4	11	15
31	11	23	6:1	15	5	12	16
2:1	12	24	2	16	6	13	17
2	13	25	3	17	7	14	18
3	14	26	4	18	8	15	19
4	15	5:1	5	19	9	16	20
5	16	2	6	20	10	17	21

217

22	10	8	11	24	31	15	21
23	11	9	12	25	32	16	22
24	12	10	13	26	33	17	23
25	13	11	14	27	34	18	24
26	14	12	15	28	35	19	23:1
27	15	13	16	29	36	20	2
28	16	14	17	30	37	21	3
29	17	15	18	31	38	22	4
30	18	16	19	32	20:1	23	5
31	14:1	17	20	33	2	24	6
32	2	18	21	19:1	3	25	7
12:1	3	19	22	2	4	26	8
2	4	20	23	3	5	27	9
3	5	21	24	4	6	28	10
4	6	16:1	25	5	7	29	11
5	7	2	26	6	8	30	12
6	8	3	27	7	9	31	13
7	9	4	18:1	8	10	32	14
8	10	5	2	9	11	33	15
9	11	6	3	10	12	34	16
10	12	7	4	11	13	22:1	17
11	13	8	5	12	14	2	18
12	14	9	6	13	15	3	19
13	15	10	7	14	16	4	20
14	16	11	8	15	17	5	24:1
15	17	12	9	16	18	6	2
16	18	13	10	17	21:1	7	3
17	19	14	11	18	2	8	4
18	20	15	12	19	3	9	5
19	21	16	13	20	4	10	6
20	22	17:1	14	21	5	11	7
13:1	23	2	15	22	6	12	8
2	24	3	16	23	7	13	9
3	15:1	4	17	24	8	14	10
4	2	5	18	25	9	15	11
5	3	6	19	26	10	16	12
6	4	7	20	27	11	17	13
7	5	8	21	28	12	18	14
8	6	9	22	29	13	19	15
9	7	10	23	30	14	20	16

17	57	30	27:1	41	13	18	15
18	58	31	2	42	14	19	16
19	59	32	3	43	15	20	17
20	60	33	4	44	16	21	18
21	61	34	5	45	17	22	19
22	62	26:1	6	46	18	23	20
23	63	2	7	28:1	19	24	21
24	64	3	8	2	20	25	22
25	65	4	9	3	21	26	23
26	66	5	10	4	22	27	24
27	67	6	11	5	23	28	25
28	25:1	7	12	6	24	29	26
29	2	8	13	7	25	30	27
30	3	9	14	8	26	31	28
31	4	10	15	9	27	32	29
32	5	11	16	10	28	33	30
33	6	12	17	11	29	34	31
34	7	13	18	12	30	35	32
35	8	14	19	13	31	36	33
36	9	15	20	14	32	37	34
37	10	16	21	15	33	38	35
38	11	17	22	16	34	39	36
39	12	18	23	17	35	40	37
40	13	19	24	18	30:1	41	38
41	14	20	25	19	2	42	39
42	15	21	26	20	3	43	40
43	16	22	27	21	4	31:1	41
44	17	23	28	22	5	2	42
45	18	24	29	29:1	6	3	43
46	19	25	30	2	7	4	44
47	20	26	31	3	8	5	45
48	21	27	32	4	9	6	46
49	22	28	33	5	10	7	47
50	23	29	34	6	11	8	48
51	24	30	35	7	12	9	49
52	25	31	36	8	13	10	50
53	26	32	37	9	14	11	51
54	27	33	38	10	15	12	52
55	28	34	39	11	16	13	53
56	29	35	40	12	17	14	54

55	8	28	8	5	9	19	13
32:1	9	29	9	6	10	20	14
2	10	30	10	7	11	21	15
3	11	31	11	8	12	22	16
4	12	35:1	12	9	13	23	17
5	13	2	13	10	14	40:1	18
6	14	3	14	11	15	2	19
7	15	4	15	12	16	3	20
8	16	5	16	13	17	4	21
9	17	6	17	14	18	5	22
10	18	7	18	15	19	6	23
11	19	8	19	16	20	7	24
12	20	9	20	17	21	8	25
13	34:1	10	21	18	22	9	26
14	2	11	22	19	23	10	27
15	3	12	23	20	24	11	28
16	4	13	24	21	25	12	29
17	5	14	25	22	26	13	30
18	6	15	26	23	27	14	31
19	7	16	27	24	28	15	32
20	8	17	28	25	29	16	33
21	9	18	29	26	30	17	34
22	10	19	30	27	39:1	18	35
23	11	20	31	28	2	19	36
24	12	21	32	29	3	20	37
25	13	22	33	30	4	21	38
26	14	23	34	31	5	22	39
27	15	24	35	32	6	23	40
28	16	25	36	33	7	41:1	41
29	17	26	37	34	8	2	42
30	18	27	38	35	9	3	43
31	19	28	39	36	10	4	44
32	20	29	40	38:1	11	5	45
33:1	21	36:1	41	2	12	6	46
2	22	2	42	3	13	7	47
3	23	3	43	4	14	8	48
4	24	4	37:1	5	15	9	49
5	25	5	2	6	16	10	50
6	26	6	3	7	17	11	51
7	27	7	4	8	18	12	52

53	33	32	45:1	38	3	9	24
54	34	33	2	46:1	4	10	25
55	35	34	3	2	5	11	26
56	36	44:1	4	3	6	12	27
57	37	2	5	4	7	13	28
42:1	38	3	6	5	8	14	29
2	43:1	4	7	6	9	15	30
3	2	5	8	7	10	16	31
4	3	6	9	8	11	17	32
5	4	7	10	9	12	18	33
6	5	8	11	10	13	19	50:1
7	6	9	12	11	14	20	2
8	7	10	13	12	15	21	3
9	8	11	14	13	16	22	4
10	9	12	15	14	17	49:1	5
11	10	13	16	15	18	2	6
12	11	14	17	16	19	3	7
13	12	15	18	17	20	4	8
14	13	16	19	18	21	5	9
15	14	17	20	19	22	6	10
16	15	18	21	20	23	7	11
17	16	19	22	21	24	8	12
18	17	20	23	22	25	9	13
19	18	21	24	23	26	10	14
20	19	22	25	24	27	11	15
21	20	23	26	25	28	12	16
22	21	24	27	26	29	13	17
23	22	25	28	27	30	14	18
24	23	26	29	28	31	15	19
25	24	27	30	29	48:1	16	20
26	25	28	31	30	2	17	21
27	26	29	32	31	3	18	22
28	27	30	33	32	4	19	23
29	28	31	34	33	5	20	24
30	29	32	35	34	6	21	25
31	30	33	36	47:1	7	22	26
32	31	34	37	2	8	23	

From this chart, it is immediately apparent that in spite of what Driver would suggest, the toledoths and the genealogies are not always related, as the first toledoth, and the final genealogy are both isolated.

The first cluster of toledoths and genealogies found from 5:1 to 11:29 may seem to support the view that toledoths are related to genealogies, and introduce them, but the toledoths of 2:4 and 6:9 are completely unattached, as are the genealogies of 4:1–2 and 4:16–22. The second cluster found in 25:1 to 25:19 seems to be the reverse of Driver's scheme, as here, although there is a gap at 25:5–11, the genealogies clearly precede the toledoths. The practice occurs again in the final cluster found from 35:22–37:2, where there is only a gap of one verse at 37:1. In this cluster, undoubtedly the genealogies precede the toledoths. Finally, as was said above, the genealogy of 46:8–27 is unattached to any toledoth.

There are altogether twelve toledoths in the Pentateuch, eleven of them occurring in the book of Genesis. The twelfth toledoth is to be found in Numbers 3:1, "These also are the toledoth of Aaron and Moses in the day that the Lord spake with Moses in Mount Sinai." This toledoth has an interesting connection with the very first toledoth of Genesis 2:4. Both contain the phrase, "in the day", a phrase found only in one other toledoth (Genesis 5:1). It should also be noted that this phrase "in the day" as used in Numbers 3:1 very obviously cannot relate to one particular day, as there were *very many* days indeed when the Lord spake with Moses in Mount Sinai, which means that the phrase is used idiomatically here, a fact recognized by the scholars Keil and Delitzsch who render it correctly as *at the time*, as does the orientalist Ferrar Fenton,[328] and, not surprisingly, the Jewish Publication Society's *New Translation Of The Holy Scriptures*.[329] Thus there would appear to be a real connection between the two toledoths of Genesis 2:4, and Numbers 3:1, which means that although the subject of this chapter is the book of Genesis, an examination of the toledoth of Numbers 3:1 is also called for. There are only two other toledoths in the Hebrew canon, that of Ruth 4:18, and I Chronicles 1:29. The toledoths found in the Pentateuch are named as the following table indicates;

---

[328] Op. cit., Volume I, op. cit., and *The Holy Bible In Modern English*, translated by Ferrar Fenton, London, A. & C. Black, 1938, in. loc.

[329] *Tanakh: A New Translation Of The Holy Scriptures,* Philadelphia, U.S.A., The Jewish Publication Society, 1985, in. loc.

Toledoths found in the Pentateuch	
The toledoth of the heavens and the earth.	Genesis 2:4
The toledoth of Adam.	Genesis 5:1
The toledoth of Noah.	Genesis 6:9
The toledoth of the sons of Noah.	Genesis 10:1
The toledoth of Shem.	Genesis 11:10
The toledoth of Terah.	Genesis 11:27
The toledoth of Ishmael.	Genesis 25:12
The toledoth of Isaac.	Genesis 25:19
The toledoth of Esau.	Genesis 36:1
The toledoth of Esau.	Genesis 36:9
The toledoth of Jacob.	Genesis 37:2
The toledoth of Aaron and Moses.	Numbers 3:1

Genesis 2:4, And Numbers 3:1

As we saw above, Genesis 2:4 is the very first toledoth, and is completely unattached to any genealogy. It is often the case that the first occurrence of a word or phrase in Scripture defines its true meaning, thus the fact that it is unattached to a genealogy is significant. Furthermore, contrary to the popular and modernist view that toledoths always *introduce* portions of narrative, this verse seems actually to *conclude* the first account of the creation, rather then introduce the second account of the creation. An obvious indicator of this is the fact that the heavens are mentioned only in the *first* account of the creation, yet this toledoth is said to be that "of the *heavens* and the earth." Clearly, in order to relate it to the heavens, it must be attached to the *first* account of the creation, and therefore, seems definitely to conclude the section of Scripture which contains this account.[330]

---

[330] It should be noted that chapter divisions of the Hebrew Canon were only introduced in 1330 C.E., thousands of years after Genesis was written. See Bullinger, *How To Enjoy The Bible*, op. cit., p. 34.

Snaith is clearly of the view that the toledoth of Genesis 2:4 belongs to the first account of the creation,[331] as is Moffatt, who, in his *New Translation*, actually removes this verse from its normal position, and makes it the initial verse of his translation, with 1:1 following![332] According to Simpson writing in *The Interpreter's Bible*, Gunkel was also of the view that 2:4 was originally the first verse of Scripture.[333] Even the *Revised Version* carries a marginal note at this point relating 2:4 to 1:1,[334] and it is clear from the construction of the paraphrases found in *Today's English Version* and *The New English Bible* that their compilers relate 2:4 to the first account of the creation as well.[335]

While I would certainly not agree that verse 2:4 should be placed before 1:1, nonetheless it does seem that 2:4 must be related to the first account of the creation.   P. J. Wiseman observes that in the case of the toledoth of Genesis 2:4, commentators generally have located it correctly, realising that the context shows that it can only be related to the *preceding* narrative, as what follows contains no mention of the heavens referred to in the toledoth.[336]

It would appear that in antiquity, it was very well known that the first toledoth belonged to the first account of the creation, as the current-day title for the first book of Moses, *Genesis*, derives via the Septuagint, from the toledoth of Genesis 2:4,[337] a fact most good commentaries on Genesis will confirm.

The Hebrew Traditional teaching referred to earlier, also connects Genesis 2:4 to the first account of the creation, stating that תלד, from whence comes toledoth, has a gematria value of 434, as ת = 400,

---

[331] Snaith, Norman H., *Notes On The Hebrew Text Of Genesis I–VIII*, London, The Epworth Press, 1947, p. 22.

[332] *A New Translation Of The Bible*, translated by Moffatt, James, London, Hodder & Stoughton, 1950, in. loc.

[333] See his commentary on Genesis in *The Interpreter's Bible*, Volume I, op. cit., in. loc. According to P. J. Wiseman, Schrader, Carpenter, and Battersby-Harford were also of this opinion. Wiseman, op. cit., p. 49.

[334] *The Holy Bible: Revised Version*, Oxford, Oxford University Press, 1928, in. loc.

[335] *Good News Bible: Today's English Version*, London, Collins/Fontana, 1976, in. loc, and *The New English Bible*, Oxford, Oxford University Press, 1970, in. loc.

[336] Wiseman, op. cit., p. 48.

[337] Swete, op. cit., pp. 214–215.

ל = 30, and ד = 4. Now it is a curious fact that the first account of the creation is completed in the Masoretic text in exactly 434 words. This fact, according to the tradition, provides a vital clue that the first toledoth must definitely be linked with the first account of the creation with which it is associated by the gematria value of toled.[338]

A similar situation is to be found with the final toledoth of the Pentateuch, Numbers 3:1. This is named the toledoth of Aaron and Moses, and according to the modernist view, must introduce the genealogy that follows. However, as has frequently been observed, there is no mention of any descendants of Moses in the following genealogy or narrative, which is a real obstacle to accepting the modernist view. Young mentions this difficulty in his *Concise Critical Comments,*[339] as does Matthew Poole in his commentary.[340] P. J. Wiseman also comments on this verse, making the point that it cannot be made to introduce the next section of text owing to the complete absence of a reference to any descendants of Moses, and therefore, like the toledoth at Genesis 2:4 must conclude the previous section of text.[341]

The Meaning Of Toledoth

Steinmueller,[342] Davies,[343] Davidson,[344] and Gesenius[345] all make the point, that while the word toledoth is clearly connected with procreation, and therefore suggestive of genealogies, it also means *histories*, the concept of *origins* connecting the two meanings. That this is a genuine way in which the word is used by Jews is seen clearly by the title of a Hebrew book I possess. Its Hebrew title is

---

[338] I have personally verified this word count. For details, see Weinreb, op. cit., pp. 77ff.

[339] Young, Robert, op. cit., p. 93.

[340] Poole, Matthew, op. cit., Volume I, in. loc.

[341] Wiseman, op. cit., pp. 49f.

[342] Steinmueller, John E., *Some Problems Of The Old Testament*, New York, Bruce Publishing, 1934, p. 41.

[343] Davies, Benjamin, *A Compendious And Complete Hebrew And Chaldee Lexicon*, London, Asher & Co., 1889, in. loc.

[344] Davidson, op. cit., in. loc.

[345] Gesenius, H. W. F., *Hebrew And Chaldee Lexicon To The Old Testament*, Grand Rapids, Michigan, U.S.A., Baker Book House, 1979, in. loc.

ספר תולדות ישרון,[346] The publishers of the book have transliterated this into our alphabet as *Toldoth Yeshurun*, but it is literally, *The Book Of The History Of Yeshurun, Yeshurun* is a cherished name for Israel.[347] So too, the blasphemous antichristian work that is highly derogatory of Christ is named the *Toldot Yeshu*, and actually means *The History Of Jesus,* and certainly does not mean *The Descendants Of Jesus,* or some such.[348] Thus toledoth is most definitely used to refer to a written account of a history of some kind. This means that Genesis 2:4 should not be translated as *These are the generations of the heavens and of the earth*, as the heavens and the earth do not reproduce themselves, but, *These are the <u>origins</u> of the heavens and of the earth*; similarly, Numbers 3:1 should read, *These are the <u>histories</u> of Aaron and Moses.* The Jewish Publication Society's translation cited above renders Genesis 2:4 as "Such is the *story* of heaven and earth when they were created," and by the paragraphing, makes it obvious that it acts as the conclusion of the first account of the creation.[349]

Conclusion 21. The distribution of genealogies and toledoths within the book of Genesis, and the Jewish use of the word toledoth show that Driver is wrong to connect toledoth so closely with genealogies.

So far then we have seen that the Jews use the word toledoth of written historical records, and that, at least in the case of Genesis 2:4

---

[346] Freidman, *Toldoth Yeshurun*, Brooklyn, New York, The Hebrew Publishing Company, undated.

[347] See Deuteronomy 33:5, & 26.

[348] See Riggans, W., *Yeshua Ben David: Why Do The Jewish People Reject Jesus As Their Messiah?* Crowborough, Sussex, Marc, 1995, pp. 127–128. I refer to this scandalous work only to demonstrate that *Toldoth* is used routinely by Jews of *histories* recorded in a book. There are in existence, old Hebrew manuscripts of The Gospel Of Matthew, which might well have been written originally in Hebrew. The opening words of the du Tillet MS contain the following, אלה תולדות ישו בן דוד. (*These are the histories (toledoth) of Jesus the son of David*). Again, it cannot be taken to mean it is an account of the *descendants* of Jesus! It is obviously the title of the Gospel. (See *An Old Hebrew Text Of St. Matthew's Gospel*, translated Schonfield, Edinburgh, T & T Clark, 1927, in. loc.) *The New Testament In Hebrew And English* (Edgware, The Society For Distributing The Holy Scriptures To The Jews, undated) offers a very similar Hebrew rendering, although the Hebrew version of the United Bible Societies, (Jerusalem, 1979) does not use the word תולדות at all.

[349] Op. cit., in. loc.

which is the initial occurrence of the word, it *concludes* a section of narrative, and has no special association with genealogies. These two thoughts will take us a long way, but first we must take notice of one other characteristic of the toledoths of the Pentateuch.

An Introduction, Or A Conclusion?

The first toledoth that is attached to a personal name is that of Adam in 5:1, yet, despite what Driver says above, Adam does not form the subject of the text which follows, although it is true that his descendants do. It is a fact however, that beyond this point all we learn about Adam is his age when he died, the narrative concerning the events of his life concludes in the preceding chapter! Wiseman draws our attention to a most interesting and relevant fact. He noted that after the phrase, "This is the book of the toledoth of Adam" nothing further is reported about Adam, apart from his age when he died. Similarly, after the phrase, "These are the toledoth of Isaac", we encounter, not a history of Isaac, but the stories associated with Jacob and Esau. Also, after the phrase, "These are the toledoth of Jacob" we read mostly of Joseph. These facts have been a conundrum to many commentators. It is conspicuously clear therefore that toledoths do not introduce the history of an individual as is often suggested.[350] I would add that the last example where the Joseph narrative follows the phrase *these are the toledoth of Jacob*, also shows that this toledoth does not introduce a passage which concerns even the descendants of Jacob, as the narrative focuses mainly on <u>one</u> of them; Joseph. The *preceding* narrative gives more information about Jacob's descendants *generally*!

Now it is true however that *genealogies* very often introduce the most ancient of records that have come down to us.[351] We see this situation very clearly from the books of I Chronicles and the Gospel of Matthew. But, if toledoths *conclude* sections of narrative, very often toledoths and genealogies would be brought into juxtaposition, but not because they are *directly* related as Driver says, for we have just seen that they are not; but because the end of one section will

---

[350] Wiseman, op. cit., pp. 46–47.

[351] Wiseman, op. cit., p. 50.

frequently be marked by a toledoth, and the start of a new section, by a genealogy.

The Literary Practices Of Antiquity

It is important when we consider the content of truly ancient records, to pause to remember the practices of antiquity, and how they differed from what we accept as normal. Commenting on these archaic literary methods, P. J. Wiseman makes the point that in ancient Hebrew, and in ancient Semitic languages generally, one reads *from right to left*, and from what we would regard as the *back* of the book, towards what we would consider to be the *beginning*. Everything is back-to-front. This is reasonably well-known, but what is less well known, is that it was the *end* of a text that contained the vital information concerning the date of composition, the nature of the document, and the name of the owner or scribe. In effect, the title-page was the last part of the text![352] This explains of course why the writers of the Septuagint took the title for the first book of Moses from the concluding words of the first section of the book. They knew where to find the title-page in ancient documents. This ancient method is a practice the modern-day West has returned to in television and cinema production, where the list of credits comes at the very end of the work.[353]

Anciently, this information was recorded in what is known as a colophon.[354] It is Wiseman's contention that the toledoths of Genesis are the colophons of the original source material of the book. Thus when we read in Genesis 5:1, "This is the book of the histories of Adam, in the day that God created man, in the likeness of God made He him, male and female created he them, and called their name Adam, in the day when they were created." and at 2:4, "These are the histories of the heavens and the earth when they were created, in the day that the Lord God made the earth and heavens," we are reading the

---

[352] Ibid., p. 63.

[353] A survival of this practice might well be found in many a preface, where it is customary for the author to give his or her name or initials, and the date and place of writing, at the *end* of the preface.

[354] For independent confirmation of the presence and function of the colophon in cuneiform tablets, see Parrot André, *The Flood And Noah's Ark*, translated Hudson, London, SCM Press, 1955, pp. 32ff.

colophons at the conclusion of the series of clay tablets these documents would originally have been recorded on, such as have since been unearthed as we saw above. Steinmueller makes the point that it is from the toledoths we learn the object of the narrative to which they pertain,[355] which encourages the belief that Wiseman is correct.

The endings of ancient records are in fact, as with modern-day film production, often far more elaborate than their introductions, which generally are extremely brief indeed. We find this with the first account of the creation. We plunge straight into the action at Genesis 1:1 with, "In the beginning God created the heavens and the earth." But the ending is far more elaborate, occupying the first four verses of chapter two. For Wiseman, the conformity of the records presented to us in the Pentateuch with the practices found in the most ancient literary remains ever discovered, provides particularly compelling evidence for the authenticity of the Pentateuchal narrative, and for its freedom from corruption. The method of giving only the briefest of prefaces, or none at all, coupled with noticeably formal, and at times elaborate conclusions, are striking testimony of the immense antiquity of the Pentateuchal texts. Wiseman cites as examples, the concluding words of Leviticus, "These are the commandments, which the Lord commanded Moses for the children of Israel in mount Sinai", and the conclusion of Numbers, "These are the commandments and the judgments, which the Lord commanded by the hand of Moses unto the children of Israel in the plains of Moab by Jordan near Jericho". Wiseman, by way of illustration, gives the concluding words of the ancient law code of Hammurabi, which, significantly, is far more lengthy than the preface, showing again how the Pentateuchal texts conform to the literary practices of antiquity. The inscription ends with the following words, "The righteous laws which Hammurabi the wise king established... my weighty words I have written upon my monument." Wiseman, having shown this conformity of the Pentateuch, particularly Genesis with the known literary practices of the remotest antiquity, observes that the overwhelming majority of commentators, although realising that the toledoths of Genesis are an important key to unlocking the book, have

---

[355] Op. cit., p. 41.

used this key "upside down", to use his own words, because they have failed to understand that toledoths conclude passages of Scripture, and, instead, have assumed that they introduce them. Thus, for such commentators, the problems of Genesis remain unresolved, even though, as we shall see, the key lies ready to hand. Wiseman quotes from Professor Skinner who wrote the following shortly before he passed away in 1929, "The problem of the *toledoth* headings has been keenly discussed in recent writings, and is still unsettled (Genesis p. lxvi)."[356] Skinner's statement was made over seventy years ago, but is still true in the majority of cases. Usually Wiseman is denied the credit for unravelling the sources of Genesis, because he thereby undermined modern Source Criticism. But as we shall see, the evidence for Wiseman's views is very clear.

Adam The Compiler Of The History Of The Line Of Cain

As we saw above, after the words "The Book Of The Histories Of Adam", we read no more about Adam at all. All we know about his life precedes these words, but now let us examine the narrative that leads up to this phrase. It concerns the line of Cain, Adam's First-Born son (Genesis 4:1). However, the account of this line ends abruptly with Jabal, Jubal, Tubal-Cain, and Naamah in the eighth generation. Why does it not go right up to the Flood, as the line of Seth does in Genesis 5? The reason is that Adam died in 930 A.M. (Anno Mundi or Year of the World) shortly before Enoch was 'taken', and early in the life of Methuselah. Thus, in all probability, the account of the line of Cain ends where it does, because it was the literary work of Adam himself, and he had died before the next generation of the line of Cain appeared.

Using Wiseman's theory, we see why, by contrast, we have a complete account of the line of Seth down to the Flood. It was compiled by Noah, who was born late enough, and lived long enough to give its *entire* history. The history of this line ends with the words, "These are the Histories of Noah (Genesis 6:9)." Noah lived to see the end of the line of Cain at the Flood, and therefore could also record the entire history and survival through the Flood of the line of Seth:

---

[356] Wiseman, op. cit., p. 51.

Adam, recording the history of his First-Born son Cain, died before the history of that line could be completed. This solves a riddle that has puzzled commentators for years. Why should the account of the line of Cain be incomplete, while the account of the line of Seth is given in full? The answer lies in the lifespans of the different compilers of these histories, which Scripture itself points out to us very clearly, but which few, if any, realised before P. J. Wiseman. Perhaps we begin to see that Scripture itself, not Higher Criticism, gives us the identity of the sources behind the text of the Pentateuch.

A Review Of The Toledoths Of The Pentateuch

As a result of his studies, Wiseman was able to claim that in none of the histories that precede the toledoths of Genesis, is there to be found any incident which could not have been written by the person or persons named in the toledoths. In every case, the subject or subjects of the toledoth would either have been fully acquainted with the facts of the matters narrated, or was in a position to acquire the necessary information from a reliable source. He then adds, "*It is most significant that the history recorded in the [toledoths] ceases in all instances before the death of the person named* [in the toledoth], yet in most cases it is continued almost up to the date of death, or the date on which it is stated the tablets were written." [Emphasis his, the words in square brackets are my own].[357] This is a particularly significant, and easily verifiable piece of evidence in favour of Wiseman's views.

The History Compiled By Noah

We now need to test this claim. After the Histories of Adam, the next we encounter is that of Noah which concludes with the toledoth of Genesis 6:9. This concludes the history of the line of Seth, and gives an account of the state of the earth prior to the Flood. As Noah survived the Flood, he could easily have written this history, the earlier parts of his history he could have acquired very readily from his grandfather, Methuselah, who, as we have already seen, was for a few decades, a contemporary of Adam.

---

[357] Wiseman, op. cit., pp. 53–54.

The History Compiled By The Sons Of Noah

Next we find the Histories of the sons of Noah ending with the toledoth of 10:1. This history gives an account of the Flood, the events immediately afterwards, and relates the death of Noah, who was survived at least by Shem, and probably by all three of his sons. Thus, those named in the toledoth, the sons of Noah, could easily have written the history it contains.

The History Compiled By Shem

We then move on to the histories of Shem, which ends with the toledoth of Genesis 11:10. The history continues to the fifth generation from Shem, namely the sons of Joktan (10:26–29), and we have seen already that Shem lived until the time of Jacob, the eleventh generation from Shem, meaning that there is no difficulty at all in believing that Shem could have compiled this history.

The History Compiled By Terah

Next comes the histories of Terah, which conclude with the toledoth of Genesis 11:27. This history terminates with the birth of Terah's sons, Abram, Nahor and Haran, and therefore is quite consistent with the proposal that it was written by Terah. We should also note that the chart in Appendix IX shows that Terah was alive before the death of Noah, which removes any difficulty associated with his compilation of the beginnings of his history.

The History Compiled By Ishmael And Isaac

We then encounter the histories of Ishmael and Isaac, which end with what might be called a double toledoth of Genesis 25:12 (Ishmael) and 25:19 (Isaac). This history ends with the death and burial of Abraham, meaning it is quite credible that the eldest son Ishmael could have compiled the basic framework of the history without any difficulty, as is indicated by the reference to the *toledoth of Ishmael* in Genesis 25:12. Abraham was 86 when Ishmael was born (Genesis 16:16), and lived to be 175 (Genesis 25:7). This means Ishmael was 89 when Abraham died. As Ishmael lived to be 137 (Genesis 25:17), he lived for 48 years after Abraham's death. I suggest that Isaac used the basis of Ishmael's histories, but inserted portions which Ishmael could not have witnessed himself, after he was expelled from Abraham's household (Genesis 21:9–21), and then added a 'post-script' to this history, which included a brief notice of the death of Ishmael, followed by his own toledoth or colophon in Genesis 25:19. The retention of Ishmael's toledoth would be the equivalent of a modern day citation of a source. Again there is no difficulty attached to this 'post-script', as Isaac outlived Ishmael by 57 years, as Ishmael died aged 137 (Genesis 25:17), while Isaac, 14 years younger than Ishmael (Genesis 16:16 cf. 21:5), lived to be 180 (Genesis 35:28). (180 – 137 = 43 and 43 + 14 = 57.)

The History Compiled By Esau And Jacob

The histories of the half brothers, Ishmael and Isaac, lead into the histories of the twin brothers, Esau and Jacob, and end with the toledoth of Genesis 37:2. P. J. Wiseman makes a very interesting point concerning this history. In his *New Discoveries In Babylonia About Genesis*, he writes, "Jacob is the central figure in the [histories preceding the toledoth of Jacob], and the latest chronological statement in them is that of the death of Isaac. Immediately before the ending formula, 'These are the origins of Jacob,' we read, 'and Jacob dwelt in the land of his father's sojourning, in the land of Canaan.' This sentence has seemed so isolated, that it has been regarded by many as to have little relation to the context, yet… it is evidence of the date, when and where the tablets were written. Within a few years Jacob had moved down to Egypt, but this sentence indicates where he was living when he closed his record, for although he tells of the death of Isaac, he says nothing whatever of the sale of Joseph into slavery, which occurred eleven years before Isaac's death, neither does he tell of Joseph's interpretation of the butler's dream, or of any other event in Egypt. Until Jacob went down to Egypt (ten years after he had buried his father), thus leaving 'the land of his sojourning,' he could not know anything whatever about these things. Thus the record of Jacob closes precisely at the period indicated in the sentence in chapter xxxvii. I. He had gone back to the South Country, Hebron (where his father lived), only ten years before Isaac had died, and he records his death, and within ten years of this latter event, Jacob was himself living in Egypt. So this hitherto obscure verse of chapter xxxvii clearly indicates not only that Jacob wrote the tablets, but when and where they were written."[358]

It would seem that Esau had himself added a postscript to these histories after revising them, as the phrase *the toledoth of Esau* occurs twice within the span of nine verses (Genesis 36:1 & 9). Jacob could have acquired his own copy of these histories after he met with Esau when together they buried their father Isaac (Genesis 35:29). The reconciliation of Esau and Jacob found in Genesis 32:3–33:15 does seem to have been permanent. He then could have added his own postscript and colophon, which we now know as the toledoth of Genesis 37:2. It is interesting to note from this that it is possible that Pfeiffer was correct in detecting what he called a Southern Source to the book of Genesis, which he designated S, for here, as Harrison, taking Wiseman's lead observes, we do actually find such Southern or Edomite material.[359]

The History Compiled By Aaron And Moses

It is remarkable how many of these histories are the work of brothers. There is firstly *the histories of the sons of Noah*, the three brothers, Shem, Ham and Japheth, which follows the history compiled by their *father*, and precedes that given by only one of the brothers, Shem. Then there are *the histories of Ishmael and Isaac*, and *Esau and Jacob*, and finally that of the two brothers *Aaron and Moses*. In each of the other cases, it seems as if the oldest brother, Ishmael, and Esau, has begun the work, but that it has later been supplemented by the youngest of the brothers, Isaac, and Jacob. So too we find that the toledoth of the youngest brother Shem, follows that compiled by the sons of Noah, which obviously included work by the older brothers.

So now we find that from Genesis 37:2 to Numbers 3:1, we have *the histories of Aaron and Moses*, with Aaron the older brother named first, followed by the rest of the book of Numbers and Deuteronomy, seemingly compiled only by Moses, as we have already seen. Thus there seems to be great consistency in the method of compilation.

---

[358] Ibid., pp. 56–57.

[359] Harrison, op. cit., p. 550.

We also now see the answer to the riddle of Numbers 3:1 referred to earlier. It is simply not possible to relate Numbers 3:1 to the narrative that follows as so many commentators have found. But we see now how clearly it relates to the preceding histories. Now this is also where the differences between Genesis chapters 1–36, and 37–50 become so crucial. As I suggested earlier, I believe that the records concerning the life of Joseph and how it relates to the descendants of Abraham Isaac and Jacob, which is the exclusive theme of the last fourteen chapters of Genesis could easily have been deposited in the Egyptian Royal Archives by Joseph himself, or possibly Manasseh, his eldest son, following the precedents noted above. Years later, I propose, this history of Joseph, and probably all the other earlier histories we have looked at as well, were retrieved by Aaron and Moses, enabling them to finish what we now know as the book of Genesis by adding Joseph's history to the earlier histories already dealt with. It is this section of Genesis, as we have already noted, that is famous for its inclusion of Egyptian words, indicating an Egyptian provenance. The rest of Genesis, particularly the earliest parts, are equally noticeable for their employment of Babylonian words. Given that Abraham, Isaac, and Jacob descended from a Babylonian family, this is hardly surprising, and, affords great authenticity.

Are Wiseman's Views Viable

Throughout this dissertation I have cited Doctor Duane Garrett, whose work I esteem greatly. It must be said however, that he would disagree with what I have said above, as he is unconvinced by the case made by P. J. Wiseman. Criticism from someone of the standing of Doctor Garrett, may not be ignored. It must be both acknowledged, and answered, which I now intend to do. Doctor Garrett's main concern centres on the toledoths of Ishmael, and Esau. He finds it difficult to accept that *they,* rather than Isaac and Jacob would have compiled the histories of Abraham, and Isaac respectively.[360] I believe there is a credible explanation for this however.

Throughout the narrative concerning the Patriarchs, it is very obvious that the rights, privileges, and responsibilities of the first-born are

---

[360] Garrett, op. cit., pp. 91–92.

very much to the fore. This is particularly evident in the histories of the two men we are dealing with, Ishmael and Esau, both of whom were passed over in favour of younger brothers, but it is prominent also in the cases of Leah and Rachel, Manasseh and Ephraim, Reuben, Judah and Joseph. From what we have seen, I suggest that it was the normal practice for the first-born son to take responsibility for the preservation of the family records. For me the real difficulty therefore, is not how to account for the eldest sons' names being attached to these histories, to me that is exactly what ought to be *expected* with any ancient family history; instead the question is how we account for the *younger* sons, Isaac and Jacob acquiring their own copies of these histories.

We must take notice of the fact that Abraham had a real fondness for Ishmael. In Genesis 17:18 he says to the Lord, "O that Ishmael might live before thee!" The Lord heard Abraham's plea, and promised blessings for Ishmael as well as Isaac, even though Isaac was the Child of Promise. We see even that an amphictyony of twelve nations would also spring from Ishmael. (vv 20–22). Even after the expulsion of Ishmael, we read in Genesis 21:20 that God was *with* him. From the fact that Ishmael and Isaac together buried their father Abraham, it seems that ultimately they managed to get on together (Genesis 25:9), and this I believe would have allowed the acquiring of a copy of the family records by Isaac from Ishmael, which he would then have been in a position to supplement as we saw above.

A similar situation existed, I propose, in the case of Esau and Jacob. We know that Esau was particularly aggrieved by Jacob's usurping his position of first-born (Genesis 27:36–41), and it is easy to imagine therefore that he would give every emphasis possible to his position as elder son, and the production of a family history would further this aim. We saw above that the happy reconciliation of the brothers seems to have been permanent, again permitting the acquisition of a copy of the records by the younger son, who then was able to supplement them.

This seems also to be the case with Shem, whose history follows that of all three brothers, and Moses, whose individual work follows on from the work compiled with his elder brother Aaron. Therefore what I have proposed seems to be in line with the general practice.

Doctor Garrett protests that an account of the Ishmaelite clans follows the toledoth of Ishmael in Genesis 25:12,[361] but this I propose was added as a supplement by Isaac in deference to the major work undertaken by Ishmael, after he had acquired a copy of the records, inserted the details of Abraham's life following the expulsion of Ishmael, and then attached his own colophon a few verses later in 25:19.

It should also be pointed out that no less a man that Professor R .K. Harrison, author of one of the best known Old Testament Introductions for theological students was a stalwart defender of P. J. Wiseman's views, and has done much to revive them. A substantial and very interesting defence of Wiseman's views is included in this Introduction which I warmly recommend.[362] There is however another consideration.

The Hebrew Traditional Understanding Of The Toledoths

We have seen on several occasions already how many features of the Scriptures have been noticed by the Jews for centuries before knowledge of them reached gentile believers in God's Word. It would seem that for a very long time, the Jews have known that the toledoths mark the end of sections of narrative rather than their beginnings, a fact, which I am sure P. J. Wiseman was unaware of. I can see no evidence that Wiseman ever knew this, and feel certain he would have capitalised on it, had he known. Similarly, the Jewish material which reports that the toledoths mark the conclusion of narrative material, does not use the evidence offered by Wiseman. It seems likely therefore that this Jewish belief is quite independent of

---

[361] Ibid.

[362] Harrison, op. cit., pp. 543–551. D. J. Wiseman of the British Museum, and the General Editor of the Tyndale Old Testament commentaries was also a very firm supporter of this view. Some might attribute this to family loyalty, as he is the son of P. J. Wiseman, but having studied oriental languages at Oxford and London; been present on many archæological expeditions to Iraq; undertaken the rôle of editor of the journal of the British School Of Archæology In Iraq; written many specialist books and articles; and having occupied the position of Assistant Keeper in the Department of Western Asiatic Antiquities at the British Museum, it is difficult to believe that his views were not founded on objective evidence.

Wiseman, and the fact that it endorses all he says, seems therefore to constitute very substantial evidence for Wiseman's views.

In his *Roots Of The Bible*, the tradent Friedrich Weinreb states that there are two types of toledoth. These two types are clearly distinguishable by their Hebrew morphology. Four of the toledoths in the book of Genesis are preceded by the word, אלה, translated, *these are*; six are preceded by ואלה, which has the prefix ו added. This is the Hebrew conjunction usually translated by the English word *and*. The Hebrew word ואלה is translated, *and these are*. This difference may seem trifling, but not for the Traditionalists, or Tradents. The toledoths preceded by אלה relate to the toledoth of Genesis 5:1, and together with it, compile the 26 generations from Adam to Moses which spell out the Sacred Name, as we saw earlier. Thus, all these toledoths look *backwards* to that of Genesis 5:1.

The toledoths preceded by ואלה however are distinct from these, as is evidenced by the Hebrew conjunction ו. The meaning of this letter which is called *waw*, is a *nail* or *hook*.[363] As a hook couples things together, so does a conjunction of course. Waw has the numeric value of 6, and the traditionalists make much of the fact that there are exactly six toledoths in the book of Genesis which are preceded by ואלה. These are the toledoths of 10:1, 11:27, 25:12, 25:19, 36:1 & 36:9. These are the toledoths of the sons of Noah, Terah, Ishmael and Isaac, and the two toledoths of Esau. Now according to the tradition, although the other toledoths look backward to that of Genesis 5:1, the presence of the waw, the hook, or conjunction actually *connects* them to the narrative immediately preceding the toledoth, exactly as P. J. Wiseman found, albeit on different grounds altogether of course. Weinreb writes that these toledoths are, "directly connected with a preceding story."[364] It is interesting to note that the toledoths Doctor Garrett cites as demonstrating the invalidity of Wiseman's views, are all attached to the Hebrew word ואלה which, according to the Tradition, gives *special emphasis* to the connection of the toledoth to the narrative that immediately precedes it!

---

[363] See Steele-Smith, W. E. *Wonders Of The Hebrew Alphabet*, Sydney, Australia, The Central Press, undated, pp. 33 & 54.

[364] Weinreb, op. cit., p. 78.

That the Tradition is so emphatic about this link, which has nothing to do with Wiseman's views, is, for me, a very strong indicator that Wiseman is correct. There is even more evidence that this is so however.

The Characteristics Of Ancient Literature

As we saw earlier, the usual material employed in the near east for the production of written records during the Patriarchal, and Pre-Patriarchal Periods of Genesis was clay in tablet form. Because of the weight and brittle nature of baked clay, such tablets were usually quite small, and therefore could not accommodate a lengthy text. Where the text could not be made sufficiently brief, so as to be contained on one tablet, a series of tablets would be produced. Naturally, a problem then arose concerning the preservation of the correct sequence of a series of tablets that contained a single text. To overcome this difficulty, definite procedures were introduced, by which the opening words of a tablet became its title, and were written at the end of every succeeding tablet together with a number, which indicated that tablet's location in the series, much like a page number. In addition to this, the first few words of a tablet in a series, would also be written at the end of the preceding tablet, linking the tablets together. These repetitions are known as a *catch-lines*.

It is truly remarkable that these techniques are discernible *today*, in the very text of the Pentateuch itself! Uniquely amongst the books of Scripture, the Hebrew titles for each of the books of the Pentateuch follow this most ancient method; they are all named from the opening words of the books themselves. Whereas we know the books as Genesis, Exodus, Leviticus, Numbers and Deuteronomy, their Hebrew titles translated into English are, *In The Beginning, And These Are The Names, And He Called, In The Wilderness*, and *These Are The Words*.[365] The fact that the writers of the Septuagint took their title of the first book of Moses from Genesis 2:4, shows that by their day, this ancient practice had died out. However, printed versions of the Hebrew text seem to retain the *catch-lines* referred to above.

---

[365] תורה נביחים וכתובים edited, Snaith, London, The British And Foreign Bible Society, in. loc.

At the bottom of each page, will be found, usually unpointed, the first word of the *following* page. This seems to be a remarkably long-lived carry-over from antiquity, when such practices were essential to the preservation of the text. But there is even more! I will let Commodore Wiseman explain in his own words. He writes, "Evidence of these literary aids may be observed in the following significant repetition of words and phrases connected with the beginning or ending of each of the series of tablets now incorporated in the Book of Genesis.

Chap.	Ver.	
i.	1.	"God created the heavens and the earth."
ii.	4.	"Lord God made the heavens and the earth."
ii.	4.	"When they were created."
v.	2.	"When they were created."
vi.	10.	"Shem, Ham and Japheth."
x.	1.	"Shem, Ham and Japheth."
x.	1.	"After the Flood."
xi.	10.	"After the Flood."
xi.	26.	"Abram, Nahor and Haran."
xi.	27.	"Abram, Nahor and Haran."
xxv.	12.	"Abraham's son."
xxv.	19.	"Abraham's son."
xxxvi.	1.	"Who is Edom."
xxxvi.	8.	"Who is Edom."
xxxvi.	9.	"father of the Edomites" (lit: Father Edom).
xxxvi.	43.	"father of the Edomites" (lit: Father Edom).

The very significant repetitions of these phrases exactly where the tablets begin and end, will best be appreciated by those scholars acquainted with ancient methods of writing in Babylonia, for similar arrangements were then in use to link tablets together. I submit that the repetition of these words and phrases precisely in those verses attached to the colophon, 'These are the origins of...' cannot possibly be a mere coincidence, for in most instances they are not used elsewhere, in others rarely used. They have remained buried in the text of Scripture, their significance apparently unnoticed."[366]

This, is truly remarkable! Wiseman has succeeded in turning the tables on the Source Critics in a most spectacular manner. Who would have anticipated that the repetitions, of which Critics make so much, and parade so triumphantly before believers as their best evidence for Genesis being nothing more than a cut and paste patchwork of different documents, turn out to be the clearest evidence imaginable for the *integrity* of the text, and its enormous *antiquity*, validating its claims of originating from the beginning of human history itself? To God be the glory!

Conclusion 22. The evidence derived from known literary practices of antiquity, and from the structure of the book of Genesis show that Driver is wrong in stating that toledoths introduce new sections of narrative; on the contrary, they conclude them.

The Dating Of The Original Sources

Throughout the books of the Kings we find events are dated by the numbers of years a king had reigned when the event in question occurred. For instance in II Kings 15:1 we read, "In the twenty and seventh year of Jeroboam king of Israel began Azariah son of Amaziah king of Judah to reign." This system is referred to by historians as regnal dating, but it was not in use during the Pre-Patriarchal Period. Instead, events were dated in a more elementary manner. P. J. Wiseman gives some examples; "The year in which the throne Nabu was made," "Year Sumulel the king built the wall of Sippar," "Year of the canal Tutu-hengal" (presumably the year the canal was cut), "Year Samsu-iluna made a throne of gold," "Year in which canal Hammurabi was dug."[367]

Wiseman proposes that we find this type of dating in the book of Genesis in the colophonic passages. He writes, "The end of the first tablet (ch. ii 4) reads, '…in the day that the Lord God made the earth and the heavens.' At the end of the second tablet (ch. V. 1) we read:

---

[366] Wiseman, op. cit., pp. 63–64.

[367] Ibid., p. 65.

241

'This is the book of the origins of Adam *in the day that God created man.*' Later tablets are dated by indicating the dwelling place of the writer at the time that the colophon was written and these dates are immediately connected with the ending phrase, 'these are the generations of...' Instances of this are:

Chap.	Ver.	
xxv.	11.	"And Isaac dwelt by Beer-lahai-roi."
xxxvi.	8.	"And Esau dwelt in Mount Seir."
xxxvii.	1.	"And Jacob dwelt in the land wherein his father sojourned, in the land of Canaan" (R.V.).

This primitive method of dating is in agreement with the then current literary usage of that early age and also with the rest of the text."[368]

Further Evidence Of Antiquity

In Genesis 10:19, we find a reference to Sodom and Gomorrah that is so striking because it is so casual. It reads, "The border of the Canaanites was from Sidon, as thou comest to Gerar, unto Gaza; as thou goest unto Sodom and Gomorrah, and Admah, and Zeboim, even unto Lasha." Sodom and Gomorrah are again mentioned of course, in 14:2, but this time they are central to the narrative. These two instances are evidence that these portions of the text derive from a time before the overwhelming of Sodom and Gomorrah through Divinely contrived convulsions in the natural order. There is more evidence of the antiquity of the narrative to be found in other place names used in Genesis.

Wiseman noticed that frequently these place-names found in the book of Genesis were of such high antiquity, even in the lifetime of Moses, that he had to add to them explanatory details, so that the Israelites who were to enter the Land of Promise under Joshua would be able to locate them. Wiseman gives several examples from Genesis 14, written originally four hundred years before the time of Moses, during the days of Abraham. Clearly the place-names given in this chapter, were those that were current in Abraham's day. Between then and the

---

[368] Ibid., pp. 65–66.

time of Moses however, many of these names had changed, and Moses, acting as an editor, inserted his own explanatory comments, resulting in readings such as;

Genesis 14:2, 7 8,   "Bela (*which is Zoar*)."

Genesis 14:3,   "Vale of Siddim (*which is the Salt Sea*)."

Genesis 14:7,   "En-mishpat (*which is Kadesh*)."

Genesis 14:15,   "Hobah (*which is on the left hand of Damascus*)."

Genesis 14:17,   "Valley of Shaveh (*which is the King's Dale*)."

Wiseman points out that these ancient place-names are used nowhere else in the Bible. I would add, that this is in spite of the fact that the localities themselves are referred to very often in later passages of Scripture, but not by these names as Wiseman says, which gives a real emphasis to their enormous antiquity.

These are not the only examples that Wiseman discovered. He drew attention also to the following texts;

Genesis 16:41,   "Beer-lahai-roi; *behold, it is between Kadesh and Bered*."

Genesis 35:19,   "Ephrath, *which is Bethlehem*."

Genesis 23:2,   "Sarah died in Kirjath-arba; *the same is Hebron in the land of Canaan*."

Genesis 23:19,   "Machpelah before Mamre: *the same is Hebron in the land of Canaan*."

Wiseman shows how with these last two examples, not only was the name by which this location was known in the time of Moses given, but Moses even felt obliged to add that Hebron was in Canaan. As Wiseman notes, this intriguing detail shows that the comments were added before the Israelites had settled in the land under Joshua, as Hebron was granted to Caleb, the contemporary of Joshua (Judges 1:20). This means we may be sure that the first generation of Israelites to enter the Land would certainly have known where Hebron was. Moreover, Hebron was one of the Cities of Refuge (Joshua 20:7), meaning its location would continue to have been known of by ordinary Israelites throughout the Period of the Judges. Further, David was king in Hebron for seven and a half years (II Samuel 5:3–5), raising the status of Hebron to such a level, that from the days of the United Monarchy onwards, it became one of the most important cities of ancient Israel. It is inconceivable therefore, that there would have been any need at all to tell the Israelites that Hebron was in the land of Canaan, unless those Israelites were of the generation that were about to leave the Wilderness and conquer the Land under Joshua. In other words, these comments only make sense by accepting the Mosaic authorship of Genesis! Wiseman adds that the terms "South country" and "East country" found in Genesis 20:1 and 24:62 respectively, also speak eloquently of a very early date of composition, as such designations never recur, owing to the later establishment of recognized place names for these areas.[369]

The Dating Of The Oldest Of The Tablets

We see from all of this then how compelling is the evidence that Moses, when he compiled the Book of Genesis, was working with texts which were particularly ancient even in his day. But how old might the oldest of them have been?

We read in The Histories of Adam, that all manner of arts and sciences developed in his own life-time. These include animal husbandry and agriculture (4:2, 20), the construction of buildings, and the establishment of civil administration and government (4:17), tent making (4:20), the manufacture of musical instruments, and the disciplines concerning their use (4:21), as well as mining, metallurgy, and metal-working (4:22). With the stress given to the clothing of man in Genesis 3:7–11, 21, it is safe to assume that the art of garment production was also practiced in those days.

In addition to this, Adam himself had ability in biology as he had classified the fauna of the earth in Genesis 2:20, a work not encountered again in Scripture until we meet with the natural history work of Solomon (I Kings 4:33).

Furthermore, we know from the account of the building of the ark, that the basic skills of carpentry were very well advanced by the time of Noah, which meant that they must have begun much earlier than him. It is plain also that the metal tools required for cutting and working wood were also readily available, and that the methods of extracting

---

[369] Ibid., pp. 60–61.

and applying pitch for waterproofing were well known (6:14). It is also clear from the references to cubits in Genesis 6:16–17 that a recognized system of metrology, or measurement was also established, enabling the manufacture of artefacts to previously agreed designs and specifications (6:15). Considering the colossal size of the ark, at least basic arithmetic must be presumed to have been in existence too, if not higher forms of mathematics, enabling geometrical calculations, and even stress-load calculations. We notice also from Genesis 7:11 that a calendar system recognising months, as well as years, was also in common usage, and, this would certainly involve careful record-keeping, and also presumes the basic arithmetical skills alluded to above.

It should be noted that much of this degree of civilisation almost presumes the presence of writing. City and business life with its inevitable book-keeping requires records of transactions, ownership of goods and animals, lists of people and products of various kinds, receipts and so on. And administrative life, including the operation of a calendar, requires calculations and tables. The industries of carpentry and metalworking could hardly be practiced without a means of marking work pieces to enable accurate cutting or manipulation.

From all of this we see that while it is true that there is no reference in Genesis 4 to the art of writing, the *presumption* of its existence is more than merely reasonable, it seems a pre-requisite for what we read in the first chapters of Genesis.

But there is a definite clue to us from the Book of Jude. In verses 14–15 Jude refers to the prophecies of Enoch, whom he identifies as "the seventh from Adam" making it very plain indeed that he is referring to the great-grandfather of Noah, and not some other Enoch of later years. How could these prophecies have survived till the time of Jude if they had not been written down? And there is no evidence anywhere, despite what Form-Critics might say, that there was an oral tradition that existed for centuries before the invention of writing permitted such prophecies to become literary works. However, what really clinches the argument, is that the list of arts and sciences given in The Histories of Adam, occurs in what Scripture actually calls, _The Book_ Of The Histories Of Adam! (Genesis 5:1) This is why the art of writing is unmentioned in Genesis 4. It is expected to be *obvious* to the reader that as one is reading from *The Book* Of The Histories Of Adam, writing certainly existed![370]

Conclusion 23. The picture presented to us by the Scriptures, of life before the Flood, makes it clear that the art of writing was known and practised, not just by the antediluvians generally, but even by Adam!

Conclusion 24. From a consideration of the two last Conclusions, it would appear to be correct to view the toledoths as colophons, as proposed by P. J. Wiseman.

The Two Accounts Of The Creation

It is evident that Adam could have written the history of the line of Cain as it appears in Genesis chapter 4, and could also have written the account of the Fall in chapter 3, but how could he have written the second account of the creation in chapter 2 which goes back to the

---

[370] It is sometimes objected that the list of advances in the arts and sciences recorded in Genesis 4 could not possibly have been achieved in the timescale presumed by the narrative, but such Critics have underestimated the effect on human progress of phenomenally long lifespans. Discounting Enoch, whose taking by the Lord is exceptional, the average life span of the antediluvians listed in Genesis 5 is 907·5 years. Allowing generous amounts of time at each end of this average life span for achieving maturity, and a gradual diminution of ability towards the end of life, we may safely assume 800 years' duration of normal ability after maturity. This is something like *twenty times* the normal amount of time today between achieving proficiency in a chosen occupation, and the beginning of a gradual decline at the close of a normal working life. The effect of compressing the experience of twenty of our generations' learning, experience, and innovation into one life time must have accelerated advancement prodigiously. When we consider that this would not be limited to a few exceptional people, but would have been the norm, so that for centuries, men and women could have worked together on specific projects, the potential for the development of the arts and sciences would be, compared with our experience, quite breathtaking. I suggest that believers themselves have rarely contemplated, let alone made a study of, the effects upon human development of immense and productive longevity. To me this is yet another instance where the Scriptures hold the answer to a problem that has teased intellects for centuries, namely, by what agent was man propelled into a state of civilisation from savagery? It is I believe an invalid question, as the presumed primeval state of savagery never existed it seems. The rapid accumulation of practical, scientific, and administrative skills occurred because of the synergy that flowed from uninterrupted centuries of innovating on the basic skills of each individual's chosen occupations, coupled with the effects of 'cross-fertilisation' between disciplines, that also would have continued for centuries. It would be a worthwhile task for any suitably qualified believer to assess systematically the prospects for the flowering of civilisation in the pre-Flood years, through the effects of the longevity of the antediluvians.

time before he was formed? and what about the toledoth of the heavens and of the earth, the first account of the creation in chapter 1 that goes back to before the earth itself was formed? In order to answer this question, I draw on the separate findings of P. J. Wiseman, and Duane Garrett who have both made acute observations that, when taken together solve this riddle I believe.

It seems from Genesis 3:8 that it was habitual for Adam and Eve to meet with the Lord in the garden, "in the cool of the day." It is from these meetings with the Lord before the Fall, that Adam learned of the method of creation as outlined in Genesis 1, I believe, as well as the details recorded in Genesis 2 which preceded his receipt of the breath of lives that was breathed into him.

That this is a tenable proposition is seen by Wiseman's observation concerning the sun and the moon. He makes the point that their being referred to as *the greater and lesser lights*, shows that the story goes back to before everything around us had received names, to the very first beginnings of human history, to a time so remote, it is beyond the reach of any secular account. I must say, that this suggestion is to me very persuasive. Wiseman emphasises the importance of the absence of names for either the sun or moon in this passage, which being the chief foci for man's idolatrous impulses are among the first objects ever to receive names. Wiseman also draws our attention to the remarkable simplicity of style with which the First Account of the creation is written. The repetition of key words, and the elementary style reinforces the conviction that in Genesis 1 we encounter the very birth of literacy; "Let there be *lights* in the firmament... and God made two *great lights*, the *greater light* to rule the day and the *lesser light* to rule the night." Were Genesis to have been written when the Critics suggest we would find here the regular Hebrew names for both the sun and the moon (שמש and ירח). As Wiseman points out, this would be the case even if it had been written in the days of Abraham. The fact that instead of this we encounter the descriptive phrases, *the greater light,* and *the lesser light,* reveals that we have here an account that is so ancient, there can be nothing that predates it.

Speaking of the first account of the creation generally, Wiseman asks us to pay attention to the most remarkable way in which the account is written. It is highly suggestive of the way Adam had learned of the facts of the Creation directly from the Lord. Wiseman draws to our notice the way it seems that we are reading the words of Adam himself, "And God *said*... and God *called*..." He also tells us the names given by God to the things that He made, "And God called the light *day* and the darkness called He *night*," "and God called the firmament *heaven*: and God called the dry land *earth* and the gathering together of waters called He *seas*." The account is written with a directness that is both striking, and very significant. It is as if Adam were striving for absolute precision in passing on to his descendents, all that the Lord had told him. On top of this is the absence of expressions associated with the reception of a vision. As Wiseman says, there are no phrases such as, "I saw," "I beheld," "I heard." Instead, we find direct speech, "and God said, Behold I have given you every herb yielding seed which is upon the face of all the earth, and every tree in which is the fruit of a tree yielding seed to you, and it shall be for meat." Wiseman concludes that in the First Account of the Creation in Genesis 1, we find words that were delivered to the first human being by his Maker, and which that first human being, our earliest father has passed on to us.[371]

Higher Critics are naturally predisposed to think it impossible that Adam really existed, and therefore cannot accept the possibility that the Lord Who had HimSelf executed the work described in Genesis 1, could have spoken to Adam about it. But if special creation is possible, so is the encounter between the Lord and Adam as described in the Scriptures, and there certainly would be no problem at all in Adam learning of the method of creation directly as proposed by Wiseman. Indeed, as Wiseman points out, there are good textual reasons for believing this suggestion to be correct.

It must be understood therefore that there are no *literary* problems in accepting that Adam could have written both of the accounts of the creation, albeit there may be some non-literary problems. Those who are troubled by such non-literary problems are referred to Supplement Two which investigates such matters, but the credibility of Genesis on *literary grounds alone* is unchallenged by either of the two accounts

---

[371] Wiseman, op. cit., pp. 71–72.

of the creation. But how do we account for the similarity of structure between the first and the second accounts of the creation that we noticed earlier, especially as the structure in the second account is veiled far more heavily than it is in the first account? Here I draw on Duane Garrett's findings.

When considering the heptadic structure of Genesis 1 and 2, Garrett notes that their similarity has implications for the composition of the two chapters. Garrett believes that the heptad of Genesis 1:1–2:3 seems to have been written before that of Genesis 2:4ff. I agree with Garrett here, as it is likely that Adam received the teaching from the Lord that became the First Account of the Creation before he compiled what became the Second Account, the drama of which he himself played a significant rôle in. Garrett goes on to make the point that if we did not have the heptadic structure of Genesis 1, it is extremely unlikely that we would ever have discovered the heptadic structure of Genesis 2:4ff, which is a deliberate echo of that found in Genesis 1. Again I fully agree with Duane Garrett's suggestion here, believing that Adam would have taken the Divinely-given first account of the creation as providing the methodology for the setting out of the second account.[372]

Adam then used the pattern revealed in the first account as the framework for the second account of the Creation, which does not fall naturally into a heptad as there is no reference to a series of seven days. Nonetheless, he constructed the account to reflect both the heptadic structure of the first account, based on the seven days, and the tenfold structure of the first account, based on the ten instances of the formula, "and God said" that we discussed earlier.

This also accounts for the existence of the toledoth of Genesis 2:4. It marked the completion of the first account of the creation, and its separation from the rest of *the book of Adam*, the first part of which imitated the structure of the First Account of the Creation. In fact the structure of the First Account of the Creation influences the structure of the rest of the canon as we saw earlier. The fact that the First

---

[372] Garrett, op. cit., p. 196. I do not agree with Garrett's further point, namely that Genesis 1:1–2:4 was directly revealed to Moses, and that the sources of Genesis 2:4ff. antedate this incident.

Account of the Creation is based upon intimate conversations between the Lord and Adam, and was wholly beyond Adam's direct experience, explains why it is distinguished from the rest of his histories, and yet still attached to them. It was written by Adam, like the rest of his book, yet not directly composed by him.

Conclusion 25. The first account of the creation is an addition to the Book Of The Histories Of Adam.

Conclusion 26. The very significant consequence of the last three Conclusions is that we now see that the separate literary sources of Genesis are actually revealed to us in the book itself, and by the toledoth of Numbers 3:1, the final Pentateuchal toledoth, as the researcher P. J. Wiseman has maintained. Unlike sceptical and cynical Modernist Source Critics with their anonymous sources and redactors, we may now provide the actual names of the writers who provided these literary sources.

1. Adam	4. Ham	7. Ishmael	10. Jacob
2. Noah	5. Japheth	8. Isaac	11. Aaron
3. Shem	6. Terah	9. Esau	12. Moses

Part C:
The Descent Of The Tablets

The Descent Of The Tablets

Finally, we have to examine how the tablets written thousands of years ago, became the Pentateuch we know today from our English printed Bibles.

As Noah, his wife, and their three sons and their wives were the only members of the human race who survived the Flood, it is obvious that Noah must have had *The Book Of The Histories Of Adam* in safekeeping in the ark during the Deluge, and in fact we find in Noah's own tablets in Genesis 5:29, that there appears to be a reference to *The Book of Adam*, by the allusion to Genesis 3:17 which refers to the cursing of the ground. This clearly implies that Noah not only had access to *The Book Of Adam*, but that he had read it.

It seems logical to suppose therefore, that just as Adam probably attached his book to the first account of the creation, revealed to him by the Lord, so too, Noah attached his tablets, which began with a genealogy, to those of Adam. This meant that Noah's history of the line of Seth, ending with himself, immediately followed the colophon at the end of Adam's tablets, and the history of the line of Cain.

This juxtaposition allowed the Higher Critic to come along and *assume* that the colophon of Adam's tablets introduced the genealogy of Noah's tablets. To be fair this is a very easy mistake to make, but it is completely out of step with the literary practices of antiquity as we have seen, and Higher Critics ought really to have acquainted themselves with these practices. Their assumption also introduces a problem which really is non-existent, concerning the human authorship of the first four chapters of Genesis of course.

We must not forget that the Prophecy of Enoch must also have been in the ark with Noah. I believe that the occurrence of the Flood is the reason for us having such a small portion of Scripture that describes man's earliest history. While the ark was of colossal size, there can be no doubt that space would most definitely have been at a premium, thus, the numbers of clay tablets Noah could have taken with him would have been small, and only the most essential would have been kept by him I believe. Thus the situation may be depicted diagrammatically as given below.

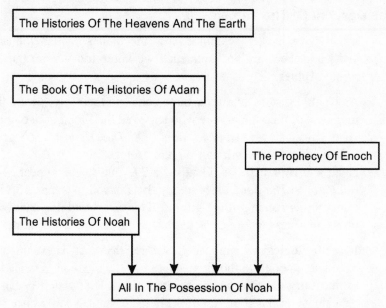

Figure 3 Histories in the possession of Noah

In spite of what I said above, there may well have been other writings in the possession of Noah, but these are all of which we may be certain.

The Account Of The Flood

The next series of tablets we encounter is *The Histories Of The Sons Of Noah*, and contains the account of the Flood. Now there is some interesting evidence attached to these tablets, which even the most sceptical of Higher Critics must answer, or else lose credibility. The Scriptures show that the whole world has been repopulated after the universal Flood from the descendants of The Sons of Noah. It is extremely worthy of note therefore that Flood Legends may be found on every continent, and in the vast majority of mythologies and folklore. Is this not exactly what we would expect if it really was the Sons of Noah who not only passed on to us the account of the Flood, but whose descendants repopulated the entire world as the Scriptures report?

Reginald Daly, an investigator into the world-wide evidence for the Flood writes, "The early aborigines of nearly every country of the world have preserved records of the universal flood. Dr. Richard Andree collected 46 flood legends from North and South America, 20 from Asia, 5 from Europe, 7 from Africa and 10 from The South Sea islands and Australia."

He then cites excerpts of Flood legends from Hawaii, Babylon, Persia, Syria, Wales, Cuba, Brazil, Transylvania, Alaska, The East Indies, Fiji, Greece, Lapland, The Leeward Islands, Switzerland, Russia, Rome, The Himalayas, China, India, as well as from the North and Central American Indians. The common basis of these legends is apparent when they are compared, an exercise undertaken by Daly in his book, *Earth's Most Challenging Mysteries*.[373]

This ubiquity of the Flood legend is well-known amongst those who study mythology but has never been explained satisfactorily apart from by believers who accept the veracity of the Scriptures. A strictly local flood would not induce a *global* distribution of Flood legends. A global phenomenon needs a global explanation; and the fact that the account of the Flood occurs in the tablets ending with the colophon of the Sons of Noah, for the believer providers just such an explanation of course. The descendants of the Sons of Noah who would have been keenly aware of the causes, nature, and consequences of the Flood, spread out by degrees all over the world, even to its remotest corners, and took with them, amongst other things, the memory of the terrible Deluge, and the saving of humanity through one righteous family.

---

[373] Daly, Reginald, *Earth's Most Challenging Mysteries*, New Jersey, U.S.A., The Craig Press, 1972, pp. 47–56. See also, Whitcomb, John C. Jnr., & Morris, Henry M., *The Genesis Flood*, Grand Rapids, Michigan, U.S.A., 1966, pp. 36–54.

After *The Histories of The Sons Of Noah*, we find *The Histories of Shem*, followed by *The Histories of Terah*, after which comes the narrative concerning Abraham. I propose that all of these records came into the hands of Abraham, although the method is unable to be defined, but given that the histories of Noah, the Sons of Noah, Shem, and Terah were all written by members of the same family, I imagine that the growing collection of tablets passed from one generation to another by inheritance, and that would usually have been by the eldest son. The exception to this would have been Shem, who was singled out for blessing by his father Noah (Genesis 9:26), and presumably would have become his heir, reversing the natural order, as happened years later with Isaac, Jacob, and Ephraim. It is highly possible therefore that Shem took the place of the first-born, and inherited the tablets containing the histories from Adam down to his own time.

I have given my reasons for thinking that Abram was Terah's first-born son, and was born when Terah was 70 years old, as Genesis 11:26 would seem to indicate in Appendix XI.

It is just possible however that all the tablets down to and including *The Histories of Shem,* were passed directly to Abraham from Shem, who was alive until the time of Jacob as we have seen already, and that Abraham set out for Canaan with the Histories of his father Terah. There are persistent Jewish legends that Melchizedek may have been Shem, but of course this is completely unprovable. Nevertheless, one way or another all the tablets we encounter in Genesis up to the end of chapter 11, I believe would have been found with Abraham, through one means or another. This then may be illustrated diagrammatically as indicated below.

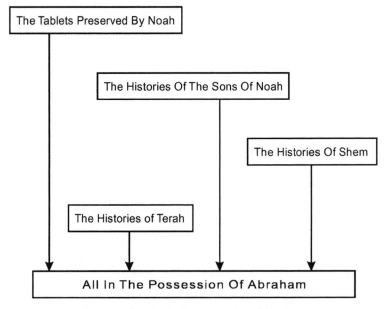

Figure 4 Histories in the possession of Abraham

From the time of Abraham on I propose that the collection of tablets became a part of the legacy received by those who inherited the Abrahamic Blessing. This meant that the tablets would have passed in turn to Isaac, Jacob and Joseph, acquiring additions along the way. Thus Isaac would have inherited all the tablets held by his father Abraham, but also incorporated with them his own Histories, as well as *The Histories Of Ishmael* as we saw above. So too Jacob would then have acquired these from Isaac, but added his own Histories as well as those of Esau. Finally these were all received by Joseph, where I propose, they were lodged in safekeeping in an archive in Egypt, where Moses, brought up in the Egyptian Royal Court, would have easily gained access to them.

We see from Numbers 3:1 that Moses and Aaron together compiled the story of Joseph found in the latter part of the book of Genesis (37:2 to 50:26), and which occurred mostly in Egypt and would derive from Egyptian sources therefore. This is the part of Genesis which has a thoroughly Egyptian background in terms of its vocabulary, again indicating the correctness of Wiseman's views. The final diagram for the book of Genesis is given below.

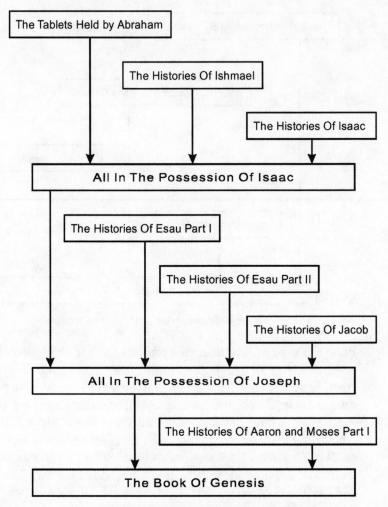

Figure 5 Compilation of the book of Genesis

The second part of *The Histories of Aaron And Moses*, together with *Moses' Travel Journal* have resulted in the books of Exodus to Numbers, while Deuteronomy is, as we saw earlier, *The Foundation Treaty Of Israel-as-a-nation*, or, we might say, *The Constitution of Israel*. Thus the diagram for the completion of the Pentateuch would be as given below.

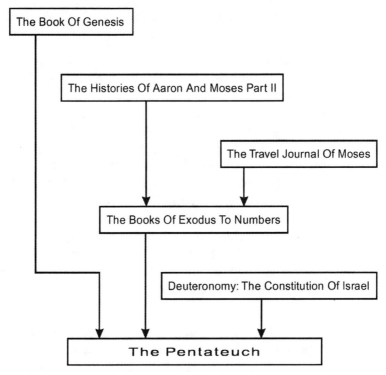

Figure 6 Compilation of the Pentateuch

Before concluding this section, two more points ought to be made. Firstly, there are very many notices in the Scriptures that speak of Moses writing the Law,[374] but in the main they seem to relate specifically to the Legislation of the Torah. There are some references however, notably Luke 16:29–31, 24:27, and 24:44, which imply that Moses was the human author of _all_ of the Pentateuch. From this it is safe to deduce I believe, that Moses played a prominent rôle in the final shaping of the book of Genesis, a fact that is of importance to the believer. Much of the material that forms the literary sources of Genesis could be described as being secular. The obvious sources that

---

[374] For example, Exodus 24:4, 30:11, 30:17, 33:1, 33:5, 39:1, 39:5, 39:29; Leviticus 1:1, 4:1, 6:1; Numbers 4:1; Deuteronomy 1:1, 1:5, 5:1, 31:22, 31:30, 33:1; I Chronicles 15:15, 22:13; II Chronicles 23:18, 24:6, 25:4, 30:16, 35:12; Ezra 3:2, 7:6; Nehemiah 1:7, 8:1, 13:1; Matthew 8:4; Luke 16:29-31, 24:27, 24:44; John 1:17; and Acts 3:22.

spring to mind are The Histories Of The Sons Of Noah, (which would have included Ham), as well as those of Terah, Ishmael, and Esau.

The fact that Moses, referred to as *the man of God* (e.g. Ezra 3:2), played a significant editorial rôle in the compilation of the book of Genesis, which would have required him being suitably Inspired (II Peter 1:21), just as Bezaleel was Inspired for his work (Exodus 31:1–3), means that we may be sure that although this study has revealed the *human* literary sources of the book of Genesis, we still may believe it to be the very Word-of-God. The Inspired redactional work of Moses, had a sanctifying effect on the human writings, as is evidenced by the Equi-Distant Letter Sequences and associated structural phenomena considered earlier. Secondly it is also apparent that editing of the Pentateuch subsequent to the work of Moses, was undertaken by persons who were enabled by God to do so. The most obvious early example of this, is the account added to Deuteronomy of the death of Moses, which, in all probability, was inserted by Joshua who we know added to the Torah (Joshua 24:26).

Given the zeal of Samuel for religious reform mentioned earlier in this study, a further editing by Samuel is not at all improbable, and it is particularly likely that when Ezra caused the whole of the Canon that then existed to be re-written in the square-charactered script we know today, that another recension was made. This is when verses such as Genesis 36:31, which refers to a time before there was a king over the sons of Israel, were added I believe. The people of Ezra's day would have been in need of several small editorial explanations such as this example, as they lived so much later than the events described in the Pentateuch, and their spell in captivity in Babylon would have prevented their acquiring a full understanding of their nation's history. Our earlier findings have shown that before this work of Ezra was undertaken, the Samaritan Pentateuch had already appeared. After Ezra, no Inspired revision of the Pentateuch occurred, and what we see today in our English printed Bibles, is a translation of the Pentateuch in the square-charactered text, substantially as it left Ezra's hand, although it was some centuries before the Masoretic Text appeared. Before that event, the Septuagint had appeared in Egypt. It is from the Septuagint that most of the quotations of the Old Testament found in the New Testament are made. The descent of the

Pentateuch itself may be illustrated diagrammatically as indicated below.

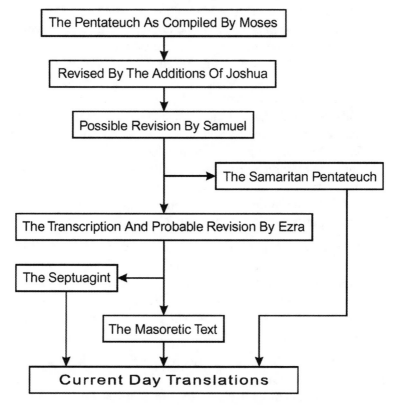

Figure 7 Descent of the Pentateuch

Conclusion 27. The revealing of the human literary sources of the book of Genesis does not militate against its being accepted as The Word Of God.

Conclusion 28. The Pentateuch was revised after the death of Moses, by Joshua, and later probably by Samuel, and Ezra.

Conclusion To Chapter Eight

It is supremely ironic that Higher Critics attempting to identify the literary sources of Genesis have passed over the answers for centuries, while all the time they have lain before their eyes in the text itself. This is all the more remarkable when we consider that the way in which we refer to the book, that is by the name of *Genesis*, is owing to the fact that the compilers of the Septuagint, from which the name comes, while they ignored the most ancient literary practice of taking the opening words of the book as its title, still realised what a colophon is, and took their title from the first colophon of the book. This act in itself provides a real clue to the construction of the book, and also shows again what we have seen throughout this dissertation, namely that Higher Criticism is actually based upon *ignorance*, and collapses in the face of knowledge. This ignorance is exacerbated by the dismissal of Wiseman's views by most commentators, R. K. Harrison being a very notable exception, but this is mainly owing to prejudice I believe, as well as an unawareness of the support for Wiseman's views to be found in Hebrew Traditional thought, English translations of the Hebrew Canon made by Jews, and the Septuagint's naming of the book of Genesis.

This ignorance is also partly induced by the radical differences in mental outlook between the occident and orient. In a most fascinating work entitled *Hebrew Thought Compared With Greek*, Thorlief Boman has shown how radically different is the Hebrew mind from our own. I hope the reader will excuse a small digression now in order to illustrate this point.

To those who know a little Hebrew, but have not made a study of the manner of Hebrew thought, this difference is most obvious from a consideration of the Hebrew and Greek verbs. Greek has many tenses, including some, for example the aorist 1 and 2, which English lacks, but broadly speaking, the similarities are sufficient to enable the English man or woman to understand without undue effort, the thought conveyed by the word. With Hebrew, there are no proper tenses as such. An action is either complete, and thereby likely to be in what we would call the past; or incomplete. But there is also this difference, which has an enormous theological impact; for the Hebrew, a completed action, that is, one that we would designate by the past tense, is actually *present* to him or her, if its nature is such that the individual lives life through its effects. This *contemporaneity*, to use Kierkegaard's word, borrowed by Boman, means that to the Hebrew, the events of the Sacrifice of Christ at Calvary, and the Resurrection of Christ from the tomb, may be really *present* with the individual believer because of the impact made by them on that individual's life. This is because time is not considered spatially, as being a line stretching from the future to the past, but is considered by the events which occurred at particular moments within that time: it is considered by its *content* rather than its position, and this content might impact upon any individual, thereby uniting that individual with the event in question, even though the event might be complete, and, therefore, in what we might call the past.[375]

Another simple but radical difference is the way the ancient Hebrew regarded the past and future. We speak usually as though the future is in front of us, and we therefore look towards it. The opposite was true for the ancient Hebrew. Boman explains, "From a psychological viewpoint it is absurd to say that we have the future before us and the past behind us, as though the future were visible to us and the past occluded. Quite the reverse is true. What our forebears have accomplished lies before us as their completed works; the house we see, the meadows and fields, the culture and political system, are congealed expressions of the deeds of our fathers. The same is true of everything they have done, lived, or suffered; it lies before us as completed facts, and we could unroll their genesis individually as much as we want. Just as in a motion picture."[376]

These two brief examples will show, I hope, how unwise it is to impose our own mental paradigms upon the ancient mind, particularly the ancient Hebrew mind, which works in a manner we are not accustomed to, and whose ways we must learn. Thus, to return to our subject now; it certainly does seem strange to us that the title of a series of tablets would be found at the end of the text, in a literary colophon, rather than at its beginning, simply because we do not work in such a way. The answer however is not to *deny* that this could be so, but to educate our minds in the custom and practices of the ancient culture we are investigating, and then to adapt <u>our</u> ways of thinking accordingly.

---

[375] See Boman, Thorlief, *Hebrew Thought Compared With Greek,* London, SCM Press, undated, pp. 145–150.

[376] Boman, op. cit., p. 150.

If such an effort is made, we will behold much which the sceptic and cynic misses because he or she uses the wrong viewpoint. Similarly, we must not insist that repetitions in an ancient text are evidence of different source documents, when a proper understanding of literature based on clay tablets shows that such repetitions were the normal method of controlling the sequence of tablets. Source Critics have failed to move from their own times, to those of the people whose literature they study.

The Authority Of Genesis

The naming of the literary sources of Genesis is a remarkable testimony to the honesty and integrity of the character of Moses. He refused to give the impression that the work was his own, but named his sources via a bibliography incorporated into the text itself. In including the colophonic statements within the text as well, he dated his sources, a device, which we have just seen, allows for the corroboration of at least some of the sources.

Inevitably, the authority of Genesis is enhanced greatly by what we have seen, as I trust, is the discipline of *faithful* Source Criticism, which is able actually to propose a viable alternative to the Graf–Wellhausen type speculations of the cynic. The believer does not have to be completely negative therefore, confining himself or herself to attacking sceptical theories; he or she may now offer a credible alternative, that is based upon the known literary practices of antiquity, is absolutely consistent, and yet exonerates the text itself, revealing it to be worthy of our acceptance.

We now move on to Part Four, where we will consider an alternative to sceptical Form Criticism as applied firstly to the book of Genesis, and secondly, to the entire Pentateuch.

Part Four

Positive Form Criticism And The Pentateuch

Chapter Nine

Positive Form Criticism
And The Book Of Genesis

Part A:
Introduction

In 1985 Isaac M. Kikawada and Arthur Quinn published their joint work, *Before Abraham Was*.[377] The two authors provide clear evidence that the first eleven chapters of the book of Genesis correspond in terms of their structure, to a recognized ancient literary form. Duane Garrett has extended this type of analysis, examining the entire book of Genesis in a similar manner. He has shown that the structure of Genesis, outlined by the toledoths and genealogies, corresponds with that revealed by analysing the book by these ancient literary forms.[378] This coincidence corroborates both types of analysis of course, but also virtually disproves the results of the New Documentary Hypothesis, as the structure revealed by the literary genres cuts right across the divisions of the text into the portions attributed to J, E, and P et cetera. We must now look at the forms discovered by Kikawada and Quinn, and Duane Garrett and examine the evidence for ourselves.

---

[377] Op. cit.

[378] Op. cit., cps. 5–10.

Atrahasis

Reference has already been made to the Assyrian *Epic Of Gilgamesh* which includes in its 326 lines of cuneiform text, 200 that are devoted to the Flood.[379] A similar account known as *The Epic of Atrahasis* has also been unearthed in various versions and in differing states of preservation.[380] Kikawada and Quinn, refer to the definitive Oxford edition of Atrahasis, that of Lambert and Millard,[381] which delineates a fivefold structure of the Epic which they report as shown below. Firstly there is A, the account of the creation, followed by three specific threats to the survival of humanity, the last of which is the Flood, (B, C, and D.). These threats are followed by E, a resolution of the problem. The Second Threat, C, has two specific stages. The table below is based on a similar table given by Kikawada and Quinn.[382]

The Structure Of The Epic Of Atrahasis

A	Creation	I	1–135
B	First Threat	I	352–415
C	Second Threat	II	i 1–11 v.21
	Part I,		
	Part II.		
D	Final Threat	II	v. 22–III vi. 4
E	Resolution	III	vi. 5–Viii. 18

Kikawada and Quinn claim that this fivefold structure is also found in the Iranian Avesta, in the story of the Trojan War, and also in the book of Genesis.[383] Their comparison between Atrahasis and Genesis is shown in the table below;

---

[379] Parrot, op. cit., p. 24.

[380] For details see Parrot op. cit., pp. 32ff.

[381] Lambert, W. G., & Millard, A. R., *Atra-Hasis: The Babylonian Story Of The Flood With The Sumerian Flood Story*, Oxford, Oxford University Press, 1969.

[382] Op. cit., p. 46.

[383] Op. cit., pp. 36–52.

Atrahasis	**Genesis**
A Creation (I. 1–135).	A Creation 1:1–2:4.
Summary of work of gods,	Summary of work of God,
Creation of man.	Creation of man.
B First Threat to survival, (I. 352–415).	B First Threat to man's survival, 2:5–3:24.
Plague.	Death introduced by the sin of Adam.
C Second Threat (II. i. 1–11 v. 21).	C Second Threat to man's survival, 4:1–26.
Part I Drought,	Part I Death by murder (Cain),
Part II Intensified Drought.	Part II Death by murder (Lamech's taunt).
D Final Threat (II. V. 22–III vi. 4).	D Final Threat to man's survival, (5:1–9:29).
Flood of Atrahasis.	Death by the Flood of Noah,
Salvation via a boat.	Salvation via ark.
E Resolution (of problem of human population growth) (III. vi 5–viii 18.).	E Resolution (ensuring human population growth) (10:1–11:32).
Birth Control.	Dispersal of nations.

Kikawada and Quinn see as confirmation of their theory the fact that each element of the fivefold structure they locate in Genesis 1–11, is separated from its neighbour by a toledoth or a genealogy or both, which would seem to indicate that the text falls *naturally* into the appropriate divisions. The first account of the *Creation* is separated from the second account, with the details of the forming of Eve, which leads into the account of the *First Threat* of the Fall, by the toledoth of 2:4–5. The account of the Fall, the *First Threat*, is separated from the First Part of the *Second Threat* by the genealogy of 4:1–2. The two parts of the Second Threat are separated by the genealogy of 4:16–22. The *Second* and *Final Threats* are separated by the toledoth of 5:1–2 and the genealogy of 5:3–32. The *Final Threat* is separated from the *Resolution* by the toledoth of 10:1 and the following genealogy of 10:2–32, and the end of the *Resolution* is marked by the *two sets* of toledoths and genealogies of 11:10–29. Although neither Garrett or Kikawada and Quinn mention it, the ending of this section with a *pair* of toledoths and genealogies validates the view that the first eleven chapters of Genesis do indeed comprise a distinct section, as the divisions of the book of Psalms are marked out in a similar manner as we saw above. The final result may be presented diagrammatically as follows. The Linking Material is in italics, the Structure Elements are in bold.

Introduction, 1:1–2:3, The Creation.

Toledoth 2:4–5

First Threat to man's survival, 2:6–3:24, Death through The Fall.

Genealogy: Part One 4:1–2

Second Threat to man's survival: Part One, 4:3–15, Death through murder.

Genealogy: Part Two 4:16–22

Second Threat to man's survival: Part Two, 4:23–26, Death through murder.

Toledoth & Genealogy 5:1–32

Final Threat to man's survival, 6:1–9:29, Death of most of mankind through the Flood.

Toledoth & Genealogy 10:1–32

Resolution, 11:1–9, the repopulation of the earth after the Flood.

Toledoth, Genealogy, Toledoth, Genealogy 11:10–29

We see also that every genealogy in the first eleven chapters of Genesis acts as a division within the narrative, although not every toledoth does. The toledoth of 6:9 is unused in this scheme. Thus the statement made by Driver, claiming that the toledoths form a framework of Genesis needs qualifying,[384] as it would appear that the genealogies definitely do form such a framework, supported by some of the toledoths.

From these facts Kikawada and Quinn claim that Genesis 1–11 conforms to the genre of Ancient Epic Literature. Duane Garrett prefers the classification Ancestor Epic, but either way it would appear that the first eleven chapters of Genesis are recognisable as a literary form, and are far from being the literary patchwork that Source Critics would have us believe.

The Blending Of The Structures Of The Ancestor Epic And The Hebrew Tradition

Although neither Garrett or Kikawada and Quinn mention it, there is available a striking confirmation of the legitimacy of viewing the first eleven chapters of Genesis as Ancient Epic Literature, with its

---

[384] See page 216.

recognized structural form. This confirmation is based upon the conformity of the pattern revealed by the Ancient Epic form, with that revealed by the Hebrew Traditional method referred to in Chapter 5, Part C.

There, we saw that the Hebrew Tradition has its unique way of analysing the structure of passages of Scripture. This was seen in the two cycles, each comprising three days, found in the First Account of the Creation. In each cycle, the Traditional Scheme positions the *last* of each set of three days in the *centre* of the scheme. Each of these days, the third and sixth, differed from the others inasmuch as they each contained two creative acts, and the others contained only one each. This meant that in *both* the Traditional Scheme, and the Ancestor Epic analysis, the central elements reveal a basic duality. Furthermore the form of the 'threats' of the Ancestor Epic, also follow the Hebrew Traditional Scheme as I will show.

In The Hebrew Traditional Scheme on pages 144–145, we noticed that the First and Second accounts of the creation occupied the First and Second Places of the Scheme respectively; those of *Fire/Heat/Light/Burning*, followed by *Water*, and that the account of the two lines of descent from Cain and Seth, showed again the duality of the Third Position of the scheme, the Place-of-the-Child, that concerns plant, animal and human life. Now the First Threat of the Ancestor Epic, coming after the *Second* Account of the Creation, would be located in this *Third* and central Position of the Traditional Scheme, and therefore ought to relate to plant, animal, and human life. Remarkably it does, as the central issue of obedience to God involves *plant life* in the form of the-tree-of-the-knowledge-of-good-and-evil and its fruit, and *animal life* as the evil one's assumed guise was that of the serpent. The impact of this episode upon *human life* is wrought out in the awful fact and consequences of the Fall, of course.

With the Second Threat, the threefold cycle of the Traditional Scheme begins again, so now we must expect a connection with the First Place of that Scheme, associated with *Fire/Heat/Light/Burning*. The issue is again conformity with the Will of God, but here this is worked out through the offerings of Abel and Cain, and offerings traditionally are consumed by *fire*, therefore the Scheme and Epic form are again in harmony.

The Final Threat, the Flood, occupies then the Second Place of the Scheme of course, the place of *water*! It seems quite unnecessary to demonstrate the conformity between the two methods of analysis here! But after the Flood there is no other threat, yet the Third Place of the Scheme is still unoccupied. How do we explain this? Well, after the account of the Flood ends, we read of Noah's drunkenness (Genesis 9:20–29), and here indeed we find the things of the Third Place of the Scheme; namely, plant and human life. The drunkenness was induced by the drinking of wine that Noah had prepared from the vine he had planted, and the human life is present inasmuch as this episode led directly to the cursing and blessing that fell upon the lives of Noah's three sons, from whom the whole world was repopulated. This also suits the fact that with this incident we have reached again the Place-of-the-Child in the Scheme. Thus the Scheme of the Hebrew Tradition, and the Threats of the Ancestor Epic coincide in a most satisfying manner, which corroborates both forms of analysis simultaneously. (I have since discovered new evidence for the genuineness of the Ancestor Epic Literary Form, which is to be found in Appendix XII.) The literary form of the Ancestor Epic then seems to be quite genuine, and we may press on with its application elsewhere.

Conclusion 29. The first eleven chapters of the book of Genesis are presented in the recognisable literary form of Ancestor Epic Literature.

Genesis 12–50

Kikawada and Quinn, while concentrating on the first eleven chapters of Genesis, make the point that the fivefold pattern of an Opening Section, a Tripartite Centre, and a Conclusion or Settlement are to be found in the book of Genesis when considered as a whole.[385] They relate the Opening Section to all of the first eleven chapters which they designate as Primeval History, the Tripartite Centre to Abraham, Isaac and Jacob, whose wives were barren, and therefore offered a threefold threat to the Abrahamic Blessing. The Conclusion they related to the story of Joseph, and the settlement of the tribes of Israel in Egypt. They do admit to two difficulties with this view however; firstly Isaac is given a prominence that the amount of Scriptural

---

[385] Op. cit., pp. 119ff.

narrative devoted to him does not seem to warrant; secondly the story of Joseph seems to be different in nature from that of the previous three patriarchs.[386]

Duane Garrett modifies this scheme by suggesting instead that the Triadic Centre should be as follows; 1) *The Abraham Cycle*, 2) *The Jacob Cycle*, and 3) *The Joseph Cycle*. Garrett's scheme has two positive merits. Firstly, Abraham, Jacob and Joseph do have one thing in common, namely the basic experience of the threat imposed by *alienation*. All are driven far from home, Abraham from Ur to Canaan, Jacob from Canaan to Padanaram, and Joseph from Canaan to Egypt. Isaac's experiences do not compare with these, and evidence will be submitted later to show that his story conforms to a different literary form.

Secondly, just as the text of Genesis 1–11 fell naturally into the form of the Ancestor Epic, by the divisions created by the genealogies, so too does Garrett's scheme through utilising every single remaining genealogy, showing to my mind, the purpose behind their intelligent positioning within the narrative material.

The scheme outlined below is based on that offered by Garrett, with slight modifications of my own, including the adding of the opening genealogy of the book of Exodus, which marks the end of the fifth part of the Ancestor Epic Form, the Conclusion, or Settlement. This also links together the books of Genesis and Exodus which seems most fitting. The two references to the names of Joseph and Jacob (and Israel, Jacob's new name), in Exodus 1:1–7 seem a positive confirmation of this continuity. The Linking Material is in italics, the Structure Elements are in bold.

---

[386] Ibid.

Introduction: Primeval History: Genesis 1:1–11:9

Toledoth, Genealogy, Toledoth, Genealogy: Genesis 11:10–29

First Threat: The Abraham Cycle: Genesis 11:30–24:67

Genealogy, Toledoth, Genealogy, Toledoth: Genesis 25: 1–19

Second Threat: The Jacob Cycle: Genesis 25:20–35:22b

Genealogy, Toledoth, Genealogy, Toledoth, Genealogy: Genesis 35:22c–37:2

Final Threat: The Joseph Cycle: Genesis 37:3–46:7

Genealogy: Genesis 46:8–27

Resolution: Settlement in Egypt: Genesis 46:28–50:26

Genealogy Exodus 1:1–7

We see again here clues that we are on the right track, as the pattern of a pair of genealogies and toledoths that closed the first section of Genesis, namely chapters 1–11, is repeated but in reverse order between the *First* and *Second Threats*. This obviously forms a connection between the two pieces of linking material, which a mere repetition would not do so clearly. The next link receives the greatest emphasis of them all, being a fivefold link, emphasising the Great Divide in Genesis that we have noticed previously. This is the point at which Aaron and Moses ceased to use the material preserved by their ancestors on clay tablets, and used their own Egyptian sources instead, as the shift from a Babylonian vocabulary, to an Egyptian vocabulary referred to earlier, testifies to.

There is every indication then that Duane Garrett is correct in his analysis and we may proceed on the basis that the entire book of Genesis appears to be cast in the form of Ancestor Epic Literature.

We notice as well of course that the intelligent placement of the genealogies has in the main produced the Ancestor Epic form, and that it is noticeably different from the structure produced by the toledoths. This I take to be textual evidence of a Mosaic editing of the sources available to him. I propose that the toledoths reveal the sources of the material used by Aaron and Moses in the compilation of Genesis, as stated in Conclusion 26, but that the genealogies reveal the Ancestor Epic literary form Moses then cast that material into, in producing the book of Genesis. The reason for using genealogies to

272

separate the Threats of the Ancestor Epic form, would be to emphasise the defeat of those Threats to population growth, by data which showed how rapidly the population was growing in spite of the threats.

Conclusion 30. The entire book of Genesis has a recognisable literary form, namely that of Ancestor Epic.

Conclusion 31. A comparison of the structures revealed by the toledoths and genealogies confirms an extensive editing by Moses of the source material at his disposal.

Conclusion 32. The genealogies of Genesis provide the true framework for the book rather than the toledoths. Every single genealogy of Genesis is used as a narrative division to create the Ancestor Epic Literary Form.

Part B:
Individual Epics

A) The Epic Of Jacob

We must now see how extensive the occurrence of these literary forms is. We begin with the Jacob Cycle in the very centre of the General Ancestor Epic. The Abraham Cycle concerns the descendants of Ishmael, Moab and Ammon as well as Israel, and the Joseph Cycle is a cycle about the ancestor of only two of Israel's tribes; Ephraim and Manasseh. The Jacob Cycle concerns all the tribes of Israel exclusively. As this Cycle has come down us though, it includes other literary forms which will be dealt with shortly. These are, firstly the account in Genesis 26, which concerns Isaac, and the account in Genesis 34 concerning the rape of Dinah. The episode concerning Isaac is a part of the Wife-As-Sister genre, and that concerning Dinah forms a part of what might be called, following Garrett, a set of Negotiation Tales. With these two elements removed, (to be dealt with later), the Jacob Cycle is outlined below, and conforms to the now familiar Ancestor Epic form.

Prologue	Esau and Jacob born; start of conflict. 25:21–28.
First Threat: Part One	Jacob acquires Esau's Birthright. 25:29–34.
First Threat: Part Two	Jacob acquires Esau's Blessing, and runs for his life. 27:1–28:22.
Second Threat: Part One	Jacob cheated by Laban. 29:15–27.
Second Threat: Part Two	Jacob hated by Laban. 31:1–16.
Third Threat: Part One	The meeting with the Angel. 32:24–32.
Third Threat: Part Two	The meeting with Esau. 33:1–20.
Resolution	Jacob at Bethel, birth of Benjamin, death of Rachel. 35:1–22b.

I have deviated from Garrett's scheme here by including two events he omits. The first addition I have made is the reference to the acquiring by Jacob of Esau's birthright, which is definitely referred to

274

in the episode concerning the subsequent acquisition of Esau's Blessing which Garrett does refer to (Genesis 27:36). The second, is the reference to the struggle with the Angel (Genesis 32:24–32), which is a distinct episode buried within Jacob's preparations to meet with Esau, to which Garrett refers.

I believe that Garrett is too eager to emulate the classic Ancestor Epic form here, and overlooks the fact that this Cycle is in the *centre* of the book of Genesis, and taking my lead from the Hebrew Tradition, I believe that duality is therefore likely to be found at every point. Jacob is run through with duality in fact, being a *twin*, having *two* wives and *two* concubines, and even *two* names. He is always responding to *another power*, either Esau or Laban. To my mind this constant duality does not reduce the parallelism with the recognized Ancestor Epic form at all, it merely gives it a distinctively Scriptural character. We must now move on to consider the episode from Isaac's life in Genesis 26 that we excluded from the Jacob Cycle.

B) The Epic Of The Matriarchs

This episode is one of the Higher Critics' favourite passages of Genesis. On three different occasions (12:10–20, 20:1–18, 26:1–17) we read of a patriarch, (Abraham twice, and Isaac once) who, travelling into a foreign land, says that his attractive wife (Sarah or Rebekah) is his sister, not his wife. The critic triumphantly parades these accounts as obvious narrative duplications, and, therefore, evidence that the New Documentary Hypothesis is true.[387]

One of the supposed problems relates to Abimelech, who was the Philistine king of Gerar, while both Abraham and Isaac stayed there during the second and third incidents. 'How can this be?' asks the critic, 'there must be a duplication here as Abimelech would have been dead by the time of Isaac's sojourn!' The positioning of the first episode featuring Abimelech in Genesis 20, shows that it occurred in the year between the Covenant of Genesis 17, when Abraham was 99 years old (17:1–16) and the birth of Isaac when Abraham was

---

[387] See S. H. Hooke in *Peak's Commentary*, op. cit., pp. 191–192 for a presentation of the Critic's viewpoint.

aged 100 in chapter 21:1–5. This is confirmed by the fact that the new names of Abraham and Sarah, which had only been given them within the year prior to the birth of Isaac (cf. 17:1–15 with 21:1–5), are found in the narrative concerning their encounter with Abimelech (20:1–18), yet clearly the incident occurred before Isaac had been born.

Now we know that Isaac married Rebekah when he was aged forty (Genesis 25:20). We do not know when exactly in Isaac's married life he stayed in Gerar, but it could certainly be within fifty years of Abraham's visit. Given the longevity of those days, which has been alluded to previously, there would appear to be no difficulty at all in accepting that Abimelech could have ruled for fifty years or more. It is clear from the account of Isaac's stay in Gerar that the threat to Rebekah was not directly from Abimelech himself (26:8–1) as it had been in the case of Sarah in the previous incident (20:3), but could have come from a number of his male subjects. This fact might well be an indicator of Abimelech's advancing age. So then, having dealt with the supposed problem of Abimelech, how do we answer the Critic's main charge about duplicate narratives?

As the first episode involved a Pharaoh of Egypt (12:14–18), and the others both involving Abimelech do not present a chronological difficulty in spite of what is often thought, there is no reason why the incidents reported may not all be genuine. Garrett rightly points out that the recurring theme of the-beloved-but-barren-wife found in the histories of Sarah (11:30), Rebekah (25:21), Rachel (29:31), Hannah (I Samuel 1:1–2) (and Elisabeth (Luke 1:5–7)),[388] do not mean that we must disbelieve them because there are similarities in their stories. Nonetheless, there are important parallels within the three accounts relating to the-wife-as-sister deception that need to be addressed. The insertion of the story within the Jacob Cycle seems to unite Isaac somehow with Jacob. Similarly, when we look at some elements of the lives of Abraham and Isaac, most of which are found in the proximity of the wife-as-sister stories we see also how closely Isaac's life in some respects, mirrors that of Abraham, thereby uniting him

---

[388] Op. cit., p. 132.

with his father as well. The following table based on suggestions made by Garrett shows these parallels.

Abraham

A 12:1–3 Abram and the Call and Promises of God.

B 12:10–20 Sarai as Abram's sister.

C 13:1–12 Strife of the men of Lot and Abram, Abram parts from Lot to prevent a fight.

D 15:1–21 Encouragement from the Lord, followed by a sacrifice.

E 21:22–34 Agreement at Beersheba with Abimelech.

Isaac

a 26:2–6 Isaac and the Call and Promises of God.

b 26:7 ff. Rebekah as Isaac's sister.

c 26:14–22 Strife with the men of Abimelech, Isaac leaves to prevent a fight.

d 26:23–25 Encouragement from the Lord, followed by a sacrifice.

e 26:26–33 Agreement at Beersheba with Abimelech.

As Garrett says, we see from this that the episode concerning Rebekah and Abimelech, *depends* upon the earlier story of Sarah and Abimelech, in order to reinforce the parallel between Isaac and Abraham. Not only this, but the second episode involving Sarah, depends upon the original episode involving Sarah and a Pharaoh of Egypt. We see this from the fact that no reason is given for Abimelech's taking of the by then elderly Sarah; the reader is expected to *know* why this should be because of the remarks found in the original account which refer to her great beauty, in spite of her age (12:11, 14). The original account is complete in itself and does not require the reader to be aware of any facts outside its compass, but this is quite different from the other two episodes.

Thus we find that the third episode is dependent upon the second, and the second upon the first. We may deduce therefore that the inclusion of all three episodes in the narrative is deliberate, and not a blunder made by an overworked editor or redactor, in spite of what Higher Criticism might say. As we have found so frequently, sceptical Source Critics, who make so much of their learning and erudition, fail when it comes to understanding the basics of the structures of Scripture.

The Findings Of Duane Garrett

Duane Garrett is to be congratulated for finding an unusual pattern which binds all three narratives together in an interesting manner. The table below, which is based on his findings, illustrates these.

Genesis 12:10–20, The First Cycle.

Event	Verses	
Event	*Verses*	
Journey	10	Owing to a famine, Abram travels to Egypt.
Deceit	11–13	Owing to Sarai's beauty, Abram calls her his sister.
Seizure	14–16	Sarai is taken by Pharaoh, and Abram receives gifts for her.
Release	17	Pharaoh plagued by the Lord.
Scolding	18–19	Pharaoh scolds Abram.
Journey	20	Departure of Abram, with his gifts.

Genesis 20:1–18, The Second Cycle.

Event	Verses	
Event	*Verses*	
Journey	1	Abraham travels to Gerar.
Deceit	2a	Abraham refers to Sarah as his sister.
Seizure	2b	Sarah is taken by Abimelech.
Release	3-7	Abimelech warned by the Lord in a dream.
Scolding	8–16	Abimelech scolds Abraham but offers gifts to him.
Journey	17–18	Abimelech healed after Abraham prays. Abraham leaves.

Genesis 26:1, 7–17, The Third Cycle.

Event	Verses	
Event	*Verses*	
Journey	1	Owing to a famine, Isaac travels to Gerar.
Deceit	7	Isaac refers to Rebekah as his sister.
Seizure	–	Rebekah not abducted.
Release	8	Abimelech sees Isaac and Rebekah and realizes they are married.
Scolding	9–13	Abimelech scolds Isaac, who is blessed by the Lord.
Journey	17	Isaac leaves Abimelech to prevent problems.

Garrett points out that a dominant feature noticeable when all three passages are compared, is that an important element of the narrative is present in only *two* out of the three accounts, and absent in the third. I have set out Garrett's interesting findings, which he refers to as *the two out of three pattern*, in the table below. Garrett refers to the first account as A, the second as B, and the third as C.

Feature	A	B	C
A and C begin with a famine. (No famine in B.)	✓	–	✓
Abraham & Sarah are the subjects in A & B. (Isaac & Rebekah in C.)	✓	✓	–
B & C occur in Gerar, with Abimelech as host. (Egypt & Pharaoh in A.)	–	✓	✓
Beauty of wife mentioned in A & C. (Unmentioned in B.)	✓	–	✓
Host's servants first to notice wife's beauty in A & C. (Not so in B.)	✓	–	✓
Wife taken into harem in A & B. (Not so in C.)	✓	✓	–
Direct intervention by God in A & B. (Providential incident in C.)	✓	✓	–
Host rewards Patriarch in A & B. (Not so in C.)	✓	✓	–
Name of Yahweh used in A & C. (Elohim in B.)	✓	–	✓
A & C speak explicitly of Patriarch's departure. (Only implicit in B.)	✓	–	✓

The fact that C is dependent upon B, and B is dependent upon A, clearly shows that the three episodes are meant to be understood as *distinct* from each other; yet the effect of the two-out-of-three pattern, to borrow Garrett's phrase, binds them all together nonetheless![389] This binding together of the three separate incidents means that we have here yet another Ancestor Epic, this time a Matriarch Epic, in composite form, with three direct and frightening threats to the Coming Seed. Further, in the second episode, or Second Threat, we learn that Abraham *often* portrayed Sarah as his sister (Genesis 20:13). Thus, again, there are two parts to the Second Threat, a general, and a particular threat to Sarah.

Yet again it is seen that the triumphalism of the sceptic is unfounded, and that the facts actually endorse the Scriptural narrative through the revealing of yet another recognized literary form. I give the outline of the Matriarchal Epic below.

---

[389] Garrett, op. cit., p. 131.

Prologue	Migration to a foreign land.
First Threat	Sarai introduced into Pharaoh's harem as Abram's sister.
Second Threat: Part 1	General threat: Sarah frequently introduced as Abraham's sister.
Second Threat: Part 2	Particular threat: Sarah introduced to Abimelech's harem as Abraham's sister.
Final Threat	Rebekah introduced to Abimelech (and his men) as Isaac's sister.
Resolution	Explanation of true situation and release of matriarch.

Conclusion 33. Both the Jacob Cycle and the Matriarchal Epic are examples of Ancestor Epic literary forms.

C) The Epic Of Lot

Garrett identifies one more individual Ancestor Epic discernible in the book of Genesis, one that concerns Lot, and this too needs to be built up from separate episodes. The first that we learn of Lot is that he is the nephew of Abram (Genesis 11:27–31) and journeyed with him from Ur to Canaan (Genesis 11:31 & 12:5).

The next episode that mentions Lot is found in chapter 13, and refers to the strife between the herdsmen of Lot and Abram over pasturing (verses 5–7.). This situation posed a threat to both Abram and Lot, who up till that moment had been accompanying Abram, and sharing in his blessings. Lot was in the weaker position of course, being younger than Abram, and not having received the direct calling from the Lord as Abram had. Graciously Abram proposed to Lot that he should take his pick of the land and take his herds wherever he would choose, and Abram would take a different course, and thus by Abram's actions, the conflict between their men would be ended (verse 8–9). Lot, decided to take for himself the best of the pasturing, namely the Jordan valley, with its relatively level ground, and copious amounts of water (verses 10–11). This left Abram on the higher ground, in both senses of the word, but the report ends with the unsettling words, "and Lot dwelled in the cities of the plain, and pitched his tent toward Sodom. But the men of Sodom were wicked and sinners before the Lord exceedingly." (Verses 12–13).

The next event which features Lot is in the very next chapter, where we find he has been captured, along with all his possessions, after the kings, Chedorlaomer, Tidal, Amraphel, and Arioch launched a military assault on the region of Sodom to punish a rebellion that had broken out there (Genesis 14:1–12). Abram learns of what has happened and manages to surprise the four kings, and succeeds in rescuing the prisoners, including Lot, and all the women, as well as all the possessions that had been seized. Thus Lot for the second time is saved from a threatening situation by his uncle Abram. Interestingly, in verse 17, we notice that Abram refused to accept any personal gifts from the king of Sodom (verses 21–24), which, probably, is another comment on the sinfulness of the city in which Lot resided.

The final references to Lot are to be found in Genesis 19, which concerns the overthrow of Sodom, but the story itself begins a little earlier in chapter 18. Abraham had been warned by the Lord about the imminent destruction of Sodom and Gomorrah, where Lot had decided to set up his home, and entreated the Lord on behalf of the righteous people who might be found there. He began his plea by asking the Lord to refrain from destroying Sodom and Gomorrah if there were but fifty righteous people there. Encouraged by the Lord's favourable response, eventually, by degrees, Abraham won agreement that if only ten righteous people might be found, the cities would escape destruction (Genesis 18:23–33).

When in the next chapter we see that both Sodom and Gomorrah are overthrown with the most awful violence, we are left to conclude that there were not even ten righteous persons within the two cities. But in verses 15–30 we see that Lot, his wife and two daughters were urged by angels to run for their lives from the doom that was about to fall, and in verse 29 we are told that this occurred because God remembered Abraham's plea, and as a consequence spared Lot and his family from sharing in the fate of the two cities. Thus, for the third time, Abraham saved Lot from a very real threat. Before we read of the destruction of the cities, we are informed in very graphic terms of the nature of the wickedness practised there in verses 1–14, thus this threat too gives an emphasis to the wickedness Lot associated himself with.

We now come to the conclusion of this most sombre of all Epics. In all the Ancestor Epics the three threats are to the continuity of mankind in general, or to a particular line of human descent. In each case, the resolution removes the threats and permits population growth in accordance with the primeval blessing of being fruitful and multiplying (Genesis 1:28). In the Epic of Lot, we find that after the threats to the continuity of his line had been removed, he too was free to multiply. In keeping with this disturbing epic however, we find the offspring of Lot derived from incestuous relationships between him and his two daughters, which resulted in the births of Moab and Ammon, who went on to become the founders of the two eponymous nations (Genesis 19:30–38). This is certainly the most uncomfortable epic we have seen.

It is particularly noteworthy that this epic includes the encounter between Abraham and Melchizedek (14:17–20), which often amongst Critics is thought to be an episode that is incongruous with the material either side of it.[390] However, seeing it as a fundamental part of the Ancestor Epic of Lot, shows the opposite to be true, namely that it forms *an integral part of the narrative,* and has clear associations with other parts of the epic, especially with the angelic visitations (18:1–21 & 19:1–23), and the discourse between Abraham and the Lord (18:23–33).

Although I depend heavily on Garrett in this section, I have again departed from his structure here, as he has not utilised all the material available on Lot,[391] nor has he shown the intensification of the Second Threat, which I believe definitely to be present in the narrative. With real respect to Duane Garrett for his many valuable contributions, and the help I have gained from him in this chapter, I submit that the true structure of the epic is as set out below.

---

[390] See for example, Hooke, S. J., in *Peake's Commentary* op. cit., p. 176., and Whybray, op. cit., p. 21.

[391] See Garrett, op. cit., p. 137.

Prologue	Migration to Canaan from Ur with his uncle Abram.
First Threat	Dispute between herdsmen. Abram's intervention rescues Lot from this situation. Lot chooses to dwell in Sodom.
Second Threat: Part 1	Lot is captured.
Second Threat: Part 2	Lot's women folk, and all his possessions are also captured. Abraham's direct intervention saves Lot, his family and possessions.
Final Threat	Lot is in danger of being engulfed by the overthrow of Sodom but is led to safety, owing to the intercession with the Lord by Abraham.
Resolution	Lot is safe and fathers incestuous offspring, ensuring in a manner typical of this grim epic, the continuity of his line.

Lot's Wife

Finally, a word ought to be said concerning the matter of Lot's wife. The critic loves to portray the incident of Genesis 19:26 as if the text suggests that by some magical metamorphosis, Lot's wife underwent an alchemical change and became salt as a punishment. After the discoveries of perfectly preserved human forms at Pompeii and Herculaneum, it is difficult to believe that Critics cannot understand that any individual who dallied as did Lot's wife, so close to a scene of catastrophic destruction which must have resembled very closely the fate of the two Roman cities just mentioned, would be in very real danger of becoming overwhelmed by debris akin to burning volcanic ash, and thus becoming entombed wherever he or she collapsed or slumped against a rock, cliff, or tree. Afterwards, given the environment, such an ash-covered human form could very readily become encrusted with a very heavy deposit of salt. Keil and Delitzsch comment, "We are not to suppose that she [Lot's wife] was actually turned into [a pillar of salt], but having been killed by the fiery and sulphurous vapour with which the air was filled, and afterwards encrusted with salt, she resembled an actual statue of salt; just as even now, from the saline exhalation of the Dead Sea, objects near it are quickly covered with a crust of salt."[392]

---

[392] Op. cit., p. 236.

The authors of the book *Volcanoes*,[393] make the point that, purely from an archaeological point of view, burning volcanic ash is the very best type of preservative known to man. Erich Lessing and Antonio Varone in their book *Pompeii*,[394] cite as an example of the instantaneous 'freezing' of the forms adopted by men and women acting in the most desperate of circumstances, a preserved family group, overwhelmed at the instant at which a dying man was attempting to surrender a very small child to a woman, whose arms were fully outstretched in an attempt to receive it. This pathetic and profoundly moving find illustrates perfectly how suddenly overwhelming the descent of burning ash may be.

Conclusion 34. The story of Lot is another example of Ancestor Epic Literature to be found within the book of Genesis.

The Story Of Hagar

There appears to be one more Ancestor Epic within the book of Genesis, but it is different in form from those of Jacob, the Matriarchs, and Lot, inasmuch as it lacks the classic threefold threat, having instead, merely a dual threat. Duane Garrett nonetheless categorises it as Ancestor Epic, but I suspect it is an amalgam of true Ancestor Epic, and the Negotiation Tales that will be examined shortly. The Epic of Hagar is set out below based on Garrett's work.

Genesis 16:1–16, The First Cycle.

A   1   Sarai unable to conceive.

B   2–3   Sarai reacts by proposing that Abram sleeps with Hagar.

C   4   Hagar conceives and despises Sarai.

D   5–6   Sarah objects and calls for Hagar to be expelled.

E   7–9   The Angel of the Lord commands Hagar to return.

F   10   The Angel of the Lord will increase Hagar's descendants.

G   11–14   The Angel of the Lord says that Ishmael will be a 'Wild Man'.

H   15–16   Ishmael is born.

---

[393] Fisher, Richard, Heiken, Grant, & Hulen, Jeffrey, *Volcanoes: Crucible Of Change*, Princeton, New Jersey, Princeton University Press, 1997, p. 247.

[394] Lessing, Erich, and Varone, Antonio, *Pompeii*, Paris, Terrail, 1996, pp. 14–15.

Genesis 21:1–21, The Second Cycle.

A   1–5   Sarah conceives.

B   6–8   Sarah reacts with: joy and laughter.

C   9   Ishmael mocks Isaac.

D   10   Sarah objects and calls for Hagar to be expelled.

E   11–12 The Lord commands that Hagar should leave.

F   13   The Lord promises to make a nation from the son of the bondwoman.

G   14–18 The Angel of the Lord promises that Ishmael will become a great nation.

H   19–20 Ishmael's life is saved.

The Negotiation Tales

Before turning to the Abraham and Joseph Cycles, there is one more literary form to consider, namely the Negotiation Tale, a category to which the account of the rape of Dinah in the Jacob Cycle was removed.

Duane Garrett gives as a classic secular example of a Negotiation Tale, an Ugaritic story in which the goddess Anath, desires from the human hero, Aqhat, a bow which the god Kothar wa-Khasis had given him.[395] Negotiations between Anath and Aqhat proceed, but Aqhat refuses all of Anath's offers, resulting in Anath causing Aqhat to be murdered. A drought then occurs and the sister of Aqhat seeks revenge for her brother's murder, but the outcome is unknown, as the tablets which record this story are broken. Nonetheless from this tale Garrett builds up the typical Negotiation Tale structure which always begins with a major challenge. An illustration of the Negotiation Tales' structure is given below, based upon Garrett's findings.

---

[395] Op. cit., pp. 146–147.

Negotiation Tale Structure

1. A Challenge looms.

2. The Challenge Deepens.

3. The Initiative of the Central Figure to meet the Challenge.

4. The Immediate Consequence of the Initiative, and

5. The Lasting Effect of the Initiative.

Garrett finds three such Tales in Genesis; 1) the negotiations concerning the burial of Sarah in Genesis 23:1–20, 2) the negotiations concerning the securing of a wife for Isaac in Genesis 24:1–67, and 3) the negotiations resulting from the rape of Dinah in Genesis 34:1–31. The structures of all three Tales are set out below.

Genesis 23:1–20, The First Negotiation Tale

1. 1–2   *The Challenge.*   The death of Sarah.

2. 3–5, 10–11 *The Challenge Deepens.* Burial site needed: Hittites offer site as gift.

3. 7–9, 12–13 *The Initiative.*   Abraham insists on purchasing the site.

4. 14–16   *The Consequence.*   Settlement reached.

5. 17–20   *The Lasting Effect.*   Site legally Abraham's (& his family's).

Genesis 24:1–67. The Second Negotiation Tale

1. 1–4   *The Challenge.*   Isaac single as Abraham close to death. Oath.

2. 5–9   *The Challenge Deepens.* Isaac must not return.

3. 10–14 *The Initiative.*   Request to the Lord for a sign.

4. 15–61 *The Consequence.*   A sign is granted; successful negotiations.

5. 62–67 *The Lasting Effect.*   Isaac marries Rebekah.

Genesis 34:1–31, The Third Negotiation Tale

1. 1–2   *The Challenge.*   The rape of Dinah.

2. 3–12 *The Challenge Deepens.* Love of Shechem for Dinah: tries to negotiate marriage with her.

3. 13–17 *The Initiative.*   Deceitful negotiations of Dinah's brothers.

4. 18–29 *The Consequence.*   Hamor & Shechem deceived, town looted.

5. 30–31 *The Lasting Effect.*   Simeon and Levi censured by Jacob.

Dinah And Rebekah

Although the episode concerning the rape of Dinah is the last of Garrett's Negotiation Tales, it is the one we encountered first of all, when we noticed its occurrence in the Jacob Cycle. It was then put on one side together with the final episode of the Matriarchal Ancestor Epic, in which Rebekah was placed at great risk through the deceit of Isaac. We noticed also that within the structure of the life of Jacob, these two episodes correspond with one another.[396] Therefore if the structure of the life of Jacob has any genuinely objective existence, we must expect a real connection between the Matriarchal Ancestor Epic, of which the episode concerning Rebekah formed a key part, and the Negotiation Tales. A failure to find such a vital connection would tend to invalidate the objective reality of the structure of the life of Jacob, which in turn, would compromise its witness against the errors of the Documentary Hypothesis.

Given Garrett's remarkable work on the Form Critical study of Genesis, and his special contribution of what he terms the two-out-of-three pattern that characterises the Matriarchal Epic, I am surprised that he has not seen the importance of the connection between the Matriarchal Epic and the Negotiation Tales. I thought it would be interesting to take Garrett's *two-out-of-three pattern*, and see if it could be found in the Negotiation Tales as well. If this could be done, then it would be a very positive indicator of a close relationship between the two, which would then confirm the objective reality of the structure of the life of Jacob, while simultaneously invalidating the tenets of the New Documentary Hypothesis.

The Two-Out-Of-Three Pattern In The Negotiation Tales

Duane Garrett located ten instances of the two-out-of-three pattern in the distinct episodes of the Matriarchal Epic; I set this as my target for the Negotiation Tales therefore. To my surprise this is exactly the number of times I detected its presence! Following Garrett and calling the first Tale A, the second, B; and the third C, this is what I discovered.

In B and C, the central character, Rebekah, or Dinah, is alive, but not in A (Sarah). A and B relate to Abraham, but C relates to Jacob. In C a

---

crime was committed against the central character (Dinah), but not in A or B. A and C occur within the Land of Promise, but B is based partly outside the Land as well. C shows a hidden agendum, but this is not the case in either A or B. C reveals deceit, but there is none in A or B. A and B end positively, but not C. In A and B the theme of the death of an ancestor is prominent (Sarah, and Abraham), but in C the death of gentile peers is a feature. In B and C the subject of marriage is key, but not in A. In A and C negotiations are with the natives of the Land of Promise, but not in B. I have set out my findings in the table below.

Feature	A	B	C
In B & C the central character is alive. (But not in A.)	–	✓	✓
A & B relate to Abraham. (C to Jacob.)	✓	✓	–
In C the central character is a victim. (But not in A or B.)	✓	✓	–
A & C occur in Canaan. (B is based in part outside Canaan.)	✓	–	✓
C reveals a hidden agendum. (But this is not so is A or B.)	✓	✓	–
C reveals deceit. (But this is not so is A or B.)	✓	✓	–
A & B end positively. (But not C.)	✓	✓	–
A & B relate to the death of an ancestor. (But C to the death of peers.)	✓	✓	–
B & C relate to marriage. (But not in A.)	–	✓	✓
Negotiations are with people of Canaan in A & C. (But not in B.)	✓	–	✓

This parallelism simultaneously validates Garrett's assessment of the separate episodes of the Matriarchal Epic, the inter-relationships and genuine existence of the Negotiation Tales, and the close connection between them and the Matriarchal Epic, by which the structure of the life of Jacob, and its witness against Graf–Wellhausen is authenticated. We noticed also that while the distinct episodes of the Matriarchal Epic bind together Abraham, Isaac and Jacob, so do the Negotiation Tales, showing again the unity of chapters 12–36 of the book of Genesis, and the baselessness of the New Documentary Hypothesis. Finally, we see the reason for the similarity of some of the stories within Genesis. They are not the work of a redactor fusing different sources, but are the consequence of utilising common literary forms.

Conclusion 35. The Negotiation Tales, by their consistency, and close relationship to the distinct elements of the Matriarchal Epic, seem to form a recognisable literary genre as Garrett maintains.

D) The Pentateuch As A Whole

There is one more instance of the Ancestor Epic literary form to consider, and it is arguably the most important instance there is. Kikawada and Quinn[397] point out something which is truly remarkable. The fivefold Ancestor Epic literary form is not only clearly evident within the first eleven chapters of Genesis, in the stories of Jacob, the Matriarchs and Lot and in the book as a whole; it is also equally discernible that *the entire Pentateuch* is set out in this manner.

Genesis of course, forms the Opening Section, and the book of Deuteronomy, as the Treaty Document of Israel-as-a-nation, forms the Settlement. In the middle where we should find the Tripartite Centre, within the books of Exodus to Numbers, following Gordon Wenham we noticed very clearly three distinct cycles; the journeys of: 1) Egypt-to-Sinai, 2) Sinai-to-Kadesh-Barnea, 3) Kadesh-Barnea-to-the-plains-of-Moab.

The Fulcrum Of The Pentateuch

This conformity to the Ancestor Epic form is particularly striking, especially as the central element, which is usually twofold, covers both the cycle from Sinai to Kadesh-Barnea as Wenham points out, *and the journey of the spies*, as the next cycle of movement did not commence until after the people gave their verdict on the spies' report. It is surprising that neither Kikawada and Quinn, or Garrett noticed this. We now see that every characteristic of the Ancestor Epic literary form is to be found at the level of the Pentateuch as a whole.[398]

Not only this, but in terms of the Ancestor Epic literary form, we see that the centre of gravity of the entire Pentateuch is the decision to be made following the report of the spies, and here there is a lesson for us. That in terms of literary form, the entire Pentateuch should turn on the decision to accept in faith what God offered freely to the

---

[397] Op. cit., pp. 119–125.

[398] Kikawada and Quinn simply refer to the *books* of Exodus, Leviticus, and Numbers as forming the Tripartite Centre (op. cit., p. 122f.), but every other cycle has been personality or activity based, which makes this division unlikely in my mind. We have already seen the merit of Wenham's scheme, and the duality of the central cycle brought about by the inclusion of the mission of the spies seems to authenticate his system very clearly.

Israelites; or to reject it through fear and unbelief is both dramatic and startling and should bring home to us most keenly, the importance of our own individual response to what God offers us freely in Christ.

For me the fact that this monumentally important decision now becomes no less than the _fulcrum_ of the Pentateuch is one more piece of evidence, and probably the most telling so far, that this analysis is genuine, and that the imaginings of the sceptics must collapse like the proverbial house-of-cards before it.

Neither The Hexateuch Or The Tetrateuch Have Any Objective Existence

The importance of this Pentateuchal literary form is seen also in two very significant consequences of this discovery.

Firstly it means that the Hexateuch of Higher Criticism is seen again to be devoid of any real existence, as the Ancestor Epic literary form is _completed_ by the book of Deuteronomy, which fulfils the concluding rôle as the Settlement. Thus, the division between the Pentateuch, and Joshua, the first of The Former Prophets, is a true division, as we now see that the Pentateuch is recognisable as a distinct literary corpus, as the Jews have insisted for centuries.

Secondly, by the very same token, the Tetrateuch of Martin Noth is also seen to be a fiction, as, although the book of Deuteronomy is distinguishable from the preceding books by its different style, it is now seen to be inextricably bound up with them, as their logical, and literary conclusion. The Ancestor Epic form embraces it emphatically and irreversibly, locking it into the rest of the Pentateuch.

This really marks the end of the road for the academic genius of Martin Noth and his Deuteronomist History from Deuteronomy to II Kings. Deuteronomy, by the literary form of Ancestor Epic is inseparable from the other four books of the Pentateuch, and we may now assert that the Deuteronomists, as Noth understands them, could never have existed![399] Thus, the literary source of D is now debunked,

---

[399] Of course, as was stated earlier, there are bound to be Deuteronomic resonances to be found in the books of Joshua to II Kings, and in the prophets, as Deuteronomy is the Foundation Treaty of Israel-as-a-nation. If the Priests were to safeguard the worship, ritual, and ceremony from corruption, and maintain Israel's adherence to it; the

and seen to be a fantasy of unspiritual intellectualism, which, dazzled by its own seeming brilliance, cannot perceive what is obvious to those who are aware of the methodology of ancient writing. The tiers of Ancestor Epic literary form to be found within the first eleven chapters of Genesis, the complete book of Genesis, and the Pentateuch as a whole are shown below.

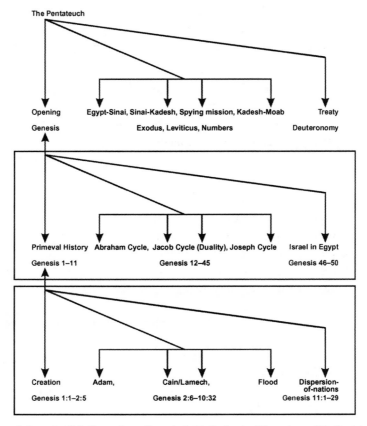

Figure 8 Ancestor Epic literary form: Genesis 1–11, the book of Genesis, and the Pentateuch

prophets were to undertake the same responsibilities with regard to the Word-of-God. Thus, the books of Joshua to II Kings, designated in the Hebrew Canon as The Former *Prophets*, are bound to include Deuteronomic phrases and sentiments. The prophets were the *real* Deuteronomists therefore, inasmuch as they worked for adherence to the Word-of-God generally, and to the Foundation Treaty in particular, in order to preserve the Covenant with the Lord. This is also why the writings of the Latter Prophets have similar characteristics of course, as we have seen.

Conclusion 36. This fivefold Ancestor Epic literary form unites each individual book of the Pentateuch, to every other book of the Pentateuch. This special characteristic builds an unique literary corpus from which no single book may be withdrawn, and to which no other book might be added, without completely destroying the Ancestor Epic form.

Conclusion 37. It follows from Conclusion 36, not only that the so-called Tetrateuch, Hexateuch, and Octateuch can have no real existence, but also that the existence of the supposed literary source of D, is now untenable.

Conclusion 38. Given that we have already seen that E and P are just as Yahwist as J, with the demise of D, the entire Pentateuch may now be classified as Yahwist! The New Documentary Hypothesis must now be abandoned therefore as untenable.

The Unity Of The Joseph Cycle

We have seen on previous occasions that the narrative concerning Joseph is significantly different from the rest of the book of Genesis. This is discernible in terms of the vocabulary, which, as would be expected, contains many Egyptian words, and from the lack of toledoths, showing that the really ancient records written on clay tablets have given way to Egyptian accounts that Aaron and Moses would have had direct access to through the royal court. But we see that the literary form is also different; the Ancestor Epic form is absent in the Joseph Narrative, instead it comes to us in a different genre as we will see shortly. Before that however, there is one difficulty that needs to be resolved. Inserted within the beginning of the Joseph narrative is an episode concerning Judah. This is to be found in Genesis 38, and details his relationship with Tamar. Initially it does seem odd that this incident should interrupt the Joseph material, so why has it been located here? Once again Garrett I believe has the answer to this problem. We need to look again at the structure of the life of Joseph. Although this was given earlier in a very simple form, a much more detailed structure is discernible which reveals that this account truly belongs to the Joseph Cycle, in spite of how incongruous it might seem at first. The detailed structure following Garrett is given below.

The Detailed Structure Of The Life Of Joseph[400]

A Hostility of brothers to Joseph (37:3–11)

  B Apparent death of Joseph, Jacob mourns (37:12–35)

    C Judah and Tamar (38:1–26)

      D Unfair reversals

      Da Pharez and Zarah (38:27–30)

      Db Potiphar's wife and Joseph (39:1–23)

        E Wisdom of Joseph (40:1–42:57)

        F Movement to Egypt (42:1–46:7)

        Fa Jacob sends brothers, brothers threatened

        Fb Brothers tricked by Joseph, and arrested; Joseph reveals himself

        Fc Jacob sets out for Egypt

          G Genealogy (46:8–27)

        F' Settlement in Egypt (46:28–47:12)

        F'a Jacob arrives in Egypt but sends Judah ahead

        F'b Joseph welcomes Jacob, introduces him to Pharaoh

        F'c Jacob moves to Rameses

        E' Wisdom of Joseph (47:13–26)

      D' Unfair reversals

      D'a Jacob favours Joseph (48:1–12)

      D'b Ephraim preferred over Manasseh (48:13–22)

    C' Irony in blessing on Judah (49:8–12)

  B' Death of Jacob, Joseph buries him (49:29–50:14)

A' Joseph reassures brothers (50:15–21)

As Garrett points out, immediately we see that structurally the story of Judah and Tamar leads in naturally to the story of Joseph and Potiphar's wife. Both concern irregular relationships which result in reversals, and both relate by their corresponding structural links (D'a & D'b) to irregular rankings amongst siblings, resulting in advancement of the younger brothers (Joseph and Ephraim). Merely at a superficial level then, it is apparent that the story of Judah and Tamar is not quite as incongruous with the Joseph material as might at first be thought. We will shortly look a little closer at Tamar, and see precisely what her story reveals.

---

[400] Based on a structure given in Garrett, op. cit., p. 172.

The Quest For Leadership

Some years ago I realised that there was a real issue during the lifetime of the twelve tribal patriarchs, as to which of them was to be the leader of the group. The more I studied this, the more I realized how central the issue is to the narrative of Genesis.[401] To my great surprise Duane Garrett also noticed this is a key issue, and in a most convincing manner shows it to be a major theme of the Joseph narrative, and shows how the incident involving Judah and Tamar helps illuminate this theme.

Reuben

The first incident concerning this is often seen as unrelated to anything else in the narrative of Genesis, but as we have seen with so many other matters, this is only because of ignorance of the practices of antiquity. In Genesis 35:22 there is the briefest of references to Reuben, the firstborn son of Jacob (29:32) committing adultery with Bilhah, Rachel's maid who became Jacob's concubine (30:1–5). Seldom is it realised that this was a common ploy in making a bid for family or tribal leadership. The crime must not be viewed as merely motivated by sexual greed, it was a crime of ambition, an attempt by Reuben to seize what was Jacob's. This seizing of Jacob's concubine was but a token signifying the ambition to seize all that was Jacob's. We see that this is so from a parallel incident during the rebellion against David of his son Absalom. Immediately after this revolt, when David had left Jerusalem, the rebel Absalom received advice to erect a tent on the palace roof, where it would be seen by all, and within it, lie with David's concubines. This public demonstration of the seizure of the concubines would make plain the political statement that Absalom had seized all that hitherto had been under David. (II Samuel 16:20–23).

A very similar incident is recorded in I Kings 2. We read in verses 11–12 of the death of David, and the subsequent advancement of Solomon to the throne of Israel. From verses 13–15 we are reminded

---

[401] My preliminary work on this subject is to be found in Part I of *Beyond The Law*, Brighton, Paradosis, 2000.

that Adonijah (the eldest surviving son of David) had hoped to become king himself. In the naïve view of Bathsheba, Adonijah had accepted the younger Solomon as king, who graciously had spared his life in spite of his recent attempt at a coup (I Kings 1:5–53). Adonijah approached Bathsheba, and persuaded her to petition her son Solomon for permission for him to marry Abishag, who, crucially, had been a maid for king David (I Kings 1:1–4). Solomon was not fooled by this and viewed it as another attempt to usurp the kingdom, and answered Bathsheba, "And why dost thou ask Abishag the Shunamite for Adonijah? ask for him the Kingdom also; for he is mine elder brother; even for him, and for Abiathar the priest, and for Joab the son of Zeruiah (confederates with Adonijah, see I Kings 1:7)." Then king Solomon sware by the Lord saying, "God do so to me, and more also, if Adonijah have not spoken this word against his own life." (I Kings 2:22–23) There was no doubt in Solomon's mind that the desire to have the king's maid, was but a preliminary to having the kingdom itself.

So then, it seems most likely that Reuben's adultery with Bilhah was motivated by ambition to usurp the family leadership and control its wealth, but as Genesis 49:3–4 shows, it resulted only in ignominy. It is against this background of Reuben's failed leadership bid that we read of his rôle in the capture of Joseph by his brothers. It might be that Reuben was detached from his brothers when their plan to kill him was hatched (Genesis 37:20), for in Genesis 37:21 we find "when Reuben *heard* it." At any rate, he managed to dissuade the brothers from murder, and planned to restore Joseph to his father (verse 22). As the eldest son, the greatest burden for protecting the youthful Joseph obviously fell on him, and keenly aware of his loss of prestige after the incident with Bilhah, it was vital to Reuben's interests that he seize this opportunity, as failure to save his father's favourite would have the most serious repercussions imaginable. Hence Reuben's cry when he discovered Joseph had been sold in his absence. Reuben's prime concern was for his *own* position, "whither shall I go?" or "What am I going to do *now*?" (verses 29–30).

Joseph And Judah

Unknown to Jacob of course, it had been Judah's plan to sell Joseph (Genesis 37:25–28). Now we notice that after Reuben, the next eldest sons of Jacob, Simeon and Levi (Genesis 29:32–34), had disgraced themselves in the reaction to the rape of Dinah (Genesis 34:25–31) that we dealt with earlier. They were debarred from receiving any territorial inheritance in Genesis 49:5–7. Judah then was the eldest son of Jacob who had not ruled himself out of consideration for the leadership of the brothers. We begin to see that the story of Joseph is concerned with the actions of his murderous brothers, and in fact results in their reform.

Joseph undoubtedly was the favourite of his father Jacob. Thus, with the fall of Reuben, Simeon and Levi, we might expect the Joseph narrative to reflect in particular the relationship between Joseph and Judah, making it far less surprising that we should encounter the story involving Tamar, which provides early on in the narrative concerning Joseph, a biographical sketch of Judah, whose position the prophetic dreams seem to indicate that Joseph would occupy (Genesis 37:5–11).

The Story Of Tamar

Garrett shows that the story of Tamar is really the story of Judah's attitude to his own family. We learn that Judah had three sons, Er, Onan, and Shelah (Genesis 38:1–5). Tamar was chosen to be the wife of Er, Judah's eldest son (verse 6). For some unspecified wickedness, the Lord slew Er (verse 7), and Judah required Onan to marry Tamar and father children in his brother's name (verse 8).[402] Onan apparently went ahead with the marriage, but was clearly unwilling to father children by Tamar, as they would be attributed to his deceased elder brother (verse 9). Of course, had children been born to Onan and Tamar in the name of his brother Er, then the benefits of the First-Born son would by-pass Onan and his family. However, if no child was born of their union, these benefits would ultimately become Onan's. This is why Onan took the action described in verse 9, he coveted the position

---

[402] Through the practice of Levirate Marriage. Cf. Matthew 22:24ff. For details, see Hastings, op. cit., in. loc.

of First-Born for himself and his own heirs. Thus we see a definite connection between this story and the jealousies arising among the sons of Jacob (and Jacob and Esau).

Onan displeased the Lord by his actions, and he too was slain (verse 10). Tamar was then in a position to claim the last son, Shelah, as her husband, but Judah, who had become very wary about Tamar, employed delaying tactics, telling her to go back to her father and wait until Shelah was older (verse 11a). In verse 11b however, we find that the real reason for Judah delaying was fear for the safety of Shelah, and possibly suspicion of Tamar's rôle in the deaths of his two sons.

Judah continued to withhold Shelah from Tamar, so that in the end, when she heard that Judah happened to be close by, she determined to adopt the desperate measure of posing as a harlot and enticing him to avail himself of her. Before this was done, Tamar secured some personal possessions from Judah, which she retained (verses 12–23). Judah, not knowing that the woman he had used was Tamar, eventually heard that Tamar was pregnant, and determined to punish her for her harlotry. It was at this point that Tamar produced the personal possessions of Judah that she had kept by her, and sent them to Judah saying that they belonged to the man who had fathered her child. Confronted by the indisputable evidence of his own culpability, Judah announced Tamar more righteous than him, as she should have been granted Shelah by whom she could have raised up grandchildren of Judah. Judah's failure to allow this to happen meant that he had himself fulfilled the rôle he was reluctant to award to his last remaining son (verses 24–26). Clearly there were lessons here for Judah about not meddling in the affairs of the rights, privileges, and responsibilities of the First-Born.

When Tamar came to give birth, it was found that she was carrying twin boys. One boy thrust out his hand, and the midwife, obviously keenly aware of the importance of identifying the First-Born tied a scarlet thread around the boy's finger, but, no doubt to the surprise of those present, the boy withdrew his hand with the thread still attached, and his younger brother who was then named Pharez emerged instead, followed by the one with the scarlet thread, who was named Zarah (verses 27–30).

Garrett rightly points out that this was yet another lesson for Judah on the rights of the First-Born. No doubt he would have seen the hand of God in this strange event, especially as it has such a strong resemblance to the birth of his father Jacob, who was chosen above his twin brother Esau, who was also distinguished by the colour red. There were also echoes of the election of Isaac over Ishmael of course. Judah must have realised two things; firstly that the re-appearance within his line of the obvious preferment of the younger brother showed that God graciously had marked out his descendants in some special way to follow in the line of Isaac and Jacob, and secondly, that while the Lord HimSelf might single out for advancement a younger son, man must never meddle in such affairs, and thus cave in to ambition and jealousy. As Garrett observes, the episode of Tamar marks a real change in the life of Judah. From that point on he matures enormously, and wins his father's confidence, and in the absence of Joseph becomes the leader of the brothers.[403]

Judah In The Joseph Cycle

In Genesis 43:3–14, it is only after listening to Judah that Jacob agrees to a second trip to Egypt, this time with Benjamin. This is after, in 42:29–38, Reuben had tried and failed to persuade Jacob to allow the trip. Thus, in terms of influence with his father, Judah had surpassed Reuben the First-Born. When Joseph had caught Benjamin in a trap, it is Judah who pleaded for him in 44:16–34, and we notice that before this in 44:14, the brothers are referred to as "Judah and his brethren," again showing the leading rôle played by Judah. Finally, we see that in 46:28, Jacob sent Judah ahead of him, to prepare the way. Judah it seems had learned the lessons associated with Tamar, and as a consequence, the position of leader became his naturally.

The final episode in the story of the relationship of Judah and Joseph comes near the close of Jacob's life. In Genesis 48:1–5 we see that Jacob adopted Joseph's two sons Ephraim and Manasseh as his own, in the place of Reuben and Simeon. That this adoption of Ephraim to the position of First-Born was effective we see from Jeremiah 31:9 where the Lord HimSelf, while speaking of Israel, refers to Ephraim

---

[403] Garrett, op. cit., pp. 174ff.

as His First-Born. We notice also that when Jacob blesses Joseph's two sons, he deliberately, and in the face of Joseph's protest, crosses his arms so that Ephraim, the younger son receives the primary blessing, while Manasseh, the older son, is relegated to the secondary position. Jacob had learned what Judah had had to come to terms with, namely, that in the line of succession of the chosen family, it is a characteristic that the younger son receives the greatest prominence.

Thus we find that both Judah and Joseph have pairs of sons, the younger of which was raised to prominence. And we see also that in the blessing of his sons, the only two that Jacob lavishes his praise upon are Judah and Joseph (Genesis 49). In this chapter we see that Judah is clearly granted the leadership of the family of Jacob (verse 10), but the birthright remains with Joseph (verses 22–26). This position is clearly ratified for us in I Chronicles 5:1–2, "Reuben the firstborn of Israel, (for he was the firstborn; but forasmuch as he defiled his father's bed, his birthright was given unto the sons of Joseph the son of Israel: and the genealogy is not reckoned after the birthright. But Judah prevailed above his brethren, and of him came The Chief Ruler; but the birthright was Joseph's.)" Here we see that both Judah and Joseph emerge with positions of leadership, and that both were distinguished by pairs of sons, the younger of which was pre-eminent. Thus the story of Judah in Genesis 38, detailing the births of Pharez and Zarah is not an interruption of the Joseph narrative, but is an integral part of one of its major themes.

Conclusion 39. The Joseph Cycle of Genesis 37–50 is incomplete without the story of Judah and Tamar in chapter 38. The critic who objects to this, has failed to see the parallelism in the lives of Judah and Joseph that the story of Joseph gives emphasis to.

The Literary Form Of The Joseph Narrative

Now that we see that the Joseph Narrative is an uninterrupted corpus it needs to be classified in terms of its literary form. We have seen clearly that the general literary form of the Pentateuch as a whole, is that of Ancestor Epic, although beneath this Primary Level, are several subsidiary, or secondary literary forms; the Migration Epic of Exodus to Numbers, the Ancient Treaty Form of Deuteronomy, and the individual Ancestor Epics and Negotiation Tales of Genesis.

Clearly the Joseph Cycle in its own right does not fit the complete Ancestor Epic form in terms of the classic fivefold structure. Equally clear are the links with Egypt through its vocabulary as has been noted previously, and the fact that as with the books of Exodus, Leviticus, and the first portion of Numbers, it is associated directly with Aaron and Moses by the toledoth of Numbers 3:1. This affinity is further emphasised by the reference to Joseph at the very start of the book of Exodus at 1:8, showing the literary and conceptual dependence of the book of Exodus, and the rest of the Pentateuch in fact, on the Joseph Narrative of Genesis 37–50.

I propose then, that the Joseph Narrative be classified in the same way as the books of Exodus to Numbers, namely as Migration Epic, a conclusion I share with Duane Garrett, albeit I go beyond Garrett's position. To me it seems patently clear that the Migration Epic of the Joseph Cycle seems to be the correlate of the Migration Epic of *The-Escape-From-Egypt*, being instead, the account of *The-Descent-Into-Egypt*. If it is objected that it is difficult to believe that the same author or authors, Moses and Aaron in our case, would write two different but related epic works on different aspects of the same subject, we have the examples from antiquity of Homer's *Iliad*, and *The Odyssey* to appeal to. Thus, it seems to be the case that all the Pentateuchal narrative from the toledoth of Jacob in Genesis 37:2a until the end of the book of Numbers, where the tribes are encamped upon the plains of Moab, comprises Migration Epic, albeit, the bulk of it forms the Tripartite centre of the overall Ancestor Epic which is the primary literary form for the Pentateuch *as a whole*. Thus the Joseph Narrative cements Genesis to the rest of the Pentateuch.

There is one more important point that should be noted however. The continuous narrative from Genesis 37:2b, the start of the Joseph Cycle, to Deuteronomy 33, that comes directly from Moses (initially with Aaron), does seem to a certain extent to be *a self-contained narrative*. As such, the Joseph Narrative may be viewed not merely as the Introduction to the book of Exodus, it may also be viewed as the essential heart of the Introduction to the rest of the Pentateuch, which means that the narrative of Genesis 37:2b to Deuteronomy 33 could be classed as Ancestor Epic narrative, *in its own right*. This has important implications as we will see shortly.

Conclusion 40. The Joseph Narrative *by itself* could be understood as the Opening Section of an Ancestor Epic that would embrace Genesis 37 to Deuteronomy 33.

Conclusion To Chapter Nine

On several occasions now, we have noticed, as have many Critics of course, the Great Divide between Genesis 1–36, and Genesis 37–50. This is noticeable by the change to Egyptian vocabulary, the change in the subsidiary literary form from individual Ancestor Epic to Migration Epic, and the Egyptian milieu, which we find again, as we would expect, in the book of Exodus.

Now our careful examination of the toledoths revealed that it was exactly at Genesis 37:2b that the use of the ancient sources based on family histories preserved on clay tablets gave way to the writings of Aaron and Moses. Moses, with Aaron is himself the *author* of Genesis 37–50, whereas he is but the *editor,* we might even say *redactor* of Genesis 1-36.

This crucial fact explains the very noticeable difference in composition, which otherwise has no explanation that would satisfy the believer. In fact understanding that Genesis 37:2b to Deuteronomy 33 is a distinct literary corpus, being the *direct* work of Moses, confirms the understanding of the toledoths as suggested by Wiseman, as the toledoth of Numbers 3:1, *alone*, associates Genesis 37:2b–50:26 with the books of Exodus to Deuteronomy.

There is no other explanation available that may account for the change from a Babylonian to an Egyptian vocabulary that occurs at Genesis 37:2b, and that has been noticed by believer and cynic alike. But, what is more natural, when, following Wiseman's understanding of the toledoths, we see that at this precise point we move from the writings of Jacob, the grandson of a native of Ur of the Chaldees, who married within the same Chaldean family, to the writings of Moses who was brought up in the height of Egyptian culture, in the Household of Pharaoh? Naturally the vocabulary would change, and in precisely the way that we observe it to change!

Now as has been noticed already, the narrative of Genesis 37:2b to Deuteronomy 33, that is the writings directly attributable to Moses, follow the classic fivefold Ancestor Epic literary form as illustrated below;

Prologue	The Joseph Cycle: The Descent to Egypt, and the background to the Exodus.
First Cycle	Egypt to Sinai.
Second Cycle: Part 1	Sinai to Kadesh-barnea.
Second Cycle: Part 2	The mission of the spies.
Final Cycle	Kadesh-barnea to the plains of Moab.
Settlement	The Foundation Treaty of Israel-as-a-nation (Deuteronomy).

We have seen already that the book of Deuteronomy must be attributed a Mosaic provenance. We have noticed also that it has a literary dependence on the book of Numbers, and a conceptual dependence on the books of Exodus and Leviticus, and that the distribution of subject matter of all three of these books witnesses to a Mosaic provenance for them as well.

It follows from this that as Genesis 37:2b to 50:26 dovetails into the literary form of the books of Exodus to Deuteronomy, that this too must be given a Mosaic provenance, precisely as Wiseman's understanding of the toledoths requires. Thus we see that as Genesis 37:2b to Deuteronomy 33, that is, the entire body of Moses' direct writings, conforms to the Ancestor Epic literary form, the one who cast this material into that literary form was Moses himself. There are important consequences of this which will be discussed in Chapter Ten, which will also include an examination of the Abraham Cycle that we may not now delay for much longer.

Conclusion 41. Moses himself is the one who has cast the narrative of Genesis 37:2b to Deuteronomy 33 into the literary form of Ancient Ancestor Epic.

Chapter Ten

Positive Form Criticism And The Testimony To Christ

Consistency

In Chapter Eight we identified the literary sources of Genesis through analysing the nature, usage, and locations of the toledoths. In Chapter Nine, using the genealogies as well as certain of the toledoths, we have seen that the narrative falls naturally into what Kikawada and Quinn refer to as Ancient Epic literary form, and what Garrett refers to as Ancestor Epic literary form. Whatever term is deemed to be the most accurate, one thing has become abundantly clear, there is a remarkable parallelism of literary form to be found within;

1. the Pentateuch as a whole,

2. the Pentateuchal Narrative authored directly by Moses, namely Genesis 37:2b to Deuteronomy 33,

3. the book of Genesis as a whole, and,

4. the first eleven chapters of Genesis.

Having concluded that it was Moses who cast the narrative of Genesis 37:2b to Deuteronomy 33 into the literary form of Ancestor Epic, the presence of the parallel literary forms in the rest of the book of Genesis are very highly suggestive of the organising hand of Moses, marshalling the ancient family histories that had descended all the way from Adam to Jacob, into a Form which made them compatible with his own direct work. Thus the persistent literary form found in the first eleven chapters of Genesis, the histories of the Matriarchs, of Lot, and Jacob, and the book as a whole, acts as a water-mark, seal, or badge-of-authenticity, revealing to those with eyes-to-see I suggest, the hand of Moses *throughout* the Pentateuch.

This explains the insistence of pious Jews, Scripture itself, and the Lord Jesus Christ in referring to the Pentateuch as the work of Moses.[404] Moses I believe, *extended* the Ancestor Epic literary form he had produced which embraced the subsidiary literary forms of the Migration Epic of the Joseph Narrative, the associated Migration Epic of Exodus, Leviticus and Numbers, and the Treaty Document of Deuteronomy, to include within its compass, the ancient family histories going back all the way to Adam. Thus the entire Pentateuch is suffused with the presence of Moses.

It is interesting to note that there is genuine linguistic evidence to support this view. Biblical Hebrew, as does all language, reveals a gradual development of style, and nowadays three distinct categories are recognised; namely,

1. *Archaic*,

2. *Standard*, and

3. *Late*.

The books of Ezra, Nehemiah, Esther, Ecclesiastes, and I and II Chronicles, all display the Late style of Biblical Hebrew. This is precisely what we would expect from the Scriptural narrative itself.[405] Now significantly, the books of the Pentateuch are all in the same style. This is not what the New Documentary Hypothesis would predict of course, as it places P and D so much later than J and E. If the New Documentary Hypothesis were true, we should expect the book of Deuteronomy to be far closer to the Late style of Biblical Hebrew than the books of Genesis, Exodus, Leviticus and Numbers. But the fact is, it is in exactly the same style; Standard Hebrew. Further, we should also expect to see a mixture of styles within the first four books of the Pentateuch, but we do not. We see only

---

[404] For example, Exodus 24:4, 30:11, 30:17, 33:1, 33:5, 39:1, 39:5, 39:29; Leviticus 1:1, 4:1, 6:1; Numbers 4:1; Deuteronomy 1:1, 1:5, 5:1, 31:22, 31:30, 33:1; I Chronicles 15:15, 22:13; II Chronicles 23:18, 24:6, 25:4, 30:16, 35:12; Ezra 3:2, 7:6; Nehemiah 1:7, 8:1, 13:1; Matthew 8:4; Luke 16:29–31, 24:27, 24:44; John 1:17; and Acts 3:22.

[405] Whybray op. cit., p. 44. See my *The 'Greeks' Of The New Testament* for evidence that I & II Chronicles is cöeval with Ezra. Birmingham, The European Theological Seminary, 2002.

consistency of style, even though there is a vocabulary change, as previously noted, from Babylonian to Egyptian.

This to my mind is compelling evidence that Moses took the ancient records, with their Babylonian vocabulary, and added them to his own writings, using his own contemporary linguistic style, instead of the Archaic, in order to make them intelligible to his own people. Here again we see that the linguistic facts are opposed to the New Documentary Hypothesis, but actually give credence to the Mosaic authorship of the Pentateuch.[406]

Conclusion 42. Acting in an editorial capacity, Moses organised the ancient family histories possessed by Jacob, which went all the way back to Adam, into a literary form compatible with his own writings, and embraced both within what might be called an Extended Ancestor Epic literary form which ran from Genesis 1 to Deuteronomy 33.

Conclusion 43. The commonality of Biblical Hebrew Linguistic Style displayed by the entire Pentateuch is favourable to a Mosaic provenance suggested in Conclusion 42, but extremely unfavourable to the tenets of the New Documentary Hypothesis.

The Nature And Distinct Quality Of Scripture

Now there is a temptation we must avoid falling into at this stage in our study. We must beware of thinking that a great deal has been achieved so far. While these remarks may startle the reader, I say quite categorically that to believe such a statement would be to entertain a delusion of such magnitude, that there would be barely any difference between the adherent of such a view and the sceptic inasmuch as both viewpoints underestimate by a colossal extent, the nature and quality of Scripture. I will explain.

What has been achieved so far amounts merely to a demonstration that the Pentateuchal narrative presents itself as a credible, self-consistent history, originating from named sources, edited by Moses, which embraces several subsidiary literary forms, and which reveals an overall conformance to the literary form of Extended Ancestor Epic.

---

[406] Whybray, op. cit., pp. 44–45, and Hartwell Horne, op. cit., Volume I, pp. 46–47.

As such we may believe it to be the work of Moses, and to be an accurate statement of the matters it reports. We must now ask ourselves a significant question; *How does this situation answer the cynic in his or her attack upon Christian belief?* The truthful answer is that it does not! We have merely shown that it is perfectly reasonable to accept the accuracy of Pentateuchal history, but that action does not in itself witness for Christianity.

The statement that the square erected on the hypotenuse of a right-angled triangle, is equal to the sum of the squares on the other two sides, is completely accurate, capable of rigorous proof, but, of course, does not at all comply with the standard required of Scripture. Very many such statements, summing up the discoveries of man may be equally as valid as Pythagoras' theorem, and may be utterly dependable, but Scripture is more than merely *accurate*.

Whether we view the Pentateuch as an amalgam of literary fragments, cobbled together by unknown and unknowable redactors, which reflect the so-called evolution of Israelite religious life, or the accurate records of named individuals that conform to known literary genres, makes little difference if they are regarded merely as the writings of man, and thereby, display only the qualities of this world.

The Scriptures however claim for themselves much more than mere accuracy and conformance to the characteristics of this world. The Scriptures declare themselves to be *Holy and Inspired,* to be invested with *a moral authority over us* (II Timothy 3:15–16, cf. II Peter 1:21), to be *unbreakable* (John 10:35), *everlasting* (Psalm 119:89, Matthew 5:18, I Peter 1:23), and *authoritative,* (Psalm 119:160). Now how could the Pentateuch possibly be described as *Holy*, and *Inspired*, when it contains the writings of, among others, Ham, Ishmael, and Esau?

On top of this, is the consideration of the <u>Supreme Characteristic of Scripture</u>: the overriding and definitive quality of Scripture is that <u>it testifies of Christ</u>, and does so uniquely, emphatically, consistently, and effectively (Luke 24:27, 24:44, John 5:39, 5:46). This, above all else is what distinguishes Scripture from every other class of literature. It has a Spiritual and life-changing power, which transcends any power that is purely natural, of speaking to sinners of their desperate need of Christ, and of the way Christ fulfils this need graciously and abundantly. It is of greater benefit to us than the food which we must eat in order to stay alive (Job 23:12, Matthew 4:4). It is also, by the power of the Scriptures *alone*, that is more potent that we can ever imagine (Hebrews 4:12), that we may defeat the evil one (Ephesians 6:17).

In overturning the attacks of cynical Source Criticism, we have to do more than show its gross errors and failure to understand the practices of antiquity; we need to demonstrate the essential character of Scripture. We merely meet the cynic on his or her own ground when we restrict our answers to such as we have discussed up till now. The debate must move forward onto the higher ground, untrodden by the cynic, where we encounter the Spiritual qualities of Scripture including the testimony to Christ, of which the world knows nothing (I Corinthians 2:12–16).

Gaussen, referring to the crucial difference between learning about the Scriptures, and learning about the God of the Scriptures, speaks wisely when he says, "If you penetrate, in fact, into the sanctuary of the Scriptures, then not only will you find inscribed by the hand of God on all its walls that God fills it, and that He is everywhere there, but, further, you will receive the proof of it experimentally. There you will behold Him everywhere; there you will feel Him everywhere. In other terms, when one reads God's oracles with care, he not only meets with the frequent declaration of their entire inspiration, but, further, through unexpected strokes, and often through a single verse or the power of a single word, he receives a profound conviction of the divinity stamped upon them throughout... It too often happens that a prolonged course of study, devoted to the extrinsic parts of the sacred book (its history, its manuscripts, its versions, its language), by entirely absorbing the attention of the men who give themselves to it, leaves them inattentive to its more intrinsic attributes, its meaning, its object, the moral power which displays itself there, the beauties that reveal themselves there, the life that diffuses itself there. And as there exist, nevertheless, necessary relations between these essential attributes and those exterior forms, two great evils result from this pre-occupation of the mind. By this absorption the student stifles his spiritual life as a man, and compromises his final salvation. This, however, is not the evil we have to do with in these pages: as a learned enquirer, he compromises his science, and renders himself incapable of forming a sound estimate of the very objects of his studies. His learning is wanting in coherence and consistency, and from that very cause becomes contracted and creeping. How can a man become acquainted with the temple, when he has seen but the stones, and knows nothing of the Shekinah? Can the types be understood, when he has not even a suspicion of their antitype? He has seen but altars, sheep, knives, utensils, blood, fire, incense, costumes, and ceremonies; he has not beheld the world's redemption, futurity, heaven, the glory of Jesus Christ! And in this state he has been unable so much as to comprehend the relations which these external objects have amongst themselves, because he has not comprehended their harmony with the whole."[407]

What we must do now is examine the process by which the accurate but ordinary historical records contained in the Pentateuch have been lifted above the level of the mundane, to that supreme height of which the texts we looked at above speak. By what agent might this transformation have been achieved?

The Transforming Power Of The Spirit Of God

As usual, the answer to this Pentateuchal question is to be found within the Pentateuch itself. There, in the book of Exodus we learn that the Israelites when they fled from Egypt, took as payment for their slave-labour, and as compensation for the appallingly bad treatment they suffered during the Oppression, large amounts of jewels, precious metals and high quality cloth (Exodus 12:35–35). Later, much of this was collected from the people to be used as the material from which the Tabernacle was to be made (Exodus 35:4–29). From this, we see that even though the gold and silver and jewels, and fine cloth had come from a *pagan and polytheistic* culture and background, yet the

---

[407] Gaussen, L., 'Theopneustia:' The Plenary Inspiration Of The Holy Scriptures, translated, Scott, re-edited Carr, revised Wiles, London, Chas. J. Thynne, fourth edition, 1912, pp. 84–85. It is interesting to note that this edition carries a preface by A. H. Sayce, the one-time critic, whose archaeological discoveries caused him to turn his back on Higher Criticism. See also Collett, Sidney, The Scripture Of Truth, London, Partridge & Co., sixth edition, undated, cap. VII.

Lord was pleased to use it in the making of the Tabernacle, within which His Own Presence was manifested.

But, we notice too how this was achieved. A man called Bezaleel was selected by the Lord, to do the work, but before it could begin, he was "filled with the Spirit of God, in wisdom, in understanding, and in knowledge (Exodus 31:1–3, 35:30 cf. 28:3)." The consequence of this was the enabling of the construction of the Tabernacle and its furnishings, which included the Holy Place, The Holy of Holies, and the ark and mercy-seat, from material obtained from *pagan* Egypt.

I believe it is perfectly legitimate to take this example, and apply it to the question raised above. The ancient records which underpin Genesis, were, I believe located by Moses in the Egyptian archive, and used by him in the production of Genesis. Moses, like Bezaleel was a man most clearly set apart by God for the tasks he was commissioned to complete, as the episode at the burning bush, and the events at Mount Sinai make abundantly plain. From Numbers 11:16–17 and Deuteronomy 34:9–10 we may see that Moses also was truly *Inspired* by the Lord to enable him to execute his work, which, according to the words of Christ, included the production of the Pentateuch (Matthew 8:4, 19:7–8, 12:19, Luke 16:29–31, 24:27, John 5:46, 7:19–23).

Here, I believe, is the answer. The toledoths reveal the non-mosaic textual sources for the first thirty-six chapters of Genesis, but Moses, under Divine Inspiration, then took these separate documents, and made from them one complete book, blending them together, and 'smoothing' over the joins, so that the reader passes easily from one source to another, and like Bezaleel with the Tabernacle and the ark, transformed them into a work within which the Presence of God might be revealed. The Transforming work of the Spirit of God superintended the work of Moses, so that these ordinary historical records have been handed down to us as Holy Scripture, which is not merely inerrant, although that is marvellous enough, but is also the Unique Witness to, and Testifier of, the Lord Jesus Christ as we saw earlier.

This proposal is certainly consistent with the Scriptures as a whole. From Genesis chapter 1, we see that the earth was transformed from a formless and empty mass into the well-ordered setting for the

Image-and-Likeness-of-God (Genesis 1:26ff), only after the moving of the Spirit of God over the dark waters that covered the earth. So too, with the creation of Adam, the Spirit-of-Lives had to be breathed into him by the Lord before he could become a living soul (Genesis 2:7). The miracle of the Word becoming flesh, was only achieved after the Spirit of God had first come upon, and overshadowed the 'dark waters' of Mary's womb (Luke 1:35). Finally, from John 3:5–8 we see that the transforming power of the Spirit is essential in the Birth-from-Above by which an ordinary man, woman, or child, becomes a New Creation; a child of God.

We notice from Exodus 25 verses 9 (twice) and 40, that all that was made for the Tabernacle was made in accordance with *patterns* revealed to Moses upon the Mount. No deviations from these patterns of any kind were allowed; they had to be adhered to in the most meticulous manner, every detail was crucial. I suggest that the patterns of the structures, literary forms, Equi-Distant Letter Sequences and associated phenomena of the Pentateuch that we have examined earlier, also emanated from the Lord HimSelf and were used to direct the Inspired Moses in his work in forming the Pentateuch.

This is not to suggest that Divine Inspiration is to be compared in any way with the occult practice of automatic writing, I have set out my views elsewhere on the vital differences between true and false Inspiration, to which I refer the interested reader.[408]

The Nature Of Inspiration

Adolph Saphir writes, "Some people (especially in recent times) have objected to the doctrine of the inspiration of Scripture, on the plea that Scripture itself does not assert such a fact. But this is erroneous. And not merely does Scripture fully and distinctly assert the doctrine, but the whole teaching of Scripture indirectly confirms this view. In most cases where the 'inspiration of Scripture' is doubted or assailed, the opposition is not so much against a particular *theory* of inspiration (which would be of little importance), but it is based

---

[408] Phelan, M. W. J., *The Spirit And The Word*, Birmingham, The European Theological Seminary, 2001.

on ignorance of what is meant by 'the Holy Ghost.' It would be better to direct the attention of people more to the general truth, that there is no Creator beside the Father, and no Redeemer beside the Son, so there is none who can enlighten our minds and renew our hearts except the Holy Ghost, Who is, like the Father and the Son, Divine in majesty and power. It is because people do not believe that *only* the Spirit of God can reveal the things of God and Christ to our spirit, that they have no firm belief and enlightened view as to the Spirit's special work—the Scriptures. Had a Scriptural view of the Person and work of the Holy Ghost been more powerfully present in the Church, and not merely in her formularies, but in reality and life, there would never have been so much occasion given to represent the teaching of the Church on the inspiration of Scripture as 'mechanical,' 'converting men into automata,' etc.; and the whole question would not have assumed such a scholastic and metaphysical form. For then the living testimony and the written testimony would appear both as supernatural and Spirit-breathed. The more the Supremacy of the Holy Ghost, Divine, loving, and present, is acknowledged, the more the *Bible* is fixed in the heart and conscience. But if the 'Book' is viewed as the relic and substitute of a now absent and inactive Spirit, Bibliolatry and Bible-rejection are the necessary results."[409]

The Abraham Cycle

Outstanding from our examination of the literary forms of Genesis in the previous chapter, is the Abraham Cycle. This has been left until now, because it provides a good illustration of the Inspiration of Scripture just discussed.

With the first eleven chapters of Genesis removed from consideration because they have already been dealt with, and treating the Joseph Narrative, the Jacob Cycle, and the other Ancestor Epics and Negotiation Tales in a similar manner, only four sections of text are

---

[409] Saphir, Adolph, *Christ And The Scriptures*, London, Morgan & Scott, undated, pp. 82–83, see also, Hodge A. A., *Evangelical Theology: Lectures On Doctrine*, Edinburgh, The Banner Of Truth Trust, 1976, pp. 61–83.

left to us, which taken together comprise the Abraham Cycle. These passages are;

A. Genesis 12:1–9,

B. Genesis 15:1–21,

C. Genesis 17:1–17, and

D. Genesis 22:1–19.

When these passages are compared, an inter-relationship is revealed, albeit one that is rather more loose than we have seen before. Nonetheless the correspondences are real, showing us that the Abraham Cycle is genuine, and possesses its own distinct identity.

A. Genesis 12:1–9

I) The Word From God, verse 1.

 II) Promise of Seed and blessing, verses 2–3.

  III) Abraham moves to the place God has commanded, verses 4–6.

   IV) Two altars, verses 7–8.

    V) Abram leaves, verse 9.

B. Genesis 15:1–21

VI) The Word From God, verse 1.

 VII) The request for an heir, verses 2–3.

  VIII) God will surpass Abram's request, verse 4.

   IX) Promise of Seed, verse 5.

    X) Abraham's Faith, verse 6.

     XI) The Land of Canaan promised to Abram, verse 7.

      XII) The Covenant Of The Pieces is required of Abram, verses 8–9.

       XIII) The Covenant Of The Pieces is undertaken, verses 10–11.

        XIV) Abram's horror, verse 12.

         XV) Prophecy about Abram's seed, verses 13–16.

          XVI) The establishment of The Covenant Of The Pieces, verse 17–18a.

           XVII) Foreigners under Abram's rule embraced by the Covenant, verses 18b–21.

C. Genesis 17:1–7

vi) The Word From God, verses 1–2.

   x) Abraham's Worship, verse 3.

Abram renamed as Abraham, verse 5.

  ix) Promise of Seed and blessing, verses 4–7.

   xi) The Land of Canaan promised to Abraham, verse 8.

    xii) The Covenant of Circumcision is required of Abraham, verses 9–14.

Sarai renamed as Sarah, verse 15–16.

    xiv) Abraham's laughter, verse 17.

 vii) The request for an heir, verse 18.

 viii) God will surpass Abraham's request, verse 19.

    xv) Prophecy about Abraham's seed, verse 20.

    xvi) The establishment of The Covenant Of Circumcision, verses 21–22.

   xiii) The Covenant Of Circumcision is undertaken, verses 23–26.

     xvii) Foreigners under Abraham's rule embraced by the Covenant, verse 27.

D. Genesis 22:1–19

i) The Word From God, verses 1–2.

  iii) Abraham moves to the place God has commanded, verses 3–5.

  iv) Two sacrifices, verses 6–14.

ii) Promise of Seed and blessing, verses 15–17.

  v) Abraham leaves 19.

We see that A most definitely corresponds with D, and that B and C are clearly related, although C has some elements which have no counterparts in B, nevertheless the existence of a relationship is clear. The looseness that is present though shows that the structure is far less formal than we have been used to, and, as such, the Abraham Cycle is different from all that we have seen before.

This unique characteristic of the Abraham Cycle means that we are left in a quandary as to how it should be classified in terms of its literary form. Although it contains negotiation, especially in regard to the promise of an heir for Abraham, it is certainly much longer than the Negotiation Tales, and much more rich in content than they are; but nor is it true Ancestor Epic, lacking the classic fivefold structure, although, undoubtedly it concerns the greatest Israelite ancestor of all! There are elements of Migration Epic discernible, but again the Cycle contains so much more. There are also hints of it containing a Treaty Document! In short it resembles in part all we have seen elsewhere in the Pentateuch, yet cannot be made to comply to anyone of these other Forms. Nevertheless, this similarity to all of the other literary forms we have observed cannot be accidental, and in the absence of anything else, ought to be taken up as the only clue we have. So then, let us proceed with this clue and see where it leads.

Abraham And Paul

The Abraham Cycle begins at the very start of the first great division of the book of Genesis, at 12:1, and therefore commences before any of the separate, or individual Ancestor Epics, Negotiation Tales or Migration Epics make their appearance. When they do appear however, crucially, they all arise from within narrative connected with Abraham. The Matriarchal Epic begins with two episodes featuring Abraham and Sarah (Genesis 12:10–20, & 20:1–18), the first of the individual Ancestor Epics, that of Lot, features Abraham in association with the removing of each of the Three Threats (Genesis 13:5–13, 14:1–24, & 18:16–19:38), and the Negotiation Tales begin with Abraham (Genesis 23:1–20, & 24:1–67). Even the Migration Epic of Joseph has its precedent in the story of Abram's journey to Egypt to escape a famine (Genesis 12:10–20). Thus all the literary forms we have seen so far, seem to be anticipated by elements within the Abraham Cycle.

In some respects then the Abraham Cycle forms what the Hebrew Tradents call a *Root Story*, that is, a story which contains themes or patterns which recur in later parts of the Scriptures, and which forms one of the mechanisms which facilitate the phenomenon of typology.[410] Significantly for us, this is seen in an unusually clear manner, inasmuch as the story of Abraham appears to be foundational for the Acts Period ministry of Paul.

---

[410] Weinreb, op. cit.

314

It is evident from the remarks of the Jews in John's Gospel that physical descent from Abraham was regarded by ordinary people at the time of Christ as enormously beneficial (John 8:39, 53). We know from Christ's words that He viewed mere physical descent from Abraham entirely differently, and regarded *Spiritual* descent as the vital element in an individual's life, yet nonetheless, the faith of Abraham was in Christ's eyes most definitely a normative standard (John 8:39–40). This was also the case for John the Baptist (Luke 3:8) and for Paul (Romans 4).

It is from Paul we get our next clue. While referring to the foreknowledge of the Scriptures in Galatians 3:8, Paul declares the subject of that foreknowledge to be Abraham and the Gospel preached to him! "And the Scripture, foreseeing that God would justify the nations through faith, preached before *the Gospel unto Abraham*." Throughout the entire chapter, Paul makes a contrast between the Law and the Promise to Abraham, showing that what was promised anticipated the blessing bestowed by Christ. Paul speaks to his readers about being blessed with faithful Abraham (verse 9), and says that the blessing of Abraham might come upon the nations through Jesus Christ; that we might receive the Promise of the Spirit through faith (verse 14). Similarly, in Romans 4, it is equally clear that the foundation of Paul's dealing with those who were uncircumcised lay with the faith of Abraham.

We saw that Paul refers to the *Self-Consciousness* of the Scriptures,[411] inasmuch as he speaks about them possessing genuine *foreknowledge*. It would seem that, technically, it is the Holy Spirit, as the Ultimate Author of Scripture, Who is the One Who *foreknows*,[412] but this statement shows such a close connection between the Spirit

---

[411] See Rotherham, *Our Sacred Books*, op. cit., p. 10. Compare this also with Galatians 3:22 which refers to the Scriptures *concluding* "all under sin."

[412] See, *Η Καινη Διαθηκη: The Greek Testament With English Notes*, edited Bloomfield, S. T., Volume II, London, Longman, Orme, Brown, Green, & Longmans, 1861, in. loc., *The Greek Testament*, edited Alford, Henry, Volume III, London, Rivingtons, fourth edition 1871, in. loc., and Bengel, John Albert, *Gnomon Of The New Testament*, edited Bengel, M. Ernest, revised Steudel, translated Bryce, Edinburgh, T. & T. Clark, seventh edition, 1877 in .loc.

and the Inspired, or God-breathed Word as to suggest practical *identification* at times.[413]

Now from all of this we begin to see how we should categorise the Abraham Cycle. According to the Scriptures themselves, the Spiritual significance of Abraham is his faith, and the fact that the Gospel of faith was preached to him. The potent phrase, sealed by the special emphasis given it by the reference to the Scriptures' foreknowledge, "the Gospel unto Abraham" gives us the literary form for the Abraham Cycle we have been looking for. The Abraham Cycle conforms to the literary form unique to the Scriptures of *Gospel Narrative.* *The Gospel Of Abraham* is the Root Story from which sprung the Synoptic Gospels, and the Acts Period ministry of Paul.[414]

The Abrahamic Gospel

At the heart of the Gospel is the Sacrifice of God's Only-Begotten Son, the Lord Jesus Christ, which enabled the Promises made to Abraham to be realised. At the heart of the story of Abraham is the longing, Promise, and miraculous birth of a son, and the subsequent requirement of the sacrifice of that son. Numerous commentators have over the years seen clearly how the Sacrifice of Christ was prefigured by the call for the sacrifice of Isaac. This has been seen in the common location of both events, the way both victims carried the wood to be used in the sacrifice, the way in which both were stretched out upon the wood to await their death, in the presence of the hand of the victim's father in both acts, and of course the presence of the element of substitution in both sacrifices.[415] This however, is only a part of the story; there are parallels between Abraham and Christ to be found throughout the Abraham Cycle.

---

[413] Cf. John 6:63, "The words that I speak unto you, they are Spirit, and they are Life."

[414] See Lightfoot, J. B., *Saint Paul's Epistle To The Galatians,* London, MacMillan, 1921, pp. 158ff.

[415] See, as examples, Poole, op. cit., Volume I, in. loc., Keil and Delitzsch, op. cit., Volume I, in. loc, Darby, J. N., *Notes And Comments On Scripture,* Volume I, Bath, P. A. Humphrey, 1884, pp. 128ff., and McIntosh, C. H, *Notes On The Book Of Genesis,* London, Morrish, undated, pp. 205–218.

Although Duane Garrett fails to mention the reference in Galatians 3:8 connecting the Gospel with Abraham, he does agree that the Abraham Cycle is in the same literary genre as the four canonical Gospel narratives, and has found many correspondences. He points out how in both the Gospels and the Abraham Cycle, the fulfilment of the promises given to the fathers, and the blessing of all families of the earth (Genesis 12:3) is utterly dependent upon the coming of a Son; a Son, Who, uniquely, is given directly by the Power of God. Garrett shows clearly that until this Son had come, everything was in abeyance, but, once He had been given, Joy was found (Luke 2:28–32).

Garrett goes on to show how the theme of sacrifice permeates the Abraham Cycle, and the Gospel story. The uniqueness of the Covenant of the Pieces, during which the Angel of the Lord passed along a way between the pieces emphasises the very special nature of the event (Genesis 15:17–18). The only Sacrifice to surpass this in significance, is that of the Son of God in the Gospels, opening up the New and Living Way *for us* into the heavens (Hebrews 10:20), but, even that was foreshadowed by that other sacrifice made by Abraham, that of his own dear son, upon whom all the Abrahamic Promises and Blessings depended.

Likewise, as Garrett reveals, while believers in Christ emphasise their covenanted unity with Christ through Baptism and the Lord's Supper, so too the descendents of Abraham united themselves with him through the Covenant of Circumcision.

But this is not all. Garrett invites us to consider how Abraham was called to leave his homeland, which resulted in him becoming a sojourner for the rest of his days. He was also warned that his people will see affliction. So too, believers in Christ have 'left' their home in the world, in which they will henceforth find tribulation (John 16:33), for their citizenship is in heaven.

Finally, the seeming incompatibility of the command for Abraham to offer his son in a sacrifice, with the many promises God had made concerning that very son, is compared by Garrett with the parallel situation concerning Christ. How utterly incongruous the news of the coming Death of Christ seemed to those who, convinced of the truth of His Messiahship, had given themselves to His cause, is plain to see from Matthew 16:21–23. In both situations however, the soteriological glory of Divine Substitution and Victory over death is brought forth with a clarity and triumph that obliterates doubt, and re-establishes belief in the goodness, the grace, and the power of God.[416]

I have shown elsewhere that the stories included in the book of Genesis would have been used to educate the Hebrews while they were in captivity,[417] but undoubtedly it is this story above all else that built the faith of the Israelites while they were in Egypt. Here indeed we find their Gospel offering them hope, deliverance and a New 'Kingdom'. But that it should parallel in so many ways the New Testament Gospel of Christ is amazing and is only possible because the editor of the story, Moses, was set aside by God for the task, and Inspired by His Spirit for this rôle of receiving the ancient family records, and transforming them into Scripture, that, as we have just seen, and we noted above, testifies to Christ.

Conclusion 44. The Abraham Cycle conforms to the literary form, unique to the Scriptures, of Gospel Narrative, with its compelling witness to Christ.

Conclusion 45. The classifying of the Abraham Cycle as authentic Gospel Narrative, means it must be regarded as Scripture. This makes it necessary to accept that its editor, Moses, must have been Inspired, so that the text he produced would be infused by The Holy Spirit, with the testimony to Christ that is the unique characteristic of Scripture.

Conclusion 46. As all the Pentateuch has a Mosaic provenance, as we have seen, we may conclude that the balance of the book of Genesis, and the books of Exodus, Leviticus, Numbers and Deuteronomy, also comprise Scripture.

---

[416] Garrett, op. cit., pp. 163–167.

[417] Phelan, M. W. J., *Beyond The Law Part I,* op. cit.

Conclusion To Chapter Ten

We began this Section with an attempt to identify the literary forms found in the Pentateuch; but now in this chapter, we have revealed the *character* of the Pentateuch, and the identity of its Ultimate Author. The Pentateuch is not merely a collection of extremely ancient family records, and Migration Epic, it is identifiable as *Scripture* through its anticipation of, and witness to, Christ. There is only One Power in existence that is able to equip an editor or writer with all that is necessary for his work to be used to demonstrate the vital elements of the ministry of Christ, thousands of years before the Word became flesh; and that Power is none other than Divine Inspiration given only by and through the Holy Spirit. We must grasp the fact that only Deity is able to reveal Deity: no mere creature, constricted by finitude's limitations may embrace the Infinite, Ultimate, Absolute, and Eternal.[418] Therefore any authentic witness to Christ may only derive from a Divinely Inspired source. Further, and every bit as significantly; it is *absolutely inevitable* that a truly Divinely Inspired work, *will* be a perfect witness to Christ.

We must keep this very firmly in mind as we consider the following. The consistency displayed by the evidence of Ancestor Epic literary form and Standard Biblical Hebrew throughout the Pentateuch indicates it to be the work of but one overall editor, whom our previous findings have shown to be Moses. We saw earlier that Moses was definitely Inspired of God in order to complete the work he was commissioned to do. Thus it follows that *all of the work* of this Divinely Inspired editor, Moses, must, necessarily and inevitably, form a potent witness to Christ; that the Pentateuch, *throughout its compass*, must speak eloquently of Christ. While this might be particularly conspicuous in the case of Abraham and Isaac, by no means would this witness be confined to the Abraham Cycle. And is this not what is found?

---

[418] A vital argument for the Deity of the Son and the Spirit of course. Unitarians must consider seriously that without the Deity of the Word and the Spirit, the undisputed Deity of the Father could never be communicated to man. We would inhabit a universe that would be quite literally, God-forsaken!

From the Primeval Messianic Promise, the so-called proto-evangelium of Genesis 3:15, where the Seed-of-the-woman Who will bruise the serpent's head, is promised, with its witness to the virgin-birth of Christ,[419] to the ritual associated with the Passover lamb, and the shielding from the power of death by the shed blood, it is all a supreme witness to Christ.[420] He is the true Jacob's Ladder,[421] the Ruler from Judah,[422] the true Propitiation,[423] the true Mercy-Seat,[424] the true Bread-from-heaven,[425] the true Rock,[426] and He offers the true Redemption,[427] and the True Rest, and, as He goes beyond the Law, He too has the same Name as Moses' successor, Yeshua (Joshua).

But the *timing* of this work is just as vital. Being given to the Israelites by Moses during the time of the making of the Sinaitic Covenant, and the institution of the Tabernacle worship, the reception of the books of the Torah would have been seen as an integral part of the inauguration of the New Economy initiated at Sinai, and, by virtue of this fact, would have been regarded immediately and universally as intrinsically Sacred, or, what we would term as Scripture. The release of these books, in the days of the pillar-of-fire, when the heavens

---

[419] McIntosh, op. cit., pp. 47–51.

[420] See McIntosh, C. H., *Notes On The Book Of Exodus*, London, Morrish, undated, pp. 121ff.

[421] (Cf. John 1:51.) See McIntosh, *Notes On The Book Of Genesis*, op. cit., pp. 257ff., and Hoskyns, E. C., *The Fourth Gospel*, edited Davey, F. N., Volume I, London, Faber and Faber, 1940, pp. 189–191.

[422] See Keil & Delitzsch, Volume I, op. cit., pp. 393–401.

[423] See Strong, Augustus Hopkins, *Systematic Theology*, Glasgow, Pickering & Inglis, 1981, pp. 722–728.

[424] See the Greek of Romans 3:25, and Sanday, W., and Headlam, A. C., *A Critical And Exegetical Commentary On The Epistle To The Romans,* Edinburgh, T. & T. Clark, 1900, pp. 85–86.

[425] There are numerous works on the typology of the Tabernacle, see for example, Slemming, Charles W., *Made According To Pattern* (revised edition, 1956), *These Are The Garments* (revised edition 1955), *Thus Shalt Thou Serve* (1966), all London, H. E. Walter, Rouw, J., *House Of Gold*, London, Chapter Two, 1984, Edersheim, A., *The Temple: Its Ministry And Its Services,* London, The Religious Tract Society, undated.

[426] See I Corinthians 10:4, and Robertson and Plummer, *A Critical And Exegetical Commentary On The First Epistle Of St. Paul To The Corinthians*, Edinburgh, T. & T. Clark, second edition reprinted 1963, pp. 201–202.

[427] See Berkhof, Louis, *Systematic Theology*, London, The Banner Of Truth Trust, 1969, pp. 265–272.

were bowed, and the Lord descended to the Mount, and when the cloud filled the tabernacle, clothed them with a sense of the sacred and unspeakably holy that accounts fully for the regard Israelites have always had for them; to my mind, nothing else may explain the sanctity, that in the eyes of Israel, is inalienably theirs. Forged documents cobbled together well after the nation was established would never be capable of inducing such feelings of reverence; but the coming of these books to the Israelites in the midst of the days of their greatest encounter with the Divine apart from the Incarnation itself, does so utterly, irresistibly, and inevitably. Higher Criticism fails to confront this matter, or even comprehend it, it would seem.

The recognition of the Pentateuch as Scripture has major consequences, the two most relevant to this study being;

1. It is absolutely authoritative, and not simply a literary corpus. Thus from now on, I will cease to use the Source and Form Critical word *Pentateuch*, which but means, 'the five books', and will instead revert to my usual designation, the *Torah*, meaning *Direction*, not merely *law*.

2. It will be inerrant, and the measure by which all else is judged. This applies not just to theories of Source and Form Criticism, but to theories of organic and cosmic evolution, anthropology, geology, comparative religion and ancient history as well.

Thus we see that the written Word-of-God shares with the Living Word-of-God, the characteristic of being at once, fully human, and fully Divine. In our study of Scripture, we must consider both of these aspects continually.

Part Five

Propositions And Conclusion

Chapter Eleven

Main Conclusion And Propositions

Our findings so far have established *who* wrote the Torah. Its human authors have been found to be Adam, Noah, Shem, Ham, Japheth, Terah, Ishmael, Isaac, Esau, Jacob, Aaron and Moses. Its Ultimate Author however, is none other than The Holy Spirit. This leads into the fact that in the last chapter we have discovered *what* was written by these authors; it was material which by the Inspiration of Moses became Divinely Inspired Scripture. We know also *where* it was written to a large extent. The books of Exodus to Deuteronomy were written in the Sinai desert, which is where Genesis was also edited. This tells us also *when* the Torah was written of course. It was written during the interval between the Exodus and the entry into the Land of Promise. We know also *how* it was written. The first 36 chapters of Genesis were written using the ancient family histories going right back to Adam. The last 14 chapters of Genesis were in all likelihood derived from records in the Egyptian Royal archive. The books of Exodus to Numbers were probably written from a travel journal of Moses, while Deuteronomy was written as a Treaty Document. This leaves us to answer the question *why* the Torah was written. I believe it was written firstly, to give the new nation of Israel a Foundation Treaty (Deuteronomy), secondly, to give the new nation an account of its own origins (Exodus to Numbers), and thirdly, to locate the nation's position within the history of Redemption, beginning from Adam (Genesis). This would enable the Israelites to see the faithfulness of God in fulfilling the Promises made to the patriarchs, and showing thereby the character of God, and how He is worthy of our trust. It then became the foundation upon which the rest of the Hebrew Canon, and the entire Christian Canon was built.

Thus all the essential questions concerning the origin of the Torah have been answered. The method used has been primarily one of letting the Scriptures speak for themselves. The internal evidence of the literary structures and affiliated phenomena have revealed the unity of the Torah; the toledoths have revealed their sources; and the literary forms and linguistic style have revealed the omnipresence of Moses as chief editor. We have also resorted to relevant external evidence in examining the antiquity of the art of writing, ancient literary remains, and the Samaritan Pentateuch. Finally the special quality of the testifying power of Scripture to Christ has also been considered, enabling us to see the Torah as being a part of the Word-of-God. It is my belief that these methods have been applied logically and consistently, and that the three aims outlined in the Introduction have been achieved.

Thus we may conclude with a set of Propositions, which, curiously, and perhaps rather fittingly, number five in total.

Proposition One

The first 36 chapters of Genesis comprise records based upon the ancient family histories preserved by Adam, Noah, Shem, Ham, Japheth, Terah, Ishmael, Isaac, Esau, and Jacob. The last fourteen chapters of Genesis were compiled by Aaron and Moses from material uncovered in the Egyptian Royal archive. The books of Exodus, Leviticus, and the first two chapters of Numbers, were compiled by Aaron and Moses, and were based upon their own experiences. Numbers 3 to Deuteronomy 33 was compiled by Moses, apart from Aaron, who was then preparing for his High Priestly duties, and later executing them.

Proposition Two

Moses compiled the entire Torah by editing the ancient family histories from Adam to Jacob, and amalgamating them in their edited form, with his own material, namely the Joseph Narrative, and what became known as the books of Exodus, Leviticus, Numbers, and Deuteronomy.

Proposition Three

Moses was divinely Inspired and set apart by the Lord in order to accomplish all he was commissioned to do (Numbers 11:16–17 and Deuteronomy 34:9–10). This fact explains how the Torah he compiled is recognisable as _Scripture_ through its undeniable witness to Christ.

326

Proposition Four

Since the times of Moses, minor revisions of the Torah have taken place. These would include a revision by Joshua, under which would have been added the details concerning the death of Moses (Deuteronomy 34), and probably another under Samuel. Finally, there may have been a minor revision when the whole work was re-written in the square-charactered script under the direction of Ezra, after the return from Babylon. It is likely that it was then that the reference to the time before Israel had a king was added (Genesis 36:31). This last revision was minimalist, as the Torah displays from one end to the other, the *Standard* Biblical Hebrew linguistic style, whereas the works that date from the time of Ezra, display the *Late* Style.

Proposition Five

The Torah is the foundation for the rest of the Canon; Hebrew and Greek, and is absolutely and verifiably uncompromised in its integrity.

I submit that these five propositions account for the characteristics of the Torah, more readily than any other explanation.

They account for the occurrence and intelligent placing of the toledoths and genealogies. The function of the toledoths is the revelation of the literary sources of the Torah, the function of the genealogies is to reveal the literary forms of the Torah. These propositions also account for the different types of literary composition in the Torah, ranging from Treaty Document, to travel narrative, and the many different compositional types of Genesis 1–36, which was the work of many different, but named, hands.

They account also for the presence of Babylonian and Egyptian vocabularies in the book of Genesis, and also for the common linguistic style of Standard Biblical Hebrew from Genesis 1 to Deuteronomy 33, as Moses was the chief editor of the entire work. They account for the presence of literary Structures, as Moses was guided in his work by The Holy Spirit, a fact which also accounts for the witness of the Torah to Christ.

Main Conclusion

As my main conclusion, I propose that the charges of cynical and sceptical Source and Form Critics are conspicuous failures, and that the Scriptures remain intact. *THE SCRIPTURE CANNOT BE BROKEN!* (John 10:35).

The Direction Of Biblical Scholarship

With the faith of the believer in God's Word vindicated thoroughly, what is to be said about the nature of Biblical scholarship? The believer must come to terms with the fact that we live in the midst of a sin-ridden society, in which every aspect of life is tainted; this applies to intellectual life as much as it does to the social, political and economic fabric of our civilisation. The Scriptures were hardly freed from the Latin tongue and the interpretations of priestcraft at the Reformation, when the move to discredit them was initiated. The satanic forces with which we contend would prefer to keep the Scriptures cut-off from public access, but if they are frustrated in this, and the Scriptures are freely circulated, then their next ploy is to discredit them. The aim of both policies is the same. Either the mass of humanity will not read the Scriptures because they are not available, or because they are deemed to be of no merit whatsoever. Sadly, believers who 'come-to-terms' with sceptical Source or Form Criticism, only end up giving credence to a satanically inspired movement designed to discredit God's Word, that is the sequel of the serpent's words to Eve. (Those particular words of course are presented as being simply a part of the J narrative, and reflect only the point-of-view of the J Source!)

We saw at the beginning of this study, that it is natural, and to be expected that unregenerate men and women will instinctively reject God's Word; it is imbued with a Spirit that is contrary to everything about them and opposes totally their view of themselves. The consequence of this opposition is that the Scriptures will actually *attract* criticism; they will draw forth the worst aspects of our civilisation, and become the focus of hostility, because they condemn the world. Nonetheless the power with which they are filled, the testimony of the Holy Spirit to the Lord Jesus Christ is, ironically, the only hope for the world, and that power, by the grace of God, may indeed overcome the world.

It is my submission that accepting God's Word at its face-value, as, I trust has been done in this study, has indeed overcome the world in that the human wisdom of three and a half centuries has been overturned simply by an honest consideration of the structures and literary forms of the Scriptures. Nonetheless, there are lessons that the history of the sceptical criticism of the last three hundred and fifty years may teach believers.

One example of this concerns a characteristic of the supposed J source, namely the frequent occurrence of anthropomorphisms in passages dominated by the use of the tetragrammaton YHWH. Believers of course must have no arguments here with the facts of the matter, only their interpretation. In fact, theologically, this pattern is precisely what we would expect. I have shown in two previous publications[428] that the Hebrew word *Elohim*, refers to the Totality of the Revealed Godhead of Father, Son and Spirit, but that YHWH is only ever used of an Individual Member of the Godhead.[429] Within the Scriptures, the Name YHWH is used of the Father, and the Son and even the Holy Spirit, but whenever it is used, it is a title used of *One Individual Member of the Godhead only*. The anthropomorphisms used of YHWH, point to what with reverence might be termed, *The Ultimate Anthropomorphism*, that is the Word becoming flesh as The Lord Jesus Christ. Again, I have shown in the publications just referred to, that the Hebrew YHWH, is most often used of The Son, and is represented in the New Testament by the Greek Κυριος, the normal designation of Christ. Thus, it is quite fitting that we encounter anthropomorphisms most often, when the narrative relates particularly to the One Who became flesh, "and was made in the likeness of men (Philippians 2:7)."

---

[428] Phelan, M. W. J., *The Fulness Of The Godhead*, Reading, The Open Bible Trust, 1987, and *The One True God And Pluralism Of Language*, Brighton, Paradosis Publications, 1996.

[429] Compare Genesis 19:24 where we find two Individuals Named YHWH. These are the Word as Theophany upon earth, and the Father in heaven. "Then YHWH rained upon Sodom and upon Gomorrah brimstone and fire from YHWH out of heaven."

By contrast, the entire Godhead of Father, Son and Spirit, could never become flesh *collectively*, which is why anthropomorphisms being associated with *Elohim* which relates to the entire Godhead are conspicuously rare. Thus, these characteristics of the Hebrew text, far from supporting Higher Criticism, actually confirm Christian theology, and Christology! From this we see that it would be most profitable to analyse the occurrence of anthropomorphisms and Theophanies in the Hebrew Canon, and relate them to the occurrence of the Divine Names and Titles, and then compare them with citations made in the Christian Canon, from the Hebrew. This would be a fine example of learning to use the techniques of Source Criticism in a positive manner, but as yet I have not seen any attempt at this.

As has so often been seen in this study, Source and Form Criticism is almost always of the destructive and cynical type. Yet, there are real alternatives. *Faithful* Source Criticism, and *Faithful* Form Criticism are both possible, and are both desperately needed. In common with Post-Critical Interpretation, I believe it is important that we understand that we cannot ignore the rise of sceptical methods of criticism. Believers must be encouraged to read the Scriptures devotionally, and to apply them to their own lives and circumstances, but they must also be encouraged to read them intelligently, even critically, and to see the literary and historical issues that need resolution, and then prayerfully to seek such resolutions. The questions that Source and Form Critics ask, are, usually, valid questions, which should induce honest, but *faithful* research. Understanding this means that we are able to extract something positive from the reign of scepticism.

Too often, scepticism has gained a foothold, simply because there has seemed to be no alternative. The irony is that believers may actually make use of the sceptic's assault upon God's Word. The Critics who have interposed between the Light of God's Word and the reader, a distorting lens which they hope will bring discredit to the Scriptures; have but shown the spectrum of glorious colours of which the dazzlingly white Light of Revelation is comprised. While believers have always understood and emphasised the unity of the Torah, an appreciation of its structure and form induced by a study of the last three and a half centuries of cynical attack actually enables believers to see how complex, multifaceted, and subtle that undoubted unity is.

The constant message of the Torah is of God's deliverance from the various threats man has encountered; sin and death, murder and violence, global destruction at the time of the Flood, dispersion and alienation, sterility, persecution, subjugation and oppression. Given this background, there can be no doubt that the Lord will indeed deliver us too from the attacks of cynics and sceptics who seek to discredit His Word. Balancing this though is the fact that it is up to us as believers to provide the alternative to cynicism and scepticism and demonstrate the validity of God's Word, and man's Only Hope, so that those caught between scepticism and faith, may be given the chance to trust, and so find the Love of God in Christ Jesus. Let us embrace that task, and hold aloft "the Word of God which liveth and abideth for ever (I Peter 1:23)." I call on others now to take up this very basic work I have undertaken, and to flesh it out with more detailed and proficient contributions, to the Glory of God. After all, "if they hear not Moses... neither will they be persuaded, though One rose from the dead!" (Luke 16:31)

Part Six

Supplementary Studies:
The non-literary problems of the Pentateuch

Supplement One

The Problem Of The Levites

Part A:
Introduction

Wellhausen's Scheme

As we have seen in the main body of the study, Wellhausen proposed that the chronology of the compilation of the alleged four literary sources of the Pentateuch, J, E, D, and P was related to what he saw as the evolution of the religious life of Israel. J was thought to be the earliest source, coming from sometime during the united monarchy, and emanated from the Southern Kingdom of Judah. E is also placed during the monarchy, but after the Disruption, and is held to originate from the Northern Kingdom of Israel. After the fall of the Northern Kingdom, it is thought that the redactor R^{JE} then amalgamated J and E to form JE, losing portions of both documents in the process, but ensuring the preservation of the teaching of the Northern source, E.

In the days of Josiah (621 BCE is the normal date), D, the book of Deuteronomy was produced. This was later amalgamated with JE by the redactor R^D, who inserted some D passages into JE, and vice versa.

Finally, after the exile P (which includes all of Leviticus) was written to promote the theology of the post-exilic priesthood. This was amalgamated with JED, by R^P to form the Pentateuch as we know it.[430]

In the eyes of Wellhausen's followers, one of his greatest contributions to Biblical scholarship was the way in which he matched the

---

[430] See Whybray op. cit., pp. 20ff., & 26ff.

335

development of the Pentateuch, to the development of the priesthood. This remains an important attraction of the New Documentary Hypothesis to this day. The question for us then is, is the evolution of the priesthood as proposed by Wellhausen real, or imaginary?

The Problem Of The Levites

It must be admitted that there is a genuine problem to be addressed concerning the Levites, and this real problem was exploited by Wellhausen to promote his views. The problem briefly described is as follows.

A superficial reading of Scripture might seem to indicate that the Levites were chosen for sacred duty owing to their readiness to follow Moses' commands after the incident of the Golden Calf as recorded in Exodus 32:28–29. The family of Aaron was chosen to be priests at the central shrine where the ark was to be installed; that is the tabernacle, and afterwards the Temple of Solomon, while the non-Aaronite Levites were called to be assistants to the sons of Aaron (see Numbers 10).

This arrangement is easy to understand and in Exodus 28:1, 28:43, Leviticus 8, Numbers 3–4, and 18, the Aaronic priests are clearly distinguished from non-Aaronic Levites. This appears not to be the case when we come to Deuteronomy however. There, in 17:9, 17:18, 18:1–8, 21:5, 24:8 and 33:8–11, it would seem that all Levites are priests (cf. Joshua 3:3, and Judges 17–18), not merely Levites who are descended from Aaron. This seems to be a contradiction of course, and generally speaking, adherents of the New Documentary Hypothesis regard such supposed contradictions as evidence of the existence of different documentary sources.

Thus it is thought by Critics that originally any in Israel could offer sacrifices (cf. Judges 6:18–27 where Gideon of Manasseh (verse 25) was *commanded* to offer sacrifices), but that D (Deuteronomy) then asserted that this right was restricted to Levites, but the later P in Leviticus and the references found in Exodus and Numbers above,[431] insists that only Levites descended from Aaron may be priests. As P is said to be later than D, this is thought to show evidence of evolutionary steps in the religion of Israel, and these steps are held to be reflected in

---

[431] See Noth, op. cit., pp. 270–274.

the documentary history of the Pentateuch. The most popular Wellhausen-type theories elaborate on this basic concept as follows.

1. In the days of the Judges there is little or no evidence of an established priesthood. Priests are mentioned only in the book of Judges in chapters 17–18, and there is no reference to descent from Aaron being a pre-requisite for the priesthood in these chapters.

2. David gave prominence within the priesthood to the Zadokites in II Samuel 8:17, who were indeed descendants of Aaron, but nonetheless the priesthood became associated with Levites in general, and by the time of Josiah when D made its appearance, every male Levite was considered to be a priest.

3. There was tension however between the descendants of Aaron in Jerusalem, and the non-Aaronic Levites outside of Jerusalem. Josiah ordered the dispersed non-Aaronic Levites to be gathered to Jerusalem where they might be brought under the control of the descendants of Aaron at the central shrine (II Kings 23).

4. Ezekiel in 44:10–31 insisted that the priesthood be restricted to the Zadokites, and that the other Levites brought to Jerusalem under Josiah, must assume a junior position as their servants. This is said to constitute the suppression of an entire category of priests, and is precisely what is found in P, and reflects the post-exilic situation under Ezra from whom we receive the Pentateuch.[432]

To enable believers to assess Wellhausen's views, two separate problems need to be addressed:

1. Why does the priesthood disappear from the book of Judges? (This is a 'standard' Old Testament problem), and,

2. How do we resolve the seeming confusion over the relationship between Levites and the priesthood?

We will examine question 1 first.

---

[432] See Garrett op. cit., pp. 199–207, and Robertson, op. cit., pp. 159–182.

Part B:
The Absence Of The Priesthood
From The Book Of Judges

The Book Of Judges

This disappearance of the priesthood from the book of Judges is indeed intriguing, especially as in Joshua, and with the history of Samuel, we see the secular or civil authority is most definitely under the control of the priests, yet the Judges seem to be free from the discipline of the priesthood, receiving their instructions directly from the Lord. How do we answer this?

Firstly, it must be pointed out that in I Chronicles 6:1–15 we are given the names of the sons of Aaron via Eleazar, Aaron's third and oldest surviving son,[433] all the way down to the Captivity. In I Chronicles 24:1–4 it is shown that the priests were drawn from both the lines of Eleazar and Ithamar, the only other surviving son of Aaron, but no lineage of Ithamar is given. Nonetheless, this is evidence of a continuous existence of two distinct lines of descent among the sons of Aaron throughout the period of the Judges.

Followers of Wellhausen could easily retort that the Chronicles were written centuries after the period of the Judges, probably under Ezra, making their history suspect, as it would be regarded by sceptics as an attempt to concoct a pedigree for Ezra and his co-workers. I would have to agree that the Chronicles probably do date from that time, as their linguistic style indicates as much, and that Ezra may well have

---

[433] Aaron's oldest sons, Nadab and Abihu perished in the wilderness, see Leviticus 10:1–8.

been their author,[434] but I do not agree that these facts invalidate their testimony.

The Samaritan Records

Deferring to the Critics' concerns however, there is another source that may be drawn upon, a source derived from the Samaritans who could not be charged with supporting Ezra in any way at all, seeing as they referred to him in a most cruel and uncalled for manner, namely, as the *'accursed Ezra!'*[435]

Now the existence of the Samaritan Pentateuch, is of course very well known, and has been discussed in great detail above. What is not so well known however, is that there is also a Samaritan Chronicle, and a Samaritan book of Joshua which have survived in Arabic versions.[436] Both of these documents report a list of High Priests starting from Aaron, a list which matches that found in I Chronicles until we reach Uzzi.

I set out both lists for comparison below. It is important to remember that the list in Chronicles registers *sons* of Aaron via Eleazar, while the list in the Samaritan sources registers *High Priests*.

Register Of The Sons Of Aaron In I Chronicles 6:3–6.	Register Of High Priests Taken From The Samaritan Records.[437]
Aaron,	Aaron,
Eleazar,	Eleazar,
Phinehas,	Phinehas,
Abishua,	Abishua,
	Shishi (*the First*),
Bukki,	Bahqi (= Bukki),
Uzzi,	Uzzi,
Zerahiah.	Shishi (*the Second*).

The fact that the Samaritan list includes Shishi I in between Abishua and Bukki or Bahqi could be because the latter was a mere child when

---

[434] See p. 304.

[435] Robertson, op. cit., pp. 72–74, & 169.

[436] Ibid., p. 174.

[437] Taken from Robertson, op. cit., p. 175.

Abishua died, perhaps necessitating a brother of Abishua (Shishi) to become Priest instead. This is only a theory of mine of course, but in a while I will show that it could well be true, and it would certainly account for the difference in the two lines. The main point to be made though, is the great *similarity* of both lines. The Samaritan evidence, endorses I Chronicles 6:3–6, even though Chronicles was very probably produced by Ezra. The infamous animosity between the Jews and Samaritans in Ezra's day, that we noticed above, virtually guarantees that the Samaritan records are completely independent of Chronicles, and establishes their credentials as being a reliable support of Chronicles. It is ironic indeed that the association of Ezra with Chronicles, which according to the Critics, makes their testimony highly suspect, actually <u>*validates*</u> the lines of descent recorded there, as the Samaritans would never have gone out of their way to support him!

Evidence Ignored

In keeping with what we have noticed before, Wellhausen seems not to have given this evidence the attention it merits. As he lived from 1844 to 1918[438] he had plenty of opportunities to research the matter, as the Samaritan lists were published in 1848,[439] and would have been widely discussed at theological faculties in universities and seminaries at the time. No academic could fail to be aware of them. I can only suppose that their support for the existence of an Aaronic High Priesthood throughout the period of the Judges was too damaging to Wellhausen's views for his comfort.

After Uzzi, we see the two lines diverge. According to the Samaritans, when Uzzi became High Priest, he was but a child. Eli, the head of the line of Ithamar, then usurped the High Priesthood

---

[438] Soulen and Kendall Soulen, op. cit., p. 207.

[439] In *The Samaritan Book Of Joshua*, published as *Chronicon Samaritanum*, Leyden, Joynboll, 1848. Further relevant publications followed; *Abul Fathi Annales Samaritani*, Gotha, Vilmar, 1865, *Chronique Samaritaine: Journal Asiatique*, Neubauer, 1869, *Une Novelle Chronique Samaritaine: Revue des Etudes Juives*, Paris, Adler & Seligsohn, 1902, and, after the death of Wellhausen, but during the lifetime of his disciples, *The Chain Of The Samaritan High Priests: Studies And Texts*, London, Gaster, 1925–1928. Cited from Robertson, op. cit., p. 174.

from the line of Eleazar.[440] This would account for the difference in the lines from then on, although it is important to see that throughout the history of the Judges, the crucial period when it comes to assessing Wellhausen's views, there is almost total agreement between the lines. Even the one minor divergence is easily accounted for as I have suggested above, and the Samaritan story about the youth of Uzzi might seem to indicate that child inheritors of the position of High Priest might be passed over. Thus we must conclude that there was indeed a line of Aaronic High Priests throughout the period of the Judges.

Eli, And The Line Of Ithamar

In support of the Samaritan claim, it is clear from a comparison of different Scriptural passages, that Eli was of the line of Ithamar. I Kings 2:27 shows us that Abiathar the priest was of the line of Eli, while I Chronicles 24:6 shows that he was also a descendent of Ithamar, meaning that Eli must also have been descended from him.[441] In Joshua 8:33, we find the ark of the covenant in Shechem at Mount Ebal, where, in accordance with Deuteronomy 27:1–8 Joshua wrote the Torah upon some stones (verse 32). The Samaritans portray the ark remaining at Shechem, but charge Eli of the line of Ithamar with making a copy of the real ark, which he then set up in Shiloh, where he established himself as a rival High Priest after leaving Shechem, when the child Uzzi became the true High Priest. This story of a counterfeit ark seems very spurious, for the Samaritans, it would seem, have to account for the disappearance of the real ark from Shechem, precisely at this time! They do this by means of another story in which the ark and the tabernacle were both placed inside a cave in Mount Gerizim for safe-keeping, the mouth of which then closed up, preventing its opening ever being located again.[442] Interestingly, Josephus, in his *Antiquities* reports that the tabernacle was indeed at Shiloh at this

---

[440] Robertson, op. cit., pp. 176–177.

[441] See also the lists of High Priests in Conder, F. R., & Conder, C. R., *A Handbook To The Bible,* London, Longmans, Green , & Co., 1880, Table VIII, p. 50.

[442] Robertson, op. cit., pp. 176–177.

time.[443] In Judges 20:26–27 however, we find the ark at Bethel, although it has been argued that the Hebrew בית--אל should be understood only as meaning the House-of-God.[444] Nevertheless, the facts are;

1. The ark of the covenant is seen clearly to be at Shiloh in the charge of Eli in I Samuel 3:3.

2. The Samaritans admit to the disappearance of the ark of the covenant from their Temple at Shechem precisely at this time.

3. At exactly the same time as the Samaritans admit the loss of the ark, there is a change of dynasty in the line of High Priests from the house of Eleazar, to that of Ithamar.

It seems most likely then that there was a rift of some kind between the houses of Eleazar and Ithamar which resulted in the priesthood, ark, and tabernacle leaving Shechem for Shiloh. A contrary view is advocated by some however, who see the hand of the Philistine occupiers of the Land in the deposing of the Shechemite High Priest, and the establishment of a High Priest, Eli of course, of their own choosing.[445] Whatever the reason for this move, from this point on, the priesthood is again clearly before the eyes of the reader of Scripture. From the time of Samuel, which is also the time of Eli, right the way through the period of the monarchy, and even down to Ezra, the priesthood is never again lost sight of in such a way, but, crucially, and for Wellhausen's views, *fatally*, the line of High Priests down to Eli is more or less agreed upon by parties who are so radically opposed to each other's point-of-view as to eliminate even the merest hint of collusion.

Conclusion I. The critic's assertion that there was no Aaronic priesthood during the period of the Judges is contrary not just to Scriptural evidence, but also to compelling external evidence, derived

---

[443] Josephus, Flavius, *The Antiquities Of The Jews*, being a part of *The Works Of Flavius Josephus*, translated Whiston, Milner & Sowerby, 1866, Book V, Chapter x, Paragraph 2.

[444] See *The Companion Bible*, in. loc.

[445] See Beecher, Willis J., in the fascinating article *Abdon*, in *The International Standard Bible Encyclopædia*, op. cit., Volume I, p. 4.

from a source which must be accepted as completely independent of the Scriptural record. This means there is no evidence at all to support the critic in his claim, but every logical reason to accept the Scriptural narrative depicting a line of High Priests throughout the period covered by the book of Judges, from Aaron to Eli.

Conclusion II. It follows from *Conclusion I* that the Aaronic High Priesthood was not the invention of the exilic or post-exilic priests.

Why Is The Priesthood 'Invisible' In The Period Of The Judges?

Having seen that there was indeed a line of Aaronic High Priests from Eleazar to Eli, throughout the period covered by the book of the Judges, we need not be detained too long by the questions concerning their absence from the narrative of the book of Judges. Nonetheless a brief word on this matter might be in order.

I have shown elsewhere[446] that during most of the history covered by the book of Judges, the twelve tribes were often broken up into separate areas of territory that were isolated from each other by the oppressors of the Israelites. Two distinct wedges of Canaanite-held territory cut right across the central highlands dividing the nation into three parts. The southernmost of these Canaanite wedges at times virtually cut-off from the Northern tribes the land of Judah, that to the East, South, and West, was bordered by the Dead Sea, Negeb Desert, and the Philistines respectively. (The Canaanite 'wedges' are shown in the maps on pages 346 and 347.) During these times of territorial fragmentation, the High Priesthood based in Shechem would have had no influence at all over events in Judah, and this lack of influence might easily have extended to other tribal areas at times. Of course, the periods when this territorial fragmentation would have been most acute, and when the influence of the central High Priesthood would consequently be at its lowest ebb, would inevitably be when the incursions of Israel's enemies were at their height, and the need for the Lord to raise up a deliverer for Israel in the form of a Judge, would have been at its most urgent. It is inevitable that when the

---

[446] Phelan, M. W. J. *The Early History Of Israel*, Birmingham, The European Theological Seminary, 2001.

young nation was on its knees, the right and proper workings of the administration could not function, and some extraordinary measures would be required. This, I believe, explains the by-passing of the High Priesthood in the phenomenon of the direct line of communication between the Lord and the Judges. It was an action necessitated by the conditions the Judges were called to resist. An example of this is discernible in Judges chapter 6, where we find Gideon, of the tribe of _Manasseh_ (verse 15) is twice commanded to offer sacrifices (verses 18–27).

Now the date and place of authorship of the book of Judges has an impact on this matter. The traditional Jewish belief is that the book was written by Samuel.[447] Although this traditional belief is scorned at by the Critics, there are a number of internal features which control the date of authorship very closely, and suggest it might be true. We know at least that the manner of the death of Abimelech recorded in Judges 9:53 is referred to in II Samuel 11:21, indicating that Judges was written before II Samuel. We know also from Judges 1:21, that it was written before the capture of Jerusalem by David recorded in II Samuel 5:6–9. Comparing this with the recurring phrase, "in those days there was no king in Israel" or similar,[448] implying that there _was_ a king in Israel when Judges was written, we see that the internal evidence is that it was written during the very first days of the monarchy, but before the capture of Jerusalem. The reference in 18:30 to "the day of the captivity of the land" cannot then be a reference to the fall of the Northern tribes, or that of Judah under Nebuchadnezzar as Critics suggest, the linguistic style is firmly opposed to that,[449] but must be, as Psalm 78:60–61, and I Samuel 4:11 indicate, a reference to the Philistine incursions, which might have been the cause of the move of the High Priesthood from the line of Eleazar to that of Ithamar.

We may conclude therefore that the book of the Judges was written during the lifetime of Samuel, and quite possibly by him, as the Jews

---

[447] See Davis, John D., _Dictionary Of The Bible_, London, Pickering & Inglis, fourth revised edition, 1972, p. 448, and Hartwell Horne, op. cit., Volume IV, p. 40.

[448] See 17:6, 18:1, 19:1, & 21:25.

[449] See Hartwell Horne, op. cit., Volume IV, p. 40.

insist. As it was written before the capture of Jerusalem, the likelihood is that it was based on records kept at David's court in Hebron in Judah, and may have been supplemented by accounts Samuel was able to gather as he undertook his journeys around the land (I Samuel 7:15–17), but nonetheless the records concerning the succession of High Priests based at Northern Shechem probably would not have been available until David was firmly established in Jerusalem, and he was the undisputed ruler of the entire land; but by that time, the book of Judges had been written. However, when I and II Chronicles were written in the days of Ezra, the details concerning the line of High Priests were in the possession of Judah, explaining the difference between the Judges and Chronicles.[450]

Conclusion III. The absence of references to the High Priesthood in the book of Judges does not militate against *Conclusions I* and *II* above, but is explainable by the historical situation the book of Judges reveals, and by the time and place of its composition, as indicated by the internal evidence.

---

[450] In fact, it has been suggested that the phrase "the house that Solomon built in Jerusalem (I Chronicles 6:10)" might be an indicator of a Shechemite origin for the lists this remark is embedded within, as it could imply a less than enthusiastic regard for the Jerusalem Temple. As E is supposed to be a Shechemite Source however, and one of the earliest, centuries before D and P the alleged last source, we would then have to accept that E originated from a Priesthood which claims descent from Aaron, a P-type claim!

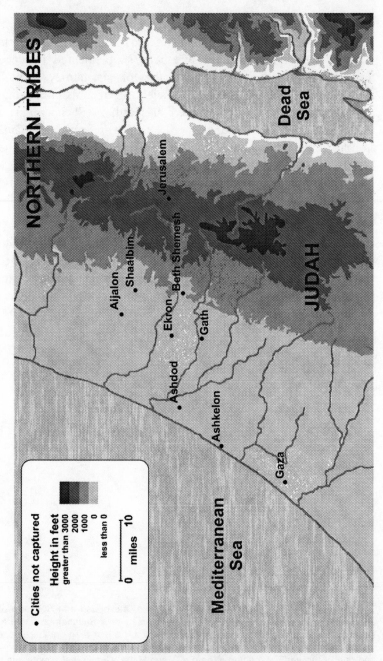

Figure 9 The Southern Wedge of Canaanite held territory during the age of
the Judges (Map 1 of 2)

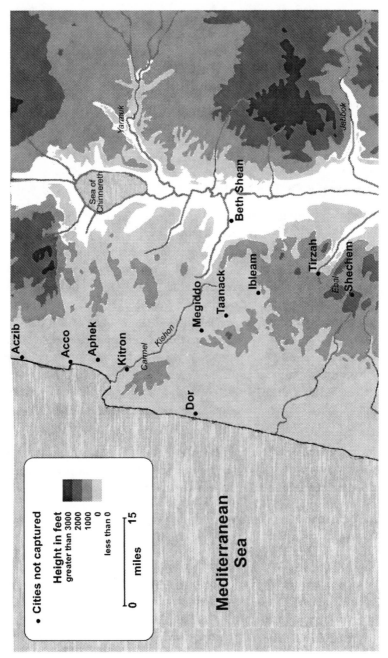

Figure 10 The Northern Wedge of Canaanite held territory during the age
of the Judges (Map 2 of 2)

Part C:
The Relationship Between
The Sons Of Aaron, And Non-Aaronic Levites

The True Status Of The Levites

Although there is no reference at all to the Aaronic High Priests in the book of the Judges, there are, in Judges chapters 17 and 18, many references to a particular Levite, who seems not to have been a descendent of Aaron, but who was most definitely a priest, albeit an idolatrous one. Does this mean that *any* Levite might have been a priest? or, is this episode to be rejected as evidence because it concerns a clear renegade? I believe that in spite of the fact that the priest did become a renegade, this incident does indicate that all Levites were priests. From 17:9 we see that descent from Levi was the ground for the Levite being accepted by his original employer, Micah, as his priest. Micah, in the next verse seems satisfied that being a Levite was all that was needed, and so, took him on as "a Father and a Priest."

From Joshua 18:7 we find encouragement for this view, for there we read, "the Levites have no part among you; for the priesthood of the Lord is their inheritance." This compares very favourably with Deuteronomy 18:1–8 of course. Here we see that the priesthood seems not to be restricted to a *minority* of Levites, namely those descended from Aaron, but to Levites in general, as no Levite received any territorial allotment.

Joshua provides further evidence that this is so in 3:3, where we encounter the Levites who were carrying the ark. There these Levites are referred to as priests, "When ye see the ark-of-the-covenant of the Lord your God, and the priests the Levites bearing it." However, in Numbers 3:29–32, we find the ark was to be carried by the Kohathites. Now, Aaron was descended from Kohath (Exodus 6:18–20), thus all

348

the Aaronic priests were Kohathites, but not all Kohathites were priests of course. It might be that the particular Kohathites who carried the ark on this occasion were priests, but then we would expect the phrase to be, "the priests the sons of Aaron," and not as it is in the text, "the priests the Levites."

There are real suggestions here then that any Levite might be a priest, albeit none of these verses is completely unequivocal, although Joshua 18:7 certainly does seem persuasive.

I Samuel 2:27–28 may clarify the matter however. These two verses indicate that the Levites were not selected to minister to the Lord in Exodus 32, but way before that, while the Israelites were still in Egypt in fact. The passage reads, "There came a man of God unto Eli, and said unto him, Thus saith the Lord, Did I plainly appear unto the house of thy father, when they were in Egypt in Pharaoh's house? And did I choose him out of all the tribes of Israel to be my priest, to offer upon mine altar, to burn incense, to wear an ephod before Me? and did I give unto the house of thy father all the offerings made by fire of the children of Israel?"

The fact that the Hebrew words rendered *thy father*, *him*, *priest* and *thy father* are all singular,[451] indicates that Levi himself is being referred to here. This would mean, firstly that the Levites were called to serve the Lord long before Exodus 32,[452] and secondly, that Levites were called to be priests even before the birth of Aaron. In turn, this would mean that all Levites were indeed priests, and that the definite calling of Aaron and his sons is to a *different category* of priesthood, presumably, the High Priesthood of the central sanctuary.[453] We would see also that

---

[451] These are respectively, אביך, אתו, לכהן, and אביך and are all singular, see Davidson, op. cit., in. loc.

[452] Given Aaron's rôle in the sin of the Golden Calf, it seems inherently unlikely that the High Priesthood would have been awarded to him because of this affair as so often is imagined. It must be more probable that he was regarded already as a priest, and that the office of High Priest was bestowed on him graciously, in spite of his involvement, and not because of any merit he displayed. On this matter see Keil & Delitzsch, op. cit., Volume I, pp. 340–341.

[453] Both Garrett (op. cit., pp. 232–233) and Weiner (in the article *Priests And Levites* in *The International Standard Bible Encyclopædia*, op. cit., Volume IV, p. 2447) point out that Minoan inscriptions found at El-'Olâ in Arabia refer to priests and priestesses of

the Israelites then would never have been without priests, which is perhaps what we would expect. Abraham, Isaac, and Jacob all offered sacrifices, but when the family of Jacob descended to Egypt the line of Levi was chosen to serve for the whole nation as priests, and, ultimately, at Exodus 32, the line of Aaron was chosen to be High Priests.

Encouragement for this view is found in the strange fact that in Exodus 4:14, Aaron is referred to as *The Levite*. This is most peculiar given that the words are addressed to Moses! Moses, being the brother of Aaron, would of course not need to be told that Aaron was *a* Levite, which means that the word must convey, for the purpose of emphasis, something other than Aaron's pedigree, which would have been identical to that of Moses. The fact that he is called *The* Levite, seems indicative that he held a particular position within the family of Jacob. Even Critics agree this is likely to be a reference indicating Aaron's profession, and probably his rank as well.[454] The reference in Exodus 4:14 to Aaron's ability in speaking would seem to indicate that this position would have involved making public addresses, and so could quite conceivably have been priestly in character, as I Samuel 2:27–28 would indicate. There would after all be very little opportunity for political meetings during the Oppression in Egypt, and the reference to sacrificing in Exodus 3:18 would seem to indicate that an Israelite priesthood was in existence in Egypt.

Different Spheres Of Activity

In the books of Exodus, Leviticus and Numbers, the focus is solely upon the services offered at the tabernacle, and these pertained to Aaron and his sons exclusively. In Deuteronomy, The Treaty Document Of Israel As A Nation, the requirements of the nation, *in occupation of the whole of the Land of Promise* are under consideration. Once in occupation of the Land, the tribes would no longer be gathered together in one place, and therefore would need to

---

Wadd as *lawî* and *lawî'at*, which might possibly be derived from the Hebrew *Levi*. If so, then it would indicate that the word *Levite* came to mean *priest*.

[454] See Smith, W. Robertson, & Bertholet, Alfred, in the article *Levites*, in the *Encyclopædia Biblica*, op. cit., in. loc.

fall back upon the general priesthood of all male Levites dispersed throughout the nation, and serving at its many shrines (e.g. I Samuel 7:17, & 20:6). Only the sons of Aaron would minister at the tabernacle, but all Levites could minister elsewhere.

We have already seen above that the Wellhausian concept of the centralisation of worship in Deuteronomy is a consequence of misunderstanding the text. Now we see it leads also to the assumption of a contradiction where none exists! The books of Exodus to Numbers address the needs of Israel in the wilderness, and therefore can relate only to the tabernacle worship, for which the sons of Aaron alone were qualified; the book of Deuteronomy is concerned with the life of the Israelites in occupation of the Land, and dealt with the needs associated with that situation.

From this, of course we can see why Joshua referred to the Kohathites carrying the ark as priests. As Kohathites they were Levites, and all Levites were priests. So too, we understand why Levites in general are said to have the priesthood of the Lord as their inheritance. Finally, we see why Micah was satisfied that his priest was simply a Levite, and was not a descendent of Aaron.

The Problems Associated With This View

There are a few passages that might appear to challenge the view expressed above, but each one, I believe, is capable of reconciliation with my point-of-view. The texts in question are;

1. Exodus 24:5

This text belongs to the section 24:3–8 and concerns the inauguration of the Sinaitic Covenant. As such, the circumstances attending this event are as unique as the event itself, and may not be taken as a pattern for working practices subsequent to the occasion. In verse 5 we see that Moses seemingly took young men from every tribe of Israel, as representatives of All-Israel, and caused them to offer burnt and peace offerings. This symbolised the turning of All-Israel to the Lord, and is absolutely neutral with regard to the understanding of the rôle of the Levites after the Covenant had become established. While some see a problem with this verse because of the by-passing of the

Levites, I submit it is not directly connected to our question owing to the special nature of the occasion.

2. Exodus 32:29

It has already been suggested that this passage concerns the calling of Aaron and his sons, not to the priesthood as such, but to the High Priesthood of the tabernacle, and also the calling of the non-Aaronic priests to the work of attending to the equipment, and materials of the tabernacle. Is this view credible?

I believe it is quite credible, and that there is a situation with some parallels that is to be found in Numbers 25:10–13. Here we find that Phinehas, the son of Eleazar, and grandson of Aaron, who it must be agreed was already honoured with the Priesthood of the tabernacle, has the priesthood confirmed for him and his seed because his zeal for the Lord overrode all other purely natural feelings. But notice the fact that he was a priest already, yet it would be possible to conclude, if this fact was unknown, that Phinehas' eligibility for the priesthood only commenced at Numbers 3:10–13. Garrett makes the point that the calling referred to in Exodus 32:29 certainly does not imply that the Levites were not priests already (as we have seen in the case of Phinehas just referred to), but only relates to the new tasks relating to the tabernacle. The Hebrew phrase translated by the Authorized Version as "consecrate yourselves" means literally "fill your hands",[455] and does not necessarily imply any kind of ordination ceremony.[456] Deuteronomy 10:8 has been understood to mean that the Levites were called to attend to the tabernacle equipment and materials long *after* the events associated with the Golden Calf, but 10:6–7 is very clearly a parenthetical statement, interrupting the narrative of 10:1–11.

3. Numbers 16–18

This passage concerns the revolt of Korah, Dathan, Abiram, and On against Moses and Aaron, over the High Priesthood itself, and is certainly the most difficult to reconcile with the Deuteronomic

---

[455] Jay. P. Green, op. cit., in. loc.
[456] Garrett, op. cit., pp. 211–212.

passages referred to above. I am grateful to Duane Garrett for showing the way forward here. It is vital to recall that the priesthood that is under dispute here, is the only priesthood that was active at the time, namely, the priesthood associated with the tabernacle services. I believe that the situation as outlined above is the only way in which the events of Numbers 16–17 may be reconciled with the statements found in the book of Deuteronomy that we have already noticed which infer that all Levites were priests. Providing it is recalled that during the desert wanderings, the only form of ceremonial worship acceptable to the Lord, after the construction of the ark and the tabernacle, is that which was based upon them, then there is no contradiction between what we find in this passage and the book of Deuteronomy. Critics make much indeed of Numbers 16–18, which to their minds is so clearly in contradiction with Deuteronomy as to be beyond dispute. As in so many similar cases, if the passage is contextualised the problem disappears. The passage in Numbers must be seen in a milieu in which only tabernacle-based service was acceptable, and it must be recalled with equal clarity that Deuteronomy caters for the local places of worship (e.g. those of I Samuel 7:17 & 20:6), as well as that based upon the central shrine.

After researching the matter Duane Garrett concluded that in the days of the Exodus, it was not the High Priesthood of Aaron, but the sacred work of the Levites generally that was considered as "fixed and inviolable." Garrett offers as evidence for this, the fact that while some of the Israelites resisted the rôle of Aaron as High Priest, the priestly rôle of the Levites was never challenged. This seems to indicate that this Levite function was regarded as being unquestionable. Ironically, according to Garrett, the truth of this situation is revealed with the greatest clarity in the great rebellion against Moses by Dathan, Abiram and the sons of Korah.

In Numbers 16 we see that the sons of Korah attempted to wrest the High Priesthood from Aaron, during which they received lay-support from Dathan and Abiram. There were two key points in this rebellion. What Garrett calls the "lay-opposition" was directed towards Moses, and was based on the charges that he had arrogated to himself far too much authority, and that he had led the Israelites into nothing but a wilderness (Numbers 16:3, 13). The complaint of the sons of Korah was that Aaron was unfit to act as High Priest owing to his association with Moses (Numbers 16:11). They attempted to supplant him therefore, seemingly through self-ambition.

What is key to the understanding of the Levites' rôle for Garrett is the fact that the lay-rebels did not feel they could act alone, but needed Levite backing. He points out that there had been lay-complaints about Moses ever since the escape from Egypt. It was only when the sons of Korah became involved however, that a serious challenge was able to be mounted, and this indicates that the Levites' part in the rebellion is what gave it credibility in the eyes of the conspirators, and, as Garrett is keen to point out, this would seem to prove that the priestly rôle of the Levites was one that had been established for many generations.

When the rebellion had been put down, what had been established, or re-established was the position of Aaron as High Priest, and the rôle of the Aaronites in ministering at the Tabernacle, it did not alter the position of the Levites in general. So too, the commands of Numbers 18:1–8 do not imply that ordinary Levites could never have any priestly duties, it simply excludes them from ministering at the central sanctuary.[457]

A point in favour of Garrett's views is that from Exodus 5:1 we see that well before the events of Mount Sinai, the Israelites were capable of holding feasts to the Lord, which would have included sacrificial offerings (3:18), which is a positive indicator that a priesthood was even then in existence amongst the Hebrews.

Samuel A Descendent Of Korah

However contrary to the normal views of fundamentalists this proposal of Garrett's is, I, at least, find it particularly attractive in answering the difficulties of reconciling this passage with Deuteronomy. We have already seen that on occasion, non-Aaronic Israelites were called to offer sacrifices at sites located away from the tabernacle (Judges 6:18–27). For me though, the most convincing aspect of Garrett's views, is that from his proposal, we see how

---

[457] Garrett, op. cit., pp. 217–219.

Samuel, a Levite, but descended from none other than the rebel *Korah* himself, was able legitimately to offer sacrifices to the Lord. This of course shows with the greatest degree of clarity possible that there was nothing against the principle of Korah officiating at any service apart from those pertaining to the tabernacle. He was excluded only because of what was current practice: in his day the only services that were offered were tabernacle-based. In the days of Samuel however, things were significantly different, and the practice was in harmony with the principle. The situation of occupancy of the Land outlined in Deuteronomy was in place. Hence Samuel as a Levite, although not of the sons of Aaron, could officiate as a priest at the local shrines as he did for example in I Samuel 7, and 16. This fact shows unequivocally, that there were indeed legitimate non-Aaronic Levitical priests, and the critic is quite wrong to believe that Deuteronomy contradicts the books of Exodus to Numbers. The descent of Samuel from Levi via Korah is shown in Appendix X.

Conclusion IV. The fact that Samuel, a descendent of Korah, could officiate at local shrines in Israel shows that all Levites could act as priests.

Conclusion V. There is no contradiction between Deuteronomy and the books of Exodus to Numbers concerning the rôle of the Levites. Deuteronomy addresses the needs of the nation in occupancy of the Land, and is not restricted in its vision only to the tabernacle or temple services. By contrast however, the tabernacle service is all the books of Exodus to Numbers could consider. These different sets of circumstances explain the different rôles, and resolve the alleged contradiction.

The Zadokites

The last High Priests of the line of Ithamar were Ahimelech, and Abiathar. Zadok, who descended from Eleazar (I Chronicles 6:50–53)[458] was joint High Priest under David, firstly with Ahimelech (II Samuel 8:15–17), and then with Abiathar (II Samuel 15:24–36).

---

[458] See Appendix X.

The issue of the succession to king David brought the downfall of the line of Ithamar via Eli however. Abiathar had sided with Adonijah in his unsuccessful bid to become king after David, while Zadok had supported Solomon (I Kings 1). After Solomon was installed as king of All-Israel, Abiathar was deposed from office, leaving Zadok as sole High Priest (I Kings 2:26–35). The High Priesthood then continued with the line of Eleazar, making all legitimate future High Priests, sons of Zadok, or Zadokites, as well as being sons of Aaron.

King Josiah's Reforms

During the dark days of Israel's decline, the nation became infested with idolatry, and this evil affected the priesthood as well. In II Kings 22 we encounter the godly king Josiah, in whose time the book of the Law (Deuteronomy) was discovered in the temple by the Zadokite High Priest, Hilkiah (II Kings 22:8 & I Chronicles 9:11). Encouraged by Hilkiah, Josiah began a massive programme of reformation, which included bringing into Jerusalem, all the priests from the outlying districts of the by then shrunken state of Judah, into the Jerusalem temple (II Kings 23:8–9).

It must be remembered that by the time of Josiah, the Northern Kingdom of Israel had fallen, and the Southern Kingdom of Judah was greatly reduced in size, making the need for non-Aaronic Levite priests to minister at local shrines almost non-existent. This move by Josiah meant that the entire priesthood was under the direct control of the godly Hilkiah, who would diligently eradicate any attempts at idolatry or syncretism. Being brought to the Jerusalem temple, these Levite priests from the outlying districts could no longer work as priests if they were not descended from Aaron, of course. Thus, from this time on, ordinary, that is non-Aaronic/Zadokite Levites had a rôle almost exactly as they did in the Sinai desert; a rôle quite distinct from the priests, whose ranks were now filled exclusively with the sons-of-Aaron via Eleazar, the Zadokites.

This is the situation we find in Ezekiel 44, where the prophet restricts the priesthood to the sons of Zadok, and is also what we find in Ezra 6:18, and also in the New Testament, in Luke 10:31–32, where again, priests are distinct from Levites.

Conclusion VI. The removal of all but the Zadokites from the priesthood was not because of a Wellhausian evolutionary step in the religious life of Israel, but because the local shrines had lost their viability with the demise of the Northern Kingdom, and the reduction in size of the Southern Kingdom, to the environs of Jerusalem. Inevitably this brought about a situation analogous in part to that of the desert wanderings, making the features of the Josianic period resemble very closely those of the Mosaic period, including the rôles of priests and Levites.

Conclusion VII. The religious history of Israel and Judah does not provide any kind of basis for The New Documentary Hypothesis, leaving it devoid of all support beyond the fanaticism of its adherents.

Supplement Two

The Credibility Of Genesis

The scope of this work as outlined in the Introduction is confined to the literary problems of the Pentateuch, however, to ignore the non-literary problems of Genesis would not be fitting, especially as they constitute one reason, albeit a negative one, for the embracing by some of the New Documentary Hypothesis. It is felt by such people that a literal acceptance of Genesis is impossible, and this feeling encourages the acceptance of an alternative view, usually a Higher Critical view. It is unfortunate that I may only skim the surface of the issues relating to the non-literary problems here. A thorough treatment of this subject would necessitate another and larger volume. I have set out the issues more or less in the order in which the reader would encounter them if Genesis were read from start to finish.

Genesis 1:1

"In the beginning God created the heavens and the earth." Conventional scientific wisdom teaches that the universe began when a point of infinitely high density, known as a Singularity, exploded at the Big Bang, to produce enormous quantities of matter and anti-matter. There was very slightly more matter than anti-matter, which meant that when the anti-matter and a corresponding amount of matter annihilated each other, a randomly distributed and tiny amount of matter was left over, from which the universe, and, ultimately all life-forms, including our own were to develop. This is a highly simplified summary of what is known as cosmic evolutionary theory.[459]

The theory cannot explain the origin of the Singularity, nor what happened to induce the Singularity to explode at the Big Bang, and

---

[459] See Davies, Paul, *God And The New Physics*, Harmondsworth, Penguin Books, 1983, cap. III., *Did God Create The Universe?* Gribbin, John, *In Search Of Big Bang*, London, Heinemann, 1986, cap. VI, *The Standard Model*, and Schroeder, Gerald L., *Genesis And The Big Bang*, New York, Bantam Books, 1990, esp. p. 24.

mathematicians certainly struggle with the concepts of a Singularity.[460] At the moment this theory is extremely popular, but so many theories have come and gone over the years, that this theory may well explode in a Big Bang of its own, and produce a large number of theories and counter-theories, which, like the proposed matter and anti-matter, might then annihilate each other. There could be a small number of randomly distributed theories left over afterwards from which a new system could be built up of course! In fact, even now there are scientists who see no need for a Big Bang at all, so, already the theories are changing again.[461]

For the believer there are alternatives. I recommend a work by the Geotechnical Engineer and university lecturer, Leander Pimenta, entitled *Before The First Day*, which offers believers credible answers to current cosmic evolutionary dogma,[462] as well as *He Made The Stars Also* by Doctor Stuart Burgess, and *Astronomy And The Bible*, by Donald de Young.[463]

The calculations of the size and age of the universe made by astronomers and cosmic evolutionists are based to a large extent upon what is known as Red-Shift, the amount by which light reaching the earth from distant stars has 'shifted' to the red end of the visible portion of the electro-magnetic spectrum through the Doppler-Effect. The higher the degree of movement, or 'shift', the faster the object emitting it is moving away from us. Objects approaching us have a Blue Shift. As the speed of light (C) is held to be a constant (299,792,458 metres per second, or 186,281 miles per second), the varying degrees of Red-Shift that are readily observable, indicate objects moving at varying speeds from the earth. They also indicate to some extent their supposed age, as galaxies appear to be separating from each other at speeds able to be measured by Red and Blue Shift,

---

[460] See Davies, op. cit., cap. III., and Gribbin, op. cit., cap. X. *The Moment Of Creation*.

[461] Gribbin, op. cit., cap. X., and Briggs, John, and Peat, F. David., *Turbulent Mirror: An Illustrated Guide To Chaos Theory And The Science Of Wholeness,* New York, Harper & Row, 1990, p. 148.

[462] Pimenta, Leander R., *Before The First Day: The Full Story Of Earth's Creation.* Chichester, West Sussex, Creation Books, 1998.

[463] Both available from The Creation Science Movement, P.O. Box 888, Portsmouth, PO6 2YD.

and this rate, assumed to be a Constant, enables the age of the universe to be extrapolated.[464]

The Creation Science Movement in Portsmouth,[465] has over the years published material produced by independent researchers from different countries which indicates that while C might now be a Constant, there appears to have been a time when it was not, but had instead a considerably higher value than that which is now attributed to it. *The Times* newspaper on the 5th. April 2000 even carried an article on this subject, and Channel 4's *Equinox* Programme of the 17th April 2000 actually seemed to offer *proof* that C was previously higher in value than it is now.[466] This would mean that calculations using Red or Blue Shift would all be open to question, and the readings which displayed the greatest amount of Shift, would need the greatest amount of correction, as it is held that C descended in a very steep curve to its present rate, making the corrections required, more and more extreme, the further back in time one went. This has enormous implications for the size and the age of the universe, and could easily rob astronomers and cosmic evolutionists of the eons of time their pet-theories require, making them untenable.

Genesis 1:27

"Male and female created He them." It has been shown recently by means of mitochondrial DNA, that every woman and girl who is alive has descended from the same human female. This speaks eloquently for the genuine existence of an original human couple, but what about the theory of evolution?[467]

The reader may not be aquatinted with the following problems for the theory of evolution;

---

[464] Gribbin, op. cit., p. 132, and cap. III., *The Expanding Universe.*

[465] P.O. Box, 888, Portsmouth, PO6 2YD.

[466] See leaflets 256, 262, 317, and *Creation* Volume 11, number 19, published by The Creation Science Movement, P.O. Box 888, Portsmouth, PO6 2YD.

[467] For details see *Creation* Volume 10, Number 7, published by the Creation Science Movement.

1. The fossil record begins very abruptly in the Cambrian rock strata. There are no pre-Cambrian fossils even though the pre-Cambrian strata, sometimes a mile thick, are perfect for fossil formation, and frequently are the same as the fossil beds above them. Fossils of perfectly formed and complex animals appear both _suddenly and abundantly_. In the pre-Cambrian there is no evidence of life; in the Cambrian, it is everywhere, and perfect and complex in form!

2. No 'half-evolved' or half-and-half creatures have been found, although they have been fabricated by evolutionists. This lack of intermediate fossil forms has been particularly challenging for leading evolutionists who have struggled to account for it, as their theories would predict _huge_ amounts of such finds. There is not merely one missing link between humans and apes; every supposed link is missing!

3. Many fish, bird, reptile, insect and mammal fossils have been found around the world, said to be several millions of years old, which are absolutely indistinguishable from living equivalents swimming, flying, crawling, or walking about today. This shows the _rigidity_ of life forms, rather than the plasticity required by evolution.

4. The best known example of alleged evolution is that of the modern horse from the tiny eohippus. Impressive displays are often given of a series of equine skeletons, each slightly larger than the other, spanning the range between eohippus and the modern horse. The reader is encouraged to suppose that the larger the skeleton the more recent the stratum it was found in. The fact that the various skeletons have been gathered from different locations around the world in a most selective manner is rarely mentioned. Nor is it ever revealed that skeletons of the modern horse have been found in strata said to be _older_ than eohippus, showing that eohippus and the modern horse were _contemporaries_. An equally impressive display could be made with ease from the various types of cats alive today. One could start from the domestic cat, and then progress to the wild cat, which is slightly larger, and then the lynx, and end up with a lion. The only problem is of

course, that all these types are alive today, although some cats, the sabre-toothed tiger for example, have died out. With the equine series, it would seem that most horse forms, including eohippus have become extinct, but that the so-called modern horse, because of its usefulness to man throughout our history has been protected. This so-called proof of evolution is merely a demonstration of special-pleading and proves nothing at all.

5. Evolution must cross the species barrier. While it is undoubtedly true that there is development within species; evolution requires one species to arise from another. Roses may be cross-bred to produce different colours and forms, but no one has ever changed a rose into a daffodil! To this extent, evolution is but the biological equivalent of medieval alchemy, requiring the transmutation, not of metals, but of species. Dog breeders may introduce different types of dogs, but have never turned a dog into a cat. Evolution preaches that every species, oak trees and jelly-fish, porcupines and humans, all came from a single-celled life-form, meaning that one species must frequently arise from another. The only evidence evolutionists offer is that of development _within_ a species, whether it's moths' wings changing colour, fruit flies mutating, or bacteria developing new strains, but where do we see new _species_ arising from old?

6. There would appear to be much evidence of devolution, inasmuch as many fossil finds seem to show stronger, more robust, and certainly larger forms of animals when compared with those now living. Fossils of giant dragonflies with 30 inch wingspans have been found, as have fossils of ten feet long frogs, ten feet high birds, six feet tall sheep, and pigs the size of current day rhinos! This is real evidence of gigantism, and the stories in the Scriptures of giants among humans may simply be reports of merely the human expression of the same phenomenon of gigantism. Huge human molar teeth have been found, and colossal human footprints.

7. There is only one place in the world in which the entire geologic column, that is the complete sequence of rock strata,

in their correct order, and with no strata missing has been found. Usually there are large gaps, and at least some of the strata are in the 'wrong' sequence! The only location in the world where it has been found in its entirety and in the correct sequence is not very far from you. Probably it is to be found in your local library as it only appears in the pages of a geological textbook; everywhere else, there are problems with the sequence! Does not this show that the text-books might be wrong?

There Is An Alternative

It is a fact that virtually no fossils are being formed today. When animals or plants die they quickly decompose, or are consumed by carrion. Even the largest trees ultimately rot away. Yet the earth's rocks are crammed with billions of fossils! Where did they come from, and why do they appear so suddenly in the strata? Seldom is it considered that most of the earth's surface is covered not by igneous, but by sedimentary rock formations, that is, rock strata laid down by *water*. These sedimentary strata are truly massive in extent, even the top of mount Everest was once under water. Here is a clue, because fossils do not mark the slow emergence of life; they mark its *sudden* extinction!

In order for a fossil to form, the dead animal or plant must be encapsulated suddenly before any natural decomposition occurs, or any hungry predator can arrive on the scene. The effect of billions upon billions of fossils found around the world, even in the peaks of the world's highest mountains requires a global cause, a cause that accounts for water-deposited rock formations covering the planet, and entombing billions of living creatures so suddenly there was no time for decomposition.

The universal deluge or Biblical Flood is the only mechanism that accounts for the sudden entombment on a global scale of every type of life known to man, and many others that since have died out. I believe that a close encounter with a large comet or similar object caused the abrupt collapse of a massively thick canopy of water vapour above the earth which brought down colossal amounts of water and ice suddenly onto the earth. At the same time the earth was moved off its axis, causing truly catastrophic destruction as huge tides swept all before them, killing all life outside the ark, and covering the earth with deposits of mud, slime, sand, gravel, organic debris and general detritus. The massive tidal surges laid down successive beds or strata of this debris and detritus which sometimes were interrupted by igneous material as volcanic activity was initiated by the trauma the earth was subject to. Billions of tons of vegetation and dead animals and fish buried under huge deposits of water laid debris that ultimately solidified into sedimentary rock, formed into coal and oil under immense pressure and the heat caused by tides in the lithosphere. This I believe is how the fossil beds were laid down, and it has enormous consequences.

When today's scientists measure water erosion or the deposition of sediment in rivers and lakes, they automatically assume the rates measured today are what they have always been. With a global flood however, and subsequent massive water drainage from the land into newly formed depressions which afterwards became the ocean reservoirs, deposition of sediment would have been phenomenally rapid. Not only this, but stalactites and stalagmites would have formed equally quickly, with very pronounced rock erosion, when the sedimentary beds were still relatively soft, like partially set concrete. All these would have occurred with prodigious speed, at rates hundreds, and possibly thousands of times faster than we see today. Within a few decades these rates would have normalised more or less to what we know today. Of course, were today's rates extrapolated back in time, as routinely they are, they would indicate an extremely great age for the earth's surface features, but the existence of a global flood and its attendant and enormously powerful mechanisms could scoop out a grand canyon or some such in only a few decades.

The four seasons we know so well probably did not exist before the Flood as the earth's axis was then vertical I believe. This would mean that annual growing cycles date only from the Flood; before then, there might have been several cycles in a year, leading to dendochronology records being misinterpreted for the years prior to the deluge. I believe that ice was also precipitated at the time of the Flood, which in turn has skewed the data extracted from ice-core samples in the Arctic and Antarctic, which, on the assumption of today's activities, again indicate a great age for the earth. Thus none of these dating methods is faulty when used of the age in which we live now; the problem lies in the assumption that today's activities are constant, when they are not, making the results derived from these techniques wildly inaccurate for the pre-Flood age. All around the world we find deep valleys with relatively small rivers flowing through them. Calculations are made in order to show how long it would take for the existing rivers to gouge out these valleys. It is seldom realised that these valleys were first cut when the rocks were soft, and that even the biggest rivers we see today are mere dribbles compared with the torrents which flowed when the earth drained off the flood waters as mountain-chains reared up, and ocean basins formed quickly after the deluge. This is what first carved out the valleys that today's rivers trickle their way through. The profoundly different qualities of the pre-Flood earth would also account for the far greater life-spans of the antediluvians, and the gigantism mentioned above, even carbon 14 dating is likely to be enormously inaccurate for the pre-Flood years.

The Ark

Those who have difficulty believing the ark could have been large enough to accommodate the load the Scriptures describe have never calculated its size, and are referred to *The Genesis Flood*,[468] where such calculations may be found. I would add though that the authors of *The Genesis Flood* under-estimated the size of the ark, as they base the cubit on relatively recent equivalents, but, given it is the length of the forearm, the pre-Flood gigantism referred to above, would have meant the cubit could easily have been twice as long as Whitcomb and Morris allow, resulting in a vessel whose size might not yet have been exceeded by even the largest ships afloat today.

Carbon 14 Dating

Carbon 14 dating is the most widely known of an entire range of dating methods which are all based on assumptions that exclude the disturbance to the earth's activities caused by the Flood, and the

---

[468] Whitcomb, John. C. Jr., and Morris, Henry M., *The Genesis Flood*, Grand Rapids, Michigan, U.S.A., Baker Book House, 1966, pp. 10–110.

enormously different regime that existed before it. I now quote from a short paper written by a friend of mine, Doctor Derek Watson, who has personally investigated the matter.

"Elements in igneous (volcanic) rocks gradually lose their radio-activity and change to non-radio elements (e.g. uranium to lead; potassium to argon). Highly complex techniques are used to measure these changes. All the methods used make a series of unprovable assumptions e.g. that decay rates have always been the same; that no losses have occurred by leakage or weathering; that none of the non-radioactive element was already present when the rock was formed. Published results show incredibly large inconsistencies. For example, volcanic laves from off Hawaii known to have been formed in 1800 gave dates ranging from 160 to nearly 3,000 million years! The rate of build-up of radio active carbon (C14) in our air has recently been measured. The results indicate that the C14 created by cosmic radiation in the upper atmosphere and permeating our earth, has not yet come into equilibrium with the C14 in living cells here. This suggests the start of life on earth must be less than 30,000 years, the calculated time required for equilibrium to be approached. Further measurements show the rate of generation of C14 to be 38% more than its rate of decay, a figure which allows our earth to be 'dated' at roughly 10,000 years. This fits remarkably well with the Biblical time-scale for history."[469]

There is fascinating chemical evidence that the earth's atmosphere at one time contained an enormously higher level of water vapour than now it does, confirming the belief that the waters of the Flood were provided by the precipitation of a vapour canopy. One effect of the existence of this vapour canopy, and its sudden loss would be the 'skewing' of data relating to C14 dating by a very large extent. See the

---

[469] Watson, Derek, D.Sc., Ph.D., F.R.C. Path., F.R.S.C., *Attempts To Answer Unsolicited Questions*, Cheltenham, published privately by the author, 1995, p. 2.

substantial section on dating methods in *The Genesis Flood* for details.[470]

The Life-Spans Of The Antediluvians

Many Flood geologists make the point that the bombardment of the earth by cosmic radiation would have been very considerably reduced by the existence of a vapour canopy, thus enhancing the quality of life on earth to such an extent that gigantism, referred to earlier would have been the norm, and by our standards, extremely long life-spans would have been commonplace. I suggest there might be some biological evidence for this.

Every female that has ever lived has an in-built calendar, inasmuch as ovulation occurs roughly every 28 days between the onset of puberty, and the menopause. When a girl reaches puberty, she possess approximately 10,000 eggs, but, on average, only a maximum of 450 would be released during her fertile life. If we take the total number of eggs as being 10,000,[471] and multiply this total by the number of days between ovulations as being the average of 28, we have of course 280,000 days. Dividing this by the number of days in the year, 365·25, gives a result of just over 766 years. If we add to this total a proportional allowance for the pre-pubescent, and post-menopausal years, we find that the age of the antediluvians seems highly compatible with the result. This, I propose, is genuine evidence that man originally lived for slightly less than a thousand years, as the Scriptures indicate. I would also point out that classic evolutionary theory states that nothing comes into existence unless it is forced to, in order for the species to survive. That being so, evolutionists have to explain why only a minority of eggs are released during a woman's fertile life, and why women's bodies waste their resources in producing thousands of eggs that can never be used?

---

[470] Op. cit., pp. 331– 453, especially pp. 374ff.

[471] *The Book Of Life*, Volume III, London, Marshall Cavendish, 1971, p. 1147.

The Dispersal Of The Nations From Babel

According to the Scriptures, after the Flood mankind kept closely together in the region of Babel, until after the judgement of the Division of Tongues, when they then dispersed across the world. Is there any evidence that this is so?

Besides the archaeological and literary evidence for the genuine existence of the Tower of Babel uncovered by the French researcher André Parrot,[472] the findings of Bill Cooper are well worth mentioning. In his most thoroughly researched work, *After The Flood*,[473] he presents reams of evidence gleaned from the most ancient records of European nations that independently trace their ancestry back to Babel, and frequently to common ancestors that are characters mentioned in the Scriptures. His book is the outcome of twenty-five years of research in this field, and shows how the Table of Nations in Genesis 10 is utterly reliable.

There are those who insist that the Scriptures present the earth as being a flat disc. I have shown elsewhere that this is completely erroneous. In fact, the Scriptures speak of the earth being the same shape as its atmosphere, and speak of the boundary between night-time and day-time as being *circular*, a phenomenon only encountered because the earth is round.[474]

Biblical History Generally

Since the 1930s enormous strides have been taken in showing how compatible with genuine historical facts, the Scriptural record is. Outstanding among the research work done is this field are the works of A. S. Yahuda, *The Accuracy Of The Bible*, London, Heinemann, 1934, Immanuel Velikovsky, *Worlds In Collision*, London, Victor Gollancz, 1950, and *Ages In Chaos*, London, Sidgwick & Jackson, 1953, Clifford Wilson, *That Incredible Book-The Bible*, Chicago, Illinois, Moody Press, 1975, Charles Taylor, *Rewriting Bible History*

---

[472] See Parrot, translated Hudson, *The Tower Of Babel*, London, SCM Press, 1955.

[473] Cooper, Bill, *After The Flood*, Chichester, New Wine Press, 1995.

[474] Phelan, M. W. J. *The Circle Of The Earth In Isaiah 40:22*, Brighton, Paradosis Publications, 1988.

(According To Scripture), Unley Park, South Australia, House Of Tabor, 1983, Emmet Sweeney, *The Pyramid Age*, Corby, Domra Publications, 1999, and especially, David Rohl in *A Test Of Time,* Volume I: *From Myth To History*, London, Century, 1995, and Volume II: *Legend*, London, Arrow, 1999. I honestly believe there is no reason at all to entertain any doubts about the veracity of the Scriptural record, and agree with Arthur Pierson's remark, "When an honest doubter comes to me, I feel perfectly safe in calmly saying, to his face, 'You have never studied the evidences, and it is likely never attentively examined the Bible.' And that arrow never misses its mark."[475]

For further reading on the subjects referred to above I recommend the following;

Balsiger, D., & Sellier, C.   *In Search Of Noah's Ark*, Los Angeles, Sun Classic, 1976.

Daly, Reginald.   *Earth's Most Challenging Mysteries,* Nutley, New Jersey, The Craig Press, 1972.

Dewar, Douglas.   *Man: A Special Creation*, Hayling Island, Evolution Protest Movement, 1975.

Dewar, Douglas.   *The Transformist Illusion*, Tennessee, Dehoff Publications, 1957.

Macbeth, Norman.   *Darwin Retried*, New York, Dell Publishing, 1971.

Meldau, F. J.   *Why We Believe In Creation Not In Evolution*, Denver, Christian Victory, 1974.

---

[475] Pierson, Arthur, *Many Infallible Proofs*, London, Morgan & Scott, undated, p. 13.

Morris, Henry M. *The Remarkable Birth Of Planet Earth*, Minneapolis, Dimension Books, 1972.

Patten, Donald W. *The Biblical Flood And Ice Epoch*, Seattle, Pacific Meridian, 1966.

Pimenta Leander. *Fountains Of The Great Deep*, Chichester, New Wine Press, 1984.

Shute, Evan. *Flaws In The Theory Of Evolution*, Nutley New Jersey, The Craig Press, 1971.

Thompson, W. R. *New Challenging Introduction To The Origin Of Species*, Hayling Island, Evolution Protest Movement, 1967.

Velikovsky, Immanuel. *Earth In Upheaval*, London, Abacus, 1973.

Velikovsky, Immanuel. *Mankind In Amnesia*, London, Sidgwick & Jackson, 1982.

Walworth, Ralph Franklin, & Walworth Sjostrom. *Subdue The Earth*, St. Albans, Granada, 1977.

Whitcomb, John C. Jr. *The Early Earth*, London, Evangelical Press, 1972.

Whitcomb, John C. Jr. *The World That Perished*, Grand Rapids, Michigan, Baker Book House, 1988.

Whitcomb, John C. Jr., & Morris, Henry M. *The Genesis Flood*, Grand Rapids, Michigan, Baker Book House, 1966.

Part Seven

Appendices, Glossary, And Bibliography

Appendix I

The Order And Divisions Of The Books Of The Hebrew Canon

The Order And Divisions Of The Books Of The Hebrew Canon

I give below the order of the books that is most commonly encountered in Hebrew Bibles. Occasionally the order of the *Writings* will change. Each other division is constant.

ENGLISH	HEBREW
The Law	תורה
Genesis	בראשית
Exodus	ואלת שמו
Leviticus	ויקרא
Numbers	במדבר
Deuteronomy	אלה הדברים

ENGLISH	HEBREW
The Prophets	נביאים
A. The Former Prophets	נביאים ראשונים
Joshua	יהושע
Judges	שופטים
Samuel (I & II)	שמואל
Kings (I & II)	מלכים

B. The Latter Prophets	נביאים אחרונים
Isaiah	ישעיה
Jeremiah	ירמיה
Ezekiel	יחזקאל
The Twelve (Hosea, Joel, Amos, Obadiah, Jonah, Micah, Nahum, Habakkuk, Zephaniah, Haggai, Zechariah, Malachi).	הושע יואל עמוס עבדיה יונה מיכה נחום חבקוק צפניה חני זכריה מלאכי

The Writings	כתובים
Psalms	תהלים
Proverbs	משלי
Job	איוב

The Five Scrolls	
The Song Of Songs	שיר השירים
Ruth	רות
Lamentations	איכה
Ecclesiastes	קהלת
Esther	אסתר

Daniel	דניאל
Ezra-Nehemiah (one book)	עזרא נחמיה
Chronicles (I & II)	דברי הימים

Appendix II

The Ugaritic Alphabet

I give below the letters of the Ugaritic alphabet discovered at Ras Shamra, and have made approximate comparisons with square-charactered Hebrew letters.[476]

Hebrew	Ugaritic	Hebrew	Ugaritic	Hebrew	Ugaritic
א		י		פ	
ב		כ		שׁ	
ג		ס		ק	
ה		ל		ר	
ד		ם		ת	
ה		ד		ג	
ו		נ		ת	
ז		ז			
ח		שׂ			
ט				שׂ	

---

[476] This table is based on the details to be found in Hooker, J. T., *Reading The Past*, London, British Museum Publications, 1990, p. 55.

Appendix III

Table Of Hebrew Alphabets

I give below the different forms of the Hebrew letters referred to in the discussion concerning the errors in the Samaritan, and Masoretic Texts, which suggest an Angular Original.[477]

Angular Script		Later Scripts	
Moabite Stone	Siloam Inscription	Samaritan Script	Square Character
			א
			ב
			ג
			ד
			ה
			ו
			ז
			ח
			ט
			י
			ך כ

---

[477] Based on tables found in Gesenius' *Hebrew Grammar*, op. cit., p. xvii, and in J. E. H. Thomson's article in *The International Standard Bible Encyclopædia*, Volume IV, op. cit., p. 2314.

Appendix III—Table Of Hebrew Alphabets

Angular Script		Later Scripts	
Moabite Stone	Siloam Inscription	Samaritan Script	Square Character
ل	ل	∠	ל
५	५	५	ם מ
५	५	५	ן נ
╪	–	ॐ	ס
○	○	▽	ע
⊃	⊃	⊃	ף פ
⊢	⅍	⅏	ץ צ
ዋ	ዋ	⊗	ק
٩	٩	৯	ר
W	w w	Ш	שׁ שׂ
×	×	∧	ת

380

Appendix IV

IV Ezra 14:1–50

I give below, in full, the account in IV Ezra (or II Esdras),[478] as translated by G. H. Box, of the alleged miraculous production of the Hebrew Canon by Ezra and five associates. I believe the unbiased reader will agree that the story bears the Hall Marks of fable.

> "And it came to pass after the third day, while I sat under the oak, lo! there came a voice out of a bush over against me; and it said, Ezra, Ezra! And I said: Here am I Lord. And I rose upon my feet. Then said he unto me: I did manifestly reveal myself in the bush, and talked with Moses when my people were in bondage in Egypt: and I sent him, and led my people out of Egypt, and brought them to Mount Sinai; and I held him by me for many days.
>
> I told him many wondrous things, showed him the secrets of the times, declared to him the end of the seasons: Then I commanded him saying: These words shalt thou publish openly, but these keep secret. And now I do say to thee: The signs which I have shewed thee, The dreams which thou hast seen, and the interpretations which thou hast heard—lay them up in thy heart! For thou shalt be taken up from among men, and henceforth thou shalt remain with my Son, and with such as are like thee, until the times be ended. For the world has lost its youth. The times begin to wax old. For the world-age is divided into twelve parts; nine parts of it are passed already, and the half of the tenth part; and there remain of it two parts,

---

[478] For an explanation of the different nomenclature used in designating this apocryphal work, and its relationship to *The Apocalypse Of Baruch*, see *The Apocrypha And Pseudepigrapha Of The Old Testament In English,* Volume II, *Pseudepigrapha*, edited Charles, Oxford, published in two volumes by Oxford University Press, 1973, in. loc.

besides the half of the tenth part. Now, therefore, set in order thy house, and reprove thy people; Comfort the lowly among them, and instruct those that are wise. Now do thou renounce the life that is corruptible, let go from thee the cares of mortality; cast from thee the burdens of man, put off now the weak nature; lay aside thy burdensome cares, and hasten to remove from these times! For still worse evils than those which thou hast seen happen shall yet take place. For the weaker the world grows through age, so much the more shall evils increase upon the dwellers on earth. Truth shall withdraw further off, and falsehood be nigh at hand: for already the Eagle is hastening to come whom thou sawest in vision.

And I answered and said: Let me speak before thee O Lord! Lo, I will depart, as thou commanded me, and will warn the people who now exist: but they that shall be born later, who shall admonish them? For the world lies in darkness, and the dwellers therein are without light. *For thy Law if burnt*; and so no man knows the things which have been done by thee, or the works that shall be done. If, then, I have found favour before thee, send unto me the Holy Spirit, that I may write all that has happened in the world since the beginning, even the things which were written in thy Law, in order that men may be able to find the path, and that they who would live at the last, may live.

And he answered me and said: Go thy way, assemble the people and tell them not to seek thee for forty days. But do thou prepare for thyself many writing tablets; and take with thee Saraia, Dabria, Selemia, Elkanah and Osiel, these five, because they are equipped for writing swiftly; and then come hither, and I will light the lamp of understanding in thy heart, which shall not be extinguished until what thou art about to write shall be completed. And when thou shalt have finished, some things thou shalt publish, and some thou shalt deliver in secret to the wise. To-morrow, at this hour, thou shalt begin to write.

Then I went forth as he commanded me, and assembled all the people and said: Hear, O Israel, these words! Our fathers were at the beginning strangers in Egypt, and they were delivered from thence. And then they received the Law of life, which they kept not, even as you also after them have transgressed it. Then was a land given you for an inheritance in the land of Sion, but ye and your fathers have done unrighteousness, and have not kept the ways which the Most High commanded you. And forasmuch as he is a righteous judge he took from you in due time that which he had bestowed. And now ye are here. If ye, then, will rule over your own understanding and will discipline your heart, ye shall be preserved alive and after death obtain mercy. For after death shall the Judgement come, when we shall once more live again: and then shall the names of the righteous be made manifest, and the works of the godless declared. Let no man, then, come unto me now, nor seek me for forty days.

So I took the five men as he had commanded me, and we went forth into the field and remained there. *And it came to pass on the morrow that, lo! a voice called me, saying: Ezra, open thy mouth and drink what I give thee to drink! Then I opened my mouth, and lo! there was reached unto me a full cup, which was full as it were with water, but the colour of it was like fire. And I took it and drank; and when I had drunk my heart poured forth understanding, wisdom grew in my breast, and my spirit retained its memory: and my mouth opened, and was no more shut. And the Most High gave understanding unto the five men, and they wrote what was dictated in order, in characters which they knew not. And so they sat forty days: They wrote in the day-time and at night did eat bread; but as for me, I spake in the day, and at night was not silent.*

So in forty days were written ninety-four books. And it came to pass when the forty days were fulfilled, that the Most High spake unto me saying: The twenty-four books that thou hast written publish, that the worthy and unworthy may read therein: but the seventy last thou shalt keep, to deliver them to the wise among thy people. For in them is the spring of understanding, the fountain of wisdom, and the stream of knowledge. And I did so, in the seventh year, of the sixth week, after five thousand years of the creation and three months and twelve days.

And then was Ezra caught up away, and taken up into the place of such as were like him, after having written all these things. And he is called the Scribe of the knowledge of the Most High for ever and ever."[479]

[479] By permission of Oxford University Press, pp. 620–624, 4 Ezra 14, (*c.* 1110 words) from *The Apocrypha and Pseudepigrapha of the Old Testament, Volume II* edited by Charles, R. H. (translated Box) (1913).

Appendix V

The Covenant Book

The parallels between the so-called *Covenant Book* of Exodus 20–23 and Deuteronomy are illustrated in the table below, based on J. A. Thompson's commentary on Deuteronomy.[480]

Exodus	Deuteronomy
21:1–11	15:12–18
21:12–14	19:1–13
21:16	24:7
22:16f.	22:28, 29
22:21–24	24:17–22
22:25	23:19–20
22:26f.	24:10–13
22:29f.	15:19–23
22:31	15:19–23
22:31	14:3–21
23:1	19:16–21
23:2f., 6–8	16:18–20
23:4f.	22:1–4
23:9	24:17f.
23:10f.	15:1–11
23:12	5:13–15
23:13	6:13
23:14–17	16:1–17
23:19a	26:2–10
23:19b	14:21b

---

[480] Op. cit., p. 27.

Appendix VI

The Usage Of חֹק And חֻקָּה

Part A

I list below every occurrence of חֹק and חֻקָּה to be found in Exodus, Leviticus and Numbers.

Reference	Remarks
Exodus 5:14	Not relevant as used prior to Sinai.
Exodus 12:14	Instruction for regulating Israel's worship.
Exodus 12:17	Instruction for regulating Israel's worship.
Exodus 12:24	Instruction for regulating Israel's worship.
Exodus 12:43	Instruction for regulating Israel's worship.
Exodus 13:10	Instruction for regulating Israel's worship.
Exodus 15:25	Statute and Ordinance.
Exodus 15:26	Instruction for regulating Israel's worship, and contrasted with Commandments.
Exodus 18:16	Instruction for regulating Israel's worship, and contrasted with Laws.
Exodus 18:20	Instruction for regulating Israel's worship, and contrasted with Laws.
Exodus 27:21	Instruction for regulating Israel's worship.
Exodus 28:43	Instruction for regulating Israel's worship.
Exodus 29:9	Instruction for regulating Israel's worship.
Exodus 29:28	Instruction for regulating Israel's worship.
Exodus 30:21	Instruction for regulating Israel's worship.
Leviticus 3:17	Instruction for regulating Israel's worship.
Leviticus 6:18	Instruction for regulating Israel's worship.

Reference	Remarks
Leviticus 6:22	Instruction for regulating Israel's worship.
Leviticus 7:34	Instruction for regulating Israel's worship.
Leviticus 7:36	Instruction for regulating Israel's worship.
Leviticus 10:9	Instruction for regulating Israel's worship.
Leviticus 10:11	Instruction for regulating Israel's worship.
Leviticus 10:13	Instruction for regulating Israel's worship.
Leviticus 10:14	Instruction for regulating Israel's worship.
Leviticus 10:15	Instruction for regulating Israel's worship.
Leviticus 16:29	Instruction for regulating Israel's worship.
Leviticus 16:31	Instruction for regulating Israel's worship.
Leviticus 16:34	Instruction for regulating Israel's worship.
Leviticus 17:7	Instruction for regulating Israel's worship.
Leviticus 18:3	Instruction for regulating Israel's worship.
Leviticus 18:4	Instruction for regulating Israel's worship, contrasted with Judgments.
Leviticus 18:5	Instruction for regulating Israel's worship, contrasted with Judgments.
Leviticus 18:26	Instruction for regulating Israel's worship, contrasted with Judgments.
Leviticus 18:30	Instruction for regulating Israel's worship.
Leviticus 19:19	Regulations for the 'walk' of Israel.
Leviticus 19:37	Regulations for the 'walk' of Israel, contrasted with Judgments.
Leviticus 20:8	Instruction for regulating Israel's worship.
Leviticus 20:22	Regulations for the 'walk' of Israel, contrasted with Judgments.
Leviticus 20:23	Instruction for regulating Israel's worship.
Leviticus 23:14	Instruction for regulating Israel's worship.
Leviticus 23:21	Instruction for regulating Israel's worship.
Leviticus 23:31	Instruction for regulating Israel's worship.
Leviticus 23:41	Instruction for regulating Israel's worship.
Leviticus 24:3	Instruction for regulating Israel's worship.
Leviticus 24:9	Instruction for regulating Israel's worship.

Reference	Remarks
Leviticus 25:18	Instruction for regulating Israel's worship, & contrasted with Judgments.
Leviticus 26:3	Instruction for regulating Israel's worship, & contrasted with Commandments.
Leviticus 26:15	Instruction for regulating Israel's worship, & contrasted with Judgments and Commandments.
Leviticus 26:43	Instruction for regulating Israel's worship, & contrasted with Judgments.
Leviticus 26:46	Instruction for regulating Israel's worship, & contrasted with Judgments and Laws.
Numbers 9:3	Instruction for regulating Israel's worship.
Numbers 9:12	Instruction for regulating Israel's worship.
Numbers 9:14a	Instruction for regulating Israel's worship, & contrasted with Judgments.
Numbers 9:14b	Instruction for regulating Israel's worship, & contrasted with Judgments.
Numbers 10:8	Instruction for regulating Israel's worship.
Numbers 15:15a	Instruction for regulating Israel's worship.
Numbers 15:15b	Instruction for regulating Israel's worship.
Numbers 18:8	Instruction for regulating Israel's worship.
Numbers 18:11	Instruction for regulating Israel's worship.
Numbers 18:19	Instruction for regulating Israel's worship.
Numbers 18:23	Instruction for regulating Israel's worship.
Numbers 19:2	Instruction for regulating Israel's worship.
Numbers 19:10	Regulations for the 'walk' of Israel.
Numbers 19:21	Instruction for regulating Israel's worship.
Numbers 27:11	Statute of Judgment.
Numbers 30:16	Regulations for the 'walk' of Israel.
Numbers 31:21	Regulations for the 'walk' of Israel.
Numbers 35:29	Statute of Judgment.

Part B

I list below every occurrence of חק and חקה to be found in the book of Deuteronomy.

Reference	Remarks
4:1	Instruction for regulating Israel's worship, contrasted with Judgments.
4:5	Instruction for regulating Israel's worship, contrasted with Judgments.
4:6	Instruction for regulating Israel's worship.
4:8	Instruction for regulating Israel's worship, contrasted with Judgments.
4:14	Instruction for regulating Israel's worship, contrasted with Judgments.
4:40	Instruction for regulating Israel's worship, contrasted with Commandments.
4:45	Instruction for regulating Israel's worship, contrasted with Judgments.
5:1	Instruction for regulating Israel's worship, contrasted with Judgments.
5:31	Instruction for regulating Israel's worship, contrasted with Judgments and Commandments.
6:1	Instruction for regulating Israel's worship, contrasted with Judgments and Commandments.
6:2	Instruction for regulating Israel's worship, contrasted with Commandments.
6:17	Instruction for regulating Israel's worship, contrasted with Commandments.
6:20	Instruction for regulating Israel's worship, contrasted with Judgments.
6:24	Instruction for regulating Israel's worship.
7:11	Instruction for regulating Israel's worship, contrasted with Commandments and Judgments.
8:11	Instruction for regulating Israel's worship, contrasted with Commandments and Judgments.

Reference	Remarks
10:13	Instruction for regulating Israel's worship, contrasted with Commandments.
11:1	Instruction for regulating Israel's worship, connected with Judgments and Commandments.
11:22	Instruction for regulating Israel's worship.
12:1	Instruction for regulating Israel's worship, contrasted with Judgments.
16:12	Instruction for regulating Israel's worship.
17:19	Instruction for regulating Israel's worship.
26:16	Instruction for regulating Israel's worship, contrasted with Judgments.
26:17	Instruction for regulating Israel's worship, contrasted with Commandments and Judgments.
27:10	Instruction for regulating Israel's worship, contrasted with Commandments.
28:15	Instruction for regulating Israel's worship, contrasted with Commandments.
28:45	Instruction for regulating Israel's worship, contrasted with Commandments.
30:10	Instruction for regulating Israel's worship, contrasted with Commandments.
30:16	Instruction for regulating Israel's worship, contrasted with Commandments and Judgments.

The Hebrew words חק and חקה are used always within the context of the Sinaitic Covenant, of Spiritual directions, and are administered by Priests rather than Magistrates.

Appendix VII

The Usage Of מִשְׁפָּט, שְׁפָטִים, And שָׁפַט

Part A

I list below every occurrence of מִשְׁפָּט, שְׁפָטִים, and שָׁפַט to be found in the books of Exodus, Leviticus and Numbers.

Reference	Remarks
Exodus 5:21	Not relevant as used prior to Sinai.
Exodus 6:6	Not relevant as used prior to Sinai.
Exodus 7:4	Not relevant as used prior to Sinai.
Exodus 12:12	Not relevant as used prior to Sinai.
Exodus 15:25	Not relevant as used prior to Sinai.
Exodus 18:13	Used of Judgment undertaken by humans.
Exodus 18:16	Used of Judgment undertaken by humans.
Exodus 18:22	Used of Judgment undertaken by humans.
Exodus 18:23	Used of Judgment undertaken by humans.
Exodus 18:26a	Used of Judgment undertaken by humans.
Exodus 18:26b	Used of Judgment undertaken by humans.
Exodus 21:1	Used of Civil Law.
Exodus 21:9	Used of Civil Law.
Exodus 21:31	Used of Civil Law.
Exodus 23:6	Used of Civil Law.
Exodus 24:3	Used of Civil Law.
Exodus 26:30	Used as instruction to follow a precedent, the precedent here being the pattern revealed on the mount.

Reference	Remarks
Exodus 28:15	Used of Judgment undertaken by humans.
Exodus 28:29	Used of Judgment undertaken by humans.
Exodus 28:30a	Used of Judgment undertaken by humans.
Exodus 28:30b	Used of Judgment undertaken by humans.
Leviticus 5:10	Used as instruction to follow a precedent (manner).
Leviticus 9:16	Used as instruction to follow a precedent (manner).
Leviticus 18:4	Used of Civil Law, contrasted with Statutes.
Leviticus 18:5	Used of Civil Law, contrasted with Statutes.
Leviticus 18:26	Used of Civil Law, contrasted with Statutes.
Leviticus 19:15a	Used of Judgment undertaken by humans.
Leviticus 19:15b	Used of Judgment undertaken by humans.
Leviticus 19:35	Used of Judgment undertaken by humans.
Leviticus 19:37	Used of Civil Law, contrasted with Statutes.
Leviticus 20:22	Used of Civil Law, contrasted with Statutes.
Leviticus 24:22	Used of Civil Law.
Leviticus 25:18	Used of Civil Law, contrasted with Statutes.
Leviticus 26:15	Used of Civil Law, contrasted with Statutes and Commandments.
Leviticus 26:43	Used of Civil Law, contrasted with Statutes.
Leviticus 26:46	Used of Civil Law, contrasted with Statutes.
Numbers 9:3	Used as instruction to follow a precedent (ceremonies).
Numbers 9:14	Used as instruction to follow a precedent (manner).
Numbers 15:16	Used as instruction to follow a precedent (manner).
Numbers 15:24	Used as instruction to follow a precedent (manner).
Numbers 27:5	Used of Judgment undertaken by humans.
Numbers 27:11	Statute of Judgment.
Numbers 27:21	Used of Judgment undertaken by humans.
Numbers 29:6	Used as instruction to follow a precedent (manner).
Numbers 29:18	Used as instruction to follow a precedent (manner).
Numbers 29:21	Used as instruction to follow a precedent (manner).
Numbers 29:24	Used as instruction to follow a precedent (manner).

Reference	Remarks
Numbers 29:27	Used as instruction to follow a precedent (manner).
Numbers 29:30	Used as instruction to follow a precedent (manner).
Numbers 29:33	Used as instruction to follow a precedent (manner).
Numbers 29:37	Used as instruction to follow a precedent (manner).
Numbers 33:4	Reference to pre-Sinai history, therefore not relevant.
Numbers 35:12	Used of Judgment undertaken by humans.
Numbers 35:24a	Used of Judgment undertaken by humans.
Numbers 35:24b	Used of Judgment undertaken by humans.
Numbers 35:29	Statute of Judgment.
Numbers 36:13	Used of Civil Law, contrasted with Commandments.

Part B

I list below every occurrence of מִשְׁפָּט, שְׁפָטִים, and שָׁפַט to be found in the book of Deuteronomy.

Reference	Remarks
1:16a	Used of Judgment undertaken by humans.
1:16b	Used of Judgment undertaken by humans.
1:17a	Used of Judgment undertaken by humans.
1:17b	Used of Judgment undertaken by humans.
4:1	Used of Civil Law, contrasted with Statutes.
4;5	Used of Civil Law, contrasted with Statutes.
4:8	Used of Civil Law, contrasted with Statutes.
4:14	Used of Civil Law, contrasted with Statutes.
4:45	Used of Civil Law, contrasted with Statutes.
5:1	Used of Civil Law, contrasted with Statutes.
5:31	Used of Civil Law, contrasted with Statutes, and Commandments.
6:1	Used of Civil Law, contrasted with Statutes, and Commandments.
6:20	Used of Civil Law, contrasted with Statutes.
7:11	Used of Civil Law, contrasted with Statutes, and Commandments.
7:12	Used of Civil Law.
8:11	Used of Civil Law, contrasted with Statutes, and Commandments.
10:18	Used of Judgment undertaken by humans.
11:1	Used of Civil Law, contrasted with Statutes, and Commandments.
11:22	Used of Civil Law.
12:1	Used of Civil Law, contrasted with Statutes.
16:18a	Used of Judgment undertaken by humans.

Reference	Remarks
16:18b	Used of Judgment undertaken by humans.
16:18c	Used of Judgment undertaken by humans.
16:19	Used of Judgment undertaken by humans.
17:8	Used of Judgment undertaken by humans.
17:9a	Used of Judgment undertaken by humans.
17:9b	Used of Judgment undertaken by humans.
17:11	Used of Judgment undertaken by humans.
17:12	Used of Judgment undertaken by humans.
18:3	Used of Judgment undertaken by humans.
19:6	Used of Civil Law.
19:17	Used of Judgment undertaken by humans.
19:18	Used of Judgment undertaken by humans.
21:2	Used of Judgment undertaken by humans.
21:17	Used of Civil Law.
21:22	Used of Civil Law.
24:17	Used of Judgment undertaken by humans.
25:1a	Used of Judgment undertaken by humans.
25:1b	Used of Judgment undertaken by humans.
25:2	Used of Judgment undertaken by humans.
26:16	Used of Civil Law, contrasted with Statutes.
26:17	Used of Civil Law, contrasted with Statutes.
27:19	Used of Judgment undertaken by humans.
30:16	Used of Civil Law, contrasted with Statutes.
32:4	Used of the Lord as the Ultimate Judge of human affairs.
32:41	Used of the Lord as the Ultimate Judge of human affairs.
33:10	Used of Civil Law.
33:21	Used of Civil Law.

The Hebrew words מִשְׁפָּט, שְׁפָטִים, and שָׁפַט are used always within the context of the Sinaitic Covenant, of the Civil Law, as opposed to directions for the Worship of Israel, and are administered by

Magistrates rather than Priests, and are often based upon precedent. They are distinguishable from laws designated as Commandments where that word is used in its special or restricted sense, as it then applies only to the Decalogue.

Appendix VIII

The Usage Of מצות

Part A

I list below every occurrence of מצות to be found in the books of Exodus, Leviticus and Numbers.

Reference	Remarks
Exodus 15:26	Used of commandments generally.
Exodus 16:28	Used of commandments generally.
Exodus 20:6	Used of the Decalogue.
Exodus 24:12	Used of the Decalogue.
Leviticus 4;2	Used of commandments generally.
Leviticus 4:13	Used of commandments generally.
Leviticus 4:22	Used of commandments generally.
Leviticus 4:27	Used of commandments generally.
Leviticus 5:17	Used of commandments generally.
Leviticus 22:31	Used of commandments generally.
Leviticus 26:3	Used of certain of the Decalogue.
Leviticus 26:14	Used in an allusion to the Decalogue.
Leviticus 26:15	Used of commandments generally.
Leviticus 27:34	Used of commandments generally.
Numbers 15:22	Used of commandments generally.
Numbers 15:31	Used of commandments generally.
Numbers 15:39	Used of commandments generally.
Numbers 15:40	Used of commandments generally.
Numbers 36:13	Used of commandments generally.

Part B

I list below every occurrence of מצות to be found in the book of Deuteronomy.

Reference	Remarks
4:2	Used of commandments generally.
4:40	Used of commandments generally.
5:10	Used of the Decalogue.
5:29	Used of the Decalogue.
5:31	Used of commandments generally.
6:1	Used of commandments generally.
6:2	Used of commandments generally.
6:17	Used of commandments generally.
6:25	Used of commandments generally.
7:9	Possible allusion to the Decalogue, cf. 5:10.
7:11	Used of commandments generally.
8:1	Used of commandments generally.
8:2	Possible allusion to the Decalogue.
8:6	Possible allusion to the Decalogue.
8:11	Used of commandments generally.
10:13	Used of commandments generally.
11:1	Used of commandments generally.
11:8	Used of commandments generally.
11:13	Used of commandments generally.
11:22	Used of commandments generally.
11:27.	Used of commandments generally.

Reference	Remarks
11:28.	Used of commandments generally.
13:4.	Used of commandments generally.
13:18.	Used of commandments generally.
15:5.	Used of commandments generally.
17:20.	Used of commandments generally.
19:9.	Used of commandments generally.
26:13a.	Used of commandments generally.
26:13b.	Used of commandments generally.
26:17.	Used of commandments generally.
26:18.	Used of commandments generally.
27:1.	Used of commandments generally.
27:10.	Used of commandments generally.
28:1.	Used of commandments generally.
28:9.	Used of commandments generally.
28:13.	Used of commandments generally.
28:15.	Used of commandments generally.
28:45.	Used of commandments generally.
30:8.	Used of commandments generally.
30:10.	Used of commandments generally.
30:11.	Used of commandments generally.
30:16.	Used of commandments generally.
31:5.	Used of commandments generally.

Thus the Hebrew word מצות has both a general and a specific application in relation the Sinaitic Covenant. The latter is restricted to references to the Decalogue.

Appendix IX

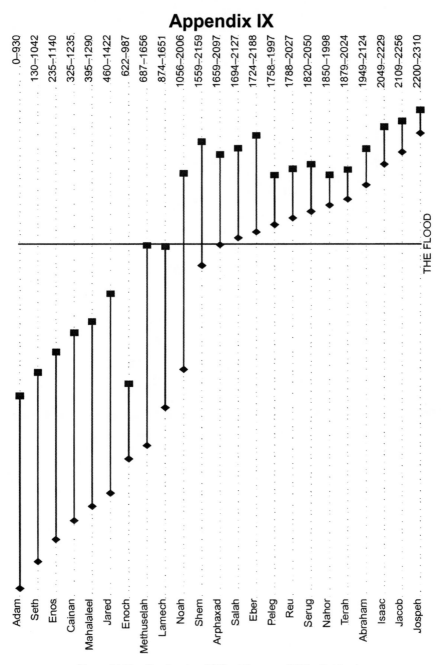

Figure 11 The Overlapping Of The Lifespans Of The Patriarchs

Appendix X

The Descent Of Samuel

The descent of Samuel from Levi via Korah is found in I Chronicles 6:33–38. In some versions Samuel is named Shemuel in verse 33, but a comparison of that verse with I Samuel 8:1–2, both of which name Samuel's eldest son as being Joel, shows that we are dealing with the same person. The line of descent of Samuel is given below, and is compared with that of the High Priests. The broken lines indicate an incomplete account of a direct line of descent.

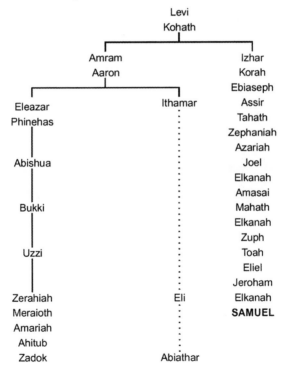

Appendix XI

The Age Of Terah At The Birth Of Abraham

A straightforward reading of Genesis 11:26 indicates that Abraham was born when Terah was 70. This is the view of Jewish chronologists. Christian chronologists, however, have to reconcile this verse with a statement found in Acts 7:4. Here, Stephen says that Abraham only set out for Canaan when his father Terah was dead. Now according to Genesis 11:32 Terah lived to be 205, and Genesis 12:4 shows that Abraham was 75 when he left Haran for Canaan.

Thus there is a seeming conflict in the data here. If Abraham was 75 when Terah was 205, then obviously Abraham was born 75 years earlier when Terah was 130, and not when he was 70, as indicated in Genesis 11:26. However, clearly something did happen when Terah was 70, and if it was not the birth of Abraham, what was it? According to most Christian chronologists this other event was the birth of an older brother of Abraham, who would have been the first-born son of Terah, even though Abraham is named *first* in the list of Terah's sons. Abraham, they say, is named first, not because he was Terah's first-born, but because he was the one through whom the Promised Seed was to come.

Christian chronologists point to the birth of Shem as a precedent for this situation. In Genesis 5:32 we read, "And Noah was five hundred years old: and Noah begat Shem, Ham, and Japheth." However, in Genesis 11:10 we find that two years after the flood, which started when Noah was 600 (Genesis 7:6), Shem was 100 years old. This means that Shem was born when Noah was 503, Ham, and Japheth being born when Noah was 500, and 501, or 502 presumably.

This seems reasonable enough, Shem it appears is indeed named first because he is in the line of the Promised Seed, not because he is the first-born. The births of the three sons of Noah are spread over a period of only four years, *and the context supplies the evidence.* But in the case of Terah, we are asked to spread the births of his three sons over a period of *sixty years*, *without there being any evidence at*

407

all from the context, or even a mere hint. Perhaps this is not such a reasonable proposition. It seems to be offered to the student, only because of the perceived difficulty of Acts 7:4. Is there an alternative to this suggestion? The Samaritan Pentateuch might give a clue here. It agrees with the Masoretic Text, on the ages of the Patriarchs from Noah to Terah except in two cases, those of Eber and Terah. The Masoretic Text states that Eber and Terah lived to be 464, and 205 respectively. The Samaritan Pentateuch in both cases reduces these ages by 60 years. This result is most interesting. In the table below I give the names and ages of these Patriarchs, and it will be seen that the data given by the Samaritan Pentateuch is more consistent with the overall trend of decline in longevity from Noah to Terah.

Patriarch	Graph Ref'	Samaritan Pentateuch	Masoretic text
Noah	1	950	950
Shem	2	600	600
Arphaxad	3	438	438
Shelah	4	433	433
Eber	**5**	**404**	**464**
Peleg	6	239	239
Reu	7	239	239
Serug	8	230	230
Nahor	9	148	148
Terah	**10**	**145**	**205**

The Masoretic Text has two Patriarchs whose life-spans go against the general trend of decline, the details of these are given in bold type. These are the very points where it differs from the Samaritan text. This is shown more clearly in the graph below. The black line shows the ages given by the Masoretic Text; the grey one, those of the Samaritan Pentateuch.[481]

---

[481] See Patten, Donald W., *The Biblical Flood And The Ice Epoch*, Seattle, U.S.A., Pacific Meridian Publishing Co., pp. 214–220, for an analysis of the curve of declining longevity from Noah to David.

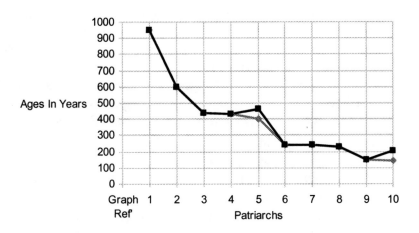

Figure 12 Decline In Longevity

I am aware that the charge of appealing to human wisdom might be levelled against me here, but, at the very least, the table and accompanying graph show that the ages given in the Samaritan Pentateuch for the Patriarchs named above, are not at all unreasonable. It must be admitted though that the ages for the births of the Patriarchs' first born sons as given by the Samaritan Pentateuch would extend the span of time between the Flood and Abraham in a way which would seem to be unacceptable.[482] What is particularly interesting about the Samaritan Pentateuch's age for Terah though, is that it reconciles *precisely* the notices in Genesis concerning the ages of Terah and Abraham with the statement of Stephen in Acts 7:4. Stephen says that Abraham only set out for Canaan when Terah had died, which

---

[482] For the data from the Samaritan Pentateuch, and a full analysis of how it compares with that from the Masoretic Text, see Owen Whitehouse, *Chronology And History Of The Bible*, being Part IV of *The Bible Readers' Manual*, or, *Aids To Biblical Study*, found in *The Teachers Edition* of *The Authorised King James Version*, London, Collins, undated, and Harrison, op. cit., p. 150.

according to the Samaritan text was when he was aged 145. According to Genesis 12:4 Abraham was 75 at this point, which means that when Abraham was born, Terah was 75 years younger than 145, or 70 years old, exactly as Genesis 11:26 appears to say. This solution does seem very appealing therefore as it almost seems to confirm Stephen's account, yet could not have been made with Stephen's statement in mind. It also invests Genesis 11:26 with far greater import and meaning, as it becomes what we have a right to expect to find, a statement concerning the birth of the greatest Patriarch of all, Abraham. It becomes a milestone in the history of Redemption.

While the normal solution to the problem that is offered by Christian chronologists, namely that Abraham is not the one referred to in Genesis 11:26 as being born when Terah was 70 is *possible*, we have to ask ourselves whether this solution is _probable_. Why would the Holy Spirit draw our attention to the birth of an individual who is of little or no consequence either to the history of Redemption, or to the Scriptural narrative as a whole, *and pass over the birth of Abraham who is unquestionably of vital importance to both?* We must conclude either that this is precisely what has occurred, or that the Samaritan Text is correct on this point, while the Masoretic text is in error.[483]

We must also consider how odd it would seem for Terah to have lived so much longer than his father, *and his son Abraham*, (who died aged 175), especially when we remember the *Abrahamic Blessing*. If we adopt the Samaritan Pentateuch's age for Terah at his death then his lifespan does fit into the general pattern of decline in longevity, but then Abraham goes against the trend, as he then lives thirty years longer than his father. In the case of Abraham however, we have a very positive and credible reason for his going against the trend, namely the *Abrahamic Blessing* just referred to. We have no such ready explanation for Terah going against the tend.[484] Abraham is

---

[483] Kenyon op. cit., pp. 46–47, is sympathetic to the view that the Samaritan dates, where they differ from the Masoretic Text, deserve serious consideration, and F. F. Bruce, op. cit., p. 121, actually refers to the case we are reviewing here, pointing out how well the Samaritan Pentateuch's data accords with the statement of Stephen.

[484] Amongst 'Flood geologists', it is usually believed that the steady decline in longevity is a consequence of the altered condition of the atmosphere after the Flood. It is proposed that the waters of the Flood were provided by the precipitation of a vapour

singled out by the Lord for particular blessing, and while we are not told that an increase in lifespan is a part of this blessing, it surely does not seem to be incongruous with it.

The difficulties associated with the Masoretic Text date in Genesis 11:32 are made all the more obvious by the extra-canonical works of the Jews. The Book of Jasher states that Terah died in the 35th year of Isaac.[485] Ginzberg's *Legends* confirms this,[486] but also records a technique of accommodating this statement with the belief, expressed by Stephen in Acts 7:4, that Terah was dead when Abraham left Haran. In order to escape the dilemma, the Jews point out that the unsaved are often spoken of as being 'dead', and that that is what is meant in this instance.[487] This ploy though, really only serves to show how desperate the situation is, for if Terah is referred to as being 'dead' after Abraham left Haran, simply because he was unsaved, *when would he have ever been referred to as anything else?* This is to confound an *event* with a *condition*! Further, why should one particular moment in his lifetime be singled out from all the others for special treatment? This explanation is conspicuously impossible, and is of interest only inasmuch as it shows us to what lengths some will go to, in order to defend the Masoretic Text, rather than abandon it in favour of that of the Samaritan Pentateuch. It also shows, of course, how absolutely *unshakeable* was the belief that Abraham was born when Terah was but 70 years old. The technique used by Christian chronologists of making Terah 130 years old when he fathered Abraham, was just as readily available for use by those Jews who felt they had to insist that the death of Terah referred to his spiritual condition, yet they would not avail themselves of it, even though it would avoid employing an explanation that must have been

---

canopy in the high atmosphere of the earth, and that after its collapse, there would be an increased bombardment of cosmic radiation striking the earth, which the vapour canopy had previously absorbed. This increased bombardment is thought to have resulted in the decline in longevity, which, it is said, follows a known 'declination curve'. For details see Pattern op. cit.

[485] *The Book Of Jasher*, translated Noah, M. M., Metairie, U.S.A., New Christian Crusade Church, 1839, Chapter 22, verse 33.

[486] Ginzberg op. cit., Volume I, p. 206.

[487] Ibid., Volume V, p. 219.

embarrassing in its simplicity. Thus for me, the 'explanations' offered in Ginzberg's *Legends*, demonstrate that the probability is that the Samaritan Pentateuch's date at Genesis 11:32 is reliable, and that Terah was only 70 years old at the birth of Abraham.

There is one further consideration. The genuineness of Stephen's statement in Acts 7:4, may be open to question. The Bezan Text[488] of the Acts of the Apostles, the foremost example of the *Western Text*, omits the reference to the death of Terah altogether, again, enabling Abraham to be born when Terah was 70, but removing the need to accept the Samaritan Pentateuch's reading at Genesis 11:32. The remarkable aspect of this variant is that, if anything, the Bezan Test is noted for the _additions_ it makes to the Book of Acts, rather than its omissions, and so, in a curious way, the fact that it should *omit* this notice to Terah, makes the omission appear more likely to be genuine.[489]

---

[488] Known as *Codex Bezæ*, or (D), which comprises two separate documents; *Codex Bezæ Cantabrigiensis*, or 'D^{ea}' (Wettstein), or '05' (Gregory) which includes the Gospels and Acts and a fragment of III John, and *Codex Claramontanus*, or 'D^p' (Wettstein) or '06' (Gregory) which contains the Pauline Corpus, see Kümmel, Werner, G., *Introduction To The New Testament*, translated, Mattill, A. J., Jr., from the 14th. edition of 1965, London, SCM Press, 1966, pp. 366–367.

[489] See Werner Kümmel's remarks, op. cit., p. 382, and those of R. B. Rackham in *The Acts Of The Apostles* London, Methuen, 1901, pp. xxi–xxvi, and those of F. G. Kenyon, op. cit. pp. 139–144.

Appendix XII

Further Evidence For The Views Of Kikawada and Quinn

T. Desmond Alexander

In a recently published challenge upon The New Document Hypothesis, the Biblical scholar, T. Desmond Alexander refers to the views of Garrett concerning the Ancient Epic literary form, and through him, to Kikawada and Quinn, and finds them wanting, saying, "To substantiate his theory Garrett must demonstrate from other extra-biblical literature that the 'ancestor epic' was indeed a widely used form in the ancient world."[490] Alexander says also, "Apart from the various examples which he isolates in the book of Genesis, he offers only one extra-biblical example, the Atrahasis Epic."[491]

These remarks ignore the fact that Kikawada and Quinn, who are the originators of the theory, refer in their book *Before Abraham Was*, to independent evidence derived from the Vendidad of the Iranian Avesta, and devote three pages to analysing its compliance with the literary form they find in Atrahasis, material concerning the Trojan war, the first eleven chapters of Genesis, Genesis as a whole and the Pentateuch.[492] Duane Garrett found several individual epics within Genesis, which, after examining personally, I found to coincide even more exactly with Kikawada's and Quinn's view than Garrett himself proposed. Further, others have also located literary forms in the Scriptures that they have classed as *epic, decades* before Kikawada and Quinn.[493] Steinmueller even refers to Homer's *Iliad* and *Odyssey*,

---

[490] Alexander, T. Desmond, *Abraham In The Negev. A Source-Critical investigation Of Genesis 20:1–22:19*, Carlisle, Paternoster Press, 1997, p. 28.

[491] Ibid.

[492] Op. cit., pp. 48ff.

[493] Steinmueller, John, E., *Some Problems Of The Old Testament*, New York, U.S.A., Bruce Publishing, 1936, p. 39.

and Virgil's *Aeneid* when he discusses Biblical epic literature,[494] a comparison Alexander castigates when writing of Garrett's referring to the *Aeneid* as "highly questionable."[495]

Thus, it seems to me that no further evidence is required, the phenomenon ought to be recognised as genuine simply on the evidence offered so far, *especially as the text falls naturally into the proposed literary form by the placement of the genealogies of Genesis*. One must wonder why they are located exactly as they are, if they were not intended to shape the text in such a manner. Yet, other evidence *is* available, and from a source that believers ought to acknowledge.

Additional Evidence

Were another book of Inspired Scripture to be identified that was laid out unequivocally in the same literary form of an *Opening Section*, a *Tripartite Centre*, and a *Conclusion*, then by itself it would constitute evidence for the views of Kikawada, Quinn, and Garrett. If such a book could also be dated credibly to the same time-frame as that accepted by believers for the composition of the Five Books Of Moses, the evidence would become extremely noteworthy. But, if in addition to this, such a book was related to a particular ancestral figure of renown amongst the peoples of the East, then the evidence would become exceptionally compelling, and would form a major support for the theories of Kikawada, Quinn, and Garrett.

Job As A Revered Ancestor

Such a book is the book of Job I propose. Job himself is described as "the greatest of all the men of the east (Job 1:3)." Centuries after the events we read of in his book, he was renowned for his righteousness (Ezekiel 14:14, 20), a reputation, that endured even until the time of Christ (James 5:11). Thus Job certainly conforms with the ancient ancestral status required by the literary form.

---

[494] Ibid.

[495] Op. cit., p. 28.

The Dating Of Job

The *precise* dating of Job is not easy, but I propose that an approximate dating is readily available. We know from Job 42:16 that he lived for 140 years after the central drama of the book had drawn to a close. From Job 1:2, we know that before the drama began, he had fathered ten children, and from verses 4–5 it would seem that each of his children had reached an age of sufficient maturity to gain independence from Job. We might allow 15 years between the births of the oldest and youngest of Job's children, and assume that Job was about 18 when the first of his children was born, and that the youngest child was also about this age when the history unfolded in the book begins.[496] This would mean that Job would have been approximately 191 when he died (18 + 15 + 18 + 140). This would be the lower limit for his lifespan. It has been suggested that as the Lord blessed Job after his ordeal with "twice as much as he had before (42:10, cf. 1:3 with 42:12)", the 140 years of 42:16, would be equal to exactly twice his age at the beginning of the book, meaning that he died aged 210. This must be the upper limit of Job's lifespan, meaning that he must be regarded as having lived somewhere between 191, and 210 years.

Now when it was the norm for people to live for approximately two hundred years or so, the average lifespans were reducing in length in accordance with a known mathematical decay curve, representing an equation used to measure decline in many areas. This seems to have been because of the enormous changes in the earth's atmosphere which were a consequence of the Flood, leading to an increased bombardment of the earth by harmful radiation from beyond our atmosphere (See Supplement Two).

This mathematical curve is discussed by Donald W. Patten in his book *The Biblical Flood And Ice Epoch*. He writes, "This curve required over 30 generations and more than 1500 years until the new norm [for the human lifespan] of 'three score and ten' years was reached by the descendants of Noah. This curve suggests that

---

[496] I have shown in my *The Dating Of The Exodus*, that this is the average generation length for the days of antiquity in the middle east. op. cit., pp. 15ff.

cumulative factors rather than single factors were involved in causing the change in the rate of ageing. This curve is a common type of decay curve, and can be duplicated in many other chemical or electrical experiments. It can be plotted when a capacitor is discharged and a new norm is ultimately reached. It can be plotted by subjecting bacteria to mild (and non-lethal) levels of germicidal ultra-violet radiation. It can be achieved by subjecting fish to ozonated water" [497] [the words in square brackets are my own]. It is remarkable that the reduction of lifespans traceable from the Scriptural data conforms to a particular decay curve known to mathematicians!

Because of this decay curve, a lifespan of 200 years or so would only represent the average for a very short space of time, and would be capable of being pinpointed by means of chronological and genealogical data from the Scriptures. From Patten's representation of the decay curve,[498] and the graph on page 409, we see that this average must be placed at around the time of Terah. We might suppose however, that because of the Lord's blessing on Job, his lifespan was longer than the average. This would mean that we might place him within the Abrahamic age. Confirmation of this is found in the fact that the Divine Name שׁדי is found frequently throughout the book.[499] This Name appears first in Genesis 17:1, when the Covenant of Circumcision is made with Abraham.

Some encouragement for this might be found in the remarks in Job 8:8–9, "For enquire, I pray thee, of the former age, and prepare thyself to the search of their fathers: (For we are but of yesterday, and know nothing, because our days upon earth are a shadow.)" Here the *former age*, might easily refer to the antediluvian world. We must remember that Shem (and probably Japheth and Ham) were still alive at this point, enabling such inquiries about this former age genuinely to be made.[500] Furthermore the words, "For we [Bildad and his contemporaries] are but of yesterday, and know nothing, because our

---

[497] Patten, D. W., *The Biblical Flood And Ice Epoch,* op. cit., p. 216.

[498] Ibid., p. 215.

[499] 5:17, 6:4, 14; 8:3, 5; 11:7, 13:3, 15:25, 21:15, 20; 22:3, 17, 23, 25, 26; 23:16, 24:1, 27:2, 10, 11, 13; 29:5, 31:2, 35; 32:8, 33:4, 34:10, 12; 35:13, 37:23, 40:2.

[500] See the graph in Appendix IX, page 409.

days upon earth [compared with the sons of Noah, and the first few generations after the flood] are a shadow" definitely seem to point in that direction. This is brought out particularly clearly in Ferrar Fenton's translation, which reads, "Ask of the primæval race, and their ancestral wisdom seek out (we are ignorant-born yesterday-our days are a shadow on earth)."[501]

During this time, people lived for enormously different lifespans, as Shem, and his immediate successors outlived many later generations. A trend is very clearly discernible however when lifespans are compared by the sequence of *birth* of the individuals concerned, however, at any given moment until the human lifespan normalised to around 70 years or so, earlier generations frequently would outlive later generations. A fact, no doubt, which led to ancestor worship, and the elevating of mortals to the status of immortals in the minds of later generations.

This dating of Job has also been confirmed using astronomical calculations, using the astronomical references in the book,[502] but I believe there may well have been disturbances to the earth's orbit during the events associated with the Exodus, the long-day of Joshua 10:12–14, and during the days of Hezekiah (II Kings 20:11) which could well modify these findings.

Nonetheless, I believe this placement to be reasonably secure, which means that the book of Job, is traceable to *the very same age* from which all the other Ancestor Epics that Kikawada, Quinn, and Garrett have identified sprung from. This is most encouraging, and means we may now turn to consider the structure of the book itself.[503]

---

[501] *The Holy Bible In Modern English*, translated Ferrar Fenton, London, A. & C. Black, 1936 edition, in. loc.

[502] Hartwell Horne, T., *An Introduction To The Critical Study And Knowledge Of The Holy Scriptures*, op. cit., Volume IV, pp. 73ff.

[503] By seeing that Job lived before Jacob, we see also how true sacrifices could be offered to the Lord by Job, even though he was a gentile. The Levitical priesthood was in his day, many years in the future.

The Literary Structure Of Job

Now, in order for our findings to be viable, any literary structure identified within the text, must be one that may not be described in any way as being artificial. The text must arrange itself naturally through its own unique features into a literary form, in order for that form to be genuine. Nothing other than this would be acceptable.

Fortunately, this is precisely the spectacle that awaits us. While the book of Job is largely poetical, distinct lines of prose are unmistakably present (39:1; 40:1; 40:3; 40:6; & 42:6), as are entire prose sections, and it is these last, with one exception, which provide the literary framework for Job. These prose sections are, the introduction of Elihu's discourses (32:1–6) which we will look at later, and the prologue (1:1–2:13), and epilogue (42:7–17). Furthermore, the connection between these last two sections is very obvious by the number of correspondences between them. Terrien writes, "The prologue (1:1–2:13) and epilogue (42:7–17) appear to form a literary piece of homogeneous character, for each needs the other."[504] The epilogue restores Job with exactly double all that he had lost in the prologue, and, this restoration also tells the reader that the accusations of Satan also found in the prologue were baseless.

The introduction or prologue then undoubtedly performs satisfactorily the rôle of what in an Ancestor Epic literary form would be the *Opening Section*, introducing us to the *dramatis-personæ* of the crisis, the interference in human affairs of Satan, strictly within what is permitted by God, and the character, position, and circumstances of the central character, Job.

Likewise, the epilogue, performs admirably as the *Conclusion* or *Settlement* of an Ancestor Epic, where there is a day of reckoning from the Lord for Job and his friends, vindicating the Lord, and refuting Satan's claims revealed in the *Opening Section,* and restoring Job's fortunes.

---

[504] Terrien, Samuel, *The Interpreter's Bible*, Volume III, op. cit., p. 884.

The Tripartite Centre

If Job is really an Ancestor Epic, then between these distinct but related prose Sections should be found the *Tripartite Centre*, and, indeed we do find between them, the main body of the work, not cast in prose, but in Hebrew poetic form; moreover, this poetic section is indeed tripartite! Mostly, in the central section we find the words of man, but from 38:1 on we encounter the words of the Lord, as He speaks directly to Job. Thus 38:1 marks a vital division within the central section. But this is not the only division in this section.

While in chapters 3–31 we have three cycles of discourses by Eliphaz, Bildad, and Zophar, and Job's replies, from 32–37 we have the discourses of Elihu, but no more speeches from Job. Significantly, Elihu's contributions are separated from chapters 3–31 by a division marked by the only other prose section of the entire book; 32:1–6, which therefore splits into two distinct parts, the section giving the wisdom of man. Thus the central section is truly tripartite.

This means the book of Job is indeed cast into the classic fivefold structure of the Ancestor Epic of Kikawada, Quinn, and Garrett. However, as the poetic form is exclusive to the three central portions, prose being found in only 11 verses of the total of 1,023 verses of all three sections combined, they do genuinely unite to form a Tripartite Centre.

It is of crucial importance of course, to note that this literary structure of Job *forms itself*, without any artificial interference whatsoever, simply by the alternation between prose and poetic forms, and the change from the words of man, to those of the Lord. The structure is given below;

The Opening Section.

Job 1:1–3:1. Introduction. *Prose.*

The Tripartite Centre.

1) The First Challenge: Job 3:2–31:37. Eliphaz, Bildad, and Zophar. *Poetry.*

Job 32:1–6. *Prose.*

2) The Second Challenge: Job 32:7–37:24. Elihu's discourses, *Poetry.*

The end of man's wisdom.

3) The Final Challenge: Job 38:1–42:6 The words of the Lord, *Poetry.*

The Settlement.

Job 42:7–17. Conclusion, *Prose.*

This fivefold structure has been noticed by others of course. R. K. Harrison comments, "The book falls quite readily into five divisions, consisting of a prose prologue (Job 1–2), the dialogue (Job 3–31), the speeches of Elihu (Job 32–37), the Theophany and divine speeches (Job 38:1–42:6), and a prose epilogue (Job 42:7–17)."[505] Samuel Terrien says, "The book falls naturally into five parts: (*a*) a prologue in prose (1:1–2:12) introducing the hero and his sudden misfortunes, as well as three friends who come to comfort him; (*b*) a poetic discussion (3:1–31:40) which goes back and forth between these friends and the hero; (*c*) a poetic rebuke and advice offered by a fourth friend hitherto unmentioned and thereafter ignored (32:1–37:24); (*d*) a series of poetic challenges and questions addressed by Yahweh to Job, and the latter's repentance (38:1–42:6); (*e*) an epilogue in prose (42:7–17) which records the hero's rehabilitation and return to happiness."[506] Finally, W. A. Irwin, says, "More than in any other book of the OT an understanding of Job is dependent upon its analysis. The book falls into five distinct parts; (*a*) the Prologue, chs. 1–2; (*b*) the Dialogue, 3–31; (*c*) the Speeches of Elihu, 32–7; (*d*) the Speeches of Yahweh (with Job's brief rejoinders), 38–42:6; and (*e*) the Epilogue, 42:7–17. The first and the

---

[505] Harrison, R. K., *Introduction To The Old Testament*, op. cit., p. 1028.

[506] Op. cit., pp. 877f.

last of these are mainly in prose, the others mainly in poetry. These facts are obvious."[507]

In the Ancestor Epic the Tripartite Centre contains three threats, and that appears not to be the case with Job. There is no doubt however that in the drama itself Job has been subjected to the most dire threats imaginable, and these indeed are threefold; the first Satanic onslaught upon his family and possessions (1:12–22), the second against his person (2:6–8), and the third from his wife who urged him to "curse God and die" (2:9–10). There is no doubt however that the *Tripartite Centre* does include three cycles of very strong *challenges* to Job, which take the form of confrontations, thus even this link is discernible. Finally, in the *Conclusion*, the ability to obey the Primeval Command of Genesis 1:28, of being fruitful and multiplying which is so plainly evident in the other Ancestor Epics is found in the fact that in spite of the loss of all his children in chapter 1, Job's line does indeed continue through the birth of ten more children (42:13–14). When we consider also that the central character is a most revered figure, the greatest man in all the East, who lived during the age of Abraham, the very time when the other Ancestor Epics began to appear, and that there is no artificiality at all about the fivefold structure of the book, then we see that all of the essential characteristics of the Ancestor Epic of Kikawada, Quinn, and Garrett are indubitably present in the book of Job. But what is of particular note is that the book of Job is the <u>only</u> book of Scripture outside the Torah that dates from the same age as the Torah. How compelling the evidence becomes then, when we see that the Ancestor Epic literary Form is found in <u>all</u> the Scriptures which date from this period.

Conclusion

The book of Job is cast in the Ancient Ancestor Epic literary form found also in the Torah, validating the theories of Kikawada, Quinn,

---

[507] Irwin, W. A., in *Peake's Commentary On The Bible*, op. cit., p. 391. See also Cheyne, in the article *Job, Book Of*, in *Encyclopædia Biblica*, op. cit., column 2465, and the article with the same title by Genung, in *The International Standard Bible Encyclopædia*, op. cit., Volume III, pp. 1679ff.

and Garrett, who, by its discovery have made a vital contribution to Faithful Form Criticism of the Scriptures.

Glossary

The purpose of bold text in the column headed 'Definition' is to refer the reader to another entry in the Glossary under the heading of the text that is emboldened.

Term	Definition
Accommodation Theory.	The supposition that Christ and the Apostles knew that the **Pentateuch** was not the work of Moses, but referred to it as such, thereby accommodating themselves to the beliefs of those they addressed.
Age-of-Enlightenment.	An intellectual movement, in seventeenth and eighteenth century Europe, hostile to conservative Christian values, which espoused social progress, and viewed rationalism, and scientific knowledge as methods by which liberation from the restraints of superstition, including religion, and the prejudices of contemporary society might be achieved.
Amosaica.	*Non-mosaic.* Small amounts of material, such as that detailing the death of Moses (Deuteronomy 34), that was added to the **Pentateuch** after it left the hand of Moses. Also referred to as Post-mosaica.
Apologia.	A defence of a particular belief or set of beliefs.
Arminianism.	A system based on the teaching of James Arminius, and is the natural opposite of Calvinism in certain respects. Arminianism rejects the idea of predestination as such, suggesting instead that God predestines those whom He knows will choose Him. It also teaches that just as salvation is freely chosen; so too, it may freely be lost.
Astruc's Clue.	The suggestion, attributed to Jean Astruc, that the occurrence of the different Names for God, YHWH and Elohim, identify different **documentary** sources (**Jahwist** and **Elohist**; later **J** & **E**) in Genesis. It is the most fundamental belief of **Source Criticism**.
Beth essentiae / ב essentiae.	A use of the Hebrew letter ב as a prefix and which suggests the meaning, "in the character/sphere/sense of."
Crystallisation Hypothesis.	The suggestion that the **Grundshrift** assumed material said to originate from the **Ergänzer**, thus destroying the **Supplement Hypothesis**. The **Crystallisation Hypothesis** proposed a number of different sources for the **Pentateuch** or **Hexateuch**. These sources were the **Elohist**, **Jehovist**, **Deuteronomist**, and three other different sources.
D.	The supposed **Deuteronomist** Source.

De Wette's Clue.	The suggestion that the book of Deuteronomy dates from 621 B.C.E., or very slightly earlier, and that its 'discovery' by Hilkiah in II Kings 22 was engineered.
Deism.	Belief in a distant, remote and aloof God who created the universe and the laws which enable it to function, and like a watchmaker, then allowed it to run without interference.
Determinative.	A sign in ancient writing which is ordinarily a **logogram**, or part of a **logogram**, used to give the context of meaning for other signs.
Deuteronomist History & Deuteronomists.	The Deuteronomists are a hypothetical group supposed to have written and embraced the outlook enshrined in the so-called Deuteronomist History of Deuteronomy, Joshua, Judges, I & II Samuel, and I & II Kings.
Deuteronomist.	Represented by the siglum **D**. The supposed literary source behind the book of Deuteronomy. A **redactor** is thought to have made occasional contributions from **D** elsewhere in the **Pentateuch**.
Document.	As a Source Critical term, it refers to a literary source traceable throughout the **Pentateuch**, as opposed to a **fragment**.
Dtr.	The first **redactor** or **redactors** of Deuteronomy in the schemes of Martin Noth.
DtrN.	The final **redactor** or **redactors** of Deuteronomy in the schemes of Martin Noth, whose motive was to present Israel's history in terms of the Law.
DtrP.	Later **redactor** or **redactors** of Deuteronomy who, in the schemes of Martin Noth, connected it with the writings of the prophets.
E.	The so-called **Elohist** Source.
Elohist.	A supposed **documentary** source of the **Pentateuch** or **Hexateuch**, identifiable by the use of the name **Elohim**, and represented by the siglum **E**.
Ergänzer.	*Supplementer*. The **Jehovistic** source that, according to the **Supplement Hypothesis**, had supplemented the **Elohist Grundschrift**.
Form Criticism.	Usually applied to the supposed pre-literary history of stories which later became sources discovered by **Source Criticism**. The study of oral tradition. It may also be applied to the literary forms, in which texts, or portions of texts have been written. One aspect of **Higher Criticism**.
Four Source Document Theory.	The application of Hupfeld's views on Genesis to the whole **Pentateuch**, and which supposes that four sources, in the sequence **P**, **E**, **J**, & **D**, account for the **Pentateuch**.
Fragment Hypothesis.	The concept that the **Pentateuch**, or **Hexateuch**, is based upon a mass of **fragments**, rather than a few **documents**.

Fragment.	A literary source found only in certain parts in the **Pentateuch**, rather than throughout its compass, as is a **Document**.
G.	The supposed **Grundlage**.
Gnosticism.	This is a generic term capable of embracing a whole host of belief-systems. It is of pre-Christian origin, and, therefore there exist Christian, Jewish, and pagan forms of Gnosticism. What unites these different systems is a belief that a special intuitive knowledge, must either supplement or replace faith, and that those who have this special knowledge, are those who are saved.
Graf's Clue.	The suggestion that the chronological sequence of the alleged **four documentary sources** of the **Pentateuch** is not **P, E, J, & D**, but **J, E, P, & D**.
Graf–Wellhausen.	The most well known Documentary Hypothesis, named after Graf, who proposed the sequence of the supposed four literary sources of the **Pentateuch** to be **J, E, P, & D**, and Wellhausen who expanded on Graf's scheme, and related it to his evolutionary Hegelian views of the religious history of Israel.
Grundlage.	A supposed common basis of **J & E**, proposed by Martin Noth, and referred to by the siglum **G**.
Grundschrift.	A term associated with the **Supplement Hypothesis**, which is used to designate a supposed **Elohistic** foundation document that has been supplemented by material from a **Jehovist** source.
H.	**The Holiness Code.**
Hebrew Canon.	The books of the Old Testament.
Hexateuch.	*The Six Books*. The books; Genesis, Exodus, Leviticus, Numbers, Deuteronomy and Joshua.
Higher Criticism.	Broadly speaking Higher Criticism refers to all forms of Biblical Criticism apart from **Textual Criticism**, and so includes, **Source Criticism, Form Criticism,** and **Historical Criticism**.
Historical Criticism.	A critical study of the connection between certain events or movements within history, and the origin or **redaction** of texts. One aspect of **Higher Criticism**.
Holiness Code.	Leviticus 17–26, often given the siglum **H**.
J.	The so-called **Jahwist/Jehovistic** Source.
Jahvist/Jahwist/ Jehovist.	A supposed **documentary** source of the **Pentateuch** or **Hexateuch**, identifiable by the use of the Name YHWH (Jehovah), represented by the siglum **J**.
JE.	The amalgamation of **J** and **E**, or, originally, the supposition that second **Elohist, E,** (not **P**, the First **Elohist**), and the **Jehovist** were actually one and the same source.
L.	A supposed Laity source.

Logogram.	A type of symbol used in ancient writing that represented entire words, rather than syllables, or letters.
Lower Criticism.	Textual Criticism.
Nag Hammadi.	The location in Upper Egypt, where, in 1945, thirteen codexes of ancient **Gnostic** Christian scriptures, including apocryphal gospels, and Valentinian type writings were discovered.
New Documentary Hypothesis.	The hypothesis that supposes four Documentary Sources for the **Pentateuch**, the chronological sequence of which is **J, E, P & D**. This is in contrast to The **Older Documentary Hypothesis**.
Niphal.	The reflexive form of a Hebrew verb.
Octateuch.	*The Eight Books*. The books of Genesis, Exodus, Leviticus, Numbers, Deuteronomy, Joshua, Judges, and Ruth.
Older Documentary Hypothesis.	The first system based directly on **Astruc's Clue**, proposing different **documentary** sources for Genesis, including a **Jehovist**, and an **Elohist** source.
Ostraca.	Broken pieces of pottery used for writing on. The singular is ostracon.
P.	Originally, Die Urschrift, the first of two **Elohist** contributors to the **Grundschrift**, according to Hupfeld. **P.** designates this contributor as a **Priestly source**. It was formally known as **Q**.
Pentateuch.	*The Five Books*; that is, Genesis, Exodus, Leviticus, Numbers and Deuteronomy.
Post-Critical Movement.	A rather loose-knit movement that saw clearly the limitations of critical methods, inasmuch as they are incapable of dealing with the eternal and religious significances of the Scriptures. The movement called for a 'return to the text' but within a community context, as they believe the text was shaped originally by religious communities. Karl Barth (1886–1968) and Hans Rosenzweig (1886–1929) were among the movement's most well known supporters.
Post-Modernism.	A revolt against authority, absolutism, and official views, and an embrace of pluralistic and relativistic views. In terms of exegesis, Post-Modernist hermeneutics, would not seek to discover the world behind the text by examining the origins of the text, nor would it seek to establish the world of the text through a scrutiny of textual variants and versions, but instead would seek out the world *in front* of the text, that is, the use (or abuse!) of a given text by any group using it and applying to their own locally coloured culture and situation. Consequently many different interpretations might simultaneously be valid.
Post-Mosaica.	See **Amosaica**.
Priestly Source.	The supposed source, **P**.

Q.	Originally a designation of the supposed **Priestly Source** now known as **P**. (Not to be confused with the New Testament Q that is usually said to derive from the German *Quelle* (source), although some say it is simply the letter following P, which designated the supposed Petrine synoptic source. Q is supposed to be a documentary source lying behind the material common to Matthew and Luke.)
Qumran.	The location, near the Dead Sea, where, in 1947, the Dead-Sea-Scrolls were first discovered in modern times.
Recension.	An editorial revision of a text.
Redactor.	One who casts into a literary form, that which previously only had an oral form, or which previously had more than one literary form.
S.	A supposed Southern source.
Sitz im Leben.	*Setting-in-life*. The original milieu in which a document or oral tradition originated.
Source Criticism.	The critical study of supposed written sources lying beneath a text as it now appears. One aspect of **Higher Criticism**.
Square Characters.	The 'normal' Hebrew characters found in printed Hebrew Bibles today.
Supplement Hypothesis.	The theory suggesting that the **Pentateuch** or **Hexateuch** comprises an **Elohistic** Foundation Document, known as the ***Grundschrift***, which had then been supplemented by a **redactor** using **Jehovist** material.
Tetragrammaton.	*The Four Letters*. The Hebrew consonants יהוה transliterated and reversed so as to read left-to-right as YHWH, not right-to-left as in Hebrew, and which spell out the Sacred Name.
Tetrateuch.	*The Four Books*. The books, Genesis, Exodus, Leviticus and Numbers.
Textual Criticism.	The critical study of texts, including manuscript and printed copies, versions, citations, and variants found in these sources. Sometimes referred to as **Lower Criticism**.
Torah.	*Commandment, law*, or *direction*. As a proper noun it refers to the books of Genesis, Exodus, Leviticus, Numbers, and Deuteronomy.
Urmarkus.	A supposed literary source underlying the Gospel of Mark. The name was first coined in 1863 by Holtzmann.
Vorlage.	*Lying under*. A text that lies beneath later texts, and is their basis.
Waw-copulative.	The Hebrew letter waw, ו, found as a prefix and used as a conjunction.

Bibliography

Texts

Green, Jay P. Sr. (Editor and Translator). *The Interlinear Bible: Hebrew-Greek-English*, Peabody, Massachusetts, Hendrickson, second edition 1986.

Snaith, N. H. (Editor). ספר תורה נביאים וכתובים, London, The British And Foreign Bible Society, undated.

Alford H. (Editor). *The Greek Testament*, Four Volumes, London, Rivingtons, sixth edition, 1868.

Bloomfield, S. T. (Editor). *Η Καινη Διαθηκη: The Greek Testament With English Notes*, Two Volumes, London, Longman, Orme, Brown, Green, & Longmans, 1841.

Non-English Versions

Brenton, Sir L. C. L. (Editor and Translator). *The Septuagint With Apocrypha: Greek And English*, Peabody, Massachusetts, Hendrickson, 1997, based on the Bagster's edition of 1851.

The New Testament In Hebrew And English, Edgware, Middlesex, The Society For Distributing The Holy Scriptures To The Jews, undated.

ספרי הברית החדשה, Jerusalem, The United Bible Societies; Israel Agency, 1979.

Jerome. (Translator). *Biblia Sacra Vulgatæ Editionis,* London, Samuel Bagster, undated.

English Versions

Good News Bible: Today's English Version, London, The Bible Societies, 1976.

Tanakh: A New Translation Of The Holy Scriptures According To The Traditional Hebrew Text, Philadelphia and Jerusalem, Jewish Publication Society Of America, 1985.

The Companion Bible, London, The Lamp Press, undated.

The Comprehensive Bible, London, Samuel Bagster, undated.

The Holy Bible: Revised Standard Version, London, Collins 1971.

The Holy Bible: Revised Version, Oxford, Oxford University Press, 1928.

The New English Bible, Oxford, Oxford University Press, 1970.

Buttrick, Bowie, Scherer, Knox, Terrien, & Harmon, (Editors).   *The Interpreter's Bible*, Twelve Volumes, New York & Nashville, Abingdon Press, 1952.

Ferrar Fenton (Translator).   *The Holy Bible In Modern English,* London, A. & C. Black, 1938.

Moffatt, J.   *A New Translation Of The Bible,* London, Hodder & Stoughton, 1950.

Schonfield, H. J. (Translator).   *An Old Hebrew Text Of St. Matthew's Gospel,* Edinburgh, T. & T. Clark, 1927.

Grammars, Lexicons And Concordances

The Hebrew Student's Manual, London, Samuel Bagster, undated.

Gesenius, H. W. F.   *Hebrew Grammar,* edited and enlarged Kautzsch, translated Cowley, London, Oxford University Press, the second English edition, from the corrected sheets, and based on the twenty-eighth German edition, 1966.

Davidson, B.   *The Analytical Hebrew And Chaldee Lexicon*, Grand Rapids, Michigan, U.S.A., Zondervan, undated, but based on the second edition by Samuel Bagster of 1850.

Davies, B.   *A Compendious And Complete Hebrew And Chaldee Lexicon,* revised Mitchell, London, Asher & Co, 1889.

Gesenius, H. W. F.   *Hebrew And Chaldee Lexicon To The Old Testament Scriptures*, Grand Rapids, Michigan, U.S.A., Baker Book House, 1979.

Strong, J.   *The Exhaustive Concordance Of The Bible*, New York, Abingdon-Cokesbury, 1890.

Wigram, G. V.   *The Englishman's Hebrew And Chaldee Concordance Of The Old Testament*, Grand Rapids, Michigan, U.S.A., Zondervan, 1970.

Commentaries

Black, Matthew, and Rowley, H. H. (Editors)   *Peake's Commentary On The Bible*, Sunbury-on-Thames, Thomas Nelson, 1962 edition, the 1977 impression.

Poole, M.   *A Commentary On The Holy Bible*, Edinburgh, The Banner Of Truth Trust, Three Volumes, the 1979 impression of the 1962 edition, based on that of 1685.

Keil, C. F. and Delitzsch, F.	*Commentary On The Old Testament,* Volume I, *The Pentateuch*, translated Martin, Ten Volumes, Grand Rapids, Michigan, U.S.A., Eerdmans, 1978.
Driver, S. R.	*The Book Of Genesis*, London, Methuen, fourth edition, 1905.
Kidner, D.	*Genesis: An Introduction And Commentary*, London, The Tyndale Press, 1967, the 1973 impression.
McIntosh, C. H.	*Notes On The Book Of Genesis*, London, Morrish, sixth edition, revised.
Sarna, N. M.	*The JPS Commentary: Genesis,,* Philadelphia, U.S.A., The Jewish Publication Society, 1989.
Wenham, G.	*Genesis 1–15*, being Volume I of the *Word Biblical Commentary* series, Waco, Texas, Word Books, 1987.
Young, E. J.	*Studies In Genesis One*, Philadelphia, U.S.A., Presbyterian and Reformed, 1964.
Cole, R. A.	*Exodus: An Introduction And Commentary,* London, InterVarsity Press, 1973, 1974 impression.
McIntosh, C. H.	*Notes On The Book Of Exodus*, London, Morrish, third edition, revised, 1862.
Wenham, G.	*Numbers: An Introduction And Commentary*, Leicester, InterVarsity Press, 1981, 1998 impression.
Thompson, J. A.	*Deuteronomy: An Introduction And Commentary*, London, InterVarsity Press, 1974.
Rotherham, J. B.	*Studies In The Psalms*, London, H. R. Allenson, 1911.
Keil, C. F. and Delitzsch, F.	*Commentary On The Old Testament,* Volume V, *Psalms*, translated Bolton, Ten Volumes, Grand Rapids, Michigan, U.S.A., Eerdmans, 1976.
Maclaren, A.	*The Psalms*, Volume II, being a part of *The Expositor's Bible,* London, Hodder & Stoughton, 1895.
Hoskyns, E. C.	*The Fourth Gospel*, edited Davey, Noel, Two Volumes, London, Faber & Faber, 1940.
Rackham, R. B.	*The Acts Of The Apostles*, London, Methuen, eleventh edition, 1930.
Sanday, W., & Headlam, A. C.	*A Critical And Exegetical Commentary On The Epistle To The Romans*, Edinburgh, T. & T. Clark, fourth edition, 1900.
Robertson, A., and Plummer, A.	*A Critical And Exegetical Commentary On The First Epistle Of St. Paul To The Corinthians,* Edinburgh, T. & T. Clark, second edition, 1963 impression.
Lightfoot, J. B.	*Saint Paul's Epistle To The Galatians*, London, MacMillan, 1921.

General

Creation Volume 10, number 7, the journal of the Creation Science Movement, Portsmouth, The Creation Science Movement.

Creation Volume 11, number 19, the journal of the Creation Science Movement, Portsmouth, The Creation Science Movement.

Reading The Past: Ancient Writing From Cuneiform To The Alphabet, London, British Museum Publications, 1990.

The Bible Readers' Manual, found in *The Teachers Edition* of *The Authorised King James Version,* London, Collins, undated.

The Book Of Jasher, Metairie, U.S.A., New Christian Crusade Church, undated.

The Book Of Life, Seven Vols., London, Marshall Cavendish, 1971.

Alexander, P. S.   *Textual Sources For The Study Of Judaism*, Manchester, Manchester University Press, 1984.

Alexander, T. Desmond.   *Abraham In The Negev: A Source-Critical Investigation Of Genesis 20:1–22:19,* Carlisle, Paternoster Press, 1997.

Allison, D. C.   *The New Moses: A Matthean Typology,* Edinburgh, T. & T. Clark, 1993.

Anderson, Sir R.   *A Doubter Doubts About Science And Religion*, London, Pickering & Inglis, third edition, 1924.

Anderson, Sir R.   *The Bible And Modern Criticism*, London, Hodder & Stoughton, 1902.

Angus, J.   *The Bible Handbook: An Introduction To The Study Of Sacred Scripture*, London, The Religious Tract Society, undated.

Ball, C. J. (Editor).   *Aids To The Student Of The Holy Bible*, London, Eyre And Spottiswoode, 1897.

Balsiger, D., & Sellier, C. E.   *In Search Of Noah's Ark*, Los Angeles, Sun Classic Books, 1976.

Bengel, J., A., translated Faussey.   *Gnomon Of The New Testament*, Three Volumes, Edinburgh, T. & T. Clark, 1877.

Bennett, W. H., & Adeney, W. F.   *The Bible And Criticism*, London, T. C. & E. C. Jack, undated.

Berkhof, L.   *Systematic Theology*, London, The Banner Of Truth Trust, 1969.

Boman, T.   *Hebrew Thought Compared With Greek*, London, SCM Press, undated.

Bowden, M.	*Decrease In The Speed Of Light*, Portsmouth, The Creation Science Movement, undated.
Bowden, M.	*The Speed Of Light–The 2nd Monograph*, Portsmouth, The Creation Science Movement, undated.
Boys, T. (Edited Bullinger).	*A Key To The Psalms*, London, published privately by the Editor, 1890.
Briggs, J & Peat, F. D.	*Turbulent Mirror: An Illustrated Guide To Chaos Theory And The Science Of Wholeness,* New York, Harper & Row, 1990.
Bruce, F. F.	*The Books And The Parchments*, London, Marshall Pickering, 1991.
Bullinger, E. W.	*Figures Of Speech Used In The Bible*, Grand Rapids, Michigan, U.S.A., Baker Book House, third impression 1971.
Bullinger, E. W.	*How To Enjoy The Bible, Or The "Word," And "The Words," How To Study Them*, London, Eyre & Spottiswoode, 1928.
Bullinger, E. W.	*The Names And Order Of The Books Of The Old Testament*, Shetland, The Open Bible Trust, 1996.
Charles, R. H. (Editor).	*The Apocrypha And Pseudepigrapha Of The Old Testament*, Two Volumes, Oxford, Oxford University Press, 1913.
Cheyne, T. K., & Sutherland Black, J., (Editors).	*Encyclopædia Biblica*, London, A. & C. Black, 1903.
Childs, B. S.	*Introduction To The Old Testament As Scripture*, London, SCM Press, 1979.
Clement.	*The Clementines Homilies*, edited Roberts & Donaldson, Edinburgh, T. & T. Clark, 1870.
Collett, S.	*The Scripture Of Truth*, London, S. W. Partridge, 1905.
Conder, F. R., & C. R.	*A Handbook To The Bible*, London, Longmans, Green & Co., 1880.
Cooper, B.	*After The Flood*, Chichester, New Wine Press, 1995.
Daly, R. M.	*Earth's Most Challenging Mysteries*, Nutley, New Jersey, U.S.A., The Craig Press, 1972.
Darby, J. N.	*Notes And Comments On Scripture*, Seven Volumes, Bath, P. A. Humphrey, 1884.
Davies, P.	*God And The New Physics*, Harmondsworth, Penguin Books, 1983.
Davis, J. D.	*Dictionary Of The Bible*, London, Pickering & Inglis, 1972.

Dewar, D.	*Man: A Special Creation*, Hayling Island, Evolution Protest Movement, 1975.
Dewar, D.	*The Transformist Illusion*, Murfreesboro, Tennessee, Dehoff Publications, 1957.
Dodd, C. H.	*The Authority Of The Bible*, London, Nisbet & Co., 1928.
Dowley, Tim. (Editor).	*The History Of Christianity*, Berkhamsted, Lion Publishing, 1977.
Drosnin, M.	*The Bible Code*, London, Weidenfeld & Nicolson, 1997.
Drosnin, M.	*The Bible Code 2: The Countdown*, London, Weidenfeld & Nicolson, 2002.
Edersheim, A.	*The Life And Times Of Jesus The Messiah*, Two Volumes, London, Longmans, Green, & Co., 1899.
Edersheim, A.	*The Temple: Its Ministry And Services As They Were At The Time Of Jesus Christ*, London, The Religious Tract Society, undated.
Evans, J. H.	*Bible Chronology*, Bournemouth, published privately by the author, undated.
Fisher, R., Heiken, G., & Hulen, J.	*Volcanoes: Crucible Of Change*, Princeton, New Jersey, Princeton University Press, 1997.
Friedmann, D. A. B. L.	*Toldoth Yeshurun*, New York, The Hebrew Publishing Co., 1892.
Garrett, D.	*Rethinking Genesis: The Sources And Authorship Of The First Book Of The Bible,* Fearn, Ross-Shire, Christian Focus Publications, 2000.
Gaussen, L.	*Theopneustia: The Plenary Inspiration Of The Holy Scriptures,* London, Chas. J. Thynne, 1912.
Gayer, G. W.	*Old Testament Chronology*, London, The Covenant Publishing Co., 1933.
Ginzberg, L.	*The Legends Of The Jews*, Seven Volumes, Baltimore, Johns Hopkins University Press, 1998.
Grenz, S. J., Guretzki, D., & Nordling, C. F.	*The Hodder Pocket Dictionary Of Theological Terms*, London, Hodder & Stoughton, 2000.
Gribbin, J.	*In Search Of Big Bang*, London, Heinemann, 1986.
Harrison, R. K.	*Introduction To The Old Testament*, London, The Tyndale Press, 1970.
Hartwell-Horne, T.	*An Introduction To The Critical Study And Knowledge Of The Holy Scriptures*, Five Volumes, London, Cadell, ninth edition, 1846.
Hastings, J., & Selbie, J. A.	*Dictionary Of The Bible*, Edinburgh, T. & T. Clark, 1909.

Hawkes, N.   *Is Einstein About To Be Dethroned?* article in *The Times*,
                               London, 5th April, 2000.

Hills, E. F.   *The King James Version Defended!* Junction City, Oregon,
                               U.S.A., Eye-Opener Publishers, 1979.

Hodge, A. A.   *Evangelical Theology: A Course Of Popular Lectures*,
                               Edinburgh, The Banner Of Truth Trust, 1976.

Ifrah, G.   *The Universal History Of Numbers*, translated Bellos,
                               Harding, Wood, & Monk, London, Harvill Press, 1998.

Jeffrey, G. R.   *The Signature Of God: Astonishing Biblical Discoveries*,
                               London, Marshall Pickering, 1998.

Jonas, H.   *The Gnostic Religion*, Boston, U.S.A., Beacon Press,
                               1967.

Josephus, F.   *The Works Of Flavius Josephus*, translated Whiston,
                               London, Milner & Sowerby, 1866.

Kaiser, W. C.   *The Old Testament Documents: Are They Reliable?*
                               Leicester, InterVarsity Press, 2001.

Kelley, P. M.,   *The Masorah Of Biblia Hebraica Stuttgartensia*, Grand
Mynatt, D. S., &   Rapids, Michigan, U.S.A., Eerdmans, 1998.
Crawford, T. G.

Kenyon, F. G.   *Our Bible And The Ancient Manuscripts: A History Of The
                               Text And Its Translations*, London, Eyre & Spottiswoode,
                               1895.

Kikawada, I. M. &   *Before Abraham Was: A Provocative Challenge To The
Quinn, A.   Documentary Hypothesis*, Nashville, U.S.A., Abingdon
                               Press, 1985.

Knapp, C.   *The Old Testament: Studies In Teaching And Syllabus*,
                               London, Thomas Murby & Co., 1926.

Kümmel, W. G.   *Introduction To The New Testament*, translated Mattill,
                               London, SCM Press, 1970.

Lessing, E., & Varone, A.   *Pompeii*, Paris, Terrail, 1996.

Lofthouse, W. F.   *Israel After The Exile*, Oxford, Oxford University Press,
                               1928.

MacBeth, N.   *Darwin Retried: An Appeal To Reason*, New York, Dell
                               Publishing, 1973.

Magnusson, M.   *BC: The Archaeology Of The Bible Lands*, London, BCA,
                               1977.

Margolis, M. L., &   *A History Of The Jewish People*, Philadelphia, U.S.A., The
Marx, A.   Jewish Publication Society Of America, 5707 (1947).

Marston, C.   *The Bible Comes Alive*, London, Eyre & Spottiswoode,
                               1937.

Mead, G. R. S. — *Fragments Of A Faith Forgotten*, New York, University Books, 1960.

Meldau, F. J. — *Why We Believe In Creation Not In Evolution*, Denver, U.S.A., Christian Victory Publishing, 1974.

Milman, H. H. — *The History Of The Jews*, Two Volumes, London, J. M. Dent, & Sons, 1909.

Morris, H. M. — *The Remarkable Birth Of Planet Earth*, Minneapolis, U.S.A., Dimension Books, 1972.

Morton, A. H. — *The Principle Of Structure In Scripture*, Worthing, published privately by the author, 1950.

Naveh, J. — *Origins Of The Alphabet*, London, Cassell & Co., 1975.

Noth, M. — *A History Of Pentateuchal Traditions*, translated Anderson, Englewood Cliffs, New Jersey, U.S.A., Prentice-Hall, 1972.

Oesterley, W. O. E., Loewe, H., & Rosenthal, E. I. J. — *Judaism And Christianity*, Three Volumes, London, The Sheldon Press, 1937.

Orr, J., Nuelsen, J. L., Mullins, E. Y., Evans, M. O., & Kyle, M. G. — *The International Standard Bible Encyclopædia*, Five Volumes, Grand Rapids, Michigan, U.S.A., Eerdmans, 1946.

Pagels, E. — *The Gnostic Gospels*, Harmondsworth, Penguin Books, 1982.

Panin, I. — *Bible Chronology In Three Parts*, Vancouver, The Covenant People, undated.

Parrot, A. — *The Flood And Noah's Ark*, translated Hudson, London, SCM Press, 1955.

Parrot, A. — *The Tower Of Babel*, translated Hudson, London, SCM Press, 1955.

Pate, C. M. — *Communities Of The Last Days*, Leicester, Apollos, 2000.

Patten, D. W. — *The Biblical Flood And Ice Epoch*, Seattle, U.S.A., Pacific Meridian, 1966.

Patterson Smyth J. — *The Old Documents And The New Bible*, London, Samuel Bagster, 1890.

Phelan, M. W. J. — *The 'Greeks' Of The New Testament*, Birmingham, The European Theological Seminary, 2002.

Phelan, M. W. J. — *The Circle Of The Earth In Isaiah 40:22*, Brighton, Paradosis Publications, 1988.

Phelan, M. W. J. — *The Dating Of The Exodus*, Birmingham, The European Theological Seminary, 2001.

Bibliography

Phelan, M. W. J.   *The Fulness Of The Godhead*, Reading, The Open Bible Trust, 1987.

Phelan, M. W. J.   *The One True God And Pluralism Of Language*, Brighton, Paradosis Publications, 1996.

Phelan, M. W. J.   *The Spirit And The Word*, Birmingham, The European Theological Seminary, 2001.

Pierson, A.   *Many Infallible Proofs*, London, Morgan And Scott, undated.

Pimenta, L.   *Before The First Day*, Chichester, Creation Books, 1998.

Pimenta, L.   *Fountains Of The Great Deep*, Chichester, New Wine Press, 1984.

Porter, R. D.   *Evolution And The End Of An Era*, Needham Market, published privately by the author, 1970.

Rendle-Short, A.   *Modern Discovery And The Bible*, London, InterVarsity Fellowship, fourth edition, 1955.

Richards, L. O.   *The Applied Bible Dictionary*, Eastbourne, Kingsway, 1990.

Riggans, W.   *Yeshua Ben David: Why Do The Jewish People Reject Jesus As Their Messiah?* Crowborough, Monarch Publications, 1995.

Robertson, E.   *The Old Testament Problem*, Manchester, Manchester University Press, 1950.

Robinson, J. A. T.   *Redating The New Testament*, London, SCM Press, 1976.

Rohl, D.   *A Test Of Time*; Volume I, *The Bible—From Myth To History*, London, Century, 1995.

Rohl, D.   *A Test Of Time;* Volume II, *Legend—The Genesis Of Civilisation,* London, Arrow, 1999.

Roseveare, D.   *Was There A Big Bang?* Portsmouth, The Creation Science Movement, undated.

Rotherham, J. B.   *Our Sacred Books Being Plain Chapters On The Inspiration, Transmission And Translation Of The Bible*, London, H. E. Allenson, 1903.

Rouw, J.   *House Of Gold*, London, Chapter 2, 1981.

Sanders, N. K.   *The Epic Of Gilgamesh*, Harmondsworth, Penguin Books,
(Translator).   revised edition, printed 1971.

Saphir, A.   *Christ And The Scriptures*, London, Morgan & Scott, undated.

Satinover, J.   *The Truth Behind The Bible Code*, London, Sidgwick & Jackson, 1997.

Scholem, G.　　　　　　*On The Kabbalah And Its Symbolism*, translated Manheim, New York, Schocken Books, 1996.

Schroeder, G. L.　　　　*Genesis And The Big Bang*, New York, Bantam Books, 1992.

Shute, E.　　　　　　　*Flaws In The Theory Of Evolution*, Nutley, New Jersey, U.S.A., 1971.

Slemming, C. W.　　　　*Made According To Pattern: A Study Of The Tabernacle In The Wilderness*, London, H. E. Walter, 1964.

Slemming, C. W.　　　　*These Are The Garments: A Study Of The Garments Of The High Priest Of Israel*, London, H. E. Walter, 1955.

Slemming, C. W.　　　　*Thus Shalt Thou Serve: An Exposition Of The Offerings And The Feasts Of Israel*, London, H. E. Walter, 1966.

Smart, N. (Editor).　　　*Historical Selections In The Philosophy Of Religion*, London, SCM Press, 1962.

Snaith, N. H.　　　　　*Notes On The Hebrew Text Of Genesis I–VIII*, London, The Epworth Press, 1947.

Soulen, R. N, &　　　　*Handbook Of Biblical Criticism*, Louisville, Kentucky,
Kendall Soulen, R.　　　U.S.A., Westminster John Knox Press, third edition, 2001.

Stanton, P.　　　　　　*The Bible Code: Fact Or Fake?* Eastbourne, Kingsway, 1997.

Steele-Smith, W. E.　　　*Wonders Of The Hebrew Alphabet For The Plain English Reader,* Sydney, Australia, undated.

Steinmueller, J. E.　　　*Some Problems Of The Old Testament*, New York, Bruce Publishing, 1936.

Strong, A. H.　　　　　*Systematic Theology*, London, Pickering & Inglis, 1981.

Sweeney, E. J.　　　　　*The Pyramid Age*, Corby, Northants, Domra, 1999.

Swete, H. B.　　　　　*An Introduction To The Old Testament In Greek*, Peabody Massachusetts, Hendrickson, 1989.

Taylor, C.　　　　　　　*Rewriting Bible History (According To Scripture),* Unley Park, South Australia, House Of Tabor, 1983.

Thompson, W. R.　　　　*New Challenging 'Introduction' To The Origin Of Species*, Hayling Island, Evolution Protest Movement, 1967.

Van Lennep, C. G. O.　　*The Measured Times Of The Bible*, London, Heath Cranton, 1928.

Various.　　　　　　　　*The Bible Under Attack*, Welwyn, Hertfordshire, Evangelical Press, 1978.

Velikovsky, I.　　　　　*Ages In Chaos*, London, Sidgwick & Jackson, 1953.

Velikovsky, I.　　　　　*Earth In Upheaval*, London, Sphere, 1973.

Velikovsky, I.　　　　　*Mankind In Amnesia*, London, Sidgwick & Jackson, 1982.

Velikovsky, I.   *Worlds In Collision*, London, BCA, 1973.

Virgil.   *The Aeneid*, translated Fitzgerald, London, Penguin
                          Books, 1990.

Walworth, R. F. &   *Subdue The Earth*, London, Granada, 1980.
Walworth Sjostrom, G.

Watson, D.   *Answers To Unsolicited Questions,* Cheltenham, published
                          privately by the author, 1995.

Watson. W. G. E.   *A Review Of Kugel's 'The Idea Of Biblical Poetry,'* in
                          Journal For The Study Of The Old Testament, Issue 28,
                          Sheffield, The University Of Sheffield, 1984.

Weinreb, F.   *Roots Of The Bible*, translated Keus, Braunton, Devon,
                          Merlin Books, 1986.

Welch, C. H.   *The Prize Of The High Calling*, Banstead, Surrey, The
                          Berean Forward Movement, 1950.

Whitcomb, J. C.   *The Early Earth*, London, Evangelical Press, 1972.

Whitcomb, J. C.   *The World That Perished*, Grand Rapids, Michigan,
                          U.S.A., revised edition, 1988.

Whitcomb, J. C. &   *The Genesis Flood*, Grand Rapids, Michigan, U.S.A.,
Morris, H. M.   Baker Book House, 1966.

Whybray, R. N.   *The Making Of The Pentateuch: A Methodological Study*,
                          being Supplement Number 53 of the *Journal For The
                          Study Of The Old Testament*, Sheffield, Sheffield
                          Academic Press, 1999.

Wilson, C. A.   *That Incredible Book—The Bible*, Chicago, U.S.A., Moody
                          Books, 1975.

Wilson, I.   *The Bible Is History*, London, Weidenfeld & Nicolson,
                          1999.

Wilson, R. D.   *Is The Higher Criticism Scholarly?* London, Marshall
                          Brothers, 1922.

Wiseman, D. J.   *Illustrations From Biblical Archaeology*, London, The
                          Tyndale Press, 1958.

Wiseman, P. J.   *New Discoveries In Babylonia About Genesis*, London,
                          Marshall, Morgan & Scott, 1958.

Wright, G. E.   *The Old Testament Against Its Background*, being Number
                          2 in the original series of *Studies In Biblical Theology*,
                          London, SCM Press, 1962.

Yahuda, A. S.   *The Accuracy Of The Bible*, London, Heinemann, 1934.

Young, R.   *Concise Critical Comments On The Holy Bible*, London,
                          Pickering & Inglis, undated.